A HANDBOOK OF COGNITIVE PSYCHOLOGY

A HANDBOOK
OF COGNITIVE PSYCHOLOGY

Michael W. Eysenck

Birkbeck College, University of London

LAWRENCE ERLBAUM ASSOCIATES, PUBLISHERS
London   Hillsdale, New Jersey

Lawrence Erlbaum Associates, Ltd., Publishers
Chancery House
319 City Road
London EC1V 1LJ

British Library Cataloguing in Publication Data

Eysenck, Michael W.
    A handbook of cognitive psychology.
    1. Cognition
    I. Title
    155.4'13 BF311

    ISBN 0-86377-016-9
    ISBN 0-86377-017-7 Pbk

Typeset, printed and bound by A. Wheaton & Co. Ltd., Exeter.

To Chris, Fleur,
and Willie With Love

Though syllogisms hang not on my tongue,
I am not surely always in the wrong!
'Tis hard if all is false that I advance—
A fool must now and then be right, by chance.

William Cowper

Contents

Preface

Over the past 20 years or so, experimental psychology has increasingly become synonymous with cognitive psychology. That is to say, most laboratory research attempts to identify the processes and mechanisms that underlie human cognition. How did cognitive psychology achieve its current pre-eminent position? Some people are inclined to regard the publication in 1967 of Neisser's book, entitled *Cognitive Psychology*, as the crucial event that provided the greatest impetus to the field of cognitive psychology. However, it seems to me that Broadbent's book *Perception and Communication*, published in 1958, has had greater seminal influence. Whatever its precise origins, there are good grounds for supposing that the intellectual dynamism of cognitive psychology has proved extremely fruitful. I hope that the reader will agree with this supposition when he or she has read this book.

One of the more intractable problems that any author has to face up to when attempting to chart the progress of cognitive psychology is the extremely diverse and sprawling nature of the current scene. What we may loosely term the 'cognitive approach' is to be found increasingly in such disparate areas as neuropsychology, artificial intelligence, applied and 'real-life' research, developmental psychology, and social psychology. Of course, only a knave or a villain would claim to possess expertise in all of these areas, and I would not be so presumptuous as to make that claim. What I have endeavoured to do between these covers is to provide as extensive a coverage of the expanding field of the psychology of human cognition as my knowledge permits me to do.

I am very grateful to various people who contributed useful ideas while I was engaged in the lengthy business of writing this book. They include Bob Hockey, Margaret Harris, David Jones, Paul Barber, and Gill Cohen. Needless to say, any deficiencies that are present in the text are entirely the responsibility of the author.

Finally, I would like to express profound gratitude to my family. I have been far more blessed than I deserve to have such a wonderful and beautiful wife, who put up with the long hours that I spent away from my family, during the writing of this book, with great tolerance and good humour. My children Fleur and Willie did their best to prevent Daddy writing at all, but in spite of that they are both sources of immense pride and pleasure to me, and it will be delightful to have more time to be with all of my family. For these (and many other) reasons, this book is dedicated to them with my love.

Michael W. Eysenck
London, 8th December 1983

1 Introduction

Anyone attempting to come to grips with the booming, buzzing confusion that is contemporary cognitive psychology is likely to be left with an actual or metaphorical headache. Among the headache-inducing qualities of cognitive psychology are its tremendous range, covering most of human experimental psychology; the huge volume of published research into human cognition; and the fragmentary and disorganised nature of much of this research. Cognitive psychology often seems to resemble the messenger in *Alice in Wonderland* who went in all directions at once. The author would like to be able to transform all of this confusion and uncertainty into systematic coherence, but has instead opted for the more modest (and more achievable!) goal of describing contemporary cognitive psychology as clearly as possible.

This chapter fulfils a scene-setting function for what follows. It begins with a discussion of the nature of cognitive psychology, including some key theoretical issues. After these rather abstract matters, there is a fairly detailed consideration of some of the main methods and techniques used by cognitive psychologists as they attempt to understand how people perform cognitive tasks.

WHAT IS COGNITIVE PSYCHOLOGY?

If the health of an academic discipline can be judged by the number of its adherents, then cognitive psychology is certainly thriving. Indeed, in a recent survey of academic psychologists in America, over three-quarters of them claimed to be cognitive psychologists! However, at least part of the reason for the growing army marching behind the banner of cognitive psychology is the increased vagueness with which the term is used. Virtually all those interested in perception, learning, memory, language, concept formation, problem solving, or thinking call themselves cognitive psychologists, despite the great diversity of experimental and theoretical approaches to be found in these various areas.

1

Paradoxically, it may help to decide what cognitive psychology is by considering what it is not. There is no doubt that contemporary research in the field of cognition represents a strong reaction against the facile approach of Behaviourism. In its pristine form, Behaviourism was a school of psychology based on the notion that psychology can only be scientific if it focuses on what is observable (i.e., environmental stimuli and behavioural responses). As a consequence, early Behaviourists made considerable theoretical use of stimulus–response connections. Later Behaviourists, such as Hull and Tolman, were prepared to include organismic or intervening variables in their theoretical formulations. However, the kinds of variables which were proposed (e.g., drive, habit) typically had marginal relevance to cognitive processes. One of the few points of agreement among cognitive psychologists is the need to provide as detailed and explicit an account of these internal cognitive processes as possible.

There are various ways in which cognitive psychologists have attempted to conceptualise the workings of these cognitive processes. Much of the early impetus was provided by the computer analogy. The computer is an example of a complex machine that processes information efficiently by means of a variety of internal mechanisms. The way in which a computer functions can be represented in a flow chart showing the sequence of processing stages and indicating the interrelationships between the various internal component functions. As a direct result, psychologists began to produce similar-looking flow charts designed to reveal the internal functioning of human beings when confronted with various problems. However, the manifold differences between computers and humans have led many cognitive psychologists to abandon the computer analogy. Despite the problems there is still much interest in simulation techniques, which attempt to program a computer to perform tasks in the same ways as people do them.

Cognitive psychologists differ enormously in the extent to which they rely on the computer in their endeavours to understand human cognition. Some cognitive psychologists prefer to make extensive use of physiological findings when constructing theories, whereas others depend on data collected from studies in social psychology or from work on sub-human primates. One of the aims of this book is to compare different approaches with respect to their relative success in furthering our understanding of cognition.

These heterogeneous approaches are likely to make the task of understanding cognitive psychology appear rather daunting, particularly because of the rather fragmentary nature of much research and theory, in which apparently interdependent processes, such as perception, attention, and memory, are rarely discussed together. In view of these complexities, the reader may find a brief discussion of general theoretical views about cognition of some use.

For a period of several years, covering the 1960s and much of the 1970s, it was the fashion to regard much of cognition as consisting of a sequential series of processing stages. When a stimulus is presented (so the reasoning went), basic perceptual processes occur, followed by attentional processes that transfer some of the products of the initial perceptual processing to a short-term memory store. Thereafter, rehearsal serves to maintain information in the short-term memory, and some of that information is transferred to a long-term memory store. One of the most sophisticated theories of this type was put forward by Atkinson and Shiffrin (1968).

This kind of theoretical orientation, in which information processing involved an invariant sequence of stages, provided a simple and coherent framework for writers of textbooks. It was possible to follow the stimulus input from the sense organs to its ultimate storage in long-term memory by means of successive chapters on perception, attention, short-term memory, and long-term memory.

One slight problem with this theoretical approach is that it cannot readily accommodate quintessentially cognitive activities, such as thinking or problem solving, but many textbook writers dealt with this in a robust manner by simply omitting such topics. A far more significant difficulty is that the sequential stage model is a gross over-simplification and is demonstrably wrong in several respects. In particular, the model appears to make the erroneous assumption that stimuli impinge on an inactive and unprepared organism. In fact, while processing is substantially affected by the nature of presented stimuli, it is also affected crucially by the individual's past experience, expectations, and so on.

Matters can be clarified by reference to a distinction that is often made between bottom-up or stimulus-driven processing and top-down or conceptually-driven processing. Bottom-up processing refers to processing directly affected by stimulus input, whereas top-down processing refers to processing affected by what an individual brings to a stimulus situation (e.g., expectations determined by context and past experience). As an example of top-down processing, it is easier to perceive the word "well" when poorly written if it is presented in the context of the sentence, "I hope you are quite ―――," than when it is presented on its own. The evidence discussed in this book demonstrates conclusively that most cognitive activity involves these two kinds of processing in combination. The sequential stage model deals almost exclusively with bottom-up or stimulus-driven processing, and its failure to consider top-down processing is its single greatest inadequacy.

According to contemporary thinking (e.g., Neisser, 1976), what normally happens is that cognitive activity comprises concurrent and interactive bottom-up and top-down processes. This appears to be the case for virtually all cognitive processes. On the face of it perception and remembering might seem to be exceptions, because perception obviously depends heavily on the precise stimuli presented (and thus on bottom-up processing) and remembering depends crucially on stored information (and thus on top-down processing). In fact, perception is also much affected by the perceiver's expectations about to-be-presented stimuli, and remembering depends far more than was thought at one time on the exact nature of the environmental cues provided to facilitate recollection.

In spite of the fact that cognition typically involves an amalgam of bottom-up and top-down processing, it is still true that the relative importance of these two kinds of processing varies considerably from one cognitive activity to another, and from one task to another. The details will be fleshed out at several points during the book.

Another general issue that is relevant to most of cognitive psychology concerns the way in which the several component processes involved in the performance of a complex cognitive task relate to each other. If, for example, a task necessitates the use of five separate cognitive processes, then one possibility is that one process is completed before the second process starts, the second process is completed before the third one starts, and so on. This is what is known as serial processing, in which different stages of processing occur in a sequential manner. Alternatively, all five cognitive processes might take place during the same period of time, in which case parallel processing would be occurring. It is also possible that what is really happening is some mixture of serial and parallel processing.

Cognitive psychologists differ among themselves as to the relative importance of serial and parallel processing in cognition. While the distinction between serial and parallel processing seems clearcut, it turns out to be disappointingly difficult to decide which kind of processing is used on any particular task. Indeed, Anderson (1976) has shown convincingly that it is always possible to produce a serial processing model that will make the same predictions about behaviour as a parallel processing model, and vice versa.

The power of the brain's processing mechanisms suggests that parallel processing is the norm rather than the exception. However, some kind of central control system operating in a serial way seems essential to prevent chaos resulting from several independent parallel processing operations. In addition, it sometimes seems obvious that a problem will be solved by means of sequential processing stages, because the later stages cannot occur until the results of earlier processing stages are available. From the psychologist's point of view, serial processing models tend to be much more tractable than those allowing for the possibility of temporal overlap of processing stages. Partly for this reason, most of the techniques for identifying processing stages assume that processing stages are sequential.

A further general issue relates to the nature and organisation of the processing system. It has often been assumed that there is a hierarchical system of processes or capacities involved in information processing. The workings of the system stem from a central processor at the top of the hierarchy. This central processor has limited capacity, and is often referred to as "attention." This hierarchical view can be contrasted with the notion that there are many processes involved in performance, none of which can be identified uniquely with attention. What happens is that different capacities assume executive control at different times, and so the system is hetarchic rather than hierarchical. These issues remain unresolved, but the relevant evidence is considered in detail later in the book.

Psychologists attempting to increase our knowledge of human cognition have to make several decisions about the kind of research that they undertake. It is important to realise that most cognitive psychologists have made the same decisions, and this has greatly influenced cognitive psychology as it is today. Some of these decisions relate to the following issues:

1. *Basic versus applied research.* It is possible to examine human cognition either "for its own sake" (basic research) or in the context of real-life problems (e.g., academic failure, dyslexia). Advocates of basic research typically confine their activities to the laboratory, whereas applied researchers are more likely to explore cognition in "real-life" settings. Cognitive psychologists (at least until quite recently) have decided to concentrate on basic research.

2. *Specific versus general focus.* Cognitive psychologists can devote their research and theoretical efforts to relatively narrow and specific problems (e.g., analysis of a single task) or to broader and more general problems. Most cognitive psychologists have decided to deal with rather specific problems.

3. *Interest in motivation and emotion.* Philosophers of yesteryear used to distinguish between cognition, conation (or motivation), and affect (emotion). Cognitive psychologists have the choice of attempting to keep the motivational and emotional states of their subjects constant (so that these factors can be ignored), or of systematically manipulating both motivation and emotion in order to observe their effects on cognition. With very few exceptions, cognitive psychologists have made the former choice.

The reader may find it worthwhile, as he or she reads this book, to question the contemporary emphasis on basic research into specific problems that is conducted with a total disregard for emotional and motivational factors. The author's personal opinion is that all of these decisions are ill-advised, and the treatment of cognitive psychology in this book reflects this opinion. Basic laboratory research is extremely important, but there is an obvious danger that such research may lack ecological validity (i.e., direct relevance to normal, everyday experiences and events). There is too often a failure to distinguish between statistical and practical significance. For example, months of laboratory research under ideal conditions may produce a complex interaction that is just statistically significant, but the chances that such an interaction could be replicated under other circumstances are minimal. For the purposes of applying research findings to "real-life" settings, it is necessary to focus on substantial laboratory effects, and this is rarely done.

The tendency to focus on specific problems or tasks naturally leads to very narrow conclusions. What we are really interested in are people's cognitive processes and mechanisms rather than exhaustive analyses of unrepresentative tasks. It is, of course, easier to made detailed and successful predictions about performance on a single, well-researched task than across a wide range of different tasks, but prediction is not the only goal of science. Understanding is more important.

Finally, the failure of contemporary cognitive psychology to consider the ways in which cognition is affected by motivation and emotion has been justified by the argument that it would complicate matters unduly to extend the scope of cognitive psychology in this way. However, it is probable that limiting the study of cognitive performance to people who are in a relatively unemotional, but motivated, state seriously restricts the usefulness of much research into cognition.

We will return to the question of the inadequacies of cognitive psychology in the final chapter of this book when the reader has had more of an opportunity to study the work of cognitive psychologists. However, it seems advisable to forewarn the reader that there are discernible biases in the approach taken by most cognitive psychologists, so that he (or she) can decide for himself (or herself) whether cognitive psychology is moving in the right direction.

TASK ANALYSIS

Introduction

We have discussed some general theoretical issues in cognitive psychology, and it is now appropriate to consider the more practical matter of the research techniques that the cognitive psychologist has available in his armament for investigating human cognition. In particular, several techniques have been developed in the attempt to identify the component processes involved in the performance of cognitive tasks. A discussion of some of the most popular ones follows.

The emphasis on analysing in detail the processing components of tasks is a distinguishing feature of cognitive psychology that is missing from earlier approaches. The reluctance of the Behaviourists to speculate on the precise processing mechanisms intervening between stimulus and response is perhaps understandable, but it might be thought that theorists concerned with human intelligence would have been interested in discovering the processes and mechanisms involved in solving the items found in intelligence tests. This was not the case, however, until comparatively recently.

There are various reasons for this neglect. One reason is that intelligence was for a very long time investigated primarily by means of factor analysis based on analyses across items and across individuals. As a result, it is almost impossible for this approach to uncover processes common to all people trying to solve a particular problem. Factor analysis is not concerned with an analysis of intra-item structure, because the only information which is usually included in the factor analysis is whether or not a particular item or set of items is answered correctly. While factor analysis can be used to look at an individual's performance, it is far more common for it to be used to analyse patterns of individual differences across subjects. Thus, there is no way in which factor analysis can discover the processes used by an individual solving (or failing to solve) an item in an intelligence test. One must agree with McNemar (1964), who came to the following pessimistic conclusion: "It is difficult to see how the available individual difference data can be used even as a starting point for generating a theory as to the process nature of general intelligence or of any other specified ability [p. 881]."

The particular method or technique chosen in the attempt to provide a systematic analysis of a task naturally depends on the nature of the task in question. A very relevant factor is whether the task involves fast or slow processes. Fast-process tasks last for no longer than a few seconds, and often occupy only fractions of a second; typically, there is little or no conscious awareness on the part of the subject of the processes involved in task solution. Examples of such tasks are various simple and complex reaction-time tasks. In contrast, slow-process tasks last for up to several minutes, and include complex mental arithmetic and several problem-solving tasks. Whereas fast-process research relies heavily on reaction-time data, slow-process research often makes use of subjects' introspections and/or computer simulation. We will initially consider some methods appropriate to fast-process research before embarking on a discussion of methods used to identify the processes involved in slow-process research.

The Additive-factor Method

The additive-factor method of analysing stages of processing was introduced into psychology by S. Sternberg (1969). The method can be applied only when certain assumptions are made about the way in which a particular task is processed. Firstly, it must be assumed that task performance consists of a series of independent processing stages. Secondly, it is assumed that at each stage of processing, information received from the immediately preceding processing stage is transformed in some way and then passed on to the succeeding stage. Thirdly, and somewhat controversially, it is assumed that the nature of the transformation produced at any particular stage and the speed with which it is produced are both unaffected by the duration of any earlier processing stage.

According to S. Sternberg (1969), the total length of time taken to perform a task is simply the sum of the times taken at each of the processing stages. In essence, the technique used to identify task stages is to introduce various experimental manipulations singly or in pairs; their effects on task solution time are then observed. The following rule of thumb is then applied to the resulting data: If two different experimental factors have independent or additive effects on solution time, then they are deemed to affect two different processing stages; if their effects are interactive (i.e., they mutually modify each other's effects), then it is concluded that they affect the same processing stage. These predictions depend crucially on the third assumption given in the previous paragraph.

The discussion of the additive-factor method so far has been rather abstract—how does it work in practice? The high-speed memory scanning task devised by S. Sternberg (1969) provides an example. It involves presenting a small memory set of items followed by a probe; the subject makes a positive response if the probe belongs to the memory set and a negative response if it does not. The behavioural measure that is of primary interest is the time taken to respond to the probe.

S. Sternberg (1969) considered the effects of four different factors on response time. These were probe quality (intact or degraded); size of the memory set; response type (positive or negative); and relative frequency of each response type. He looked at five out of the six possible relationships between pairs of variables, and discovered that the effects were always independent or additive. According to the logic of the additive-factor method, this means that there must be at least four separate processing stages contributing to the time taken to respond to the probe. S. Sternberg incorporated this information into his theoretical model. More specifically, he assumed that probe quality affected a stage of stimulus encoding; size of the memory set affected a serial comparison stage; response type affected a binary decision stage; and, finally, the relative frequency of each response type affected a stage of translation and response organisation. It should be emphasised that this model did not follow solely from the application of the additive-factor model, but also made use of plausible conjectures and speculations.

How successful is the additive-factor method in revealing processing stages? One obvious limitation is that it explicitly assumes that processing is serial rather than parallel, so that its usefulness may well be rather limited.

However, a more telling criticism is that there are doubts concerning the validity of using additive and interactive effects to identify the number of processing stages. As Pachella (1974) has pointed out, "In situations where stages have some independent definition, it is perfectly conceivable that two factors might affect a single stage in an additive manner or that they might affect different stages and interact [p. 58]." Suppose experimental factor A affects not only the duration of an early processing stage but also its output. Under such circumstances there might be a "knock on" effect producing an interaction between factor A and another factor B, which only affects a later stage of processing.

There are other limitations to this method. In particular, it cannot discover the duration of each stage; all it can do is reveal the less interesting fact of the amount by which a particular factor lengthens the duration of a particular stage. Furthermore, the method does not, in and of itself, indicate the order of processing stages, although considerations of plausibility usually eliminate some of the possibilities.

The Subtraction Method

An alternative to the additive-factor method is the so-called subtraction method. This was originally put forward by Donders (1868), and can be used when a task consists of a series of processing stages. The basic logic of the method is that the temporal duration of a single processing stage can be measured by comparing the time to solve a version of the task, which includes that processing stage, with a second version of the task that differs from the first version only by the deletion of that processing stage. The difference in solution time for the two versions of the task represents the time spent on the processing stage of interest. In principle, successive deletions can be used in order to obtain an estimate of the duration of each processing stage.

A well-known example of the subtraction method is research carried out by Clark and Chase (1972) into the sentence–picture verification task. A sentence, such as, "Star isn't below plus," is followed by a picture, such as, "$*\atop+$," and the task is to decide as rapidly as possible whether the sentence is a true description of the picture. The sentence can take one of eight forms: The preposition can be either "above" or "below"; the subject of the sentence can be "star" or "plus"; and the statement can be positive ("is") or negative ("isn't").

To account for performance, when the sentence precedes the picture in their model, Clark and Chase assumed that the first step involves representing the sentence in terms of its underlying deep structure propositions. They claimed that a so-called "marked" adjective, such as "below," would take longer to process than an "unmarked" adjective, like "above," (parameter

a), and that negative sentences would take longer to process than positive sentences (parameter b). The second step is to encode the picture into propositional form with the same preposition ("above" or "below") as used in the sentence. The next step is to compare the sentence and picture representations. It takes less time to perform the comparison when the first noun in the two propositional representations is the same than when it is different (parameter c), and the comparison time is less when neither representation contains a negative than when one of them does (parameter d). The fourth, and final, step is the production of a response, and it was assumed that the time taken for this is a constant (parameter t_o).

The subtraction method can be applied to the sentence–picture verification task by comparing response times as a function of the exact sentence and picture presented. Thus, for example, the sentence "A is below B" has parameters a and t_o assigned to it when it is true, whereas the sentence "A is above B" has only parameter t_o assigned to it if it is true. Thus, the difference in solution time should reflect the duration of parameter a. Unfortunately, parameters b and d always occur in negative sentences, but not in positive sentences, so that separate measures of each parameter cannot be obtained.

Clark and Chase (1972) applied the subtraction method to the data from their first experiment and obtained the following estimates: parameter $a = 93$ msec., parameters $b + d = 685$ msec., parameter $c = 187$ msec., and parameter $t_o = 1763$ msec. The theoretical model based on these parameter estimates was found to account for over 99% of the variance in the group means. Furthermore, Clark and Chase discovered that the parameters were applicable to other versions of the sentence–picture comparison task.

The work of Clark and Chase (1972) has been widely regarded as an outstanding example of a successful use of the subtraction method. Are there any major problems with this method? One fairly obvious difficulty is that it is not always easy to delete processing stages in a precise way; in practice, a parameter will often consist of two or more conceptually distinct stages. For example, Clark and Chase argued that the amount of time required to compare the sentence "Star is above plus" with the picture "$*$" was equal to the parameter t_o. However, common sense indicates that at least four different processing activities (i.e., encoding the sentence, encoding the picture, comparing the sentence with the picture, and producing the response) are all contained within a single parameter.

A second common problem is the estimation of a relatively large number of parameters with a smallish number of data points (four parameters and only eight data points in the case of Clark and Chase). This leads to inflated estimates of the percentage of the variance accounted for. Indeed, while Clark and Chase were able to account for over 99% of the variance in their data, Carpenter and Just (1975) proposed a rather different model that accounted for a comparable percentage of the variance in the data of Clark and Chase. Moreover, the theoretical approach of Clark and Chase fails altogether to account for the way in which some subjects perform the task (MacLeod, Hunt, & Mathews, 1978).

A further problem limiting the usefulness of the subtraction method is that the experimenter must have a precise conceptualisation of the component processes involved in the performance of a task before the subtraction method can be utilized. Finally, and in the opinion of many most seriously, there is the problem that the subtraction method is based on the assumption of pure insertion, i.e., the notion that it is possible to insert or delete processing stages from a complex information-processing task without affecting the other processing stages in any way. In the words of S. Sternberg (1969), "Experimental operations . . . which might be thought of as deleting entire stages without altering the functions of other stages, are probably very rare; they should be considered special cases [p. 280]." In fact, the assumption of pure insertion does not necessarily pose great difficulties, especially since it is often possible to test its validity. The model put forward by Clark and Chase included the assumption of pure insertion; if that assumption had been erroneous, then their model could not have provided such an excellent fit to the data.

In sum, the subtraction method provides a reasonably effective way of discovering some of the major componential stages used in an information-processing task, and of estimating the temporal duration of each stage. However, not all tasks lend themselves to the subtraction method, and it is sometimes difficult (or even impossible) to prevent two or more processing stages combining to form a single parameter estimate.

Componential Analysis

One of the most important problems with much of the research that has employed the additive-factor and subtraction methods concerns the status of the processing stages identified. A particular processing stage may be extremely important within the confines of a single, highly specialised, information-processing task, but may have no relevance to any other task. The problem, which is perhaps the most serious one facing cognitive psychologists, is that of paradigm specificity: Typically, we just do not have the necessary information to assess the degree of generality of the processing stages which we postulate. Part and parcel of the same problem is our inability to decide whether a processing stage discovered in Task A is the same as an apparently similar processing stage uncovered in Task B. The almost total failure to grapple with such difficulties has led to the present state of affairs, which was characterised by Claxton (1980) as follows: "We are like the inhabitants of thousands of little islands, all in the same part of the ocean, yet totally out of touch with each other [p. 15]."

Some of these problems can be at least partially resolved by the use of correlational methods. If the same processing stage does occur in two different tasks, then performance on that stage in the two tasks should be highly correlated across individuals. It is true that a high correlation is only a necessary but not sufficient condition for showing equivalence of the two processing stages, but a very low correlation demonstrates conclusively that the two processing stages are different.

Several examples of the ways in which a consideration of individual differences can clarify important theoretical issues are discussed by Eysenck (1983). By way of illustration, there are two rather different ways in which short-term storage capacity has been assessed, one based on digit or word span and one based on the recency effect in free recall (i.e., the last few items in the list are especially well remembered on an immediate test). There has been some concern about the equivalence of these two measures because the number of items in the digit span is typically much higher than that in the recency effect (7 or more versus 2 or 3, respectively). The non-equivalence of these two alternative ways of measuring the capacity of short-term storage was shown clearly when it was discovered that digit span correlates approximately +.15 with the recency effect (Martin, 1978).

R. Sternberg (1977) claimed persuasively that the information-processing or cognitive psychologist's approach can be regarded as having depth but little breadth, whereas the psychometric or differential approach, based on correlational and factor analytic techniques, has breadth but not depth. As R. Sternberg (1977) argued, "Given the complementary strengths and weaknesses of the differential and information-processing approaches, it should be possible, at least in theory, to synthesise an approach that would capitalise upon the strength of each approach, and thereby share the weakness of neither [p. 65]."

R. Sternberg proposed componential analysis as an approximation to the desired synthesis. While it is customary to measure only the total time taken to solve a complex problem, componential analysis provides a more fine-grain breakdown of performance. The basic strategy can be illustrated with reference to analogy problems having the form "A is to B as C is to D" (e.g., "Hand is to foot as finger is to toe"). The problem can be divided into two parts, so that subjects are given, say, "Hand is to foot," and then, when they are ready, "as finger is to toe." The time taken to process the first fragment of the problem is known as a cue score, and the time spent processing the second fragment and solving the problem is the solution score. Obviously, the amount of information presented in each fragment can be systematically varied, and the resulting cue and solution scores provide a fairly detailed profile of the times taken to deal with the different parts of the problem.

The data obtained from interval scores are used to test theoretical models which indicate the components involved in task performance. According to R. Sternberg (1977), a component is the fundamental unit of analysis, and is defined as an "elementary information process that operates upon internal representations of objects or symbols [p. 65]." Analysis of analogical reasoning suggested that six components are involved, five of which are mandatory and one of which is optional. For problems of the form '*A* is to *B* as *C* is to *D*', the components are as follows: Encoding of the terms; inference (i.e., discover the rule relating *A* to *B*); mapping (i.e., discover the rule relating *A* to *C*); application (i.e., decide what the fourth term should be, and compare against the fourth term supplied); justification (i.e., an optional component testing the accuracy of the operations performed); and preparation-response. R. Sternberg was able to show that theoretical models postulating the existence of these six components occurring in the order given were able to account satisfactorily for the interval-score data.

What evidence is there that these six components have any general significance? Firstly, R. Sternberg (1977) investigated three quite different types of analogy problem (People Pieces, verbal, and geometric), and obtained correlational data suggesting that the five mandatory components are used in all three kinds of task. Secondly, if a component has general applicability then scores on that component should correlate highly with relevant intelligence-test factor scores. Thus, the components of analogical reasoning should theoretically correlate with tests of inductive reasoning ability, but not with tests of perceptual speed. Unfortunately, R. Sternberg's data on this point are rather messy. Reasoning ability scores were correlated with each of the six components, but only under certain conditions. The correlations were nearly always in the expected direction of high reasoning ability being associated with fast component times, with the exception that slower encoding times were sometimes linked with good reasoning ability. Quite unexpectedly, there were especially high correlations between reasoning ability and preparation-response, perhaps because this component actually amalgamates a number of processes.

In essence, the componential method of analysis initially involves an intensive task analysis based on a modified version of the subtraction method, followed by the construction and testing of component models of performance. Finally, the generality of the postulated components is assessed by correlating scores on a particular component in one task with scores on the same component in a second task, and by correlating component scores with scores on intelligence-test factors. R. Sternberg (1977) justified the latter form of analysis by suggesting that factors of intelligence are "constellations of components showing common patterns of individual differences [p. 320]."

One of the standard criticisms of attempts to provide a single theoretical model of task performance is that the existence of substantial individual differences in processing strategies vitiates and invalidates such attempts. While this criticism may have some force, it does not seem relevant to analogical reasoning. R. Sternberg (1977) applied four different theoretical models to the data from one of his studies of analogical reasoning (People Pieces), and found that the model which best accounted for the group data provided the best fit to the data of 12 out of the 16 subjects, and also fitted the data of the remaining subjects quite well.

All in all, componential analysis appears to offer a way of overcoming many of the more obvious inadequacies inherent in much research within cognitive psychology. It is often assumed that it is easier to elucidate the processes involved in low-level tasks than in cognitively demanding tasks; this makes it all the more noteworthy that R. Sternberg's successful use of componential analysis was with a task (analogical reasoning) on which performance has been found to correlate approximately +.8 with the general factor of intelligence (Spearman, 1927).

The "Open Window" Approach

Most of the ways of identifying the component processes of cognitive tasks are highly inferential and necessitate putting forward complex theoretical models. For many purposes it may be preferable to use tasks in which the component processes are relatively obvious. If it is also possible to obtain direct estimates of the duration of each component process, then we have what could be regarded as an "open window" technique.

An interesting example of this technique concerns the letter-transformation task (Hamilton, Hockey, & Rejman, 1977; Hockey, Mac-Lean, & Hamilton, 1981). Between one and four letters are presented, and the subject has to transform each one by working a predetermined distance through the alphabet. Thus, the problem "F + 3" has "I" as the answer, and "KENC + 4" has "OIRG" as the answer. For each problem, the complete transformed sequence must be reported as a single response.

The task is certainly a demanding one: Many university students require considerable practice before being able to solve four-letter problems. The sequence of processing operations seems reasonably clear: Each letter is encoded and the appropriate alphabet location is found in long-term memory (encoding stage); secondly, the transformation is carried out on the letter (transformation stage); finally, the result of the transformation is stored in the memory, and the accumulating answer is rehearsed (storage stage).

Hockey *et al.* (1981) have devised an ingenious technique for measuring the duration of each stage of processing. For example, when given a four-letter problem (e.g., "KENC + 4"), subjects press the button to see the first letter (i.e., "K"), perform the transformation out loud ("LMNO"), and then press the button again to see the second letter (i.e., "E"). This cycle of operations is repeated until all four letters have been presented, and the answer is produced. From the data collected, the duration of the encoding stage is defined as the time between the button press to see a letter and the onset of the overt transformation, the duration of the transformation itself can be measured directly from a tape recording, and the length of the storage stage is the time between the end of the transformation of one letter and the button press to see the next letter.

For a four-letter problem, it is thus possible to divide the total solution time into 12 component times representing the three stages of processing for each of the four letters. There are some potential problems with this technique. It is possible that some of the time apparently spent in performing a stage of processing is actually devoted to back-checking. The externalisation of the transformation stage may affect the way in which the task is performed. Most seriously, the storage stage may well be confounded because it probably represents an amalgam of retrieving the previously stored part of the answer, integration of the transformation just completed into the part-answer, and storage. There are important individual differences at the storage level; informal evidence in our laboratory indicates considerable variation across subjects and problems in the extent to which mnemonics are used to facilitate storage.

One of the advantages of obtaining such unusually detailed behavioural data is that many important issues can be clarified. For example, it emerges that performance is systematically affected by the control processes involved in strategic planning (Hockey *et al.*, 1981). This is shown by the fact that the time to begin transforming the very first letter is influenced by the number of letters that are to follow that trial. In addition, if one simply considers total solution times or error rates, then there are no obvious effects of either alcohol or noise on performance of the letter-transformation task (Hockey *et al.*, 1981). However, it turns out that both of these factors do affect the pattern of performance, increasing the speed with which some components are performed, but decreasing the speed for other components.

Introspection

When people are asked to solve a complex problem taking several minutes to complete, they can usually follow the instruction to "think out loud" during the time spent wrestling with the problem. Newell and Simon (1972) made extensive use of the data from such introspective reports in formulating theoretical accounts of the processes involved in cryptoarithmetic problems, solving theorems in logic, and playing chess, and other theorists have adopted the same general approach with other kinds of problem solving.

There has been considerable controversy almost throughout the history of psychology with respect to the status that should be accorded to introspection. Aristotle argued that introspection was the only method available to study thinking, and concluded that the content of the mind consisted primarily of images organised on the basis of association by contiguity. This associationistic approach was developed by the British empiricists, such as, Hobbes, Locke, and Mill.

The revolt against introspection was perhaps initiated by the brilliant Victorian polymath Sir Francis Galton. He argued in 1883 that the position of consciousness, "appears to be that of a helpless spectator of but a minute fraction of automatic brain work." The Wurzburg school, working in Germany around the end of the nineteenth century, came to a similar conclusion on the basis of rather more empirical evidence. The Wurzburg psychologists gave people simple tasks, such as producing a word association, and then immediately asked them to introspect. They discovered that trained subjects often provided peculiarly formless reports, which they regarded as evidence for "imageless thought."

With the advent of Behaviourism, introspection was discarded as a technique, and theorists, such as Watson, attempted to explain away thinking as merely sub-vocal speech. In contemporary cognitive psychology, the modal view is that introspection provides valuable evidence about some mental processes, but not about others. However, until quite recently there were only sporadic attempts to provide criteria for deciding when introspection is of use.

The middle-of-the-road consensus on the value of introspection was vehemently attacked in a well-known article by Nisbett and Wilson (1977). They argued that introspection is practically worthless, and illustrated their argument with a number of examples. Ghiseli (1952) discussed the ways in which the creative process operated in a number of distinguished people and concluded that: "Production by a process of purely conscious calculation seems never to occur [p. 15]." Indeed, several creative workers indicated that they were sometimes unaware that any process was occurring until the time at which the solution to a problem appeared in consciousness. Ghiseli (1952) quoted the words of Henry James, who deliberately consigned an idea to the unconscious:

I was charmed with my idea, which would take, however, much working out; and because it had so much to give, I think, must I have dropped it for the time into the deep well of unconscious cerebration: not without the hope, doubtless, that it might eventually emerge from that reservoir, as one had already known the buried treasure to come to light, with a firm iridescent surface and a notable increase of weight [p. 26].

At a more experimental level, Nisbett and Wilson (1977) referred to several studies in which the participants seemed entirely oblivious of the processes involved in determining their behaviour. For example, Storms and Nisbett (1970) found that insomniacs fell asleep more quickly than usual after they had taken a placebo pill which was said to produce rapid heart rate, breathing irregularities, and alertness, whereas they slept less readily than usual when the placebo was said to have the opposite effects. This paradoxical finding has been explained in terms of the imputed cause of an individual's internal state: Someone who attributes his aroused internal state to the placebo feels that he is actually fairly calm "in himself," and so sleeps easily, whereas someone who is aroused despite apparently having taken a tranquiliser feels that he must be really agitated, and so cannot sleep.

Irrespective of the adequacy of this explanation, it is clear that the alleged effects of the placebo affected the onset of sleeping. However, when Storms and Nisbett (1970) questioned their subjects about the unusual speed or slowness with which they had gone to sleep, they referred to events totally unrelated to the placebo (e.g., personal problems; time of the week). Indeed, most of the subjects claimed that they had completely forgotten about the pills after taking them.

According to Nisbett and Wilson (1977), such failure to be aware of the processes instrumental in affecting behaviour is the rule. How then can one account for the fact that people are often fairly accurate in their introspective reports about their own mental processes? Nisbett and Wilson argued that this can be explained in terms of implicit a priori theories: "We propose that when people are asked to report how a particular stimulus influenced a particular response, they do so not by consulting a memory of the mediating process, but by applying or generating causal theories about the effects of that type of stimulus on that type of response [p. 248]." This theoretical position leads to the general prediction that a subject's introspections about his own higher mental processes should be no more accurate than the guesses about such processes made by other people.

If the conclusions of Nisbett and Wilson (1977) are valid, then cognitive psychology is in big trouble. Research on human memory relies very heavily on introspection, since the most-used measures of retention, recall and recognition, both depend on conscious awareness that certain information was presented at an earlier time. It would be extremely difficult to conduct experiments on visual illusions if introspection is valueless and thus cannot be used, and the same is true of many other perceptual phenomena (e.g., after-images).

While most cognitive psychologists are reluctant to agree with Nisbett and Wilson (1977), it has to be admitted that their broadside makes it imperative to devise criteria for distinguishing between valid and invalid uses of introspection. Ericsson and Simon (1980) have undertaken this task and provided a preliminary set of criteria including the following:

1. It is preferable to obtain introspective reports during the performance of a task rather than retrospectively. In view of the fallibility of human memory, retrospective reports may be incomplete due to failures of retrieval from long-term memory.

2. Subjects are more likely to produce accurate introspections when asked to describe what they are attending to, or thinking about, than when required to interpret a situation or to speculate about their thought processes. In the study by Storms and Nisbett (1970) previously mentioned, subjects were virtually asked to provide an experimental hypothesis to account for their behaviour.

3. It is clear that people cannot usefully introspect about several kinds of processes (e.g., neuronal events, recognition processes). According to Ericsson and Simon (1980), the degree of involvement of attention is of crucial importance: "Our model assumes that *only information in focal attention* can be verbalised . . . With increase in experience with a task, the same process may move from cognitively controlled to automatic status, so that what is available for verbalisation to the novice may be unavailable to the expert [p. 235]."

Careful consideration of the studies which Nisbett and Wilson (1977) regarded as striking evidence of the worthlessness of introspection reveals that, in virtually every case, subjects provided retrospective interpretations about information which had probably never been fully attended to. In other words, the criteria proposed by Ericsson and Simon seem to work in practice.

At a rather more theoretical level, Ericsson and Simon (1980) argued persuasively that accurate introspection or verbalisation concerning cognitive processes has to be based on information contained in either short-term or long-term memory. As a consequence, introspections may be incomplete if the appropriate information never enters the short-term store (e.g., due to lack of focal attention); or if information previously available in the short-term store is not stored in long-term memory; or if information is stored in long-term memory but cannot be retrieved. Since introspection depends to such an extent on the short-term store, the limitations of that store (e.g., small capacity, detailed information not normally stored) directly affect the process of introspection.

Even if introspective reports can frequently be accepted as valid, there is the further methodological problem that requiring people to provide such reports while performing a task may change the nature of the cognitive processes that are under study. However, common sense suggests that the extent of any disruption of ongoing cognitive processes depends on the kinds of information that subjects are asked to provide in their introspective reports. Disruption should be minimal if subjects are simply asked to "think aloud"; in contrast, disruption should be maximal if subjects are asked to provide complex interpretations concerning information which would not normally be in focal attention. Probably the most crucial factor is whether or not the information required in introspective reports is accessible without changing the focus of attention.

There are many cases in which thinking aloud has been found to have no systematic effect on the structure and course of the processes involved in performing a task. For example, Newell and Simon (1972) compared the performance of subjects who were not asked to provide introspective reports with that of subjects told to think aloud on tasks involving the discovery of proofs in propositional logic. Detailed analyses of the correct and incorrect steps taken by the two groups of subjects revealed no consequential differences. Furthermore, the two groups did not differ in the number of correct solutions.

In sum, while there are various limitations on introspection as a method for identifying cognitive processes, it can be a valid and extremely useful technique under some circumstances. Ericsson and Simon (1980) have made the important point that the limitations of introspection correspond closely to the limitations of the memory system.

Computer Simulation

A technique that is often used in tandem with introspection is computer simulation. Theorists have argued that if the performance patterns of a computer and of a human being on a given task are functionally equivalent, then the programme that is directing the computer represents a good theory of how that person carried out the task.

Unfortunately, the whole issue of functional equivalence is more complicated than it appears to be at first glance. A computer programme may perform various mathematical calculations with the same degree of accuracy as a person, suggesting equivalence, but may produce solutions much more rapidly, which is indicative of non-equivalence. Indeed, it is typical for computers to simulate only some aspects of human performance. As Neisser (1963) pointed out many years ago, computer goals tend to be simple and fixed, whereas those of human beings are usually complex and fluid. Thus, a person playing chess may be concerned about the length of time taken up by the game, other commitments he or she may have, and his or her

HCP-B

interactions with his or her opponent, as well as winning the game, whereas a computer deals only with the chess game.

If complete equivalence between computer and human performance is a chimera, what degree of functional equivalence should we strive for? Firstly, a set of problems should yield the same order of difficulty for the computer and for humans. Secondly, the levels of accuracy should be comparable for the computer and for man. Thirdly, the computer should make the same kinds of mistakes as humans during problem solution. Fourthly, and of major importance, there should be reasonably close correspondence between the introspective reports of human subjects and the steps incorporated into the computer-simulation program.

There are several examples of reasonably successful computer simulation. In particular, Newell and Simon (1972) with their General Problem Solver have been able to produce reasonably good simulations of human performance on a variety of problems. The basic problem–solving strategy built into the General Problem Solver is means–ends analysis. An important difference between the current state of the world and the goal state is detected, and a method of reducing or eliminating the difference is sought and applied. If this does not lead directly to the goal state, the process is repeated as often as is necessary. When the General Problem Solver has been used to solve logical and mathematical problems, its approach, of proceeding on the basis of reducing the difference between the current state of the problem and the goal state, typically corresponds approximately to the strategies used by people.

One of the major limitations of such computer-simulation theories is that they are only applicable to well-defined problems in which the initial state, the goal state, and the permissible moves are all clearly specified. It is probably the rule rather than the exception in everyday life for problems to lack one or more of the characteristics of well-defined problems, and relevant computer-simulation techniques have not been developed. Such ill-defined problems may, for example, have no unequivocal goal state, in the sense that any possible solution has an amalgam of advantages and disadvantages associated with it.

The computer-simulation technique has also been used in several other areas of psychology. Examples include perception (see Chapter 2), imagery (see Chapter 7), and language processing (see Chapter 8). Some of the major issues concerning the usefulness of computer simulation to an understanding of human cognition are discussed at greater length in Chapter 13.

Conclusions

Six different techniques for identifying component processing stages or operations in cognitive tasks have been discussed in this chapter, and various other methods have also been used from time to time. Which technique or method has turned out to be the most successful? This question is essentially meaningless for various reasons. In the first place, each method can only be used on certain limited kinds of tasks. Secondly, within its range of applicability each method or technique has proved markedly more successful in identifying the relevant processes for some tasks than for others. As a consequence, each of the six methods is sometimes more suitable than any of the others, but is often inappropriate or inadequate.

The overwhelming emphasis in the literature has been on the identification of the processing stages in a particular task or closely related set of tasks. The next step, that of assessing the generality of the processing stages thus discovered, has been curiously neglected. A processing mechanism that is used in dealing with very few tasks might as well be consigned to Stygian darkness, whereas a mechanism that is common to numerous cognitive activities may form one of the building blocks of any adequate theory of cognition. Componential analysis is the only method that appears to have accorded the generality issue the significance it merits, and thus the basic strategy of wedding the cognitive and psychometric approaches that provides the underpinning of componential analysis may provide an adumbration of future developments.

2 Aspects of Perception

Our discussion of perception can perhaps most appropriately begin with a consideration of the concept of perception. While it is clear that perception is an activity importantly influenced by sensory information, there is no consensus regarding its definition. Bartley (1969) chose to focus on the role played by discrimination: "*Perception* is the immediate discriminatory response of the organism to energy-activating sense organs. . . . To discriminate is to make a choice reaction in which contextual conditions play a deciding role [pp. 11–12]." In contrast, Levine and Shefner (1981) offered the following definition which is more in tune with contemporary thinking: "*Perception* refers to the way in which we interpret the information gathered (and processed) by the senses. In a word, we sense the presence of a stimulus, but we perceive what it is [p. 1]."

This process of interpreting sensory information is complex and involves a considerable variety of processing mechanisms. At the very least, perception depends upon basic physiological systems associated with each sensory modality, together with central brain processes that integrate and interpret the output from these physiological systems. Not surprisingly, major contributions to our knowledge of perception have come from advances in both physiology and psychology. There is also increasing interest (see Frisby, 1979) in the possibility that certain key aspects of perception can be performed successfully by a computer. The hope is that such an achievement would shed light on the ways in which human perceptual processes operate.

It is obvious that there can be no comprehensive coverage of perception from the physiological, psychological, and artificial intelligence perspectives within the confines of a single chapter. What has been attempted is rather more limited. The emphasis will be on the more cognitive aspects of perception, but there will also be some discussion of the highlights of work on physiology and artificial intelligence. Furthermore, the focus will be on visual perception, since this has attracted more research interest than other sense modalities.

23

SUBLIMINAL PERCEPTION

Introduction

It is natural for us to regard perception as a processing activity of which the individual is consciously aware, and this orientation has been shared by most psychologists interested in perception. In line with this, it is worth noting that most perception research relies heavily on the individual subject's reports of what he or she is perceiving. This practice makes little or no sense unless there is conscious awareness of perceptual activity.

This popular view of perception appears to rule out the possibility of subliminal perception, i.e., perception occurring even though the stimulus input is presented so briefly or at such low intensity as to be below the threshold of conscious awareness. In fact, there is steadily accumulating evidence indicating the existence of subliminal perception in various different situations. Most of the relevant evidence was discussed by Dixon (1981), who arrived at the following challenging conclusions:

> The brain respond to external stimuli which, for one reason or another, are not consciously perceived. The effects of such stimuli may be almost as varied as those of sensory inflow which *does* enter consciousness. They include the evoking and determination of cortical potentials, changes in the EEG, the production of electrodermal responses, and changes in sensory threshold. They also include effects on memory, the influencing of lexical decisions, and such subjective manifestations as changes in conscious perceptual experience, dreams, and the evoking of appropriate effects [p. 262].

Subliminal perception has been demonstrated in studies of binocular rivalry, in which there is conscious awareness of the information from only one eye when entirely different visual stimuli are presented to each eye. In spite of the lack of conscious perception of information from the suppressed eye, it appears that this information is registered and analysed. In one study (Walker, 1975), a red patch was presented to one eye and a green patch to the other. When a further, but subliminal, stimulus (a moving array of randomly distributed black and white squares) was added to the suppressed visual field, that visual field almost immediately assumed dominance. In other words, conscious perception was systematically affected by perceptual processing occurring without awareness.

A rather different example of subliminal perception was reported by Rollman and Nachmias (1972). In a signal-detection task, subjects had to decide whether or not a chromatic disc had been presented. On those trials when the subject incorrectly reported that there was no visual stimulus, he or she was asked to guess what colour the disc would have been if it had been presented. These guesses showed a tendency to correspond to the colour that had actually been presented.

How can we account for the existence of subliminal perception? One reasonable possibility is that the physiological threshold for a stimulus is usually lower than its awareness threshold. As a consequence, a modest level of stimulus energy may suffice to activate peripheral sensory organs and relevant cortical areas without being intense enough to produce conscious perception. Libet (1973) recorded cortical-evoked potentials from fully-conscious subjects, and found that a weak tactile stimulus did not lead to conscious perception, but did elicit the early components of the evoked response. An increase in stimulus strength was associated with reported awareness of the stimulus, and the later components of the evoked response were elicited.

Perceptual Defence

Some of the major theoretical controversies raised by research on subliminal perception can be clarified by considering the phenomenon of perceptual defence, in which emotionally-charged stimuli are perceived less readily than relatively neutral stimuli. It has sometimes been argued that the elevated recognition threshold for emotive stimuli, such as taboo or obscene words, is due to some kind of response bias, and is thus not a truly perceptual phenomenon. For example, even when an embarrassing stimulus has been recognised there may be some reluctance to report it. It may be somewhat simplistic to suggest that perceptual defence reflects the workings of either the perceptual system or of the response system, but relevant evidence can be, and has been, obtained by making use of the measures of signal-detection theory, namely, sensitivity or d' and response criterion or β.

Hardy and Legge (1968) gave their subjects the task of detecting the presence of a faint auditory stimulus while watching a screen upon which emotional or neutral words were presented subliminally. Although nearly all of the subjects failed to notice that any words had been presented, Hardy and Legge discovered that the auditory threshold was higher when emotional words were being presented. This effect was due to a reduction in sensitivity to stimulation rather than a shift in response bias. The experimental design effectively precluded any report suppression, and the conclusion that perceptual defence is a perceptual rather than a response-bias phenomenon has been confirmed in other studies using the signal-detection theory measures.

One popular way of explaining perceptual defence has been the fragmentation or partial cue hypothesis. The basic idea is that conscious perception of part of a word stimulus (e.g., "sh*t") may inhibit further perceptual processing if it is suspected that the word may be obscene. There may be a grain of truth in this hypothesis, but it does not seem relevant to the study by Hardy and Legge (1968), since their subjects were not even aware that words had been presented. Furthermore, it is not altogether clear how inhibition of visual perceptual processing would lead to elevation of the auditory threshold.

Perceptual defence poses a problem for many theories of perception, largely because of the difficulty of deciding how it is that the perceiver can selectively defend him or herself against an emotional stimulus unless he or she has already perceived the stimulus and identified it. The essence of this paradox was expressed clearly by Howie (1952): "To speak of perceptual defence is to use a mode of discourse which must make any precise or even intelligible meaning of perceptual defence impossible, for it is to speak of perceptual process as somehow being both a process of knowing and a process of avoiding knowing [p. 311]."

How can we explain away this apparently logical paradox? The most straightforward answer (Dixon, 1981; Erdelyi, 1974) is to reject the notion of perception as a unitary event, and to replace it with a conceptualisation in which perception involves multiple processing stages or mechanisms, with consciousness perhaps representing the final level of processing. It is thus possible for a stimulus input to receive considerable perceptual processing without conscious awareness of the products of that processing, and this may well be the case with perceptual defence.

PERCEPTION: DIRECT OR INDIRECT?

Introduction

Perception of the environment through the various senses (vision, hearing, touch, taste, and so on) is a relatively effortless process for most of us. It is also amazingly efficient, allowing us to move around freely with only very occasional mishaps, some of which stem from the ill-judged use of drink or drugs rather than any inherent limitations of the perceptual system. The apparent simplicity of perception can make it rather difficult to realise that perception is in fact rather complex and poorly understood. Consider for a moment what you see when you look around a room. Perhaps you can see four walls, some tables, a clock, and a number of distant cars through a window. The walls and the tables probably appear to be rectangular, the clock looks circular, and the cars seem to be of normal size. Such mundane perceptions immediately become more mysterious when you consider the information that is being received by the eyes. The right angles that you perceive in the corners of the room or on the tables nearly all form acute or oblique angles on the retina, and the round clock is probably an ellipse

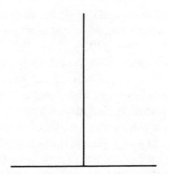

FIG. 2.1   The vertical–horizontal illusion.

in the retinal image. As for the distant cars, they occupy much less space in the retinal image than does the watch on your wrist, but you see the cars as being very much larger than your watch.

All in all, accurate perception is a far more considerable achievement than it initially appears to be. Indeed, it is of interest that even sophisticated computers cannot as yet be made to match the visual capacities of relatively primitive animals, but they can be programmed to play chess as well as expert human chess players. While perception is usually accurate, it is worth noting that the perceptual system does make mistakes, some of which can be demonstrated by means of the various well-known visual illusions. It has sometimes been suggested that such illusions are merely unusual trick figures dreamt up by psychologists to baffle ordinary decent folk, and that they are in no sense representative of normal perception. This view is certainly erroneous, as can be seen by Fig. 2.1. Which line is longer in this vertical–horizontal illusion? We tend to over-estimate vertical extents relative to horizontal ones, and this can be shown readily with real objects by taking a teacup, saucer, and two similar spoons. Place one spoon horizontally in the saucer and the other spoon vertically in the cup, and you will see that the vertical spoon looks much longer than the horizontal spoon.

Any adequate theory of perception must account for both the successes and the failures of the perceptual system. It must also explain how accurate or veridical perception is possible, given the apparently impoverished nature of the information available in the retinal image. As is explained later, there is no theory as yet able to provide full explanations of these perceptual phenomena, but some partial answers are available.

Theoretical Controversies

There are two main sources of information that can be used in the attempt to perceive the external world accurately: (1) currently available sensory information; and (2) relevant past knowledge and experience stored in the brain. There has been much controversy over the relative importance of these two factors, with Gibson (1950, 1966, 1979) emphasising the role played by stimulus information in perception, and Bruner (1957) and Gregory (1970) focusing on constructive and hypothesis-testing processes.

One of Gibson's main points is that there is much more information potentially available in sensory stimulation than is usually realized. It is possible, of course, to eliminate most of this information by presenting a visual scene very briefly in a tachistoscope,but everyday life is not generally like that. Observers normally have ample time to inspect the visual environment, and viewing the same scene from different angles greatly increases the amount of useful information that can be extracted from sensory stimulation.

According to Gibson, we are able to perceive surfaces at different slants or in depth as a result of using information from visual stimulation concerning the gradient of texture density. If a homogeneously textured surface is perpendicular to the line of sight, then the density of the texture does not vary from one part of the optic array to another, i.e., the gradient of texture density is zero. On the other hand, an object that slants will have an increased gradient, or rate of change, of texture density as you look from the near edge to the far edge. If observers "pick up" this information about the gradient of texture density from the optic array, then it could be argued that at least some aspects of depth are perceived directly.

Further valuable information about the spatial layout of objects in the external environment becomes available when we move forwards. All of the stationary objects in the visual field undergo a process of expansion; the gradient of expansion thus created produces a pattern that is determined by the orientation of each object, by the speed and direction of the observer's motion, and by the distance of the observer from each object.

The gradients of texture density and expansion illustrate some of the information inherent in the optic array that can be used to provide an observer with an unambiguous spatial layout of the environment. In more general terms, Gibson argued that certain higher order characteristics of the visual array change and others remain unaltered when an observer moves around his or her environment, and these transpositions and invariants supply crucial evidence that is picked up in a direct fashion by the perceiver. This theoretical position was expressed in the following terms by Gibson (1979): "The perceptual system simply extracts the invariants from the flowing array; it *resonates* to the invariant structure or is attuned to it [p. 249]." The concept of "invariant" has been used by Gibson (1972) in a rather broad and amorphous way: "A great many properties of the array are *lawfully* or *regularly* variant with changing observation point, and this means that in each case a property defined by the law is *invariant* [p. 221]."

How can the Gibsonian approach handle the problem of meaning? Gibson rejected the conventional view that percepts become meaningful as a result of the involvement of relevant knowledge, and argued instead that all of the potential uses of objects (i.e., their "affordances") are directly perceivable. The particular affordances of an object that are detected depend on the perceiver's species and his or her current psychological state. For example, a hungry person will percive the affordance of edibility when presented with an orange, whereas an angry wife may detect the affordance of projectile and throw the orange at her bemused husband.

What is one to make of the Gibsonian view that the stimulus itself is so rich and full of information that perception is merely a matter of "picking up" that information from the optic array? Does perception really occur in such a direct fashion? In answering these questions, it is important to bear in mind that the existence of potentially informative stimulus variables, such as the invariants emphasised by Gibson, is insufficient to provide strong support for Gibson's position. What needs to be done is to demonstrate that people actually make use of these perceptual variables in everyday perception, and the available evidence is rather inconclusive. It has to be borne in mind that people can only accept information from the visual world at a relatively slow rate (Gregory, 1970, put the limit at approximately 12 bits of information per second). Even if the perceptual system is able to make use of some higher order characteristics of the visual array, it may not do so in quite the direct fashion implied by Gibson, If, for example, detection of the gradient of texture density requires the acuity of foveal vision, then information must be picked up and integrated over a period of time from a succession of eye movements, which does not sound much like direct perception.

One of the main aims of Gibson's theory is to provide an explanation of how it is that we are able to perceive the environment in a veridical way. In a sense, his explanation is too good, because visual stimulation allegedly provides the observer with so much valuable information that space perception should normally be essentially perfect. In fact, of course, this is by no means always the case. We have already mentioned the ubiquitous vertical–horizontal illusion, and another common perceptual failure is the tendency for large objects at great distances to look much smaller than they actually are. In a nutshell, Gibson's theory of direct perception is primarily designed to account for veridical perception, and often has no plausible explanation of the systematically distorted percepts produced by illusory figures.

A radically different approach has been favoured by several theorists including Bruner (1957), Gregory (1970, 1972), and Neisser (1967). In essence, they regard perception as an active and constructive process; perception is not directly given by the stimulus input, but occurs as the end-product of the interactive influences of the presented stimulus and internal hypotheses and expectations. According to Gregory (1972), perceptual experiences are constructions "from floating fragmentary scraps of data signalled by the senses and drawn from the brain memory banks, themselves constructions from the snippets of the past." To anticipate a little, this theoretical approach can readily account for perceptual errors (e.g., in terms of inappropriate expectations), but is perhaps somewhat embarrassed by the fact that perception is normally veridical.

There are several phenomena indicating that at least some perceptual representations are not constructed solely on the basis of information from the current physical input, but make use of stored information. A case in point is the phonemic restoration effect. Twenty people were presented with a recording of the sentence, "The state governors met with their respective legi*latures convening in the capital city." The asterisk indicates a .12 second portion of the recorded sentence that had been removed and replaced with the sound of a cough. Warren and Warren (1970) found that all but one of their subjects claimed that there was no missing sound; the remaining subject identified the wrong sound as missing.

Warren and Warren (1970) then modified the basic experimental technique slightly to provide a more striking demonstration of the ways in which stored knowledge can affect perception. Their subjects were presented with one of the following sentences; the asterisk again indicates a deleted portion of the sentence:

1. It was found that the *eel was on the axle.
2. It was found that the *eel was on the shoe.
3. It was found that the *eel was on the table.
4. It was found that the *eel was on the orange.

The way in which the crucial element in the sentence (i.e., "*eel") was perceived was much affected by sentence context. Subjects listening to the first sentence tended to hear "wheel", those listening to the second sentence heard "heel," whereas those exposed to the third and fourth sentences heard "meal" and "peel", respectively.

The formation of expectations on the basis of the available information (sentence-context information in the experiments by Warren and Warren, 1970) can clearly facilitate perception, in that relatively little stimulus information may be needed in order to construct an accurate percept. However, if the current situation appears familiar, but is actually novel, then the perceptual hypotheses formed may be well wide of the mark. As an example, consider the well-known Ames distorted room. The room is actually of a most peculiar shape, but when viewed from a particular point it gives rise to the same retinal image as a conventional rectangular room.

Not surprisingly, observers decide that the room is like a normal one; they maintain this belief even when someone inside the room walks backwards and forwards along the rear wall, apparently growing and shrinking as he or she proceeds! The reason for the apparent size changes is that the rear wall is not perpendicular to the viewing point; one corner is actually much further away from the observer than the other corner. As might be expected by constructive theorists, there is a greater likelihood of the room being perceived as having an odd shape and the person walking inside it remaining the same size when that person is the spouse or close relative of the observer.

Another illustration of the possible pitfalls involved in relying too heavily on expectations comes in a study by Bruner and Postman (1949). Their subjects expected to see conventional playing cards, but some of the cards used were incongruous (e.g., black hearts). When these incongruous cards were presented briefly, subjects sometimes reported that they saw brown or purple hearts. In this case we have almost literally a blending of stimulus information and stored information.

Constructive theorists can explain many of the classic visual illusions in a general way by assuming that previous knowledge derived from perception of three-dimensional objects in space is applied inappropriately to the perception of two-dimensional figures. For example, people typically see a given object as having a constant size despite variations in the retinal image by taking account of its apparent distance; the further away from the observer that an object is, the smaller will be its size in the retinal image. Gregory's (1970) misapplied size-constancy theory argues that this kind of perceptual processing is applied wrongly to produce several visual illusions. In the Müller–Lyer illusion (see Fig. 2.2), the vertical line in the figure on the left appears longer than the vertical line in the figure on the right, although they are in fact of the same length. According to Gregory, the Müller–Lyer figures can be regarded as simple perspective drawings of aspects of three-dimensional objects. Thus the figure on the left can be

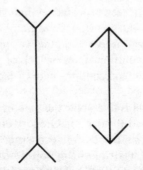

FIG. 2.2 The Müller–Lyer illusion.

thought of as the inside corner of a room, and the figure on the right as the outside corner of a building. In other words, the outgoing fins represent lines approaching us, whereas the ingoing fins stand for lines receding into the distance. Thus the vertical line on the left is in some sense further away from us than the vertical line on the right. Since the retinal images of the two vertical lines are the same size, the implication of size-constancy scaling is that a more distant line of the same retinal size as a less distant line must actually be longer, and that, of course, is the Müller–Lyer illusion.

In essence, then, the misapplied size-constancy theory claims that the internal processes that use apparent distance to gauge apparent size are misapplied to illusion figures, such as those of the Müller–Lyer. Why do the figures appear flat if they are treated in many ways as three-dimensional objects? Gregory (1970) argued that this is because the figures are seen as lying on a flat surface, and that the Müller–Lyer figures do indeed take on a three-dimensional appearance when they are presented in the dark as luminous two-dimensional outlines.

The theory is ingenious, but it has by no means gained universal acceptance. Gregory's claim that luminous Müller–Lyer figures are seen three-dimensionally by everyone is erroneous, and it has been argued (Stacey & Pike, 1970) that apparent size determines distance, rather than the reverse. It is particularly puzzling from the perspective of Gregory's theory that the Müller–Lyer illusion can still be obtained when the fins on the two figures are replaced by other attachments such as circles or squares. This suggests that the vertical line may appear longer or shorter than its actual length simply because it is a part of a large or a small object. It is likely (Day, 1980) that more than one factor contributes to the Müller–Lyer illusion, and that the various visual illusions are to be explained in different ways.

Does perception depend mainly on detailed analysis of stimulus information (sometimes referred to as bottom-up processing), or is it mainly a function of context and expectations (i.e., top-down processing)? It would be foolish to answer the question in a dogmatic fashion, because the relative importance of bottom-up and top-down processing in perception is affected by a variety of factors. It seems probable that visual perception is very largely bottom-up when the viewing conditions are good, but may increasingly involve top-down processes as the viewing conditions deteriorate because of very brief presentation times or lack of stimulus clarity, and the same is likely to be true of perception in the other sense modalities (e.g. auditory, tactile).

This line of argument helps to resolve the theoretical controversy between Gibson on the one hand and Bruner and Gregory on the other hand. Gibson has concentrated on visual perception occurring under optimal viewing conditions, whereas theorists emphasizing top-down processes in perception have tended to use very sub-optimal viewing conditions (e.g., brief tachistoscopic presentation of visual stimuli). In other words, the theoretical differences may be due in large measure to the very different perceptual environments investigated by different researchers.

In most circumstances, perception undoubtedly involves the combined influence of bottom-up and top-down processes. Total reliance on bottom-up processing would be unwise because of the ambiguous and imprecise nature of much visual stimulation, and we would always be hallucinating if we only used top-down processing. In an elegant demonstration of the importance of both kinds of processing, Tulving, Mandler, and Baumal (1964) looked at some of the factors involved in perceiving a word correctly. The role of bottom-up processing was manipulated by altering the exposure duration, and the involvement of top-down processing was varied by changing the amount of relevant sentence context provided before the word was presented. The probability of a correct identification increased directly as a function of both exposure duration and the amount of context. In addition, the impact of context was progressively reduced as the target words were presented for longer durations, suggesting that the clearer the stimulus input, the less is the necessity to make use of other sources of information.

While the interactive effects of bottom-up and top-down processes on perception have been firmly established, much remains to be discovered about the details of this interaction. For example, it seems plausible to assume that the perceiver's expectations are initially relatively vague and general, and that they become progressively more specific as more and more stimulus information is available. It seems likely, too, that expectations play a part in determining those stimulus attributes that receive attention. However, a comprehensive evaluation of these, and other, theoretical notions is a task for the future.

ORGANISATION IN VISUAL PERCEPTION

One of the most obvious facts of visual perception is that it is nearly always organised. An important part of that organisation is the segregation of the visual field into one part called the "figure" and another part called the "ground." The figure and ground are separated by a contour that appears to belong to the figure. According to Rubin (1921), the form has "thinglike" qualities, unlike the ground which is relatively uniform. In addition, the figure usually seems to be nearer than the ground, and the ground extends unbroken behind the figure.

This figure–ground organisation seems to come about fairly automatically, and Rubin (1921) and the Gestalt psychologists argued that it reflects the basic and innate functioning of the visual system. Some support for that position has emerged from investigations of blind adults whose sight has been restored following the removal of cataracts. Even though such individuals have had little or no previous visual experience, they are usually able to segregate the visual field into figure and ground. However, this may only be possible because of their previous experience with other sense modalities such as touch. It is clear that figure–ground organisation does not always occur immediately and with no difficulty. If the central object in the visual field is large, then it may take a number of glances before the figure can be perceived accurately.

The Gestaltists were interested in some of the ways in which visual perception is organised. They called those areas of a visual display that are encoded as figures, "Gestalten" or organised wholes. Their fundamental principle of perceptual organisation was the law of Prägnanz, which Koffka (1935) expressed as follows: "Psychological organisation will always be as 'good' as the prevailing conditions allow. In this definition the term 'good' is undefined [p. 110]." In practice, the Gestaltists regarded a good form as the simplest or the most uniform of the available alternatives.

While the law of Prägnanz was their key organisational principle, the Gestaltists also proposed several other laws, most of which can be subsumed under the law of Prägnanz. These laws were formulated on the basis of their use of ambiguous patterns such as those shown in Fig. 2.3. Pattern (a) shows that visual elements tend to be grouped together if they are close to each other (the law of proximity); three horizontal arrays of dots are perceived rather than vertical arrays. Pattern (b) illustrates the law of similarity, according to which elements will be grouped perceptually if they are similar to each other. Vertical columns rather than horizontal rows are seen because the elements in the vertical columns are the same, whereas those in the horizontal rows are not. The law of good continuation is shown in pattern (c); we naturally see two crossing lines rather than a V-shaped line and an

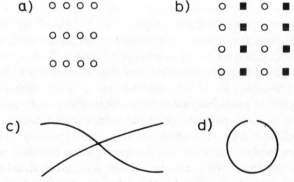

FIG. 2.3   Examples of some of the Gestalt laws of perceptual organization: (a) the law of proximity; (b) the law of similarity; (c) the law of good continuation; and (d) the law of closure.

inverted V-shaped line, because we group together those elements requiring the fewest changes or interruptions in straight or smoothly curving lines or contours. Pattern (d) illustrates the law of closure, according to which missing parts of a figure are filled in to complete the figure. Thus, a circle is seen in spite of the fact that it is incomplete.

These, and other, Gestalt laws of perceptual organisation make reasonable intuitive sense, but they are obviously descriptive statements possessing little or no explanatory power. The Gestalt laws are also rather limited in that they are only directly applicable to the perceived organisation of two-dimensional representations. With three-dimensional scenes, figure–ground separation can be facilitated by depth information or by movement of the figure (e.g., a chameleon may only be distinguishable from its background when it moves). The Gestaltists appear to have believed that their laws reflect basic organisational processes within the brain, but it is quite likely that the laws arise as a result of experience. After all, similar and spatially close visual elements are much more likely to belong to the same object in everyday life than are dissimilar and distant elements.

Some fresh insights into perceptual organisation were provided in a series of studies by Beck (e.g., 1966). He discovered that simple visual elements tended to be grouped together on the basis of line orientation: Similarly shaped elements presented in different orientations were grouped separately, whereas dissimilar elements in the same orientation were grouped together. This suggests that perceptual grouping may depend more on a relatively simple stimulus attribute, such as orientation, than on similarity as proposed by the law of similarity. In this connection, it may be relevant that there is strong physiological evidence for specific detectors for line orientation in the visual cortex (Hubel & Wiesel, 1962). Beck concluded that perceptual grouping occurs on the basis of simple stimulus properties, such as, brightness, size, and line orientation, all of which are processed at an early stage by the visual system.

It will be remembered that the major perceptual law introduced by the Gestaltists was the law of Prägnanz or good form. The notion of a "good" or simple form was left rather amorphous by Gestalt psychologists, but Attneave (1954) made a noteworthy attempt to render it more precise. He argued that a "good" figure is one with a high degree of internal redundancy; in other words, the structure of any unseen part of a "good" figure is highly predictable from the parts that can be seen. From this perspective, factors such as proximity, similarity, and good continuation all reduce perceptual uncertainty by providing redundant information. Hochberg (1978) has developed a similar theoretical position, proposing what he calls a minimum principle: If there is more than one organisation for a given visual stimulus, the one most likely to be perceived is that which requires the least amount of information to describe it.

The Gestaltists put forward the concept of the Gestalt (whole or configuration) as the major unit of analysis within perception, and perhaps their best-known view is that "the whole is more than the sum of its parts." The basic Gestaltist position was put by Wertheimer (1958): "The way in which parts are seen, in which subwholes emerge, in which grouping occurs, is not an arbitrary piecemeal . . . summation of elements, but is a process in which characteristics of the whole play a major determining role [p. 135]." This may sound like mumbo-jumbo, but there are actually various ways of testing it. For example, it follows from the Gestaltist perspective that it should be possible to replace the original parts with other parts while managing to retain the quality of the whole or the Gestalt. This is known as "transposition," and a simple example is the way in which a melody remains the same when it is transposed into a key in which all of the notes are changed.

One of the implications of the Gestaltist approach is that the overall Gestalt or whole may be perceived before the parts comprising that Gestalt. This idea may sound far-fetched, but it was put to the test in an important series of experiments carried out by Navon (1977). He drew a conceptual distinction between global and local features; local features are more specific than global features and are consequently "part-like", whereas global features are more "whole-like." If, for example, a large letter "H" were constructed out of several small "S"s, then the global feature would be the letter"H", and the "S"s would be the local features.

In one experiment, subjects looked briefly at a large letter made up of many small letters while deciding as rapidly as possible whether an "H" or an "S" had been presented auditorily. When the global letter was the same as the auditory letter, speed of auditory discrimination was increased, whereas there was an interference effect when it was different. More surprisingly, performance on the auditory task was quite unaffected by the nature of the local letters, and most of the subjects even failed to notice that the large letters were constructed out of small letters. These findings suggest that global features are perceived more readily than local features, as the Gestaltists would have expected. Why should this be so? Perhaps when there is only sufficient time for a partial perceptual analysis, it is usually more valuable to obtain information about the general structure of a perceptual scene than about a few isolated details.

The experiment that we have just discussed shows that the whole can be perceived before its parts, but it is not clear how much control people have over their perceptual processes. If, for example, someone wanted to perceive the local features while ignoring the global features, would this be possible? Navon (1977) attempted to answer this question in a further study again using large letters made out of small letters. The task was to decide as rapidly as possible either whether the global letter was an "H" or an "S", or whether the small letters were "H"s or "S"s. Decision speed with the large or global letter was unaffected by the nature of the local or small letters, but performance speed with the local letters was greatly slowed when the global letter conflicted with the local letters. This latter finding indicates that it is difficult, or even impossible, to avoid perceiving the whole, and suggests that global processing necessarily occurs before any more detailed perceptual analysis.

Navon's (1977) work implies that the notion that perceptual analysis involves building up a representation of a visual scene from its individual elements may be misguided. Instead, initial global structuring is often fleshed out by progressively more and more fine-grained analyses. There is obvious sense in having the perceptual system operate in this fashion, because it enables important objects in the visual scene to be identified and perceived with minimal delay. However, it is clear that the perceptual system does not invariably work like this. The large letters in Navon's (1977) studies were not all that large, never exceeding 5.5° of visual angle. Kinchla and Wolf (1979) used similar stimuli to those of Navon, but with sizes ranging up to 22.1° of visual angle. They discovered that the local letters were easier to respond to than the global one when the global letter exceeded 8° of visual angle. They concluded that those forms in the visual field having an optimal size are processed first.

In spite of these complexities, it still seems likely that global-to-local processing frequently occurs. A theoretical model based on that assumption was put forward by Palmer (1977), who argued that visual form is analysed hierarchically starting with the overall configuration and moving down towards the basic features or elements. At each level of the hierarchy, Gestalt principles help to determine how the lower-level units are joined together to form more organised wholes or Gestalten at that level.

Palmer (1977) tested these ideas by making simple line drawings, and also constructing parts of them that varied in degree of figural goodness. Those segments or parts possessing high figural goodness often resembled familiar and nameable shapes. The subjects initially viewed one of the complete line drawings, followed by a test figure consisting of line segments. Their task was to decide whether the test figure formed part of the original line drawing.

Theoretically, the subjects were assumed to analyse the original figure first as a total form, then in terms of its "good" component parts, and finally in terms of its individual lines. When the test figure was presented, the subjects allegedly worked their way down this memorised hierarchy until either a match occurred (on positive trials) or no match was detected at any level (on negative trials). As expected by Palmer's (1977) hierarchical model, positive responses were made faster the higher the figural goodness of the test figure. With "good" test figures, it is more likely that a match can be made at a higher level of the hierarchy.

PATTERN RECOGNITION

Introduction

One of the most important (yet least understood) aspects of visual perception is pattern recognition, which involves assigning meaning to visual input by identifying the objects in the visual field. The typically effortless way in which pattern recognition occurs poses a theoretical problem, because pattern recognition is actually more of an achievement than it might appear. In essence, what needs to be accounted for is the amazing flexibility of the human perceptual system as it copes with a multitude of different stimuli. An example of this flexibility much favoured by textbook writers is our ability to recognize different visual presentations of the letter "A" as instances of the pattern "A" in spite of considerable variations in orientation, in typeface, in size, and in writing style.

Even though it is not known in detail how pattern recognition occurs, it seems clear at a very general level that it involves matching information in one memory store (the sensory register) with information in a second memory store (permanent or semantic memory). In other words, information conveyed by the senses is matched with and related to what we know about the world. When the stimulus information has been compared with information in permanent memory, a decision is then made as to which information in permanent memory provides the best match to the stimulus.

Various kinds of pattern-recognition theory have been advanced that attempt to explain how this matching process occurs. Most of them are either template theories, prototype theories, or feature theories. Accordingly, we consider each of these three theoretical approaches in turn in our discussion.

Template Theories

The basic idea behind template theories is that stimulus information is compared directly to various miniature copies (or templates) of previously presented patterns which are stored in permanent memory. A stimulus is identified on the basis of that template producing the closest match to the stimulus input.

This kind of theory is beguilingly simple, but matters become more complicated when we consider how template theories explain the ease with which patterns are recognised in the face of changes in size, orientation, colour, and so on. It could be argued, of course, that there is a separate template for every conceivable instance of a pattern, but this would be tremendously uneconomical in storage terms, and thus seems implausible. The problem could be alleviated somewhat if it were assumed that the match between the internal representation of the stimulus input and the stored template need not be perfect. Alternatively, the number of templates required for pattern recognition can be reduced to a more realistic level if the stimulus input undergoes a normalisation process that produces an internal representation in a standard position, size, and so on, before the search for a matching template begins. However, the advantages of postulating such a normalisation process are largely illusory. The reason is that the normalisation process itself must be supplemented by some additional processing mechanism that is able to recognise the appropriate size and orientation of the visual pattern. It could be argued that normalisation is often facilitated by the fact that visual patterns are typically presented in some larger context, with this context providing useful indications as to the proper size and orientation of the pattern.

All in all, template-matching theories tend to be rather unwieldy and ill-equipped to account for the versatility of perceptual processing. These inadequacies are especially obvious when the stimulus belongs to an ill-defined category, i.e., a category for which no single template could possibly suffice (e.g., a building or a book).

Prototype Theories

Whereas most template theories treat each stimulus as a separate entity, prototype theories claim that similarities among related stimuli play an important role in pattern recognition. More specifically, prototype theories argue that each stimulus is a member of a class of stimuli, and shares key attributes of that class. Pattern recognition involves comparing stimuli to prototypes, which are abstract forms representing the basic elements of a set of stimuli. Thus, for example, a prototypical aeroplane might consist of a long tube with two wings attached.

One obvious advantage of prototype theories over template theories is that the information stored in permanent memory consists of a manageable number of prototypes rather than a virtually infinite number of templates. At the empirical level, some of the strongest evidence in favour of prototype theories was obtained by Franks and Bransford (1971). They started by constructing prototypes; this was done by combining geometric forms such as circles, stars, and triangles into structured groupings. Several distortions of these prototypes were then formed by applying one or more transformations to them. Subjects were then shown some of these distorted patterns (but not the prototypes themselves), followed by a recognition test.

The results were quite striking. The subjects were most confident that they had seen the prototypes, in spite of the fact that the prototypes had not been shown to them before! Those patterns differing from a prototype by a single transformation were next most confidently recognized, and there was a straightforward relationship between the degree of similarity of a pattern to its prototype and recognition confidence. Somewhat surprisingly, a stimulus the subjects had seen before was rated as no more familiar than a stimulus they had not seen before, if the two stimuli contained the same number of transformations from the prototype.

What do these findings mean? The simplest explanation is that the subjects used information from the various patterns presented initially to construct prototypes that were then stored in long-term memory. This prototype knowledge was then used to classify and identify new stimuli, with recognition being simply a function of the extent to which any given pattern matched the stored prototype.

Prototype theories are quite promising, but they possess certain limitations. Most of them are not very explicit about the details of the matching process between the internal representation of a stimulus and a prototype. For example, the comparisons involved in the matching process may occur either serially or in parallel. Since the matching process could take a very long time to achieve pattern recognition if it operated serially, it seems likely that comparisons between internal representations of stimuli and prototypes are made in parallel. Prototype theories also typically fail to explain how pattern recognition is affected by the context in which a stimulus is presented as well as by the stimulus itself.

Feature Theories

The various difficulties that have beset template and prototype theories have led to the development of feature theories, in which it is assumed that a pattern consists of a set of specific attributes or features. The process of pattern recognition is assumed to begin with the extraction of the features from the presented stimulus. This set of features is then combined, and compared against information stored in permanent memory.

If we return to the question of how the letter "A" is recognized, then it could be argued by feature theorists that its crucial features are two straight lines that intersect or almost intersect, with an angle of approximately 45° between them and a cross-bar intersecting both of them. One of the advantages of this kind of theoretical approach is that visual stimuli varying greatly in size, orientation, and minor details may nevertheless share the same defining features and thus be identifiable as instances of the same pattern.

Gibson (1969) indicated one way in which letters of the alphabet could be identified on the basis of a feature analysis. She identified 12 features (e.g., closed loops; horizontal line segments; and vertical line segments), and argued that any stimulus letter could be correctly identified by comparing its feature content with that of each of the letters of the alphabet. For example, only the letter "O" is symmetrical and has a closed curve. One of the most obvious predictions from this theoretical position concerns the kinds of errors that are made when a letter is identified: Those letters sharing the most features with the letter actually presented should have the greatest probability of being confused with it. There is some empirical support for this prediction, but the evidence is not very strong.

A slightly different experimental approach was taken by Gibson, Shapiro, and Yonas (1968). They measured the length of time it took to decide whether two-letter stimuli were the same or different. Their key finding was that response latencies on trials where two different letters were presented were directly related to the number of features the letters shared. Thus, for example, it took longer to decide that "P" and "R" were different than to decide that "G" and "W" were different.

We have focused so far on the way in which certain visual stimuli can be recognised on the basis of their constituent features. Precisely the same kind of reasoning can be applied to auditory stimuli. Spoken language consists of a series of sounds or phonemes, and these phonemes incorporate various features. Among the features for phonemes are the following: The consonantal feature (i.e., the presence or absence of a consonant-like quality); the place of articulation; and voicing (the larynx vibrates for a voiced consonant but not for a voiceless one). The value of a feature approach to spoken language was demonstrated by Miller and Nicely (1955). They gave their subjects the task of recognising consonants that were presented auditorily against a background of noise. The most frequently confused consonants were those that differed from each other on the basis of only one feature.

The importance of features in perception has also been shown in research on stabilised images. A stabilised image is one that remains in the same position on the retina irrespective of any eye movements. Stabilised retinal images can be achieved in many ways; for example, a visual stimulus can be projected on to the retina by means of a miniature projector positioned on a contact lens worn by the individual. When the eye moves, so does the contact lens (and thus the projector and the retinal image), but the visual image does not move relative to the retina. The stabilised retinal image fades within a minute or so, but the entire image does not disappear. What usually happens is that features disappear and then reappear as meaningful units. Thus, the visual stimulus "BEER" may come to be perceived as "PEEP," "PEER," "BEE," or "BE".

Feature theories are appealing because they replace the countless templates required by template theories with a much smaller number of features that can be combined and recombined to permit pattern recognition. They also possess the merit (as we have just seen) that they are in accord with much of the evidence. However, everything in the garden is not lovely.

Feature theories are clearly over-simplified in a number of ways, in that they de-emphasise the role played by contextual effects and by expectations in pattern recognition.

The importance of contextual effects was demonstrated convincingly by Weisstein and Harris (1974). Subjects attempted to detect a line which was embedded either in a briefly flashed three-dimensional form or in a briefly flashed less coherent form. According to feature theories, the target line should always activate the same feature detectors irrespective of the visual context, and so the coherence of the form in which it is embedded should not affect detection. In fact, target detection was highest when the target line was part of a three-dimensional form, and declined as this form became flatter and more incoherent. Weisstein and Harris (1974) called this the object-superiority effect, and it shows that some kind of modification of feature theories is needed. Perhaps the notion that the features of a pattern are extracted prior to the construction of the form and structure of that pattern is incorrect.

Further difficulties for feature theories can be identified if we reconsider some of the evidence apparently supporting the feature theory approach. It will be remembered that Gibson (1969) claimed that letters of the alphabet can be identified by means of a feature analysis. While this may be true, it is also the case that expectations play a part. For example, we often fail to notice typographical errors while reading because we rely heavily on our anticipations of what will be presented. Of course, such anticipations (which are based on our knowledge of which letters are likely to occur together in words) also serve to facilitate the reading process.

The feature theory approach to spoken language also suffers from its emphasis on bottom-up or stimulus-driven processing. We saw earlier in the chapter that a particular auditory stimulus (the sound of a cough) can be perceived as "wh," "h," "m," or "p," depending on the precise sentential context in which it is heard (Warren & Warren, 1970). In this case it would make little sense to argue that the features of the cough had much influence on pattern recognition.

At a rather superficial level of analysis it might appear that recent advances in the neurophysiology of vision provide strong evidence in favour of the feature theory approach. Simple cells, complex cells, and hyper-complex cells have been identified within the brain's visual system. The simple cells differ in terms of the kind of stimulus to which they are maximally responsive, leading them to be divided into edge detectors, slit detectors, and line detectors. These simple cells have often (rather mis-leadingly) been called feature detectors. Complex cells resemble simple cells in that the optimal stimulus is still a line, slit, or edge, but the two kinds of cells differ in that the location of the stimulus within the cell's receptive field is much more critical in determining the response of simple cells. Hypercomplex cells resemble complex cells, but their responsiveness is much affected by the length of the stimulus.

Since these various cells in the brain are maximally responsive to certain specific aspects or features of visual stimuli, it might seem that they constitute the feature detectors postulated by feature theorists. The function of a feature detector is to indicate the presence of a particular stimulus feature regardless of the presence of other stimulus features. However, the responsiveness of visual cortical cells is typically not independent of other stimulus features, being affected by additional features, such as length and stimulus location.

There is a further apparent similarity between feature theories and findings in the physiology of vision. Feature theories typically assume that processing proceeds in a serial fashion, with feature extraction being followed by feature combination and by pattern recognition. Hubel and Wiesel (1962) argued for a serial flow of information through visual cortical cells on the basis of physiological data. They reported that the output in the brain of lateral geniculate cells terminates at a group of simple cells, and that the output of these simple cells forms complex cells, and that these complex cells terminate at hypercomplex cells. However, as a recent review of the physiological evidence by Lennie (1980) makes clear, it now appears that a great deal of non-serial processing takes place in the visual cortex, and that the interrelationships between the three kinds of brain cells are more complex than was originally envisaged.

Feature theories tend to treat all features or attributes of stimuli in the same way. That this is an over-simplification seems to have been demonstrated by Garner (1974). He argued for a distinction between separable and integral attribute combinations. Attribute combinations are said to be separable if they are perceived in terms of their separate attributes (e.g., form and size), whereas they are regarded as integral if they are not perceived separately (e.g., hue and brightness of a coloured form). As a consequence, a change in just one attribute with integral attribute combinations appears to produce a stimulus that causes a difference to the whole, rather than a difference for only the changed attribute. In fact, Garner (1974) suggested that there are two types of integral combinations: Those for which such global or holistic perception is necessary; and those which people prefer to process holistically, but which can also be processed attribute by attribute when such processing is advantageous.

There are various kinds of research that support Garner's (1974) theoretical contentions (see Spoehr and Lehmkuhle, 1982, for a review). One approach is based on dissimilarity ratings, and involves ratings of pairs of stimuli for how different the two members of each pair appear to be. In general terms, dissimilarity ratings for stimuli with two separable dimensions reflect differences in the two dimensions independently, whereas ratings for stimuli having an integral structure reflect the interdependence of the component dimensions.

An alternative approach involves restricted classification in which the subject is shown three stimuli varying along two dimensions. Each set of stimuli consists of two stimuli that are the same with respect to one dimension, but differ a lot on the other dimension; the third stimulus is close to, but not identical to, one of the other stimuli on both dimensions. The subject's task is to divide the set of three stimuli into two classes on the basis of similarity. The expectation is that the two stimuli which are the same on one dimension should be grouped together (i.e., dimensional classification) when stimuli with separable dimensions are used, because it is obvious that they are identical on that dimension. In contrast, the prediction is that overall similarity should determine grouping with integral stimuli, so that the two stimuli that are similar but not identical on both dimensions should tend to be grouped together.

Both of these predictions have been confirmed. Shepp, Burns, and McDonough (1980) found that 90% of groupings involving the integral dimensions of the height and width of rectangles were based on overall similarity, whereas Burns, Shepp, McDonough, and Wiener-Ehrlich (1978) discovered that dimensional classifications were made 78% of the time when stimuli varying in the separable dimensions of circle size and angle of radius were used.

A final way of distinguishing between separable and integral attribute combinations is to measure sorting speed for stimuli that must be classified on the basis of a single attribute dimension. What happens when there is random variation on an irrelevant dimension? If the variation occurs in a dimension that is integrally related to the relevant dimension on the sorting task, this slows down the speed of classification considerably. On the other hand, variation in a highly separable irrelevant dimension usually has little or no effect on sorting speed. It appears that selective attention is less effective in suppressing the distracting effects of an irrelevant attribute dimension, as the combination of relevant and irrelevant attributes becomes more integral.

Our discussion of separable and integral dimensions has implied that any dimensional combination is either integral or separable. In fact, it is probably more realistic to regard integrality and separability as the end points of a continuum. In any case, it is obvious that there are complexities concerning the ways in which features of a stimulus are extracted that have received little attention from features theorists.

While it is customary to contrast feature theories with template theories and prototype theories, it is worth noting that in some ways they are similar. Indeed, features can quite plausibly be regarded as mini-templates. Moreover, while simple feature theories assume that pattern recognition involves merely listing the features of the stimulus, this cannot be the whole story, otherwise two oblique uprights and a dash randomly presented (\/–) would be perceived as the letter "A"! In a realistic feature theory it is necessary to consider the relationships between features, and it is likely that some features are more important than others in pattern recogniton. Complex feature theories that take such considerations into account resemble prototype theories in many ways.

COMPUTATIONAL THEORY

We have seen during the course of this chapter that there are various different approaches to the study of perception, of which the psychological and the physiological have been the most important historically. There are increasing signs that the approach based on artificial intelligence will ultimately prove important as well, especially if it becomes possible to produce a computer program that enables a machine to recognise objects in the real world. The reader may feel that what is needed is some kind of integration of information from the psychological, physiological, and artificial intelligence viewpoints, and this is exactly what the late David Marr and his colleagues have attempted to do for visual perception. Their computational theory is discussed at length in various places (e.g., Frisby, 1979; Marr, 1982).

Apart from the multi-disciplinary nature of computational theory, it is also distinguished by the way in which it deals primarily with the structure of visual processing rather than the detailed mechanisms involved in implementing the process. This emphasis is deliberate. Marr (1982) stressed the distinction between *what* vision accomplishes (which involves process) and *how* it is accomplished (which involves some mechanism or mechanisms). The mechanisms of visual perception should be examined systematically only after there is a thorough understanding of exactly what visual information is extracted from the stimulus input.

Computational theory makes extensive use of neurophysiological data, especially those obtained through use of the single cell recording technique. This technique involves inserting a microelectrode into some part of the visual system, with the tiny electrical changes produced by stimulation being amplified and displayed on the screen of an oscilloscope. Single-cell recording has led to the discovery of three important kinds of cells within the brain's visual system: simple cells, complex cells, and hypercomplex cells.

Simple cells have often been divided into edge detectors, slit detectors, and line detectors on the basis of the kind of stimulus that produces the maximum response, and it has been assumed that simple cells are feature detectors. This assumption has been challenged successfully by Marr (1982).

When he attempted to construct a computerised feature-detecting system, he discovered that the activity in any one cell is simply too ambiguous to be used directly as a feature description. Consider, for example, a cell which responds maximally to a vertical edge. Moderate activity in this cell cannot be taken as necessarily indicative of the presentation of a stimulus with a vertical edge. The reason is that moderate activity would be produced by either a faint vertical edge or a high-contrast edge that was presented just off the vertical.

If simple cells do not function as feature detectors, then how should they be regarded? According to Marr (1982), the outputs of simple cells can most appropriately be thought of as providing the first step in the analysis of the features present in the visual input. It would be possible to distinguish between a faint vertical edge and a high-contrast edge presented just off the vertical by comparing the amount of activity in different kinds of simple cells. If the stimulus contained a faint vertical edge, then the moderate activity in cells that reacted optimally to a vertical edge would exceed the activity in cells maximally responsive to different orientations. On the other hand, if the stimulus was actually a high-contrast, just-off-vertical stimulus, then the most active cells would be those specifically designed to respond to just-off-vertical stimuli. In other words, the responses of simple cells should be regarded as measurements requiring further interpretation, rather than as complete feature descriptions.

We have just seen that there are good reasons for arguing that the process of feature extraction is more complicated than is usually realised. Computational theorists go further and claim that the entire process of perception involves several successive stages. More specifically, Marr (1982) proposed that there are three increasingly complex visual representations leading up to pattern or object recognition. The first is the primal sketch. This is a fairly basic feature description that includes information about edges, contours, and blobs. The primal sketch then forms the basis for the second representation, which is known as the "$2\frac{1}{2}$-D" sketch. This sketch incorporates a description of the depth and orientation of visible surfaces, making use of information provided by shading, texture, motion, binocular disparity, and so on. It is limited in that it is observer-centred (i.e., the perspective is still retinal in nature). The third basic representation is the "3-D" sketch, which does not suffer from the limitations of the "$2\frac{1}{2}$-D" sketch. It describes three-dimensionally a representation of the stimulus objects independent of the observer's viewpoint, and it incorporates the constancies of perception.

One of the issues that any theory of visual object recognition needs to consider is that of segmentation, i.e., the way in which visual information is used to decide which regions of the visual scene belong together and form coherent structures. Marr (1976) discovered that the grouping principles proposed by the Gestaltists (discussed earlier in the chapter) were often very useful in achieving accurate segmentation even without making use of knowledge about the objects represented. He did this by constructing computer programs that made use of these principles. He applied the Gestalt principles to a teddy bear, and discovered that they led to appropriate segmentation of the teddy bear's outline, its eyes, and its nose.

However, there are some scenes that present ambiguities in segmentation that can be resolved satisfactorily only by making use of information about the object or objects presented. For example, Marr (1982) considered the segmentation problem that occurred with a bowl of flowers where two leaves overlapped substantially. The computer program could not find enough line features in the area of overlap to demarcate the two leaves clearly. Marr dealt with this problem by adding to the computer program the additional information that the line segments in the two adjacent areas belonged to two different objects.

Obviously, we have only been able to indicate the flavour of computational theory here. The most exciting aspect of computational theory is the way in which our knowledge of visual perception is enhanced by its multi-faceted approach. In one of the examples considered here, computational and computer methods were applied to neurophysiological findings, and indicated strongly that the neurophysiological findings have been misinterpreted in the past. In another example, computational methods were successful in demonstrating the potential importance of the psychological notions of the Gestaltists to the segmentation problem.

On the negative side, computational theory so far has focused mainly on only some of the major issues in perception. Most attention has been paid to the transition from the primal sketch to the $2\frac{1}{2}$-D sketch, and there has been relatively little interest in the ways in which visual processes are affected by prior knowledge of the objects in the visual scene. A further limitation was pointed out by Tenebaum, Witkin, and Wandell (1983). They noted that Marr (1982) often seemed to regard the existence of a computational theory that could achieve certain perceptual goals as proof that the computational theory described how that aspect of perception normally operates. For example, Marr (1982) found by computational methods that depth and surface orientation can be inferred without making use of knowledge about the object, and this led him to conclude that the representation of depth and orientation always precedes object recognition. It should be obvious that the conclusion does not necessarily follow.

3 Attention and Performance Limitations

The concept of "attention" has had a rather fluctuating existence during the past century. It was regarded as an important concept by many philosophers and pyschologists in the late nineteenth century, but was totally rejected by the early Behaviourists, who regarded all internal processes such as attention with the greatest suspicion. Attention became fashionable again following the publication of Broadbent's book *Perception and Communication* in 1958, but more recently the prevalent view has been that it is too amorphous to be of much value. Moray (1969) pointed out that attention is sometimes used to refer to the ability to select part of the incoming stimulation for further processing, but it has also been regarded as synonymous with concentration or with mental set. It has also been applied to search processes in which a specified target is looked for, and it has been suggested that attention co-varies with arousal (e.g., the drowsy individual is in a state of low arousal and attends little to his environment).

There is an obvious danger that a concept that is used to explain everything will turn out to explain nothing. However, attention is most commonly used to refer to selectivity of processing, and this was the sense emphasised by William James (1890):

> Everyone knows what attention is. It is the taking possession by the mind, in clear and vivid form, of one out of what seem several simultaneously possible objects or trains of throught. Focalisation, concentration, of consciousness are of its essence. It implies withdrawal from some things in order to deal effectively with others [pp. 403–404].

Within the general area of attention research there are several important issues that need to be considered. If we enquire what factors determine the contents of attention, then the usual answer is that we choose to attend to sources of information that are relevant in the context of our present activities and intentions. This is true as far as it goes, but it also has to be recognised that some stimuli draw attention to themselves. Berlyne (1960)

49

argued that such stimuli are typically those that conflict with expectation; they tend to be novel, surprising, incongruous, complex, or intense. The main evidence for this position is that such stimuli tend to elicit the orientation reaction, which is thought to reflect attention. Stimuli that are novel, incongruous, or surprising also tend to be well remembered (von Restorff, 1933; Eysenck, 1972), which suggests that they are thoroughly processed. It is disappointing that there has been little recent interest in the determinants of "involuntary" attention in view of its general significance.

There is an important distinction to be drawn between focused attention and divided attention. Focused attention is studied by presenting people with two or more concurrent stimulus inputs and instructing them to process and respond to only one. Work on focused attention can tell us how effectively people select certain inputs rather than others, and it enables us to investigate the nature of the selection process and the fate of unattended stimuli. Divided attention is also studied by presenting at least two concurrent stimulus inputs, but the instructions indicate that all stimulus inputs must be attended to and responded to. Studies of divided attention provide useful information about a person's processing limitations, and may tell us something about attentional mechanisms and their capacity.

FOCUSED ATTENTION

The Shadowing Technique

Systematic research on focused attention was initiated by Cherry (1953) who became interested in the "cocktail party" problem. This relates to our ability to follow just one conversation even when several different people are all speaking at once. He discovered that this ability involves making use of any salient physical differences among the auditory messages in order to select the one of interest; these physical differences can include differences in the sex of the speaker, in voice intensity, and in the location of the speaker. When Cherry presented two messages in the same voice to both ears at once (thus eliminating these physical differences), listeners found it remarkably difficult to separate out the two messages on the basis of meaning alone.

Cherry (1953) also conducted experiments in which one auditory message had to be shadowed (i.e., repeated back out loud) at the same time as the second auditory message was played to the other ear. Very little information seemed to be extracted from the second or non-attended message, and listeners seldom noticed when the message was spoken in a foreign language or in reversed speech. In contrast, physical changes such as the insertion of a pure tone were almost always detected. The basic conclusion that unattended information receives practically no processing was supported by other evidence. It was discovered, for example, that there was no memory for words on the unattended message, even when they were presented 35 times each (Moray, 1959).

Broadbent (1958) felt that these findings from the shadowing paradigm were important, and he was also impressed by data from a memory task in which three pairs of digits were presented to a subject dichotically, i.e., three digits were heard serially at one ear, at the same time as three different digits were presented to the other ear. Subjects demonstrated a clear preference for recalling the digits ear by ear rather than in the temporal order of input. Broadbent accounted for these, and other, findings by proposing that two concurrent stimuli or messages gain access in parallel to a sensory buffer. One of the inputs is then allowed through a filter on the basis of its physical characteristics, with the other input remaining in the buffer for later processing. This filter is necessary in order to prevent overload in the limited-capacity mechanism that transforms the input.

This theory handles Cherry's basic results quite neatly: The unattended message is rejected by the filter and thus receives minimal processing. It also accounts for performance on Broadbent's dichotic task because the filter selects one input at a time on the basis of the most salient physical characteristic distinguishing the two inputs (i.e., the ear of arrival). In spite of the theory's successes, however, it fails to explain other findings. It assumes that the unattended message is always rejected at an early stage of processing, but this is erroneous. The original shadowing experiments made use of subjects who had little or no previous experience of shadowing messages, so that nearly all of their available processing resources had to be allocated to the shadowing task. The importance of this fact was demonstrated by Underwood (1974), in an experiment in which subjects attempted to detect a single digit appearing on either the shadowed or the non-shadowed message. Naïve subjects detected only 8% of the digits on the non-shadowed message, suggesting very limited processing of that message. However, when the same task was performed by Neville Moray, a prominent researcher in this area who has great experience of shadowing, he detected 67% of the non-shadowed digits.

The early work on shadowing was also somewhat limited in that the attended and unattended inputs were usually rather similar (i.e., they were both auditorily presented verbal messages). It has been found (Allport, Antonis, & Reynolds, 1972) that combining shadowing of passages from George Orwell's *Selected Essays* with the learning of auditorily presented words leads to minimal learning of the words, a finding to be expected on the basis of Broadbent's (1958) filter theory. However, when the same shadowing task was combined with picture learning, subsequent retention of pictorial information was reasonably good. The implication is that the limitations on the processing of two concurrent inputs are less rigid than was implied by Broadbent, especially when the two inputs are dissimilar.

HCP-C

The typical result from the early shadowing studies was that, as predicted by Broadbent's (1958) filter theory, none of the semantic content of the unattended message was processed. However, this was based upon people's lack of conscious awareness of the meaning of that message, and it is at least possible that meaning can be processed without them being aware of the fact. This issue was investigated by von Wright, Anderson, and Stenman (1975). In the first stage of their experiment, subjects attended to a long list of words, and sometimes received an electric shock when the Finnish word meaning "suitable" was presented. In the second stage of the study, subjects shadowed one auditory list of words and ignored a second concurrent list. When the previously shocked word (or its homonym or synonym) was presented on the non-attended list, there was a noticeable galvanic skin response. This suggests that information on the unattended message can receive semantic analysis, in spite of the fact that the subjects were not consciously aware that the previously shocked word had been presented.

An issue that has received some consideration is the extent to which the unattended message is processed for meaning. It appears to receive less thorough semantic processing than the attended message, with words on the unattended message not being integrated into larger semantic units such as phrases or sentences. Evidence for this comes from an examination of context effects, i.e., the speeding up of the shadowing response to a word on the attended message by semantically relevant prior information presented in either the shadowed or unattended message. It has been found (Underwood, 1977) that increasing the amount of such relevant context from one word to an entire sentence enhanced this context effect only when the context occurred in the shadowed message.

There is further support for the notion that the unattended message receives less processing than the attended message in studies of memory (see Chapter 5 for details). Long-term memory for the attended message is typically fairly good, but is almost (or totally) non-existent for the semantic content of the unattended message.

In sum, there can be far more thorough processing of the non-shadowed message than was allowed for by Broadbent (1958). He proposed a relatively rigid system of selective attention that cannot account for the great variability in the amount of analysis of the non-shadowed message that is actually observed. The same rigidity of the filter theory is also evident in its assumption that the filter selects information on the basis of physical features. This assumption is supported by the tendency of subjects to recall dichotically-presented digits ear by ear, but a small change in the basic experiment can alter recall order considerably. Gray and Wedderburn (1960) made use of a version of the dichotic task in which "Who 6 there" might be presented to one ear at the same time as "4 goes 1" was presented to the other ear. The preferred order of report from subjects in this experiment was not ear by ear; instead, it was semantically determined (e.g., "Who goes there" followed by "4 6 1"). The implication is that selection can occur either before the processing of information from both inputs or afterwards. The fact that selection can be based on semantic characteristics of presented information is inconsistent with the filter theory.

How can the various findings on focused attention be explained theoretically? Treisman (1964) favoured a modified version of Broadbent's (1958) theory in which the analysis of unattended information is attenuated. Whereas Broadbent had claimed that the bottle-neck occurred early in processing, Treisman suggested that the location of the bottle-neck was more flexible. In essence, she proposed that stimulus analysis proceeds in a systematic fashion through a hierarchy starting with analyses based on physical cues, syllabic pattern, and specific words, and moving on to analyses based on individual words, grammatical structure, and meaning. If there is insufficient capacity to permit full stimulus analysis, then tests towards the top of the hierarchy are omitted. In addition, expected stimuli are treated differently to other stimuli, with the analysing systems being pre-biased towards them.

Treisman's (1964) theory clearly accounts for the extensive processing of unattended sources of information that proved embarrassing for Broadbent (1958). However, the same facts can also be explained by a rather different theory put forward by Deutsch and Deutsch (1963). They argued that all incoming stimuli are fully analysed, with one input determining the response on the basis of its importance or relevance in the situation. Their theory is similar to those of Broadbent and Treisman in postulating the existence of a bottle-neck in information processing, but it is quite different in placing the bottle-neck much nearer the response end of the processing system. The kind of theory put forward by Deutsch and Deutsch (1963) is still popular (e.g., Shiffrin & Schneider, 1977).

On the face of it, Treisman's theory is more plausible than that of Deutsch and Deutsch; in particular, it seems very uneconomical for all inputs to be analysed completely, and then to have most of the analysed information forgotten almost at once in the way proposed by Deutsch and Deutsch. However, it is much better to adjudicate between theories on the basis of empirical evidence rather than vague notions of plausibility, and Treisman and Geffen (1967) attempted to do just that. Their subjects shadowed one of two concurrent auditory messages, and at the same time monitored both messages in order to detect target words. The detection of a target word was indicated by a simple tapping response.

The crucial findings related to the detection rates on the two messages. According to Treisman's theory, there should be attenuated analysis of the non-shadowed message, and so fewer targets should be detected on that message than on the shadowed one. In contrast, the assumption made by

Deutsch and Deutsch that there is complete perceptual analysis of all inputs leads to the prediction that there should be no difference in detection rates between the two messages. In fact, the shadowed or attended message showed a very large advantage in detection rates over the non-shadowed message, with the detection rates being 87% and 8%, respectively.

Deutsch and Deutsch (1963) naturally enough argued the toss over this apparent refutation of their theoretical position. They pointed out that their theory assumed that only important inputs led to responses. Since the task used by Treisman and Geffen (1967) required their subjects to make two responses to target words appearing in the shadowed message (i.e., shadow and tap), but only one response to targets in the non-shadowed message (i.e., tap), there is clearly a sense in which the shadowed targets were more important than the non-shadowed ones.

Treisman and Riley (1969) attempted to obviate this interpretative problem by ensuring that exactly the same response was made to targets occurring in either message. They did this by telling the subjects to stop shadowing and to tap as soon as they detected a target in either message. The findings were less dramatic than in the earlier study by Treisman and Geffen (1967), but it was still the case that many more target words were detected on the shadowed message than the non-shadowed message.

Deutsch and Deutsch (1963) assumed that selection always occurs after full analysis of all inputs has taken place, an assumption which suggests that selective attention operates in a rather rigid and fixed way. In contrast, Johnston and Heinz (1978) proposed a more flexible model in which selection is possible at several different stages in processing. The more stages of processing that take place prior to selection, however, the greater are the demands on some processing capacity. As a consequence, selection occurs as early in processing as is possible in view of the prevailing circumstances and task demands.

Some of these ideas were tested by Johnston and Heinz (1979). Target words were presented binaurally at the same time as non-target words, and the target words were shadowed. In the low sensory discriminability condition, both sets of words were spoken in the same male voice, whereas in the high sensory discriminability condition the targets were spoken in a male voice and the non-targets in a female voice. According to Johnston and Heinz, selection based on sensory information can be used in the high sensory discriminability condition, but selection at a later stage of semantic processing is necessary in the low sensory discriminability condition.

In other words, Johnston and Heinz (1979) predicted that non-targets would be more thoroughly processed in the low sensory discriminability condition. On the other hand, theories of the Deutsch and Deutsch type assume that there will be essentially complete analysis of the non-target words irrespective of the amount of sensory discriminability between the target and non-target words. In fact, more processing resources were used with low sensory discriminability, and recall of non-target words was higher in the low sensory discriminability condition. It thus appears that the amount of processing of non-shadowed stimuli varies as a function of task demands in a way more consistent with Treisman's approach than with that of Deutsch and Deutsch.

Further evidence of the flexibility of processing was obtained by Johnston and Wilson (1980). Pairs of words were presented together dichotically (i.e., one word to each ear), and the task was to identify target items consisting of members of a designated category. The targets were homonyms, that is, words having at least two distinct meanings. For example, if the category was "articles of clothing," then "socks" would be a homonymic target word. Each target word was accompanied by a non-target word biasing the appropriate meaning of the homonym (e.g., "smelly"), or a non-target word biasing the inappropriate meaning (e.g., "punches"), or by a neutral non-target word (e.g., "Tuesday"). When subjects did not know which ear targets would arrive at (divided attention), appropriate non-targets facilitated the detection of targets and inappropriate non-targets impaired target detection (see Fig. 3.1).

Thus, when attention needed to be divided between the two ears, there was clear evidence that the non-target words were processed semantically. In contrast, when subjects knew that all targets would be presented to the left ear, the type of non-target word presented at the same time had no effect on target detection. This suggests that non-targets were not processed

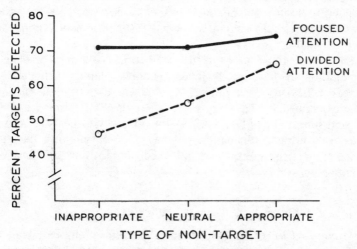

FIG. 3.1 Effects of attention condition (divided versus focused) and of type of non-target on target detection. Data from Johnston and Wilson (1980).

semantically in this focused attention condition, and that the amount of processing received by non-target stimuli is often only as much as is necessary to perform the experimental task.

In sum, evidence has accumulated over the years to indicate that the analysis of unattended inputs can be more extensive than was originally supposed. This may be due in part to the fact that the shadowing requirement does not always "capture" attention, so that so-called unattended inputs may actually receive some attention, but this is hardly the whole story. The most reasonable account of focused attention is along the lines suggested by Treisman (1964) and by Broadbent (1971), with reduced or attenuated processing of sources of information outside focal attention, but the extreme notion that all inputs are fully analysed (Deutsch & Deutsch, 1963) remains popular among several theorists in spite of its inflexibility.

What can be concluded about the controversy concerning the amount of processing of unattended stimuli? There have been many attempts to answer this question on the basis of evidence that unattended inputs are sometimes processed semantically, but such findings are consistent with both attenuation and complete analysis theories. What is needed is a somewhat broader approach to the question. Consider, for example, some of the findings on visual search reported by Rabbitt (1964, 1967). Subjects were required to locate a target letter included among a number of irrelevant letters. Search time was initially affected greatly by the number of irrelevant letters, but prolonged practice with the same set of letters reduced their interfering effects. A subsequent change in the irrelevant letters increased the interference again, unless the new irrelevant letters shared a visual feature with the old ones (e.g., possession of only straight lines). These findings suggest that irrelevant stimuli are not processed fully; instead, only the essential features of the irrelevant letters that serve to distinguish between targets and distractors are processed.

As Broadbent (1982) has pointed out, theories assuming complete processing of all inputs have usually failed to address findings such as those on visual search. In view of that failure, together with data from the shadowing paradigm obtained by Treisman and Geffen (1967), Treisman and Riley (1969), and Johnston and Heinz (1979), the full analysis theory seems rather dubious. In contrast, attenuation theories of the type subscribed to by Treisman (1964) and by Broadbent (1971) account satisfactorily for most of the findings.

Conscious Attention and Automatic Activation

One of the ways in which a fuller understanding of the nature of focal attention can be achieved is by trying to delineate the salient differences between it and some other aspect of the processing system. This strategy was followed by Posner and Snyder (1975) who drew a conceptual distinction between conscious attention and automatic activation. They proposed three criteria that need to be satisfied in order for a process to be regarded as automatic rather than reflecting the workings of conscious attention: (1) it should not lead to conscious awareness; (2) it should occur without intention; and (3) is should not interfere with any other concurrent mental activity.

The distinction between conscious attention and automatic activation can be clarified if we consider a concrete example in some detail. Lexical decision tasks involve rapid decisions as to whether or not a visually presented letter string forms an English word. The decision time for a word stimulus (e.g., "DOCTOR") is shorter when the preceding stimulus or prime is a semantically related word such as "NURSE" than when it is an unrelated word (e.g., "LIBRARY"). Why does this so-called semantic-priming effect occur? One possibility is that the priming word automatically activates the stored representations of all the words related to it due to massive previous learning. Alternatively, conscious attention may be involved, with a prime such as "NURSE" leading the subjects to anticipate or expect that a semantically related word will follow.

Neely (1977) used an ingenious technique in an attempt to disentangle the relative effects of conscious attention and automatic activation on lexical decision. The priming word was the name of a semantic category (e.g., "Bird"), and it was followed by a letter string. In the key condition, subjects expected that a particular category name would usually be followed by a member of a different, pre-specified category (e.g., "Bird" followed by the name of a part of a building). There are two kinds of trials in this condition which are of interest: (1) the category name is followed by a member of a different, but expected, category (e.g., "Bird-Window"); (2) the category name is followed by a member of the same, but unexpected, category (e.g., "Bird-Magpie").

According to the theory put forward by Posner and Snyder (1975), conscious attention speeds performance when the stimulus for lexical decision is expected, but slows it down when it is unexpected. The reason for this is that unexpected events require that attention be switched from the expected event to the event that has actually happened, and this takes time. In contrast, automatic activation speeds decision time when the word is semantically related to the priming word, and has no effect otherwise. Finally, there should be no effect of conscious attention with a very short time interval between the prime and the decision word, because conscious attention takes some time to develop an expectation.

The detailed results of Neely's trials are shown in Fig. 3.2; they conform remarkably well to the predictions of Posner and Snyder's (1975) theory. Decision speed was only slowed down when the target word was unexpected,

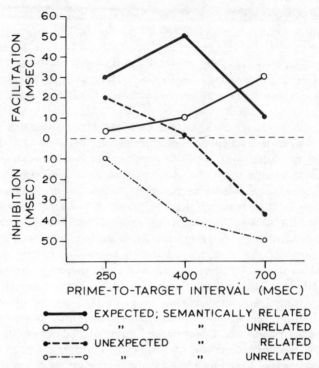

FIG. 3.2   The time course of inhibitory and facilitatory effects of priming as a function of whether or not the target word was related semantically to the prime, and of whether or not the target word belonged to the expected category. Data from Neely (1977).

i.e., when conscious attention was misled. When the target word was semantically related to the priming category name but was unexpected, there was initial facilitation from automatic activation followed by an inhibitory effect when a conscious expectation had developed. When the target was expected but semantically unrelated to the prime, there was no effect with a short interval between prime and decision word, but facilitation developed as a conscious expectation was formed.

The notion that it takes a discernible length of time for conscious attention to respond to events is a valuable one, and there is physiological as well as behavioural evidence in its favour. Posner (1978) suggested that the P300 component of the average evoked potential may reflect the operation of conscious attention. This component is known as P300 because it is a positive wave that typically occurs some 300 milliseconds after stimulus onset, and is especially likely to be found when a stimulus requires close attention. It is also found when a stimulus is omitted after a repetitive series; this suggests that P300 is affected by the subject's expectations, which is, of course, equally true of the behavioural data on conscious attention reported by Neely (1977).

In sum, Posner has managed to elucidate some of the functions of focal attention. It seems reasonable that conscious attention takes some time to develop specific expectations, and that there are associated benefits and costs. If the expectations formed are appropriate to the situation, then benefits accrue; if unexpected events occur, then there are costs involved in shifting the focus of conscious attention. Does the delay in responding to an expected event simply reflect the time taken to switch attention? Neill (1979) argued that the time to switch attention should vary directly with the degree of semantic dissimilarity between the actual and expected events, but he discovered that it sometimes took longer to switch attention to an unexpected event from the same category as the expected event, than to an unexpected event from a different category. There may actually be several determinants of the time taken to switch attention, such as the time to signal the switching mechanism; the time to disengage attention from what had been expected; the transit time between the unexpected and actual events; and the time to engage attention with the unexpected event.

DIVIDED ATTENTION

What happens when people endeavour to do two things at once? The answer obviously depends on what "things" we are referring to. Sometimes the attempt is successful, as when an experienced motorist drives a car and holds a conversation at the same time, or a tennis player notes the position of his opponent while running at speed and preparing to make a stroke; at other times, as when someone tries to rub his stomach with one hand while patting his head with the other, or a learner driver tries to control a car while talking, there can be a complete disruption of performance. In this section we are concerned with some of the factors that determine how well two tasks can be performed concurrently.

At a more theoretical level, the breakdowns of performance often found when two tasks are combined shed light on the limitations of the human information-processing system. It has been assumed by many theorists that such breakdowns reflect the limited capacity of a single multi-purpose central processor or executive that is sometimes simply referred to as "attention." Other theorists are more impressed by our apparent ability to perform two relatively complex tasks at the same time without disruption or interference. Such theorists tend to favour the notion of several specific processing resources, arguing that there will be no interference between two tasks provided that they make use of different processing resources.

HCP–C*

It is probably true to say that there has been more progress at the empirical level than there has at the theoretical level. It is now possible to predict reasonably accurately whether or not two tasks can be combined successfully, but the accounts offered of many of the findings by different theorists are very diverse. Accordingly, initially we discuss the factual evidence before moving on to the murkier issue of how the data are to be accounted for.

Dual-task Performance

When we think of pairs of activities that are performed together with no great difficulty in everyday life, the examples that come to mind usually involve two rather dissimilar activities (e.g., driving and talking; reading and listening to music). There is plenty of evidence that the degree of similarity between two tasks is of great importance. When people attempted to shadow prose passages while learning auditorily presented words, their subsequent recognition-memory performance for the words was at chance level (Allport et al., 1972). However, the same authors found that memory was reasonably good when shadowing was combined with visually presented words, and it was excellent (90% correct) when the to-be-remembered material consisted of pictures.

Any adequate analysis of the effects of similarity on dual-task performance must recognise that there are at least three different kinds of similarity that must be distinguished: similarity of the stimuli involved in the two tasks; similarity of the internal processing operations; and similarity of responses. In spite of the likelihood that similarity of processing operations is of the greatest importance, it is in fact stimulus similarity that has been more thoroughly explored than the other kinds of similarity. This has usually been investigated by manipulating the modalities in which task stimuli are presented. We have already seen that it is difficult to handle two concurrent auditory inputs, and the same is true of two visual inputs presented together. Kolers (1972) invented a headgear with a half-silvered mirror; when he wore it, the visual world in front of him and the visual world behind him were both available in the binocular field of view. He discovered that he could attend either forwards or backwards at will, with the unattended scene simply "disappearing." However, it was not possible to attend to both visual inputs at the same time.

More direct evidence concerning the importance of stimulus similarity was obtained by Treisman and Davies (1973). They found that two monitoring tasks interfered with each other much more when the stimuli on both tasks were presented in the same sense modality (visual or auditory) than when they were presented in different modalities. Subsequent work has shown that the advantage of mixed modality presentation over single modality presentation depends on the nature of the tasks, being greater when they require processing at the physical level than when they demand semantic processing (Martin, 1980).

The importance of response similarity has also been demonstrated. In a study by McLeod (1977), people were required to perform a continuous tracking task with manual responding at the same time as a tone-identification task. Some of the participants responded vocally to the tones, whereas others responded with the hand not involved in the concurrent tracking task. There were very few errors on the tone-identification task, but performance on the tracking task was worse under high response similarity (i.e., manual responses on both tasks) than under low response similarity (i.e., manual responses on one task and vocal ones on the other).

It is clear in a general sense that the extent to which two tasks interfere with each other is a function of their similarity. However, what is signally lacking is any satisfactory measure of similarity: how similar are piano playing and poetry writing, or driving a car and watching a football match? Only when there is a better understanding of the processes involved in the performance of such tasks will sensible answers be forthcoming.

Common sense suggests that the old adage, "Practice makes perfect," is especially applicable to dual-task performance. For example, people who have just mastered touch-typing would undoubtedly find their typing performance greatly disrupted by holding a conversation or listening to the radio, but expert typists do not. While there is still little theoretical understanding of exactly what is happening, recent research provides overwhelming support for the commonsensical opinion, "Practice makes perfect." In a celebrated study by Spelke, Hirst, and Neisser (1976), two students called Diane and John received 5 hours' training a week for 4 months on a variety of tasks. Their first task was to read short stories for comprehension at the same time as they wrote down words at dictation. They found this very difficult initially, and their reading speed and hand-writing both suffered considerably. After 6 weeks of training, however, they were able to read as rapidly and with as much comprehension when taking dictation as when only reading, and the quality of their handwriting had also improved.

In spite of this impressive dual-task performance, Spelke *et al.* (1976) were still not satisfied. They discovered, for example, that Diane and John could recall only 35 out of the thousands of words they had written down at dictation. Even when 20 successive dictated words formed a sentence or came from a single semantic category, the two subjects were unaware of the fact. With further training, however, they learned to write down the names of the categories to which the dictated words belonged while maintaining normal reading speed and comprehension.

Spelke *et al.* (1976) wondered whether the popular notion of man's limited processing capacity was accurate, basing themselves on the dramatic findings obtained by John and Diane:

> They understood both the text they were reading and the words they were copying. In at least this limited sense, they achieved a true division of attention: they were able to extract meaning simultaneously from what they read and from what they heard ... People's ability to develop skills in specialized situations is so great that it may never be possible to define general limits on cognitive capacity [p. 229].

There are alternative ways of interpreting these findings. Perhaps the dictation task was performed rather automatically, and so placed few demands on cognitive capacity, or there might have been a rapid alternation of attention between reading and writing. Hirst, Spelke, Reaves, Caharack, and Neisser (1980) attempted to refute these alternative interpretations. They claimed that writing to dictation was not done automatically because the subjects understood what they were writing. They also claimed that reading and dictation could only be performed together with success by the strategy of alternation of attention provided that the reading material was simple and highly redundant, but they discovered that most subjects were still able to read and take dictation effectively when less redundant reading matter was provided.

The studies by Spelke *et al.* (1976) and by Hirst *et al.* (1980) are often thought to demonstrate that two relatively complex tasks can be performed together without disruption provided that sufficient practice is provided. This is not the case. One of the subjects used by Hirst *et al.* was tested at dictation without reading, making less than half the number of errors that occurred when reading at the same time. Another reason for doubting the sweeping conclusions usually drawn from these studies is the fact that the reading task gave the subjects tremendous flexibility in terms of when they attended to the reading matter; such flexibility makes the strategy of alternation of attention much more workable than it would be with tasks where there is moment-by-moment control of the subject's processing activities.

There are other cases of apparently successful performance of two complex tasks, but the requisite skills were always highly practised. In a study by Allport *et al.* (1972), expert pianists were able to play from seen music while at the same time repeating back or shadowing heard speech, while Shaffer (1975) found that an expert typist could type and shadow at the same time. While these studies are usually regarded as evidence of completely successful task combination, there are some signs of interference when the data are inspected closely (Broadbent, 1982).

There are several reasons why practice might facilitate the concurrent performance of two tasks. In the first place, subjects may develop new strategies for performing each of the tasks so as to minimise any task interference. Secondly, the demands that a task makes on attentional or other central resources may be reduced as a function of practice. Thirdly, while a task may initially require the use of several specific processing resources, practice may permit a more economical mode of functioning that relies on fewer such specific resources.

It seems fairly obvious that the ability to perform two tasks together in an adequate fashion depends in some sense on the difficulty of the two tasks. However, the notion of "task difficulty" is rather amorphous, and there are undoubtedly several ways in which one task can be more difficult than another. In spite of the problems associated with the assessment of task difficulty, there are several studies showing the expected pattern of results. Sullivan (1976) gave her subjects the two tasks of shadowing an auditory message and detecting target words on a non-shadowed message. When the shadowing task was made more difficult by using a less redundant message, fewer targets were detected on the non-shadowed message.

The impact of task difficulty on dual-task performance was also shown by Hitch and Baddeley (1976). A verbal reasoning task was combined with rapid overt rehearsal of six digits; the digits were either "one-two-three-four-five-six" or a random sequence. When the more difficult random digit sequence was used, the time taken to carry out the verbal reasoning task increased considerably.

The effects of task difficulty on the performance of two concurrent tasks are by no means always as expected. One reason for this was suggested by Norman and Bobrow (1975), who distinguished between data-limited and resource-limited processes. If performance is resource limited, then an increase in the amount of resources invested in the task would improve performance. This is not the case when performance is data limited; here the problem is one of poor quality of the task stimuli or inadequate information in memory.

Increasing the difficulty of one task will impair performance on a second, concurrent task only if extra resources are allocated to the first task. If data limitation is involved, then quite different results to resource limitation may be obtained. Consider an extreme example of someone reading and listening at the same time. Turning out all of the lights certainly makes the reading task more difficult, but this does not lead to impaired performance on the listening task.

It has often been assumed that the demands for resources of two tasks when performed together are equal to the sum of the demands of the same tasks when performed separately. This assumption of additivity of demands is often inaccurate, because the necessity to perform two tasks together often introduces fresh demands of co-ordination and avoidance of interference. Such fresh demands were observed by Duncan (1979) in an experiment in which subjects had to respond as quickly as possible to two closely successive stimuli, one requiring a left-hand response while the other called for a right-hand response. The relationship between each stimulus and response was either corresponding (i.e., rightmost stimulus calling for response of the rightmost finger, and leftmost stimulus requiring response of the leftmost finger) or crossed (e.g., leftmost stimulus requiring response of the rightmost finger). Overall performance was surprisingly poor when the relationship between one stimulus and its response was corresponding, and was crossed for the other stimulus and its response. Under these conditions, the subjects may sometimes have been confused, as was suggested by the fact that the errors were largely those expected if the inappropriate stimulus–response relationship had been selected. In this case, the uncertainty and confusion caused by mixing two different stimulus–response relationships added a completely new complexity to performance that would not exist when only one of the two tasks was performed on its own.

In sum, it is only possible to predict the extent to which two different tasks can be performed together when account is taken of several factors. In general terms, two dissimilar, highly practised, and simple tasks can usually be combined successfully, whereas two similar, unfamiliar, and complex tasks cannot. There are other considerations, too, such as the extent to which the structure of the tasks permits alternation of attention between them. As will become obvious shortly, theorists differ in terms of which factor or factors they regard as most consequential.

Central Capacity Versus Multiple Resources

A straightforward way of accounting for many of the dual-task findings is to assume that there is some central capacity which can be flexibly deployed across a wide range of activities. This central capacity possesses strictly limited resources (and is sometimes referred to as attention or effort), and the extent to which two concurrent tasks can be performed successfully depends upon the demand which each task makes on those resources. If the combined demands of the two tasks do not exceed the total resources of the central capacity, then the two tasks will not interfere with each other. When the resources are insufficient to meet the demands placed on them by the two tasks, then disruption of performance is inevitable. The amount of disruption suffered by either task will be affected by the ways in which the available resources are allocated. More specifically, performance levels will be determined by the principle of complementarity (Norman & Bobrow, 1975), according to which an increase in use of resources by one task produces a commensurate decrease in the resources available for the other task. In addition to Norman and Bobrow (1975), theories of this basic kind have been put forward by several theorists (e.g., Baddeley & Hitch, 1974; Johnston & Heinz, 1978; Kahneman, 1973).

One of the predictions that flows naturally from the central capacity theory is that even apparently dissimilar tasks should interfere with each other if they make substantial demands on the limited resources of the central capacity. There are numerous examples of such interference effects occurring, starting with a study by Welch (1898), who found that the physical task of producing maximal hand grip interfered with mental tasks such as calculation and reading. Such findings clearly point to the existence of some very general processing system (such as attention) that is utilized across a wide range of task demands.

According to all central capacity theories, the crucial determinant of dual-task performance is the difficulty level of each of the tasks, defining difficulty in terms of the demands placed on the resources of the central capacity. We saw earlier that manipulations of task difficulty often produce the expected results, but there are numerous exceptions. In particular, any effects of task difficulty are sometimes swamped by those of the degree of similarity between tasks. In essence, the basic problem for central capacity theories occurs in situations where we consider four tasks (e.g., A, B, C, D). If we pair A with C, and B with C, and discover that A interferes more with the performance of C than B does, then central capacity theories argue that A requires more of the resources of the central capacity than B. That conclusion leads to the prediction that A will also interfere more with the performance of D than B will. If it turns out that the performance of D is less disrupted by A than by B, then no simple central capacity theory can account for the data.

This rather abstract account can be rendered more concrete by considering an example of this kind of interactive effect. Segal and Fusella (1970) combined image construction (visual or auditory) with signal detection (visual or auditory). The findings are shown in Fig. 3.3. The auditory image task impaired detection of auditory signals more than the visual image task did, suggesting to central capacity theorists that the auditory image task is more difficult and requires more resources than the visual image task. This interpretation seems rather suspect, however, since it turned out that the auditory image task was *less* disruptive than the visual image task when each task was combined with a task requiring detection of visual signals. In this case, task similarity was clearly of paramount importance, and an account based on some general capacity is otiose.

Central capacity theories are rather embarrassed by the discovery that two relatively complex tasks can sometimes be performed together with minimal disruption (e.g., Allport et al., 1972; Spelke et al., 1976; Shaffer, 1975). The reason is that complex tasks should theoretically make great use of central

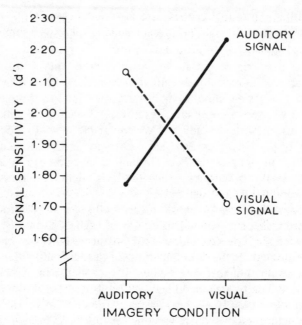

FIG. 3.3   Sensitivity (d′) to auditory and visual signals as a function of concurrent imagery modality (auditory versus visual). Adapted from Segal and Fusella (1970).

resources, and so should interfere with each other. However, it is noticeable that highly practised subjects are nearly always used in this kind of study, and it is probable that the amount of resources required to perform a task decreases as a function of practice (see Norman and Bobrow, 1975). Indeed, it has been argued (e.g., Shiffrin & Schneider, 1977) that extended practice sometimes leads to the development of automatic processes making no demands on central capacity.

Central capacity interference models owe much of their popularity to the simple explanations of dual-task performance which they provide. However, this simplicity is achieved by making use of some rather dubious assumptions. For example, it has often been assumed that questions about the limitations on performance of two concurrent tasks are very much the same as questions about the limitations of central capacity or attention. This often leads to the dangers of circular argument: limited central capacity is frequently measured by the mutual interference between two tasks, and this interference is then "explained" in terms of limited central capacity.

Even advocates of central capacity theory have been forced to admit that the original theory needs to be bolstered by a number of extra explanatory principles in order to account for the data. These include the demands on resources of task co-ordination (Duncan, 1979), the existence of automatic processes, and the notion that central capacity is elastic and flexible rather than fixed (Kahneman, 1973). The present state of play was summarised accurately and succinctly by Navon and Gopher (1979):

> The most parsimonious view of the field (i.e., the central capacity interference theory) seems to have proved inadequate; the remaining alternatives are either to augment, patch and hedge that view so that it barely resembles its original form, or to substitute it altogether with a broader, and necessarily more complex, view [pp. 247–248].

Some theorists have become so disenchanted with the notion of a central capacity or attentional system that they have argued that no such capacity or system actually exists. The strongest expression of that disenchantment was by Allport (1980). He claimed that the term "attention" is often used as a synonym for the less acceptable term "consciousness," without any proper specification of how it is supposed to operate. Perhaps his main argument against continuing to postulate the existence of attention or central capacity is that it has not proved fruitful in terms of deepening our understanding. For example, it is very easy to "explain" dual-task interference by claiming that the resources of some central capacity have been exceeded, and to account for a lack of dual-task interference by proposing that the two tasks did not exceed those resources, but such reasoning signally fails to provoke any further, and more searching, examination of what is happening.

What should replace the attention construct? According to Allport (1980), the most plausible alternative is that there are several different specific processing mechanisms or resources. If the processing system comprises such specific mechanisms, then it is immediately clear why the degree of similarity between two concurrent tasks is so important: Similar tasks compete for the same specific processing mechanisms, and thus produce mutual interference, whereas dissimilar tasks involve different mechanisms, and may thus not interfere with each other at all.

This kind of theory often seems rather unrealistic, in that chaos would probably result if several processing mechanisms were all operating totally independently of each other. Some central control is essential if behaviour is to be co-ordinated and purposeful. It is also not clear, in most theories postulating specific processing systems, exactly why entirely dissimilar tasks often interfere with each other (e.g., Welch, 1898). A further pressing difficulty is that theorists who favour the idea that there are specific processing mechanisms rarely go so far as to spell out the number and exact nature of these mechanisms. However, a start was made by Baddeley and Hitch (1974), who argued for two specific processing systems (i.e., the articulatory loop and a visuospatial scratch pad) in addition to a central capacity (i.e., the modality-free central processor). Such a theory can readily explain why overt repetition of an over-learned sequence of digits does not interfere much with verbal reasoning: Overt repetition makes use of the articulatory loop, whereas verbal reasoning relies on the central processor.

In view of the complementary strengths and weaknesses of the central capacity and specific mechanism theories, there seems to be some merit in combining aspects of both approaches (Eysenck, 1982a). While this may sound like a soggy compromise, it does enable us to make more sense of the data. Perhaps there is a hierarchical structure of processes, with the central processor at the top of the hierarchy and more specific processing resources below it. The details of such a conceptualisation were spelt out by Eysenck (1982a):

> The position of any processing system within the hierarchy is determined by two major criteria: (1) the generality-specificity of the processing system and (2) the degree of automaticity of the processing system. Relatively general and non-automatic processes appear towards the top of the hierarchy, and specific, automatic processes occur at the bottom. As a rule of thumb, the location in the hierarchy of the processes involved in the performance of a task can be assessed by a series of experiments in which the task is paired with several others: higher-level processes will more consistently produce interference than will low-level processes [p. 45].

Automatic Processing

One of the key phenomena within the dual-task paradigm is the dramatic impact that practice typically has on performance (e.g., Spelke *et al.*, 1976). While there are several possible explanations of this phenomenon, the consensual view is that, as a result of prolonged practice, some processing activities cease to make any demands on central capacity or attention; in other words, they become automatic. An influential theory based on this assumption was put forward by Schneider and Shiffrin (1977) and Shiffrin and Schneider (1977). They distinguished between controlled and automatic processes: Controlled processes are of limited capacity, require attention, and can be used flexibly in changing circumstances, whereas automatic processes suffer no capacity limitations, do not require attention, and are very difficult to modify once they have been learned.

Schneider and Shiffrin (1977) and Shiffrin and Schneider (1977) investigated controlled and automatic processes in a series of experiments. They made use of a task in which subjects memorised between one and four items (the memory set), were then shown visual displays containing between one and four items, and finally decided as rapidly as possible whether any one of the items in the visual display was the same as any one of the items within the memory set. In many of their experiments the crucial manipu-

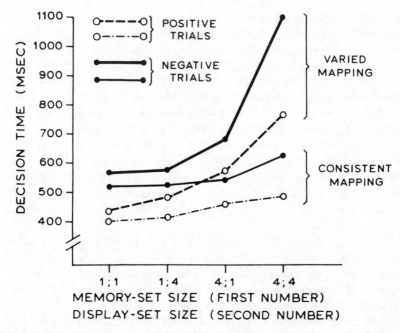

FIG. 3.4   Response latency on a decision task as a function of memory-set size, display-set size, and consistent versus varied mapping. Data from Schneider and Shiffrin (1977).

lation was the kind of mapping used: consistent versus varied. Schneider and Shiffrin (1977) utilised a consistent mapping condition in which only consonants were used as members of the memory set, and only numbers were used as distractors in the visual display (or vice versa). In other words, if a subject was given only consonants to memorise, then he or she would know that any consonant detected in the visual display must be an item from the memory set. In contrast, varied mapping involved using a mixture of numbers and consonants to form the memory set and to provide distractors in the visual display.

The results were dramatically affected by the nature of the mapping conditions (see Fig. 3.4). The numbers of items in the memory set and visual display both greatly affected decision speed under varied mapping conditions, with the effects being approximately twice as large on negative trials (i.e., when the visual display did not contain any of the memorised items.) With consistent mapping, decision speed was almost unaffected by the sizes of the memory set and visual display. According to Schneider and Shiffrin (1977), a controlled search process was used with varied mapping; this involves serial comparisons between each item in the memory set and each item in the visual display until a match is achieved or all of the possible comparisons have been made. On the other hand, performance with consistent mapping reflected the use of automatic processes operating in parallel and independently. How did these automatic processes develop? According to Schneider and Shiffrin, they evolved as a result of years of practice in distinguishing between letters and numbers.

The notion that automatic processes develop through practice was investigated in a direct fashion by Shiffrin and Schneider. They used consistent mapping, with the consonants B to L comprising one set and the consonants Q to Z forming the other set. As before, items from only one set were always used in the construction of the memory set, and the distractors in the visual display were all selected from the other set. There was reasonable evidence that the improvements in performance obtained over a total of 2100 trials reflected the growth of automatic processes.

The evidence discussed so far has suggested that automatic processes operate more rapidly and efficiently than controlled processes, but for a complete picture we must consider the potential disadvantages of automatic processing. The most obvious problem with automatic processes is their lack of flexibility, which is likely to disrupt performance when there is a change in the prevailing circumstances. This was confirmed in the second part of the study just described. The initial 2100 trials with one consistent mapping were followed by a further 2400 trials with the reverse consistent mapping. For example, if the memory-set items were always taken from the second half of the alphabet during the first part of the experiment, then they were drawn from the first half of the alphabet during the second part. This reversal of the mapping conditions had a markedly adverse effect on performance; indeed, it took nearly 1000 trials under the new conditions before performance recovered to its level at the very start of the experiment.

Of course, it could be argued that performance normally suffers when the way in which a task has been carried out in the past is no longer appropriate, and thus an explanation in terms of automaticity is superogatory. This possibility was explored by Shiffrin and Schneider (1977). They discovered that there were relatively minor effects on performance when the conditions were changed for subjects given varied mapping, which indicates that controlled processes are much more easily modifiable than automatic processes. This conclusion was further supported by other experiments in which subjects initially attempted to locate target items anywhere in a visual display, but then were instructed to detect targets in one part of the display and to ignore any targets that appeared elsewhere in the display. The key finding was that subjects were less able to ignore part of the visual display when they had developed automatic processes as a consequence of consistent mapping than when they had made use of controlled search processes due to varied mapping.

In sum, Shiffrin and Schneider (1977) discovered that attention can be divided among several information sources with reasonable success when automatic processes are used. The position is quite different with respect to focused attention, in which some sources of information must be attended to and others ignored. Under such circumstances, controlled processes largely prevent unwanted processing from occurring, whereas automatic processes disrupt performance because of automatic responses to to-be-ignored stimuli. In a nutshell, the major conclusion to be drawn from the programme of research carried out by Shiffrin and Schneider is as follows: "Automatic processes function rapidly and in parallel but suffer from inflexibility; controlled processes are flexible and versatile but operate relatively slowly and in a serial fashion [Eysenck, 1982a, p. 22]."

Of course, Shiffrin and Schneider (1977) and Schneider and Shiffrin (1977) only examined controlled and automatic processes in the context of visual tasks, and it is possible that different results might be obtained in other sensory modalities. However, Poltrock, Lansman, and Hunt (1982) investigated the effects of consistent and varied mapping on auditory target detection, and obtained very similar results to those of Shiffrin and Schneider.

The theoretical approach of Shiffrin and Schneider is important, but it is certainly not beyond reproach. There is a puzzling discrepancy between theory and data with respect to the identification of automaticity. The theoretical assumption that automatic processes operate in parallel and place no demands on capacity means that there should be a slope of zero in the function relating decision speed to the numbers of items in the memory set or in the visual display when automatic processes are used. In fact, while Shiffrin and Schneider argued that their consistent mapping conditions produced automaticity, they typically found that decision speed was slower when the memory set and the visual display both contained several items than when they did not (e.g., see Fig. 3.4 on p. 69).

Shiffrin and Schneider assumed that a non-zero slope was indicative of the use of controlled attentional processing. This assumption is only warranted provided that there is but a single capacity (i.e., controlled attention) that limits performance. If there are any other capacity limitations, then a non-zero slope cannot be taken as conclusive evidence that attention is being paid to the task in question. In a reaction-time study (Logan, 1979), 6 days of practice with consistent mapping reduced, but did not eliminate, the slope relating the number of stimulus–response alternatives to reaction time. This could be taken as evidence that controlled attentional processes were still being used. However, Logan also used a second measure of automaticity based on the impact of a concurrent memory task on reaction time; according to this criterion, consistent mapping did lead to the development of automaticity for some aspect of the reaction-time task. It thus appears that it may be easier to draw a conceptual than an empirical distinction between controlled and automatic processes.

One of the major implications of the theoretical position adopted by Shiffrin and Schneider (1977) is that two tasks can be performed together efficiently provided that at least one of the tasks involves automatic processing. The reason for this is that automatic processes allegedly place no demands on capacity. In a study on visual search, Schneider and Fisk (1982) discovered that one controlled (i.e., varied mapping) and one automatic (i.e., consistent mapping) task could be performed as well together as separately after extensive practice, whereas two controlled processing tasks could not be combined successfully. These findings provide striking confirmation of the notion that automatic processes can sometimes be performed without any measurable cost.

A more detailed account of the circumstances in which automatic processes can occur was offered by Treisman and Gelade (1980). They distinguished between features and objects, regarding a feature as a particular value on a dimension which is analysed by a functionally independent perceptual sub-system (e.g., colour is a dimension, and red is a feature on that dimension). Their key theoretical assumption was that perceptual features are processed automatically and in parallel, but objects are identified only as the result of serial processing based on focused attention. An important role of focused attention is to provide the "glue" which constructs unitary objects from the available features.

Treisman and Gelade (1980) provided strong support for their feature integration theory of attention. In one of their experiments, subjects searched for a target in a visual display containing between 1 and 30 items. The target was either an object (a green letter "T") or it was a single feature (either a blue letter or an "S"). It was predicted that focal attention would be needed to detect the former target (because it was defined by a combination of features), but automatic processes would suffice to detect the latter target.

The results on trials when a target was presented were exactly as predicted: The number of items in the visual display substantially affected detection speed when the target was defined by a conjunction of features (i.e., a green letter "T"), but there was practically no effect of display size when the target was defined by a single feature (a blue letter or an "S"). It could be argued that automatic search did not occur with the conjunctive target simply because the subjects were relatively unfamiliar with the task of searching for a specified letter presented in a particular colour. However, Treisman and Gelade discovered that lengthy practice with the conjunctive target failed to produce evidence for automatic processing in the form of parallel search.

According to the feature integration theory, lack of focused attention should produce a state of affairs in which the features of different objects are processed but remain "unglued." As a result, it seems likely that a feature from one object might be mistakenly combined with a feature from a second object to form an "illusory conjunction." This prediction was confirmed by Treisman (1977), who discovered that illusory conjunctions, involving integrating the shape of one object with the colour of a second, were often reported in the absence of focal attention.

The findings of Treisman and Gelade indicate clearly that automatic search processes can only be used successfully under certain limited conditions. The most important requirement is that the target items can be distinguished from non-targets on the basis of a single feature. If this requirement is not satisfied, then the use of automatic processes produces various problems, including those stemming from illusory conjunctions. Shiffrin and Schneider (1977) emphasised the importance of practice and consistency of mapping in the development of automaticity; the work of Treisman and Gelade (1980) suggests that they rather ignored the key issue of the kinds of information that can be processed automatically.

Is it really true, as Treisman and Gelade (1980) assumed, that unattended stimuli are necessarily processed only at the feature level? The finding (e.g., von Wright *et al.*, 1975) that the meaning of unattended words can be registered without any conscious awareness is rather troublesome for the theory, because it is rather unlikely that meaning is represented as a single feature. However, it would be unwise to pontificate too much on this issue until the notion of a semantic feature is clarified.

Although it seems clear that automatic processing can, and does, occur, the astute reader will have noticed that there are a number of unresolved issues. Firstly, there is by no means a consensus regarding the appropriate criteria for judging the existence of automaticity. As LaBerge (1981) pointed out, the proposed criteria for automatic processes include unavoidability, occurring without awareness, highly efficient, without capacity limitations, and resistant to modification. Whether all five criteria are of equal importance in defining automaticity is currently unknown.

Secondly, it is quite possible to conclude erroneously that a process does satisfy one or more of the criteria for automaticity. For example, consider the Stroop effect, in which the naming of colours in which words are printed is slowed down by using colour words. This effect has usually been thought to involve unavoidable and automatic processing of the colour words. However, recent research by Kahneman and Henik (1979) suggests the involvement of attentional processes in the Stroop effect. They discovered that the effect was much larger when the distracting information (i.e., the colour name) was in the same location as the to-be-named colour rather than in an adjacent location within the central fixation area. The processes producing the Stroop effect are not always unavoidable, and are thus not necessarily automatic.

Thirdly, while the assumption that automaticity often develops as a result of practice is probably sound, certain qualifications seem to be in order. Some processes may not become automatic simply as a result of repeated use, and may require special forms of practice. Other processes may be intrinsically incapable of automatisation (Treisman & Gelade, 1980).

PRACTICAL APPLICATIONS:

ACTION SLIPS AND ABSENT-MINDEDNESS

Some of the theoretical notions considered in this chapter are relevant to an understanding of the commonplace phenomenon of absent-mindedness. Psychologists often refer to this phenomenon by the term "action slip," meaning the performance of an action that was not intended. At the most general level, it seems obvious that attentional failures usually underlie action slips, but it may well be that there are several different kinds of action slips, each of which requires its own detailed explanation.

The first prerequisite is to collect numerous examples of action slips and attempt to assign them to a manageable number of categories. This was done by Reason (1979), who asked 35 people to keep diaries of their action slips over a 2-week period. Over 400 action errors were reported altogether, most of which belonged to five major categories. Forty percent of the action slips involved storage failures in which intentions and actions were either forgotten or recalled incorrectly. Reason (1979) quoted the following example of a storage failure: "I started to pour a second kettle of boiling water into a teapot full of freshly made tea. I had no recollection of having just made it [p. 74]". A further 20% of the errors were test failures in which the progress of a planned sequence was not monitored sufficiently thoroughly at crucial junctures. An illustrative test failure from one person's diary went as follows (Reason, 1979): "I meant to get my car out, but as I passed through the back porch on my way to the garage I stopped to put on my wellington boots and gardening jacket as if to work in the garden [p. 73]." Sub-routine failures accounted for a further 18% of the errors; these involved insertions, omissions, or re-orderings of the component stages in an action sequence. Reason (1979) exemplified such failures as follows: "I sat down to do some work and before starting to write I put my hand up to my face to take my glasses off, but my fingers snapped together rather abruptly because I hadn't been wearing them in the first place [p. 73]." There were relatively few examples of action slips belonging to the two remaining categories of discrimination failures (11%) and programme assembly failures (5%). The former category comprised failures to discriminate appropriately between stimulus objects (e.g., mistaking shaving cream for toothpaste), and the latter category consisted of inappropriate combinations of actions (e.g.,

"I unwrapped a sweet, put the paper in my mouth, and threw the sweet into the waste bucket [p. 72]").

It would be unwise to attach much importance to the percentages for the various kinds of action slips. In the first place, the figures are based solely on those action slips that were noticed, and we do not know how many cases of each kind of slip went completely undetected. Secondly, the number of occurrences of any particular kind of action slip is meaningful only when we have some idea of the number of occasions on which that kind of slip might have happened but did not. For example, the small number of discrimination failures may reflect either good discrimination on the part of the diary keepers, or the relative lack of situations requiring anything approaching a fine discrimination.

When we look in detail at slips of action, it is of interest that they nearly all occur during the performance of highly practised and over-learned activities. This is somewhat surprising and paradoxical, since what normally happens is that proneness to errors decreases as skills are acquired. Reason (1979) accounted for this apparent paradox by distinguishing between two modes of control over motor performance. During the initial stages of motor learning, extensive use is made of a closed-loop or feedback mode of control, in which visual and proprioceptive feedback is used by some central processor or attentional system to provide moment-by-moment control of behaviour. As a result of extensive practice, this closed-loop mode is increasingly replaced by an open-loop mode of control in which motor performance is controlled by motor programmes or by pre-arranged instruction sequences. A crucial aspect of the open-loop mode is that it frees the resources of the central processor to engage in processing activities that may have little relevance to the current motor performance.

The advantages of the open-loop mode are obvious in that attentional resources are not exclusively committed to the ongoing task and can thus be flexibly deployed. However, there are concomitant disadvantages. In particular, an individual who is operating in the open-loop mode and attending to non-task information may fail to return to the closed-loop mode as and when appropriate. As a consequence, slips of action occur. This theoretical position was spelt out by Reason (1979):

> The performance of a highly practised and largely automatized job liberates the central processor from moment-to-moment control; but since, like Nature, focal attention abhors a vacuum it tends to be 'captured' by some pressing but parallel mental activity so that, on occasion, it fails to switch back to the task in hand at a 'critical decision point' and thus permits the guidance of action to fall by default under the control of 'strong' motor programmes [p. 85].

How well does this hypothesis account for action slips? This question can only be answered by considering the various types of action slips separately.

One common type of action slip involves repeating an action unnecessarily because the first action has been forgotten. Common examples are attempting to start a car when the engine has already been started, or brushing one's teeth twice in quick succession. We know from studies in which listeners attend to one message and repeat it back (i.e., shadow it) while ignoring a second concurrent message that unattended information is held very briefly and then forgotten. When the initial starting of a car or brushing one's teeth occurs automatically in the open-loop mode, it would be predicted that subsequent retention of the information that that action has been performed should be extremely poor.

Many action slips can be accounted for when it is appreciated that most action sequences consist of a number of distinct motor programmes. While each individual motor programme can be carried out without close control by the central processor, a switch to the closed-loop mode of control is essential at certain points in the sequence of actions, especially when a given situation is common to two or more motor programmes, and the strongest available motor programme is inappropriate. The person who put on his gardening clothes instead of getting the car out exemplifies the way in which strong but unplanned actions can occur in the absence of attentional control, and a further illustration was given by William James (1890): "Very absent-minded persons in going to their bedroom to dress for dinner have been known to take off one garment after another and finally to get into bed, merely because that was the habitual issue of the first few movements when performed at a later hour [p. 115]." In other words, one of the consequences of relatively automatic functioning is an inflexible sequence of motor activities based on the relative strengths of the various motor programmes. Most situations call for some flexibility in the nature and ordering of the components of an action sequence, and such flexibility can only occur with the closed-loop mode of control.

On the basis of the discussion so far it might be argued that people would function more efficiently if they placed less reliance on automatic processes and more on the central processor. However, such an argument is suspect because automatised activities can sometimes be disrupted if too much attention is paid to the details of task performance. For example, it can become more difficult to walk down a steep spiral staircase if attention is paid to the leg movements involved. Moreover, Reason's diarists produced an average of only one action slip per day, which is by no means an indication that their usual processing strategies were ineffective. All in all, most people seem to use the closed-loop and open-loop modes of control very efficiently. The optimal strategy involves very frequent shifts from one mode of control to the other, and it is noteworthy that these shifts are performed with great success for the most part. Action slips are the consequence of a failure to shift from open-loop to closed-loop control at the right moment, and while they are theoretically important, action slips usually have a minimally disruptive effect on everyday life. Of course, there may be important individual differences, and the tendency of academics to attend to their own profound inner thoughts may mean that there is a grain of truth in the stereotype of the absent-minded professor!

4 The Structure of the Memory System

Most theorists interested in the phenomena of memory have drawn a distinction between storage and retrieval. The distinction certainly makes sense at the experimental level: Events occurring during the presentation of to-be-remembered information determine what is stored, whereas the conditions at the time of a subsequent retention test determine what can be retrieved. At a more theoretical level, however, matters are rather muddier. If, for example, people find it easier to recognise distinctive faces than non-distinctive ones, does this reflect superior storage of information about the distinctive faces, or does it indicate an effect of distinctiveness on ease of retrieval? Such questions can be surprisingly difficult to answer satisfactorily.

It is worth emphasising that storage and retrieval should not be regarded as being entirely independent of each other. As Tulving and Thomson (1973) pointed out, "Only that can be retrieved that has been stored, and ... how it can be retrieved depends on how it was stored [p. 359]. Storage and retrieval are only discussed in separate chapters in this book for ease of explanation, and their interdependence will hopefully become manifest in due course.

THE SPATIAL METAPHOR

When people think about the mind, they often liken it to a physical space, with memories and ideas as objects contained within that space. Thus, we speak of ideas being in the dark corners or dim recesses of our minds, and of holding ideas in mind. Ideas may be in the front or back of our minds, or they may be difficult to grasp. With respect to the processes involved in memory, we talk about storing memories, of searching or looking for lost memories, and sometimes of finding them. An examination of common parlance, therefore, suggests that there is general adherence to what might be called the spatial metaphor. The basic assumptions of this metaphor are that memories are treated as objects stored in specific locations within the mind, and the retrieval process involves a search through the mind in order to find specific memories.

One of the most intriguing features of theorising by philosophers and psychologists about human memory is the strong reliance placed on the spatial metaphor. An early use of the spatial metaphor as a guide to understanding memory phenomena was by Plato, who compared the mind to an aviary. Plato (in Hamilton, 1961) described a discussion in which Socrates asked Theatetus to consider whether possessing knowledge is not,

> like a man who has caught some wild birds—pigeons or what not—and keeps them in an aviary he has made for them at home.... Let us suppose that every mind contains an aviary stocked with birds of every sort, some in flocks apart from the rest, some in small groups, and some solitary and flying in any direction among them all [p. 904].

As with most spatial metaphors of memory, remembering information was assumed to involve a search process. Socrates asked Theatetus (Hamilton, 1961) to think of the person as, "hunting once more for any piece of knowledge that he wants, catching and holding it, and letting it go again [p. 904]." Finally, the analogy of the aviary provided a way of accounting for errors in retrieval. An error would occur when, "in hunting for some particular piece of knowledge, among those that are fluttering about, he misses it and catches hold of a different one ... as he might catch a dove in place of a pigeon [p. 906]."

Plato's bird-brain analogy is embarrassing for contemporary cognitive psychologists because some of the most recent theories of memory seem to be remarkably similar. However, while the spatial metaphor has shown extraordinary longevity, there have been some interesting changes over time in the precise form of analogy used. In particular, technological advances have influenced theoretical conceptualisations (Roediger, 1980). The original Greek analogies were based on wax tablets and aviaries; these were superseded by analogies involving switchboards, gramophones, tape recorders, libraries, conveyor belts, and underground maps. Most recently, the workings of human memory have been compared to computer functioning (e.g., Atkinson & Shiffrin, 1968), and it has been suggested that the various memory stores found in computers have their counterparts in the human memory system.

Cognitive psychologists have tended to take the spatial metaphor for granted. As a result, there have been relatively few critical evaluations of its usefulness as a theoretical framework. However, one common criticism of the spatial metaphor concerns its apparent inability to explain the fact that we can often decide very rapidly that we do not know something. The most obvious assumption based on the spatial metaphor is that there would need to be a thorough memory search in order to ascertain that some piece of information was not present. In fact, people can decide very quickly that letter strings such as "MANTINESS" are not English words, and they are sometimes able to make negative decisions about issues such as whether they know certain words well enough to be able to use them in a sentence, or whether they have visited certain cities, faster than they can make positive decisions (Kolers & Palef, 1976). The finding that non-words can often be rejected rapidly can be explained by assuming that there is, indeed, exhaustive search of the lexicon, but that it is a parallel search (Coltheart, 1978). However, it is not clear that the other findings can be accounted for so readily.

It is possible to extend the spatial metaphor to account for the ways in which we cope with novelty. However, there do seem to be some fairly intractable problems here for the spatial metaphor. Bransford, McCarrell, Franks, and Nitsch (1977) provided a thoughtful critique of the spatial or memory metaphor which emphasised the issue of novelty:

> The problem for the memory metaphor is that storage and retrieval of traces only deals [sic] with old, previously articulated information. Memory traces can perhaps provide a basis for dealing with the "sameness" of the present experience with previous experiences, but the memory metaphor has no mechanisms for dealing with novel information [p. 434].

A major limitation of the spatial metaphor is that it is mainly relevant to questions concerning the storage and subsequent retrieval of individual items of information. Such questions can perhaps be answered by means of the typical retention tests used by memory psychologists (e.g., recognition and recall). However, in our everyday lives memory is by no means always used merely to re-evoke previously experienced events. A skilful tennis player undoubtedly makes use of previous knowledge and experience, and yet it would seem ludicrous to equate the ability to play tennis with a large collection of memories of previous tennis-playing experiences. In a nutshell, the spatial metaphor leads us to ask the question, "Can this item of information be located within the memory system?" In real life, information is usually retrieved in the context of ongoing activities rather than in a vacuum, and the ability to locate previously stored specific memories is of only modest relevance.

A final problem with the spatial metaphor is that it seems to imply a rather inflexible storage system. If everything we know is stored within a three-dimensional space, then some kinds of information must necessarily be stored closer together than others. Perhaps the organisation of information within the memory system resembles a library (Broadbent, 1971), with semantically related items of information being stored together. However, the cataloguing system used in most libraries would break down completely if a novel category of books were requested (e.g., books with red covers or with more than 700 pages).

This suggests that any classification system used to organise the contents of human memory would only work efficiently provided that certain limited kinds of questions were posed. For example, if memory is organised in terms of semantic categories, then it might be fairly straightforward to select the odd man out from the words "shoe," "shirt," and "rock." If the odd man out needed to be picked from the same three words in the context of objects that could be used to pound a nail into a wall, then it is less clear that the spatial metaphor can account for efficient performance. Most versions of the spatial metaphor imply that search and retrieval processes can only be used successfully when the nature of the requested information is compatible with whatever classification system is used to organise the contents of memory. In actuality, retrieval appears to demonstrate markedly greater flexibility than this. In essence, reliance on the spatial metaphor leads to an over-emphasis on the ways in which information is represented in the memory system, and an under-emphasis on the processes operating on those memorial representation.

MEMORY STORES

Introduction

Several memory theorists (e.g., Atkinson & Shiffrin, 1968; Waugh & Norman, 1965) have attempted to describe the basic architecture of the memory system. However, it should be noted that their emphasis was very much on verbal memory rather than, for example, visual memory. Three kinds of memory store have been postulated: sensory stores; the short-term store; and the long-term store. It was assumed that information from the external environment is initially received by the sensory stores. These stores are modality-specific, with a separate sensory store corresponding to each of the sensory modalities. Information is held transiently in the sensory stores, with some of it being attended to and processed further by the short-term store. In turn, some of the information processed in the short-term store is transferred to the long-term store.

It is worth noting at this point that there is a considerable overlap between the areas of attention and memory, and so much of the material covered in Chapter 3 is relevant here. For example, Broadbent's (1958) theory of attention was in many ways the main precursor of the multi-store approach to memory, and there is a definite resemblance between the sensory stores and his "buffer" store.

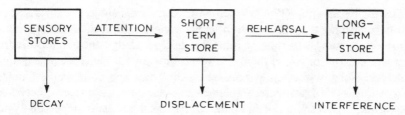

FIG. 4.1   The modal multi-store model of memory.

The modal multi-store model is shown in Fig. 4.1. As in most theoretical models of memory, it incorporates a number of structural and processing assumptions. The memory stores themselves form the basic structure, and processes such as attention and rehearsal control the flow of information between the memory stores. However, the emphasis within the multi-store approach to memory is on structure rather than on the processes operating on that structure, and that is why this approach is discussed in this chapter. The processes involved in learning and memory are discussed at length in Chapter 5.

In the following sections we discuss the basic characteristics of each of the memory stores. After that, the multi-store model proposed by Atkinson and Shiffrin (1968, 1971) is evaluated. Finally, contemporary developments, including the working memory model (Baddeley & Hitch, 1974), are discussed in some detail.

Sensory Stores

At any given moment in time, our senses are bombarded with an enormous amount of information, most of which is not attended to. For example, if you are sitting down as you read this, then tactile information from that part of you in contact with your chair is probably available; however, if you have any interest in what you are reading, you have hitherto been unaware of that tactile information. It is a matter of some considerable theoretical interest to investigate the fate of such information: is it immediately lost, or does it remain in the processing system for a brief period of time? It is clear that information in most, if not all, of the sense modalities persists for some time after the end of stimulation. The value of this persistence of sensory information is that it facilitates the task of extracting its most important aspects for further analysis.

While it is usually assumed that there are as many modality-specific stores as there are sense modalities, the evidence is much stronger with respect to the visual and auditory modalities than any of the others. So far as the visual or iconic store is concerned, the classic demonstration of its existence was provided by Sperling (1960). When he presented his subjects with a visual array containing three rows of four letters each for 50 msec., and asked them to recall as many letters as possible, he discovered that they could usually report only four or five of them. However, most of the subjects claimed that they had actually seen many more letters than they had been able to report.

Sperling (1960) wondered whether this puzzling discrepancy between performance and self-report was due to the fact that visual information was available after the stimulus had been turned off, but so transiently that the information had faded before most of it could be reported. He explored this hypothesis by asking the subjects to report only one-third of the presented information. This was achieved by presenting a cueing tone either .1 sec before the onset of the visual display (which lasted 50 msec.) or at intervals of up to 1 sec. after stimulus offset. A high tone indicated that the top row of letters was to be reported, a medium tone was used to cue recall of the middle row, and a low tone meant that the bottom row of letters was to be recalled. Since the three rows were tested at random, it was possible to estimate the total amount of information available to each subject by multiplying the number of items recalled by three.

The results with this partial report procedure were quite striking. When the tone was presented immediately before or after the onset of the display, approximately 9 letters appeared to be available, but this dropped to 6 letters when the tone was heard 0.3 sec. after the presentation of the display, and it fell to 4.5 letters with an interval of 1 sec. Thus, there is apparently a form of visual storage which fades quite rapidly (within about 0.5 sec. according to most estimates). It has been claimed (e.g., Holding, 1975) that the relatively poor performance under the whole report procedure compared to the partial report method is due in some measure to response interference rather than simply the slowness of report making the icon unavailable. This cannot be the whole story, since results similar to those of Sperling (1960) have been obtained when response or output interference was eliminated as a factor (e.g., Averbach & Coriell, 1961).

It has often been assumed that information in iconic storage is held in a relatively raw and uninterpreted form that corresponds fairly directly to the physical stimulus. This is supported by the finding that subjects can efficiently select items for report on the basis of size or colour but not on the basis of category membership (e.g., letters versus numbers). However, subjects do better on the Sperling task when the letters in non-cued rows resemble English words than when they do not (Butler, 1974), which suggests that iconic information is not necessarily in an unanalyzed form.

Where in the nervous system is the icon produced? It has been claimed (e.g., Sakitt, 1976) that the locus of iconic memory is peripheral, being based on the activity rod cells in the retina. However, this conclusion has been disputed. McCloskey and Watkins (1978) investigated what they termed the "seeing-more-than-is-there" phenomenon, which is produced by moving a stimulus figure to and fro rapidly behind a narrow opening. Although each figure was much wider than the opening, subjects reported seeing the complete figure as approximately the same width as the opening. The fact that subjects perceived the whole figure simultaneously implies that information from the icon and from the figure itself was integrated. The phenomenon occurred even when the subjects did not close their eyes, and it seems unlikely that a single set of rod cells could hold one part of the figure and then another. It is probable that the illusion, and thus the icon, is rather more centrally located than in the retinal photoreceptors.

From what we have said so far, it is rather difficult to understand how visual processing and perception normally proceed. If everything we see persists for some time in the iconic store, there ought to be considerable confusion between the current visual input and the information already in iconic storage. Averbach and Coriell (1961) resolved this problem. They discovered that a visual stimulus will often erase the information contained within the iconic store, and this erasure system serves to minimise the confusion effects that might otherwise occur.

How useful is iconic storage? A trenchant attack on its usefulness was mounted by Haber (1983), who claimed that the iconic store is irrelevant to normal perception, except possibly when attempting to read in a lightning storm. In essence, he argued that "frozen iconic storage of information" may be valuable in the laboratory when you are confronted with very brief tachistoscopic presentations of individual stimuli, but similar conditions practically never obtain normally. In the real world, the icon formed from one visual fixation would be rapidly masked by the next fixation, and so could not assist perception. As a result, our theories of visual perception would remain essentially unaltered if we pretended that the iconic store did not exist.

However, as Coltheart (1983) pertinently noted, Haber seems to have made the erroneous assumption that the icon is created at the offset of a visual stimulus, whereas in fact it is created at its onset. Thus, even with a continuously changing visual world, there is plenty of opportunity for iconic information to be used. Indeed, the mechanisms responsible for visual perception invariably operate upon the icon (or primal sketch—see Chapter 2), rather than directly upon the visual environment itself. The iconic store is thus an integral part of visual perception rather than a laboratory curiosity.

There is considerable evidence for a transient store in the auditory modality. This is often known as the echoic store, and is usually assumed to consist of a relatively unprocessed auditory input. For example, suppose that someone who is reading a newspaper or book is asked a question. The person addressed will sometimes ask, "What did you say?", and at the same time realise that he does know what has been said. This "playback" facility depends on the workings of echoic memory.

A related phenomenon was explored by Treisman (1964), who asked people to repeat back aloud (i.e., shadow) the message presented to one ear while ignoring a concurrent message presented to the other ear. She presented the same message to both ears, but in such a way that the shadowed message either preceded or followed the non-shadowed message. When the non-shadowed message preceded the shadowed message, the two messages were only recognised as being the same when they were within 2 seconds of each other. This suggests that the temporal duration of un-attended auditory information in echoic storage is approximately 2 seconds.

Echoic storage was investigated in a fashion resembling Sperling's (1960) work on iconic storage by Darwin, Turvey, and Crowder (1972). A different set of items was presented concurrently at each of three spatial locations (left, middle, and right). The task was either to recall all of the items in their correct spatial location (whole report) or to recall only one set of items (partial report). In the partial report condition, a visual cue was presented at various times up to 4 seconds after the end of the stimulus presentation to indicate which items were to be recalled. As in Sperling's work, the partial report procedure produced better recall than the whole report procedure, and the advantage of partial report decreased as the time between the end of stimulus presentation and the recall cue increased. However, there was one interesting difference. Partial report remain superior to whole report even with an interval of 4 seconds between presentation and cue. This finding is in line with several others indicating that the temporal duration of echoic storage is generally rather longer than that of iconic storage.

Short-term and long-term Stores

The distinction that multi-store theorists have drawn between a short-term and a long-term store resembles that proposed by William James (1890) between primary memory and secondary memory. Primary memory relates to information that remains in consciousness after it has been perceived, and thus forms part of the psychological present, whereas secondary memory contains information about events that have left consciousness, and are therefore part of the psychological past.

Attempting to remember a telephone number for a few seconds is an everyday example of the use of the short-term store or primary memory. It illustrates two key characteristics that are usually attributable to this store: (1) extremely limited capacity (we cannot remember a sequence of more than some eight digits); and (2) fragility of storage, since the slightest distraction usually causes us to forget the number.

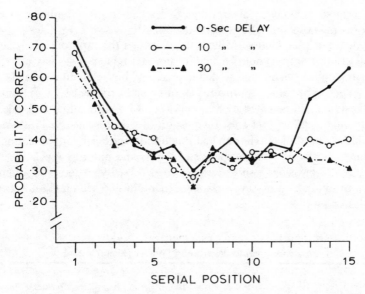

FIG. 4.2   Free recall as a function of serial position and duration of the interpolated task.
Adapted from Glanzer and Cunitz (1966).

How can we obtain evidence to support the proposed distinction between
short-term and long-term memory stores? The usual strategy is to attempt
to discover experimental manipulations having a *differential* effect on the two
hypothesised stores. A classic study using this strategy was carried out by
Glanzer and Cunitz (1966). They used a technique known as free recall, in
which a list of words is presented, and then the subject immediately tries to
recall them in any order. Performance is usually best for the first few items
(the primacy effect) and the last items (the recency effect) (see Fig. 4.2.).
Requiring the subjects to count backwards by threes for 10 or 30 seconds
after the list had been presented reduced the recency effect dramatically, but
had practically no effect on recall from the remainder of the list. Glanzer and
Cunitz concluded that the words in the recency portion of the list were in
the short-term store when the list presentation ended, and this is why they
were so vulnerable to the counting task. In contrast, the items from the
pre-recency part of the list were in the long-term store, and so unaffected
by the interpolated task. Other factors (e.g., rate of presentation; list length)
also have differential effects on the recency and pre-recency parts of word
lists, and thus support the conclusion that performance on free recall tasks
reflects recall from both short-term and long-term stores.
   One of the most obvious ways in which the short-term and long-term
stores appear to differ is in terms of their storage capacity. While the

short-term store is nearly always regarded as having very limited capacity, there are no such limitations with the long-term store. In a well-known theoretical analysis, George Miller (1956) argued that approximately seven chunks of information could be held in short-term memory at any one time. The term "chunk" is difficult to define precisely, but refers to a familiar unit of information based upon previous learning and experience. This chunking hypothesis was investigated by Simon (1974), who argued that a chunk will correspond to the highest-level integration of the stimulus material that is available to the subject. He pursued this notion further by investigating his own memory span for various kinds of words and phrases. As can be seen in Table 4.1, measuring short-term storage capacity in terms of imputed chunks produces a more stable estimate than did reliance on the number of syllables or words.

TABLE 4.1.
Memory Span for Words and Phrases (Simon, 1974)

	1-syllable Words	2-syllable Words	3-syllable Words	2-word Phrases	8-word Phrases
Span in syllables	7	14	18	22	26
Span in words	7	7	6	9	22
Span in imputed chunks	7	7	6	4	3

A problem with span measures of short-term storage capacity is that long-term memory may play a part in determining the span. When digit strings are presented for immediate serial recall, and one digit string is surreptitiously repeated several times, performance on the repeated string becomes progressively superior to that on the non-repeated strings (Bower & Winzenz, 1969). This suggests that some information about the repeated digit string is stored in long-term memory.

The question, "What is the capacity of short-term memory?", can be answered unequivocally only if there is a unitary short-term store. In fact, as we see later in this chapter, it is becoming increasingly obvious that there are actually several different components of short-term memory storage. We should, therefore, be thinking in terms of several different capacities (one corresponding to each component) rather than a single capacity.

A rather different kind of evidence relevant to the distinction between short-term and long-term stores comes from neuropsychological research into brain-damaged patients. One of the most famous cases involved a 29-year-old motor winder known as H.M., part of whose hippocampus had been destroyed. To a casual observer, H.M. appeared to be normal, and his capacity for understanding and reasoning were relatively normal. However, he had practically no ability to store new information in long-term memory.

He did the same puzzles and re-read the same magazines over and over again without realising he had done these things before.

A more formal assessment of the nature of the memory deficit of H.M. and other patients with bilateral hippocampal lesions was undertaken by Drachman and Arbit (1966). Their findings suggested that these patients had impaired long-term storage of information, but a relatively intact short-term store. A similar pattern of results has been found with patients suffering from Korsakoff's syndrome, a disorder associated with chronic alcoholism. Baddeley and Warrington (1970) discovered, for example, that such patients showed poor memory for pre-recency words in free recall, but they had a normal recency effect. They also had a relatively unimpaired digit span.

The picture painted so far is over-simplified to some extent. In particular, there are some circumstances in which brain-damaged and Korsakoff patients have reasonable long-term memory. For example, H.M. showed nearly perfect retention of a perceptual-motor skill over an interval of one week (Corkin, 1968). The complex nature of the deficit exhibited by these patients is discussed at greater length in Chapter 6.

The reverse problem to that of the patients described so far, namely impaired short-term storage combined with normal long-term storage, is relatively rare. However, a few such cases have been reported, including K.F., a patient who suffered damage in the left parieto-occipital region following a motor-cycle accident. K.F. had no difficulty with long-term learning and recall, but his digit span was grossly impaired, and he had a recency effect in free recall of only one item (Shallice & Warrington, 1970).

One of the most important distinctions between the short-term and long-term stores concerns the ways in which forgetting occurs. Forgetting from the short-term store occurred in the study by Glanzer and Cunitz (1966) discussed earlier when the subjects had to count backwards. This may have happened either because counting backwards is a source of inter-ference, or because it diverts attention away from the information in short-term memory. The available evidence suggests that both interference and diversion of attention play a part (e.g., Reitman, 1974).

Forgetting from the long-term store (discussed in detail in Chapter 6) appears to involve rather different mechanisms. As Tulving (1974) pointed out, we must distinguish between trace-dependent forgetting (i.e., the relevant memory traces are lost from the memory system) and cue-dependent forgetting (i.e., the memory traces are still in the memory system, but are inaccessible to most retrieval cues). There is much evidence of the im-portance of cue-dependent forgetting. For example, many people report that they cannot remember much about their early childhood experiences. However, if they revisit the area they were brought up in, the streets and houses often serve as powerful retrieval cues that enable them to reconstruct many childhood events.

While there is still some disagreement about the mechanisms involved in forgetting from the short-term and long-term memory stores, the crucial point is that the forgetting mechanisms appear to be quite different for the two stores. Therefore, a consideration of forgetting mechanisms provides additional support for the theoretical distinction between the two storage systems.

A final distinction between the short-term and long-term memory stores is in terms of the speed of retrieval. Since information in the short-term store is currently being attended to, and has been regarded as "the contents of consciousness," retrieval from the short-term store would be expected to be extremely rapid. In contrast, retrieval of information from the much larger long-term store may involve a more complex and time-consuming process. The usual finding is that information is retrieved much more rapidly from the short-term store than from the long-term store. Eysenck and Eysenck (1979) obtained the typical difference in retrieval speed from the two stores; they also found that more processing capacity was involved in retrieval from the long-term store than from the short-term store.

In sum, there are several ways of distinguishing between separate short-term and long-term memory stores. These include the following: Storage capacity; temporal duration; differential effects of an interpolated task; neuropsychological evidence from brain-damaged patients; the mechanism involved in forgetting; and speed of retrieval. The evidence *in toto* almost compels one to accept the reality of a conceptual distinction between two separate components of memory, although this is disputed by some (e.g., Crowder, 1982). However, it is more difficult to incorporate this distinction into an adequate overall theoretical conceptualisation of human memory, as we see in the next section of this chapter.

THEORETICAL MODELS

The Multi-store Approach

Perhaps the most thorough and influential multi-store theory was proposed by Atkinson and Shiffrin (1968, 1971). They argued in favour of three kinds of memory store: Sensory registers, short-term store, and long-term store. In addition, they claimed that two of the major processes involved in the transfer of information from short-term to long-term memory are rehearsal and coding, i.e., the attachment of additional information from the long-term store to the incoming stimulus. In practice, Atkinson and Shiffrin emphasised the notion that long-term storage of information often depends on rote rehearsal, with a direct relationship between the amount of rehearsal in the short-term store and the strength of the stored memory trace. At a more general level, they assumed that information is transferred or "copied" into the long-term store throughout the time that it is actively being processed in the short-term store.

How can we measure rehearsal activity? An ingenious solution was proposed by Rundus and Atkinson (1970). Their overt rehearsal technique allowed the subjects to rehearse any of the list items on a free recall task, but required them to rehearse aloud. They found the usual superiority in recall of the initial items in the list (i.e., the primacy effect), and also discovered that these items received a disproportionately large amount of rehearsal. This suggests that the primacy effect is due to extra rehearsal, but other factors are also involved. When steps are taken to equate the amount of rehearsal given to each of the list items, the primacy effect is reduced but not eliminated (Fischler, Rundus & Atkinson, 1970).

In spite of the data obtained by Rundus and Atkinson (1970), the assumption that the sheer quantity of rehearsal causally determines the probability of long-term retention is clearly erroneous. Consider as an example multi-trial free recall of a list of words belonging to a number of different semantic categories. When subjects rehearse aloud during list presentation, it becomes apparent that recall is determined far more by the extent to which rehearsal is organised in terms of the semantic categories present in the list than by the amount of rehearsal (Weist, 1972). In other words, the quality or nature of rehearsal can be much more important than the quantity.

Craik and Lockhart (1972) distinguished between maintenance rehearsal, which simply involves the repetition of processing activities already carried out, and elaborative rehearsal, which involves deeper or more thorough analysis of the stimulus. They assumed that only elaborative rehearsal enhanced long-term retention, an assumption that has not gone un-challenged (Nelson, 1977; Rundus, 1977). The issues are discussed more fully in Chapter 5. While it may prove more useful to regard rehearsal processes as falling along a continuum, between maintenance rehearsal at one extreme and elaborative rehearsal at the other extreme, rather than as a dichotomy, the crucial point for present purposes is that the relationship between rehearsal and long-term retention is more complex than was originally thought to be the case.

If we move away from the limited free recall paradigm, the role played by rehearsal becomes even less important. For example, when people read newspapers or novels they usually retain some information in long-term memory, but it seems intuitively unreasonable to assume that active rehearsal is usually involved. Even if rehearsal is involved extensively in learning tasks necessitating the verbatim recall of unrelated words presented rapidly, there is no good reason to extrapolate from such findings to more normal memorial functioning.

Atkinson and Shiffrin (1968, 1971) assumed that information entered into the long-term store only as a result of processing activity in the short-term store. It seems to follow that individuals suffering from reduced short-term storage capacity should necessarily experience difficulties in placing newly learned information in the long-term store. However, as was mentioned earlier in this chapter, there are a few cases of brain-damaged patients suffering from impaired short-term storage whose ability to store new information for long periods of time is normal (e.g., Shallice & Warrington, 1970).

One of the theoretical assumptions made by Atkinson and Shiffrin (1968, 1971) that has received relatively little attention is the notion that information is retrieved from the long-term store via the short-term store. This suggests that retrieval from the long-term store is more complex than retrieval from the short-term store, and Eysenck and Eysenck (1979) found that retrieval from the long-term store made greater demands on processing capacity. However, Patterson (1971) found that counting backwards for 15 seconds after each word was recalled in free recall had no effect on either the number of words recalled or on the extent to which recall was organised, despite the fact that the counting task presumably made heavy demands on the short-term store.

The central weakness of the multi-store approach can best be appreciated by referring back to Fig. 4.1 on p. 83. It is assumed that information in the modality-specific stores is in a relatively raw and uninterpreted form, whereas in the short-term store it is often in a phonological code (due to rehearsal), and in the long-term store it is predominantly in semantic form. By what magic do these dramatic changes in the nature of the information occur? Within the context of the multi-store approach, attention and rehearsal are responsible. This manifestly will not do. It is not known exactly how stimulus input receives full analysis, but the multi-store approach substantially under-specifies the processes involved.

How have Atkinson and Shiffrin responded to the various criticisms of their theory? Atkinson has moved into other areas, but Shiffrin (1976) and Shiffrin and Schneider (1977) have proposed a modified conceptualisation, in which the three kinds of memory store have become more unified. Information goes directly from the sensory registers to the long-term store, where it activates its permanent trace. This activation of information in the long-term store is equivalent to the earlier notion of placing information in the short-term store. In this conceptualisation, if the long-term store corresponds to a collection of electrical wires, then the short-term store consists of that small fraction of the wires carrying current at any given moment.

This newer formulation has the advantage that it eliminates the dubious notion of information "moving" from one memory store to another.

However, it shares with the original theory the simplistic assumption of a single long-term store. Is it really true that all of the information and knowledge that we can retain for more than a few seconds is stored in exactly the same way? Tulving (1972) argued persuasively for a distinction between semantic memory and episodic memory. Semantic memory is a mental thesaurus consisting of our general knowledge (e.g., word definitions; multiplication tables; names of the kings and queens of England), whereas episodic memory refers to memory for specific episodes in our lives (e.g., what we had for breakfast yesterday). Episodic memory has an auto-biographical flavour, and usually contains spatial–temporal information. The great majority of laboratory studies involve episodic memory, and it is doubtful that semantic memory follows the same principles as episodic memory.

In sum, the multi-store approach of Atkinson and Shiffrin and other theorists is now regarded as too rigid and simplistic. There does appear to be a valid distinction between short-term and long-term memory stores, but the cognitive processes operating within this structure are much more complicated than was thought to be the case only a few years ago.

Working memory

Baddeley and Hitch (1974) and Hitch and Baddeley (1976) attempted to obviate some of the problems inherent in the earlier multi-store approach. In particular, they addressed the criticisms that the variety of coding is much greater than was allowed for by multi-store theories and that the short-term store is a theoretical construct of strictly limited usefulness. They suggested that the concept of the short-term store should be replaced with that of working memory. The working memory system comprises a modality-free central executive; an articulatory loop; and a visuo-spatial scratch pad. The most important component is the central executive, which has limited capacity, and is thought to be used when dealing with most cognitively demanding tasks. It resembles attention, and Baddeley (1981) admitted that, "the central executive is becoming increasingly like a pure attentional system [p. 22]."

The articulatory loop and the visuo-spatial scratch pad are slave systems that can be used by the central executive for specific purposes. The articulatory loop is organised in a temporal and serial fashion, and it encodes information in a phonemic form. Important information about the articulatory loop was obtained in a word-span study Baddeley, Thomson and Buchanan (1975). They discovered that their subjects could provide immediate serial recall of approximately as many words as they could read out loud in two seconds. This suggested that the capacity of the articulatory loop is determined by temporal duration in the same way as a tape loop. In practice, the articulatory loop seems to be used to supplement the storage capacity of the central executive across a somewhat restricted range of tasks.

The defining characteristics of the visuo-spatial working memory system are less clear than those of the articulatory loop. However, Baddeley and Lieberman (1980) have made some headway. They drew a distinction between spatial and visual coding, and found that spatial coding was more important than visual coding in a variety of tasks. Accordingly, they tentatively concluded that the visuo-spatial scratch pad relies primarily on spatial rather than visual coding.

What are the immediate advantages of the working memory formulation over the unitary short-term store postulated by the multi-store theorists? Firstly, we have seen that verbal rehearsal plays a much smaller role in learning and memory than was suggested by the multi-store theorists (refer back to p. 90). The notion that verbal rehearsal is an optional process occurring within the articulatory loop seems more in accordance with the true state of affairs. Secondly, the postulation of several components of working memory, each with its characteristic form of processing, takes account of the fact that verbal rehearsal is merely one of several kinds of processing that can be applied to incoming stimulation. Thirdly, the working memory system is of more general utility than the short-term store. This is especially true of the central executive, which seems to be involved in activities such as mental arithmetic (Hitch, 1978), verbal reasoning (Hitch & Baddeley, 1976), and comprehension (Baddeley & Hitch, 1974), in addition to traditional memory tasks.

Of the various components of the working memory system, it is the articulatory loop that has been investigated most thoroughly. The notion of the articulatory loop was originally proposed to explain the strong association between verbal coding and short-term memory. The association is particularly strong when the short-term memory task involves immediate serial recall of a short list of verbal items. Short-term serial recall is reduced when the items are phonemically similar to each other, even when they are presented visually (Conrad & Hull, 1964). This indicates that the items are processed phonemically. Memory for a sequence of visually presented items is also impaired when the items in the sequence are multi-syllabled words rather than short ones (i.e., the word-length effect; Baddeley et al., 1975). This is consistent with the existence of a speech-based system of limited capacity.

Perhaps the strongest evidence in favour of the articulatory loop comes from the use of articulatory suppression, in which the subject repeatedly says something simple like "hi-ya" or "the" while the learning material is being presented. The basic assumption is that the articulatory suppression task pre-empts the use of the articulatory loop and prevents it being utilised on the learning task. Not surprisingly, articulatory suppression reduces the short-term memory span. Of far greater theoretical interest, articulatory suppression eliminates the phonemic similarity effect (Murray, 1968), and it also removes the word-length effect when the stimulus words are presented visually (Baddeley *et al.*, 1975). Thus, both the phonemic similarity effect and the word-length effect depend on the articulatory loop: Articulatory suppression prevents the loop from being used and so eliminates both effects.

The picture so far seems clear. However, some nasty complications have started to come to light. Firstly, the power of articulatory suppression to abolish word-length and phonemic similarity effects on the memory span is found with visual presentation, but not with auditory presentation (Baddeley *et al.*, 1975). Secondly, it has been discovered that immediate serial recall of visually presented letters is essentially unaffected by articulatory suppression, provided that there is concurrent auditory presentation of the letters (Levy, 1971). Thirdly, Shallice and Butterworth (1977) examined a patient suffering from grossly impaired immediate memory. The obvious assumption from the working memory model is that the patient has a deficient articulatory loop. However, this seems improbable, because the patient has normal speech patterns.

Perhaps the most plausible way of accounting for these complications is to assume that there are separate articulatory and acoustic systems. Information presented auditorily has direct access to acoustic coding whether or not it is processed by the articulatory loop. Baddeley (1982) seems to be moving in the direction of accepting the reality of a distinction between articulatory coding (the inner voice) and acoustic coding (the inner ear).

Some readers may be wondering where the recency effect fits into the picture. After all, the recency effect in free recall has often been regarded as the major measure of short-term memory. It is clear that the recency effect does not involve the articulatory loop (Baddeley, 1976). The recency effect is unaffected by word length, and phonemic similarity among the list items presented for free recall also has no influence on the size of the recency effect. In addition, articulatory suppression has equivalent effects on the pre-recency and recency portions of the free recall curve (Richardson & Baddeley, 1975), revealing that there is no special involvement of the articulatory loop in the recency effect.

It also appears that the recency effect does not depend on the central executive. Hitch (1980) has reviewed a number of studies in which subjects were required to perform some additional task during the presentation of a free recall list. The concurrent tasks used have included mental arithmetic, card sorting, and choice reaction time, and one of the few things they all have in common is that they require the use of the central executive. The modal finding is that the concurrent task impairs the long-term memory component of free recall, but leaves the recency effect intact. Since the central executive has limited capacity, the failure of concurrent tasks using some of its capacity to reduce the recency effect strongly implies that the recency effect does not depend on the resources of the central executive.

We have managed to demonstrate what is *not* involved in the recency effect, but it is less clear what *is* involved. Hitch (1980) distinguished between a relatively passive input register which holds information about recent verbal inputs and an output register which holds information about potential verbal responses (the articulatory loop). According to Hitch, the recency effect in free recall reflects the workings of the input register.

The distinction between the input register and the articulatory loop can be clarified by considering language comprehension and production. According to Hitch (1980), the input register holds a parsed representation of the most recent words spoken, and paves the way for comprehension. In contrast, the articulatory loop acts as an output buffer in the production of overt speech. It is probably involved in Spoonerisms, which are speech errors usually involving the accidental transposition of the first letters of two or more words (e.g., "He has just received a blushing crow").

The greatest difference between the working memory model and the earlier multi-store approach is the replacement of a unitary short-term store with a number of sub-systems or components. How can this fractionation be justified? The basic experimental approach has been as follows. We attempt to discover two tasks, one of which requires only component A of working memory and the other of which needs only component B. It follows that each of the two tasks can be performed as well together as when they are performed separately, because they are not competing for the same processing resources. As an example of this strategy in operation, consider a study by Hitch and Baddeley (1976). They used a verbal reasoning task depending largely on the central executive, and a digit task presumably involving only the articulatory loop (i.e, cyclical repetition of "one-two-three-four-five-six"). They discovered that the two tasks could be combined successfully with only a modest adverse effect on the verbal reasoning task. In contrast, performance on the verbal reasoning task was greatly impaired when it was combined with the task of repeating out loud a random sequence of six digits. In this case, both tasks were presumably competing for the resources of the central executive.

There have been a number of recent attempts to apply the insights of the working memory model to activities far removed from standard memory research. Among the activities considered have been reading and mental arithmetic. The research on reading is dealt with in the next section, but some of the work on mental arithmetic warrants discussion here. Hitch (1978) combined auditory presentation of addition problems with visual aids ranging from nothing to the entire problem. It could be argued that the initial information and the results of interim calculations are held in the articulatory loop, with the consequence that complete visual information greatly reduces the storage problem in the loop. Whether or not that analysis is correct, the error rate on the addition problems decreased from 22% with no visual information to 3% with complete visual information.

Somewhat more direct evidence of the involvement of the articulatory loop in mental arithmetic was obtained by Hitch (1980). He used two types of problem that were matched in arithmetical complexity, but varied with respect to the time at which intermediate results had to be remembered. Articulatory suppression produced a greater decrement in performance on those problems where the results of interim calculations needed to be stored for a longer interval of time. Thus, it appears that the articulatory loop plays an important storage role in mental arithmetic.

How useful is the working memory model? On the positive side, the assumption that there are several different processing systems is manifestly more realistic than the previous notion of a unitary short-term store. Furthermore, there is reasonable evidence for the existence of all of the postulated components of working memory (i.e., the central executive, the visuo-spatial scratch pad, the articulatory loop, the acoustic store, and the input register). At a more general level, the idea that short-term storage and attention are so closely related that they should be considered together at a theoretical level is a valuable one, as is the notion that there are common processing resources which are used in the performance of a great variety of apparently heterogeneous cognitive tasks.

On the negative side, it is unfortunate that there has been so little clarification of the role played by the key component of the working memory system, i.e., the central executive. It is claimed that the central executive is of limited capacity, but no one has been able to measure that capacity. It is also claimed that the central processor is "modality-free" and used in numerous processing operations, but the precise constraints on its functioning are quite unclear.

A further difficulty concerns the sharpness of the distinctions between the components of working memory. At one time, it was assumed that phonemic processing occurred only within the articulatory loop, and this provided one way of distinguishing between the articulatory loop and the other systems within working memory. However, it was subsequently discovered that the speed and accuracy of judgements about the sounds of words and non-words are virtually unaffected by articulatory suppression (Baddeley & Lewis, 1981). This clearly indicates that phonemic processing can occur in some component of working memory other than the articulatory loop (perhaps the acoustic store). Since we can attend to phonemic information, it seems possible that phonemic processing can also occur within the central executive. In other words, one of the erstwhile distinguishing features of the articulatory loop can no longer fulfil that role.

PRACTICAL APPLICATIONS: READING

If the working memory system really has the generality claimed for it by Baddeley and Hitch (1974), then it ought to be possible to demonstrate its involvement in an everyday activity such as reading. In recent years, Baddeley and his associates (Baddeley, 1979; Baddeley, Eldridge & Lewis, 1981; Baddeley & Lewis, 1981) have investigated the role of working memory in the reading process, focusing especially on the part played by the articulatory loop. However, the findings in this area, which are discussed in this section, have been rather inconsistent. This should not come as any great surprise. Reading covers an enormous variety of activities ranging from reading a popular newspaper to reading a poem, and from reading a light novel to checking the small print of a legal document. The involvement of the different components of working memory in reading is in all probability greatly affected by the specific requirements of the reading task.

A major theoretical issue, and one that has aroused much controversy, concerns the extent to which phonemic recoding in the form of "inner speech" is involved in the reading process. The main arguments for believing that reading depends on inner speech were expressed in a classic work, *The Psychology and Pedagogy of Reading*, written by Huey (1908):

> The carrying range of inner speech is considerably larger than that of vision. . . . The initial subvocalisation seems to help hold the word in consciousness until enough others are given to combine with it in touching off the unitary utterance of the sentence which they form. . . . It is of the greatest service to the reader or listener that at each moment a considerable amount of what is being read should hang suspended in the primary memory of the inner speech. It is doubtless true that without something of this there could be no comprehension of speech at all.

There have been several attempts to ascertain the veracity of Huey's contentions. One of the more direct approaches was that of Hardyck and Petrinovich (1970). They discovered that people show increased electro-myographic (i.e., muscle) activity of the larynx while reading. People who were trained to suppress that activity during reading showed reduced comprehension of difficult prose material, but there was no effect with simple prose passages.

A rather different approach was taken by Baron (1973). He asked people to decide whether each of a series of visually presented short phrases was or was not meaningful. The key comparison was between non-meaningful phrases that sounded the same as meaningful phrases (e.g., "tie the not") and non-meaningful phrases that did not (e.g., "I am kill"). Decision time was comparable for both kinds of non-meaningful phrase, but more errors were made on the former type. This suggests that phonemic coding (probably involving the articulatory loop) occurred during the performance of the task.

Perhaps the most satisfactory way of assessing the involvement of the articulatory loop in reading is to observe the adverse effects (if any) on reading performance of preventing the articulatory loop from being used on the reading task. This can be accomplished most readily by means of articulatory suppression. Sometimes articulatory suppression has been found to affect performance surprisingly little. Baddeley (1979) discovered that articulatory suppression produced no increase in either processing time or errors on the task of deciding on the truth of simple sentences such as "Canaries have wings" and "Canaries have gills." Levy (1978) asked subjects to decide whether test sentences conveyed the same meaning as sentences which had been presented previously. Thus, the original sentence, "The solemn physician distressed the anxious mother" might be followed either by a correct paraphrase (e.g., "The solemn doctor upset the anxious mother") or by an incorrect paraphrase (e.g., "The solemn officer helped the anxious mother"). Performance was not affected by articulatory suppression.

Stronger evidence that the articulatory loop is sometimes involved in reading processes was obtained in another experiment carried out by Levy (1978). When sentences were presented visually, and memory for the precise wording of the sentences was tested, articulatory suppression adversely affected memory performance. However, this effect of suppression disappeared when the sentences were presented auditorily. Taking Levy's various findings together, it appears to be the case that it is possible to read for meaning without making use of the articulatory loop, but the necessity to encode information verbatim can sometimes cause the loop to be utilised.

Additional evidence that the loop is used in at least certain reading situations was obtained by Baddeley et al. (1981). Their subjects read sentences in order to decide whether they were meaningful or whether they contained anomalies. These anomalies were produced either by substituting inappropriate words or by changing word order within sentences. Articulatory suppression did not affect reading rate, but greatly impaired the ability to detect semantic anomaly. It may be that sub-vocal articulation is of value in monitoring accuracy, but is merely used in parallel with other reading processes.

In sum, it is clear that the articulatory loop is used sometimes, but not always, while people are reading. What is less obvious are the precise circumstances in which the articulatory loop is likely to be used. There is some mileage in the notion that the articulatory loop is an auxiliary system that comes into play when other components of the working memory system (e.g., the central executive) are in danger of becoming overloaded. This would explain why there is greater utilisation of the loop with more difficult reading material (Hardyck & Petrinovich, 1970). It would also account for the greater adverse effects of suppression on a task requiring decisions about the semantic acceptability of sentences than on one calling for decisions about the categorical membership of individual words (Kleiman, 1975). In addition, the articulatory loop seems to be specialised for preservation of order information about verbal items, and is thus especially likely to be used when a reading task necessitates close monitoring of word order (Baddeley et al., 1981) or verbatim retention (Levy, 1978).

While it has been established that the articulatory loop can be involved in the reading process, there are many situations in which it is not used. Even when it is, it may not be used in quite the way popularly supposed. The prevalent view, dating back to Huey (1908), is that the intake of information is followed by a verbatim, ordered record of the last few words (i.e., inner speech), which in turn serves as the basis of subsequent comprehension. Apart from anything else, this viewpoint misleadingly suggests that comprehension is a time-consuming activity. In fact, comprehension usually occurs rather rapidly. If people are asked to read a sentence such as, "As she was sewing the sleeve fell off her lap," to themselves, they discover after reaching the word "fell" that the prepositional phrase that they are forming, has to be reduced to the first four words of the sentence. Since the word "fell" is fixated for an unusually long time, it appears that the inappropriateness of the initial interpretation of the sentence ("As she was sewing the sleeve") is discovered sufficiently quickly to influence eye movements within approximately 250 msecs. (Rayner, Carlson & Frazier, 1983).

The view that reading proceeds in a bottom-up fashion from inner speech to comprehension is also embarrassed by other evidence. Levy (1981) investigated the effects of articulatory suppression on memory for both thematically related and unrelated sets of sentences. If it were the case that articulatory suppression impairs the initial analysis of printed language, then it would probably also restrict semantic analysis and thus reduce the memorial advantage of thematic over unrelated sentences. In fact, the thematic effect on memory was much greater with articulatory suppression; suppression reduced memory of both wording and meaning for unrelated sentences, but had little or no effect on memory for thematic material. Perhaps there is less reliance on the articulatory loop when thematic structure permits the stimulus material to be integrated easily with existing knowledge. Such an account, of course, emphasizes top-down effects in reading, and minimises the importance of the articulatory loop. It may transpire that the role played by the articulatory loop in reading is that of a back-up system that is not normally directly involved, but may be made use of if severe problems in comprehension develop.

We have discussed the role played by the inner voice in reading, but there is also some scattered evidence (e.g., Baddeley & Lewis, 1981) that the inner ear is also involved in the reading process. It has been reported informally that the internal monologue that often appears to accompany reading continues even during concurrent articulatory suppression. More definitive evidence was provided by Baddeley and Lewis. The task was to categorise nonsense words as similar or dissimilar in sound to actual words. Examples of nonsense words sounding like real words are "cayoss" and "yorn," and of nonsense words not sounding like actual words, "bambil" and "trid." Since articulatory suppression did not affect speed or accuracy on this task, it seems probable that this task can be performed without using the articulatory loop. There may be two phonemic codes, one of which is articulatory and the other of which is acoustic (see Besner & Davelaar, 1982, for additional evidence). Introspective evidence from people taking part in the above experiment indicated that an acoustic code in the form of auditory imagery mediated performance.

Since the stimulus material in reading tasks is necessarily presented visually, it might have been expected that there would be considerable interest in investigating the relevance of the visuo-spatial scratch pad component of working memory to the process of reading. In fact this has not been the case. However, there has been some work focusing on the nature of the visual information that is stored during reading. One of the most intriguing findings was reported by McConkie (1979). He asked people to read passages in which successive letters alternated between upper and lower case. When the visual display switched between successive eye fixations (i.e., upper-case letters became lower-case letters and vice versa), the subjects were not even aware that any change had taken place. This suggests that there is no storage of the details of the visual input. However, greater changes (e.g., the switch of an entire line from upper case to lower case) were detected.

McConkie (1979) concluded that there is an integrative visual buffer that takes visual information from successive fixations and integrates them during reading. He suggested on the basis of his findings that the information in the visual buffer is stored at a relatively abstract level. A similar conclusion was reached by Morton (1979). He argued for the existence of a visual system on the basis of a study by Winnick and Daniel (1970). They found that the reading of a word was facilitated by previously presenting that word visually, but there was no facilitation when a definition of the word or an appropriate picture was presented, even though the subjects themselves produced the word. Morton replicated and extended these findings. He found that the reading of a typewritten word was facilitated as much by an earlier presentation of that word in cursive script as it was by the presentation of an identical typewritten version, indicating that information about the initial presentation was stored in an abstract visual form. On the basis of these findings, Morton argued for the notion that there are separate visual and auditory lexicons for word recognition.

Of course, this account of the ways in which working memory affects reading is a little like a performance of the play *Hamlet* that lacks its eponymous hero. The most crucial processes involved in reading are those relating to semantic analysis and comprehension of textual material, and such processes are essentially the province of the central executive. The reason why this has not been discussed is because practically no research has investigated the part played by the central executive in reading. So far we have only a partial understanding of the involvement in reading of relatively peripheral components of working memory, while the central mystery remains to be explored.

5 Information Processing and Storage

Any adequate analysis of human memory must probably consider both the structure of memory and the processes operating within that structure. Whereas the focus in Chapter 4 is on the structural aspects of memory, the emphasis in this chapter is on those processes involved in the storage of information. Of course, memory also involves the retrieval of information stored at a previous point in time, and the nature of retrieval is considered at length in Chapter 6.

One of the most obvious characteristics of learning is the great variety of processing strategies that can be used. For example, if you were asked to learn the word "CHAIR" for a subsequent retention test, you might focus on the individual letters of the word, its sound, the fact that it is printed in capital letters, its dictionary definition, its relationship to other, related words (e.g., table, settee), or the chair you happen to be sitting on. The specific processing operations performed on a to-be-remembered stimulus play a major role in influencing what information will be stored, and the nature of the stored information is of vital importance in determining the precise conditions under which remembering and forgetting occur.

In this chapter emphasis is given to the conceptual distinction between the stimulus-as-presented and the stimulus-as-encoded. Many earlier theorists assumed, whether explicitly or implicitly, that there is a direct correspondence between the stimulus-as-presented and the stimulus-as-encoded. This is definitely erroneous, because any particular external stimulus can produce an essentially infinite variety of encodings. Since memory depends far more on the stimulus-as-encoded than on the stimulus-as-presented, much experimental ingenuity has been applied to the task of ascertaining what information has been encoded. It is, of course, much more difficult to specify the stimulus-as-encoded than the stimulus-as-presented, because we are dealing with internal and inaccessible processing activities.

MEMORY FOR UNATTENDED EVENTS

It has often been assumed that only information that has been attended to can be retained over long periods of time. For example, most of the multi-store theorists whose ideas were discussed in the previous chapter argued that information entered long-term storage only as a result of processing within the short-term store, and it was usually claimed that information needed to be in the short-term store in order for it to receive attention.

It is thus of some theoretical significance to investigate the fate of unattended information. However, it is usually difficult to be certain that information is really unattended, in part because the concept of "attention" is rather nebulous. One popular approach to this general issue is sleep learning. Obviously we do not attend to the external environment in the same way when we are asleep as we do when we are awake, but it is more difficult to decide whether or not external events can receive some attention in the sleeping state.

The media have shown much interest in the claim made by some psychologists (especially those in Eastern Europe) that sleep learning is an effective way of acquiring knowledge. It would certainly be good news if the "wasted" hours of sleep could be used in a productive fashion to enable us to master foreign languages or other complicated skills, but close examination of the evidence points to a much more pessimistic conclusion.

The greatest problem with studies reporting the existence of sleep learning is a very simple one: It was assumed that people are asleep almost continuously during the time that they are in bed. All of the methodologically sound experiments have used behavioural and/or physiological criteria to establish the actual state that an individual is in during the presentation of the learning material. Simon and Emmons (1956) used brain-wave activity (i.e., the EEG) as their criterion in a study in which they presented apparently sleeping people with a different question and answer every 5 minutes. The subsequent ability to answer the questions depended on the level of sleep at the time that the question and its answer were presented. The answer was recalled 80% of the time when the EEG indicated that the subject was awake but relaxed, however this dropped to 50% when the subject was drowsy, and to only 5% when the EEG revealed a transition between drowsiness and light sleep. When the subject was actually asleep, there was practically no evidence of any learning.

A similar conclusion is suggested by the findings of Bruce, Evans, Fenwick and Spencer (1970). They presented information to people who were asleep, and then awakened them almost immediately for testing. In spite of the fact that the use of such a short retention interval should have maximised the chances of obtaining evidence of sleep learning, there was an almost total inability to remember the information presented during sleep.

At a theoretical level, it is rather difficult to make definite statements about the extent to which information is unattended in the sleeping state. A superior way of ensuring that some stimuli are unattended may be to require the subject to attend continuously to other stimuli presented at the same time. This is what happens in the shadowing technique, in which two auditory messages are presented concurrently, and the subject has to repeat back aloud (i.e., shadow) one of the messages. It is usual for one message to be presented to the left ear and the other to the right ear, with the instructions telling the subject to shadow the message on one ear (for a discussion of the shadowing task see Chapter 3).

When subjects are asked at the end of the shadowing task what they can remember about the unattended message, there is a characteristic pattern to their responses. As Cherry (1953) discovered, people can usually report on the physical characteristics of the unattended message (e.g., the sound intensity; the sex of the voice), but have no recollection of its semantic content. The lack of awareness of important aspects of the unattended message was shown dramatically by Cherry in an experiment in which the message in the unattended ear was changed from English to German during the shadowing task. When the listener was asked subsequently to state the language of the unattended message, he replied that he had no idea, but assumed that it was English.

Subjects do tend to detect some particularly salient kinds of information in the unattended message (e.g., their own names), but the usual finding is of extremely poor long-term memory for the content of the unattended message. In one experiment (Moray, 1959), listeners shadowed one message while words were presented up to 35 times in the unattended ear. A later recognition test revealed that there was practically no retention of the unattended words.

Must we conclude that there is no analysis at all of unattended messages? In fact, this conclusion would not be warranted, as other kinds of experiment have shown. MacKay (1973) wondered whether unattended information might affect the way in which the shadowed message was interpreted. Accordingly, he presented ambiguous sentences for shadowing (e.g., "They threw stones towards the bank yesterday"), and at the same time a disambiguating word was presented to the unattended ear (e.g., "river" or "money"). There was a subsequent recognition test for the shadowed sentences, on which the subjects had to choose between sentences such as, "They threw stones towards the side of the river yesterday," and "They threw stones towards the savings and loan association yesterday." Although the subjects could not remember the unattended words, these words nevertheless affected recognition-test performance. The implication is that unattended words can be encoded at a semantic level, and other findings lead to a similar conclusion (e.g., Corteen & Dunn, 1974).

We have discovered so far that there is usually extremely poor, or non-existent, long-term retention of unattended information. The picture looks rather different when much shorter retention intervals are used. Norman (1969) found that subjects could recognise what had just been presented in the unattended message, but performance fell to chance level with an interval of only 6 seconds between presentation and test. In another study (Glucksberg & Cohen, 1970), subjects shadowed prose and attempted to report digits presented in the unattended message in response to a cue. The detection rate was 26% when the cue almost immediately followed the presentation of a digit, but there was no evidence of any memory for unattended digits with retention intervals greater than 3 seconds.

These findings can probably best be understood with reference to the notion of echoic memory, a transient store in the auditory modality, which was discussed in Chapter 4. Auditory information is held in a relatively passive and uninterpreted form in echoic memory for at least 2 or 3 seconds (Darwin, Turvey & Crowder, 1972). Since echoic memory does not depend on attentional mechanisms, it is plausible to assume that unattended auditory stimuli are stored transiently in echoic memory, and that the length of time for which unattended auditory information is available is determined by the temporal duration of echoic memory.

One of the problems with many of the shadowing studies is that the subjects were usually aware that they would be tested for retention of the unattended message at some point, and so they may have attempted to encode this input. As a consequence, it may not always be strictly accurate to regard one of the messages as "unattended." Nevertheless, it seems reasonably clear that unattended words enter echoic memory and may activate their semantic representations in long-term memory, but nearly always fail to be remembered for more than a few seconds. In other words, there appears to be merit in the notion that information must normally be attended to in order to produce long-term retention.

REHEARSAL: MAINTENANCE AND ELABORATIVE

The effects of rehearsal on long-term retention were discussed at some length in Chapter 4. We saw that there is sometimes a direct relationship between the amount of rehearsal activity and long-term memory, presumably because rehearsal leads to increased storage of information. However, there are numerous situations in which rehearsal has practically no beneficial effect on subsequent retention.

How are the apparently contradictory findings to be reconciled? An interesting answer was proposed by Craik and Lockhart (1972), who distinguished between two main types of processing or rehearsal: "Type I processing, that is, repetition of analyses which have already been carried out, may be contrasted with Type II processing which involves deeper analysis of the stimulus. Only this second type or rehearsal should lead to improved memory performance [p. 676]."

The controversial part of this theoretical statement is the assumption that there is a form of rehearsal (i.e., Type I—maintenance) that does not benefit long-term retention. Some of the available evidence supports this assumption, but there is other evidence indicating that maintenance rehearsal can enhance long-term memory. Rundus (1977) discovered one of the major factors responsible for these apparently inconsistent results in a study making use of a distraction recall task. On each trial the subject was presented with a short digit string followed by attempted recall after a few seconds. During the retention interval the subject performed a distracting activity that involved the overt repetition of one or more words. Some of the words were presented for rehearsal on more than one trial.

At the end of the experiment, the subjects were unexpectedly asked to recall the words they had been repeating via maintenance rehearsal. The probability of recall was not affected by the length of time for which once-presented words had been rehearsed. However, the probability of recall increased considerably when a word was presented for rehearsal on more than one trial. The total rehearsal time was the same for a once-presented word rehearsed for 12 seconds and for a thrice-presented word rehearsed for 4 seconds on each of its presentations, but recall was 21% in the former case and 40% in the latter. It is not clear exactly why maintenance rehearsal is more beneficial for memory when it occurs for repeatedly presented items, but it may reflect the establishment of additional temporal-contextual routes to an item.

Another important factor in determining the memorial consequences of maintenance rehearsal is the type of retention test that is used. Glenberg, Smith and Green (1977) used the same paradigm as Rundus (1977). In line with the findings of Rundus, they discovered that a nine-fold increase in rehearsal time produced only a tiny 1.5% increase in recall. However, the probability of correct recognition increased from .65 to .74 as rehearsal time increased from 2 to 18 seconds. Other researchers have confirmed these findings. Recognition memory is thus more sensitive than recall to the effects of maintenance rehearsal.

In sum, it seems that a clear-cut distinction between two types of rehearsal, one of which enhances long-term memory and the other of which does not, cannot be sustained. Nevertheless, it is certainly true that maintenance rehearsal is usually less effective than elaborative rehearsal in facilitating long-term retention, and so the distinction may still have some heuristic value. However, there is a growing body of opinion that the original notion of a dichotomy between maintenance and elaborative rehearsal should be replaced by a continuum of rehearsal activities ranging between pure maintenance and highly elaborative.

If maintenance rehearsal has only a small effect on long-term memory, what purpose does it serve? One answer is that it permits the transient storage of information at relatively low "cost" in terms of processing resources. For example, mental arithmetic frequently requires the holding of parts of the answer while the individual performs further calculations, and maintenance rehearsal is adequate for this purpose.

LEVELS OF PROCESSING

Introduction

Suppose that you were interested in the memorial consequences of different processing activities. How would you set about exploring this issue experimentally? One reasonable method that has proved extremely popular is to present several groups of subjects with the same list of nouns, and to ask each group to perform a different activity or orienting task with the list. The tasks used can range from counting the number of letters in each word to thinking of an appropriate adjective for each word. In order to control the subjects' processing activities as tightly as possible, the experimenter does not tell the subjects that there will be a subsequent test of memory. Finally, all of the subjects are unexpectedly asked to recall as many of the list words as possible. Since the various groups of subjects are all presented with exactly the same words, any differences in recall must reflect the influence of the processing tasks rather than characteristics of the stimulus material (e.g., word frequency, word length, or word concreteness).

The published literature contains dozens of studies in which various different orienting tasks were used in an incidental learning situation (see Eysenck, 1982b, for a review). A study by Hyde and Jenkins (1973) provides a good example of this experimental paradigm. They used words that were either associatively related or unrelated (in terms of meaning), and different groups of subjects carried out each of the following five orienting tasks: (1) rating the words for pleasantness; (2) estimating the frequency with which each word is used in the English language; (3) detecting the occurrence of the letters "e" and "g" in the list words; (4) deciding the part of speech appropriate to each word; (5) deciding whether the list words fitted sentence frames.

Five groups of subjects performed the orienting tasks with no instructions to learn the material (orienting task plus incidental learning), and an

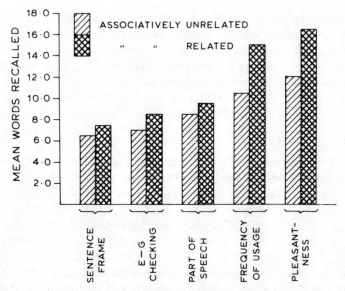

FIG. 5.1   Means words recalled as a function of list type (associatively related or unrelated) and orienting task. Data from Hyde and Jenkins (1973).

additional five groups carried out the tasks, but were also asked to try to remember the words (orienting task plus intentional learning). Finally, there were control subjects who received intentional learning instructions but no orienting task. All of the groups were given a test of free recall shortly after the completion of the orienting task.

The results are shown in Fig. 5.1. They can be interpreted most simply in the light of the assumption made by Hyde and Jenkins (1973) that rating pleasantness and rating frequency of usage both involve semantic processing, whereas the other three orienting tasks do not. If one is prepared to make that somewhat dubious assumption, then retention was 51% higher after the semantic tasks than the non-semantic tasks on the list of associatively unrelated words; with the list of associatively related words, there was an 83% superiority for the semantic tasks.

Incidental learners performing a semantic orienting task recalled as many words as intentional learners in the control groups. The implication is that intent to learn is not of critical importance; rather, it is the nature of the processing activity that determines how much is remembered subsequently. Finally, and rather surprisingly, there were practically no recall differences between intentional and incidental learners who performed the same orienting task. It might have been expected that intentional learners performing a non-semantic task would engage in additional processing of the meaning of the list words, but this was apparently not the case.

This study by Hyde and Jenkins (1973) has been discussed in detail because it is representative of work in this area. Indeed, all of the major findings from this study have been replicated many times. As we see in the next sub-section, Craik and Lockhart (1972) made use of findings such as these in proposing their extremely influential theory.

Levels-of-processing Theory

Craik and Lockhart (1972) put forward a levels-of-processing theory that attempted to provide a broad framework within which memory phenomena could be understood. Their initial major assumption was that memorial functioning should not be regarded in isolation; rather, memory traces are formed as by-products of attentional and perceptual processes. They postulated a number of different levels of processing, ranging from shallow or physical analysis of a stimulus (e.g., processing of the lines, angles, and brightness of visual stimuli) to deep or semantic analysis. The crucial notion of depth of processing was further explained by Craik (1973): "'Depth' is defined in terms of the meaningfulness extracted from the stimulus rather than in terms of the number of analyses performed upon it [p. 48]."

The single most important theoretical assumption made by Craik and Lockhart (1972) was that the level or depth of processing received by a stimulus had a substantial effect on its memorability. In their own words: "Trace persistence is a function of depth of analysis, with deeper levels of analysis associated with more elaborate, longer lasting, and stronger traces [p. 675]." It was this emphasis on the depth of processing that led Craik and Lockhart to propose a distinction between maintenance rehearsal and elaborative rehearsal. They argued that maintenance rehearsal does not enhance long-term memory because it does not involve processing the stimulus at a deeper level of analysis. Elaborative rehearsal, on the other hand, increases retention precisely because it does involve deeper processing.

In line with their emphasis on the major role played by processing activities in determining retention, Craik and Lockhart (1972) suggested that memory should be studied primarily by means of incidental learning paradigms. As they pointed out: "Under incidental conditions, the experimenter has a control over the processing the subject applies to the material that he does not have when the subject is merely instructed to learn and uses an unknown coding strategy [p. 677]."

All of these theoretical assumptions have been criticised in recent years, as is discussed in the next sub-section. However, the general notion that memory depends to a great extent on attentional and perceptual processes is sound, as is the emphasis on the nature of processing activities. If we want to identify the factors that together determine retention, then the kind of mental activity that occurs when a stimulus is presented is one of the most momentous of such factors.

The Critics Have a Field-day

The reaction of most psychologists to the levels-of-processing theory has been to admit that it contains a grain of truth, but that it represents a substantial over-simplification of a complex reality. The most obvious problem concerns the difficulty of ascertaining the depth of processing. For example, Hyde and Jenkins (1973) assumed that judging a word's frequency involved thinking of its meaning, but it is not altogether clear why this should be so. They also argued that the orienting task of deciding the part of speech to which a word belongs is a shallow processing task, but other researchers claim that the task involves deep processing.

In essence, the problem is caused by the lack of any independent measure of processing depth. This can lead to the unfortunate state of affairs described by Eysenck (1978): "In view of the vagueness with which depth is defined, there is the danger of using retention-test performance to provide information about the depth of processing, and then using the putative depth of processing to 'explain' the retention-test performance, a self-defeating exercise in circularity [p. 159]."

It could, of course, be argued that the depth of processing necessitated by the performance of an orienting task is usually fairly obvious, and it is sometimes possible to provide an adequate measure of processing depth (Parkin, 1979). However, there are many cases in which the depth of processing cannot readily be assessed or inferred, and this continues to be a major difficulty with the levels-of-processing theory.

Craik and Lockhart (1972) assumed that there was an intrinsic memorial superiority associated with deep levels of processing. Evidence such as that obtained by Hyde and Jenkins (1973) is consistent with that assumption, but suffers from the limitation that only a single form of retention test (i.e., free recall) was utilised. It is only valid to extrapolate from the results obtained from such free recall studies provided that the ordering of different orienting tasks with respect to memory performance does not vary across different kinds of retention test.

In fact, the effects of different orienting tasks on memory depend heavily on the nature of the retention test. Morris, Bransford, and Franks (1977) required their subjects to answer semantic or shallow (rhyme) questions for lists of words under incidental learning conditions. Memory was tested either by means of a standard recognition test, in which a mixture of list and non-list words was presented, from which subjects had to attempt to select the list words, or it was tested by a rhyming recognition test. On this latter test, subjects had to select words that rhymed with list words; the list words themselves were not presented.

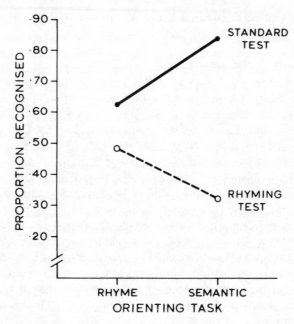

FIG. 5.2   Mean proportion of words recognised as a function of orienting task (semantic or rhyme) and of the type of recognition test (standard or rhyming). Data are from Morris *et al.* (1977), and are from positive trials only.

Performance based on those words associated with positive answers on the orienting task is shown in Fig. 5.2. It is clear that the effectiveness of different levels of processing depends on how memory is tested; this is revealed by the interaction between the type of orienting task and the nature of the recognition-memory test. If one considers only the results obtained with the standard recognition test, then the predicted superiority of deep encodings over shallow encodings was obtained. However, the opposite result was obtained with the rhyme test, and this represents an experimental disproof of the notion that deep encodings are intrinsically more memorable than shallow ones.

These findings, and others discussed by Bransford, Franks, Morris and Stein (1979), demonstrate conclusively that the ways in which memory is to be tested must be taken into account when predicting the memorial consequences of any processing activity. More specifically, Morris et al. (1977) interpreted their findings as supporting a transfer-appropriate processing view of memory. This view assumes that different kinds of processing leads learners to acquire different kinds of information about a stimulus. Whether the information stored as a result of performing a given orienting task leads to subsequent retention depends upon the *relevance* of that information to the kind of memory test that is used. For example, storing semantic information is essentially irrelevant when the memory test requires the identification of words rhyming with list words; instead, what is required for this kind of test is shallow rhyme or phonemic information.

The paradigm typically used to explore the levels-of-processing theory (i.e., incidental learning with various orienting tasks) can only be regarded as satisfactory provided that the subject's processing activities are controlled effectively by the orienting tasks. It is easy enough to be sure that the processing activities required by a particular orienting task have been performed; all that is necessary is for the subject to produce overt responses that can then be evaluated to see whether they comply with task demands.

A more worrying possibility is that the subject may engage in extraneous processing that is not strictly required by the orienting task. For example, incidental learners who checked for the occurrence of "e"s and "g"s in a list of unrelated words recalled almost seven words on average (Hyde & Jenkins, 1973). It stretches credibility to attribute this level of performance solely to encoding two letters of the alphabet. In general terms, there is more extraneous processing when subjects perform different orienting tasks on different words than when each subject performs only one orienting task (Coltheart, 1977).

It will be remembered that one of the theoretical assumptions made by Craik and Lockhart (1972) was that maintenance rehearsal does not improve long-term retention. The argument was that maintenance rehearsal does not involve deeper processing, and it is only rehearsal that leads to a deeper level of processing that enhances long-term memory. There is some support for this theoretical position, but the evidence discussed earlier in the chapter revealed that there are various circumstances in which maintenance rehearsal can be effective in improving memory.

A fundamental assumption of the levels-of-processing theory is that deep encodings are more durable and longer lasting than shallow encodings. In other words, the rate of forgetting over time is assumed to be inversely related to the depth of processing. This prediction can only be tested when the amount of learning at different levels of processing is equated, a requirement that has not usually been fulfilled. When the number of learning trials was manipulated in order to produce comparable acquisition at deep and shallow levels of processing, the rate of forgetting was not affected by processing depth (Nelson & Vining, 1978). It is thus possible that variations in depth of processing affect the speed of acquisition rather than the rate of forgetting.

A fundamental problem with the original levels-of-processing formulation is that it seems in many ways to describe rather than to explain what is happening. Why are semantic encodings usually better remembered than non-semantic encodings? According to Craik and Lockhart (1972), the answer is that retentivity is determined by the depth of processing. This obviously begs the question of *why* it is that deep processing is so effective, i.e., the observed relationship between processing depth and retention is not linked to any more general or fundamental ideas.

A final problem with the original levels-of-processing formulation is that Craik and Lockhart (1972) appear to have assumed that there is a direct relationship between the semanticity of processing and the depth of processing. They also assumed that deep processing is more meaningful than shallow processing, but this seems to involve too narrow a view of what constitutes meaningful processing. An apprentice type-setter who looks at printed pages in order to identify different type faces is surely engaged in meaningful processing, in spite of his inattention to the semantic content of the paragraphs in front of him. The mistake consists in assuming that, because we tend to possess more semantic knowledge than non-semantic knowledge, it therefore follows that semantic processing is equivalent to making use of previous knowledge to interpret presented stimuli in a meaningful fashion. The major implication of this revised conceptualisation was expressed clearly by Stein, Morris and Bransford (1978): "Rather than emphasize the superiority of semantic over non-semantic processing, it may be more useful to ask how people use what they know (whether this knowledge is non-semantic, semantic, etc.) to more precisely encode and retain information [p. 708]."

Theoretical Modifications

It is now generally agreed that the original levels-of-processing theory and the accompanying incidental learning paradigm are both too narrow in the range of factors considered. Indeed, the initial focus was on different encoding operations to the virtual exclusion of all other factors. Any complete theory would have to take account of the fact that learning and memory depend upon at least four major factors: (1) the nature of the task given to the subject; (2) the kind of stimulus materials presented to the subject; (3) the individual characteristics of the subjects (e.g., their relevant knowledge); (4) the nature of the retention test used to measure memory.

In fact, most recent studies of incidental learning fall far short of providing information about all of these factors. In the typical study, the memorial consequences of several orienting tasks are tested by means of a single retention test, there is only one kind of stimulus material (usually unrelated words), and only one kind of subject is used.

This experimental narrowness causes trouble because there are substantial interactions between the four factors described above (see Eysenck, 1982b). As we found earlier in the chapter, the nature of the orienting task interacted with the form of the retention test. Indeed, the typical superiority of semantic over non-semantic tasks, on which Craik and Lockhart (1972) relied so heavily, can even be reversed under certain retrieval conditions (e.g., Morris et al., 1977).

At a more theoretical level, there has been some interest in the notion of elaboration of processing as an adjunct to, or as a replacement for, depth of processing. As Anderson and Reder (1979) pointed out, there is usually far more scope for elaborate or extensive processing at the semantic than at the non-semantic level. For example, the word "CHAIR" has only a single phonemic representation, but numerous semantic features or attributes (e.g., an article or furniture, something to sit on, can be made of wood or metal, found in offices and living rooms, etc.). If deep encodings are usually more elaborate or extensive than shallow encodings, it follows that more information is stored in long-term memory after a deep processing task than after a shallow one. It then becomes understandable that deep encodings are better remembered than shallow encodings, since ease of retrieval is presumably affected by the amount of stored information.

Elaboration was investigated by Craik and Tulving (1975). In one of their experiments, subjects were presented with a sentence containing a blank and a word on each trial, and had to decide whether the word fitted appropriately into the blank space. Elaboration was manipulated by varying the complexity of the sentence frame between the simple (e.g., "She cooked the . . .") and the complex (e.g., "The great bird swooped down and carried off the struggling . . ."). There was also an unexpected cued recall test, in which the subject was given the sentence frame and asked to recall the word that had been presented with it.

For those words that were compatible with the sentence frame, cued recall was twice as high for words accompanying complex sentences as for words paired with simple sentences. Since the same deep or semantic level of analysis was involved in both conditions, the obvious conclusion is that some factor in addition to processing depth must be important, a factor which Craik and Tulving (1975) identified as elaboration.

Those theorists who have favoured an elaboration model of memory have often assumed, either explicitly of implicitly, that there is a direct relationship between the sheer quantity or number of elaborations and the probability of recall. However, it is probable that the precise nature of any elaborations is also important. Bransford et al. (1979) presented either minimally elaborated similes (e.g., "A mosquito is like a doctor because they both draw blood") or multiply elaborated similes (e.g., "A mosquito is like a raccoon because they both have heads, legs, jaws"). Recall of the simile with the first noun used as a cue (e.g., "mosquito") was much better for the minimally elaborated similes than for the multiply elaborated ones, indicating that the nature and degree of precision of semantic elaborations are relevant when predicting the effects of elaboration on retention.

Most experimentation on elaboration has involved varying the amount of processing received by the stimulus words (i.e., intra-item processing), and there has been little interest in elaboration that involves associating or organising the list words together (i.e., inter-item processing). Bellezza, Cheesman and Reddy (1977) compared these two types of elaboration. They manipulated intra-item semantic elaboration by varying the length of the sentences that subjects constructed to the list words, and inter-item semantic elaboration was produced by requiring the subjects to link list words together by making up sentences that formed part of a story.

Intra-item elaboration had no effect on free recall, but inter-item elaboration led to a 60% increase in recall. The latter finding makes sense if we consider that the lack of retrieval cues in free recall produces a problem in gaining access to the stored items; this problem can be alleviated if the list words are strongly associated with each other.

It is clear that the amount of processing at any given level must be considered in addition to the level itself. The amount of elaboration can sometimes be indexed, for example, by varying the number of semantic decisions that need to be made (Johnson-Laird, Gibbs & de Mowbray, 1978), but this is not always possible. As a consequence, the notion that deep encodings are more elaborate than shallow encodings has not as yet been put to any satisfactory empirical test.

An alternative way of conceptualising the basic depth effect on memory has become popular among several theorists (e.g., Bransford et al., 1979; Eysenck, 1979b; Jacoby & Craik, 1979). The fundamental assumption is that deep encodings are better remembered than shallow encodings because they are more distinctive and unique. Part of the reason for this difference in distinctiveness may be the much greater variety of potential semantic encodings of a word than, for example, phonemic encodings. A word such as "BOOK" has only a single phonemic representation but an essentially unlimited number of semantic encodings. As a consequence, phonemic encodings of words are much less affected by the context in which the words are processed than are semantic encodings, implying that different phonemic encodings of the same word would be very similar, that is, non-distinctive.

Moscovitch and Craik (1976) presented their subjects with an encoding question (semantic or phonemic) and a word on each trial, and then used the encoding questions as recall cues. Distinctiveness was manipulated by using each encoding question with only one list word or with ten list words. With semantic cues, recall was much better with single, unique cues than with shared cues; with phonemic cues, there was no effect of cue distinctiveness. These findings suggest that shallow encodings are inevitably non-distinctive, and so do not benefit from the use of unique cues. Moscovitch and Craik concluded that, "The event must be discriminable and unique *semantically* before retention is enhanced [p. 457]."

The finding that processing depth interacted with cue distinctiveness is consistent with the notion that deep and shallow encodings differ in distinctiveness. However, Postman, Thompkins and Gray (1978) failed to replicate this theoretically critical interaction between cue distinctiveness and level of processing. Eysenck and Eysenck (1980b) explored the notion that manipulations of distinctiveness are effective only at the semantic level, and also attempted to unconfound depth and distinctiveness of processing. They asked their subjects to perform the shallow orienting task of pronouncing nouns with irregular grapheme-phoneme correspondence as if they had regular grapheme-phoneme correspondence (e.g., pronouncing 'glove' to rhyme with 'cove'). This manipulation presumably produced distinctive and unique encodings. On a subsequent unexpected recognition test, these encodings were recognised as well as semantic encodings and this recognition was much better than for phonemic encodings based on normal pronunciation. It may thus be the non-distinctiveness of shallow encodings rather than their shallowness *per se* that leads to their poor retention.

How successful is the distinctiveness approach to memory? One major difficulty is that there is no adequate operational definition of distinctiveness. However, it is clear that the degree of distinctiveness depends on the context in which a stimulus is processed. For example, the name "Smith" in the list "Jones, Robinson, Williams, Baker, Smith, Robertson" is not distinctive, but it certainly is in the list of names "Zzitz, Zysblat, Vangeersdaele, Vythelingum, Smith, Uwejeyah" taken from the London Telephone Directory. A stimulus may be distinctive along one coding dimension (e.g., phonemic) but not along a second dimension (e.g., semantic), in which case the distinctiveness or otherwise of the encoding depends on exactly which coding dimensions are processed.

A further consideration is what might be called the "distinctiveness paradox." A very distinctive or unique encoding can only occur in the presence of an extremely unusual environmental event. Since such an event is, by definition, unlikely to recur, appropriate retrieval cues for remembering its occurrence will probably not be available. Thus distinctive encodings may be "strongly" represented in memory but relatively inaccessible. A case in point is the first manned landing on the moon in July 1969. That was a very distinctive event that nearly everyone remembers, and yet most people rarely think about it.

The general notion that distinctive encodings may be readily accessed only under certain retrieval conditions was explored by Eysenck (1979b). He found that distinctive shallow encodings, involving pronouncing words in unique ways, were much better recognised than non-distinctive encodings, but the findings were less clear-cut for recall.

It is not altogether obvious exactly why distinctiveness should facilitate retention, although it seems reasonable that a distinctive encoding might "stand out" in memory and be retrieved readily, in the same way as a red object can be located more easily when it is surrounded by black and white objects. A somewhat more specific theoretical suggestion was put forward by Eysenck (1979b), who related work on distinctiveness to interference theory:

> The usual memorial superiority of deep over shallow encodings is due to the fact that deep encodings are less susceptible to proactive and retroactive interference than are shallow encodings. This differential susceptibility to interference is in turn due to the greater trace distinctiveness usually associated with deep encodings [p. 114].

By now you are probably confused as to the relative merits of theoretical accounts based on depth of processing, elaboration of processing, and distinctiveness of processing.

Part of the problem is that semantic encodings are usually deeper, more elaborate, and more distinctive than non-semantic ones, and it is extremely difficult to unconfound these three factors. However, we do know that retention cannot be predicted solely on the basis of the level of processing, because more elaborate or distinctive semantic encodings are usually remembered much better than non-elaborate or non-distinctive semantic encodings. It is, in fact, entirely possible that all three factors make a separate contribution towards determining long-term retention. Of the three factors, it is likely that distinctiveness, which relates to the nature of processing and takes account of the relationships between encodings, will prove more important than elaboration, which is only a measure of the amount of processing.

IMAGERY

The emphasis so far has been on verbal and linguistic processing in the storage of information. An influential theoretical approach that distinguished between verbal and imaginal processes was put forward by Paivio (1971), and is often referred to as the dual-code theory. The quintessence of this theoretical position was expressed by Paivio (1979) in the following way:

> The theory assumes that cognitive behaviour is mediated by two independent but richly interconnected symbolic systems, which are specialized for encoding, organizing, transforming, storing, and retrieving information. One (the image system) is specialized for dealing with perceptual information concerning nonverbal objects and events. The other (the verbal system) is specialized for dealing with linguistic information.

Paivio (1971, 1979) has also pointed to other differences between the two processing systems. He assumes that the imaginal system represents information in a spatially parallel manner, so that different components of a complex scene are available at the same time, whereas the verbal system is sequentially organised in the same way as linguistic utterances.

The dual-code theory has been applied to many memory phenomena. Of particular interest is the very robust finding that pictures are more likely to be remembered than concrete words (i.e., words denoting things that can be perceived by one or more of the sense modalities), and concrete words are more likely to be remembered than abstract words. This ordering of memorability has been obtained in studies of free recall, paired-associate learning, and recognition memory (Paivio, 1971).

Paivio's (1971) preferred explanation in terms of dual-code theory is shown in Table 5.1. He assumed that pictures are most likely to be stored in both codes (i.e., verbal and imaginal), whereas abstract words are typically stored only in the verbal code. Memory for an item will be more likely when two codes have been formed, because it is possible to retrieve that item on the basis of one code even if the other code has been "lost" during the retention interval.

TABLE 5.1

Paivio's Dual-coding Theory. The Greater the Number of Plus Signs, the Greater is the Availability of the Appropriate Code (Paivio, 1971)

| Type of Stimulus | Coding System Used | |
	Imaginal	Verbal
Picture	+ + +	+ +
Concrete word	+	+ + +
Abstract word	−	+ + +

The dual-code theory certainly accounts for the basic findings. Moreover, the distinction between verbal and imaginal codes makes sense in the light of research into hemisphere differences that has suggested that verbal processing occurs primarily in the left hemisphere, whereas the right hemisphere is more involved with spatial and imaginal processing (Cohen, 1977). In addition, the claim that concrete words are more likely than abstract words to be processed imaginally receives some indirect support from the high correlation of $+.83$ that Paivio, Yuille, and Madigan (1968) reported between word concreteness and imageability.

While concrete or imageable words are better remembered than abstract or non-imageable words, this does not demonstrate that retention is causally related to imageability. The reason is that the relationship between memory and imageability is merely correlational in nature. One way of shedding some light on the factors responsible for the memorial superiority of concrete over abstract words is to manipulate the learning instructions. When standard learning instructions are compared against interactive imagery instructions (e.g., form images depicting objects interacting in some way), the imagery instructions improve performance for concrete material but not for abstract material (see Richardson, 1980, for a review). This finding makes sense if one assumes that only concrete items can be processed imaginally. However, a complicating factor is that verbal mediation instructions (e.g., form short phrases including the list items) have been found to have the same effects on memory; that is to say, they increase retention when the stimulus material is concrete but have no effect when it is abstract.

What is going on here? One possibility (Bower, 1972) is that interactive imagery instructions and verbal mediation instructions are both effective simply because they increase the organisation and cohesion of the information to be remembered. Bower (1972) presented pairs of concrete words, and give his subjects either interactive imagery or separation imagery instructions (i.e., construct a mental image of two objects separated in space). On a subsequent cued recall test, the interactive imagery subjects performed much better than the separation imagery subjects, who in turn performed no better than subjects instructed to use rote repetition. In other words, interactive imagery instructions are effective because they enhance relational organisation rather than because they involve the use of imagery.

As yet, we have not discussed any evidence providing strong support for the hypothesis that concrete words are processed in a qualitatively different manner (i.e., imaginally) to abstract words. Perhaps the most direct approach to this issue is suggested by the common assumption that imagery and perception are closely related. The basic argument is that certain kinds of perceptual task should disrupt the concurrent use of imagery if perception and imagery both depend upon the same specific processing mechanisms. For example, suppose that subjects learn concrete or abstract pairs of words either in the absence of a second task or while performing a visuo-spatial task, such as the pursuit rotor tracking task. The obvious prediction from Paivio's (1971) theory is that the concurrent visuo-spatial task will impair learning of the concrete material to a greater extent than the abstract material. In fact, Baddeley, Grant, Wight and Thomson (1975) carried out precisely that experiment, and failed to obtain the expected interaction between concreteness or imageability of the material and the effect of the concurrent visuo-spatial task. There are several other studies in which this interaction failed to occur, and it also appears that a concurrent visual task usually does not reduce the beneficial effects of imagery instructions.

One of the reasons why concurrent visuo-spatial tasks have often failed to have a selective effect is that the learning tasks, and the processing instructions used, have typically required little in the way of spatial processing. Baddeley and Lieberman (1980) compared serial recall of subjects learning a sequence of words by the method of loci (i.e., constructing an image locating each object at a particular place on a familiar route) with that of subjects using rote rehearsal. A concurrent pursuit tracking task drastically reduced performance under imagery instructions but had no effect under rote learning conditions. It is probable that both the method of loci and pursuit tracking necessitate spatial processing, and it is under such circumstances that selective interference effects are most likely to be observed.

In sum, it is by no means clear why concrete stimulus material is usually much better remembered than abstract material. However, it is probable that as a result of extensive direct experience with the referents of concrete words, there is more information about such words than about abstract words available in semantic memory. This may permit more elaborate encoding of concrete rather than of abstract words, i.e., the encodings of the two kinds of words may differ quantitatively rather than qualitatively.

It will be remembered that Paivio (1971) assumed that pictures were more likely than concrete words to be processed imaginally, and it is for this reason that they are so well remembered. It is certainly difficult to account for the retention of complex visual stimuli, which cannot be easily described verbally, without postulating some non-verbal form of coding. The notion of separate verbal and imaginal codes is also supported by the finding that instructions to subjects to name the objects depicted in pictorial stimuli increase retention; presumably this would not happen if pictures were encoded solely in verbal form.

An ingenious test of Paivio's (1971) assumption that the verbal and imaginal systems are functionally independent was devised by Paivo and Csapo (1973). They were interested in the beneficial effects of repetition on recall, and so they investigated picture-picture and word-word repetitions, as well as picture-word repetitions (in which pictures of previously named objects or names of previously presented pictures were shown). Picture-picture and word-word repetitions both produced better recall than single presentations, but not as high as would be expected if the two encodings of repeated stimuli were independent and additive in their effects. In other words, there is a considerable overlap of information between the two encodings of repeated words or pictures. However, picture-word repetitions were additive in their effects on recall, which is consistent with the hypothesis of functionally independent verbal and imaginal codes.

Paivio's dual-code theory predicts that there are at least two ways in which the usual memorial superiority of pictures over words can be reduced:

1. Use of fast rates of presentation that restrict subjects to imaginal coding of pictorial stimuli and to verbal coding of words.

2. Utilisation of learning tasks that require serial processing. The reasoning is that verbal processes are specialised for serial processing, whereas imagery is especially useful for parallel processing and spatial representation.

Paivio and Csapo (1969) presented concrete words and pictures at a fast rate of presentation (5.3 items per second) or a slow rate (2 items per second, and they used two tasks necessitating serial processing (memory span and serial learning), and two other tasks not requiring serial processing (free recall and recognition). The results are shown in Fig. 5.3, and are consistent with predictions. Pictures were remembered less well than concrete words only with the fast rate of presentation on serial tasks, and they were better remembered only with the slow rate of presentation on non-serial tasks. However, performance at the fast rate was undoubtedly influenced by purely perceptual factors, such as masking, and there may have been more perceptual interference with pictures than with words.

It may be true, as Paivio (1971) claimed, that disparate kinds of stimulus material tend to be processed in qualitatively different ways, and the evidence for this is strongest when one compares pictures and concrete words. However, one of the lessons of the levels-of-processing approach (Craik & Lockhart, 1972) is that any given stimulus can be processed in several different ways. Encoding flexibility with pictorial and verbal stimuli

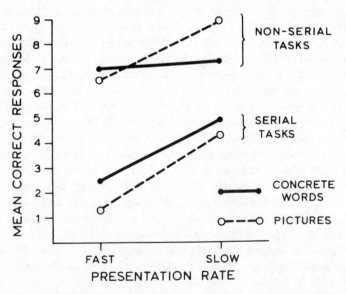

FIG. 5.3   Retention-test performance as a function of rate of presentation, type of stimulus, and task processing demands. Adapted from Paivio and Csapo (1969).

was shown clearly by Tversky (1969). After learning to associate schematic faces with nonsense names, subjects were presented on each of several trials with a name or a face followed one second later by a name or a face. The task was to decide as rapidly as possible whether the two stimuli had the same name.

Tversky (1969) found that the subject's expectations had a decisive impact on performance. When most of the second stimuli were pictorial, subjects responded faster to second stimuli that were pictorial irrespective of the nature of the first stimulus, and response speed was consistently faster to verbal than to pictorial second stimuli when most of the second stimuli were verbal. When the two stimuli had a different name, decision speed was inversely related to their similarity in terms of the modality of the second stimulus (i.e., picture or name), but the modality of the first stimulus did not affect performance. The implications of these findings is that the first stimulus was encoded either verbally or visually depending upon the anticipated modality of the second stimulus.

In sum, there is mixed support for Paivio's dual-code theory. It has by no means been established that concrete and abstract words are encoded in qualitatively different ways, and it seems more likely that the superior retention of concrete words simply reflects more elaborate processing of concrete than of abstract words. It is more tenable to assume that words and pictures are processed in qualitatively different ways, and Paivio may be correct in his assumption that the main code for pictures is imaginal, whereas the main code for words is verbal-linguistic. However, the great flexibility and variety of processing that any given stimulus can receive indicate that dogmatic statements about the way in which a kind of stimulus material is processed should be avoided.

BEYOND THE INFORMATION GIVEN

Introduction

When you study a list of words, what exactly is learned? The obvious answer that the list of words themselves are learned is true, but by no means represents the totality of what is learned. Suppose that you learned a list of words in a psychology laboratory on a particular day, and that you think back to that experience a few days later. Perhaps you remember that the walls of the laboratory were painted green, that the words were presented on a white screen by means of a slide projector, and that you had a splitting headache at the time. In other words, you actually remember many details that are not directly relevant to the list of words themselves.

Any learning task occurs in a particular context which is defined by a combination of the external environment and the learner's own internal

HCP–E*

environment (e.g., emotional state or mood). A rather different reason why we learn more than simply the to-be-remembered information is provided by the ways in which we utilize past knowledge and experience in learning. For example, if you hear the sentence, "John shot Mary," it is very difficult to avoid drawing the inference that John used a gun to shoot Mary, and there is strong evidence that such inferences are stored along with the information actually presented (e.g., Bransford, Barclay & Franks, 1972).

The theme of this section of the chapter is that the external environment, the internal environment, and relevant knowledge can all affect the nature of stored information to a considerable extent. As a consequence, what is learned is the to-be-remembered information together with salient contextual information, thus producing richer and more varied memory traces than could be formed on the basis of the learning task stimuli alone.

External Context

The basic paradigm that has been used to investigate possible influences of the external environment on the stored memory traces involves giving subjects a retention test in either the same environmental context as was present during learning or a different environmental context. If no information about the environmental context is stored during learning, then there is no particular reason why retention should be affected by the degree of similarity between the acquisition and the test environment. On the other hand, if information is stored at input about the environmental context, then using that same context at the time of test may facilitate retrieval of the to-be-remembered items.

Powerful effects of external context on recall were demonstrated by Godden and Baddeley (1975). Subjects learned a list of words either on land or 20 feet underwater, and 4 minutes later they were given a test of free recall either on land or underwater. Those who learned on land recalled more on land than underwater, whereas those who learned underwater did better when tested underwater. Retention was approximately 50% higher when learning and recall took place in the same environment than when they took place in different environments. However, Godden and Baddeley (1980) found no effect of external context when they carried out a very similar study, but used a recognition memory test instead of free recall.

Will changing the external context between input and test always reduce recall? It is possible that it might not if people attempted to think themselves back into the original learning environment at the time of the retention test. This possibility was explored by Smith (1979). A list of words was presented for learning in a carpeted room with posters on the walls and orange drapery hanging from the ceiling. An unexpected test for free recall was given the next day, either in the same room or in a different room that was filled with computer equipment and contained a soundproof chamber in which the recall test took place. Mean recall for the same-context subjects was roughly 50% higher than for the different-context subjects. Additional subjects were tested in the different context, but they were instructed to attempt to list ten objects they could remember seeing in the learning room, to think about that room, and to use their recollection of that room to aid recall. These subjects recalled virtually as many words as the same-context subjects.

Internal Context

The influence of the internal context on what is learned and remembered has been assessed in the same way as that of the external context. There is plenty of evidence that retention is often higher when the subject's state or mood is similar at learning and at test than when it is dissimilar. This phenomenon is usually known as state-dependent retrieval, and it has been discussed in detail by Eich (1980).

In many of the studies subjects learned either in a normal state or while drugged or intoxicated, and their recall was usually better when they were tested in the same drugged or undrugged state. A study that may have more relevance to everyday life (except for heavy drinkers or junkies!) was carried out by Bower, Monteiro, and Gilligan (1978). Subjects were hypnotized and asked to create a happy or sad mood while the to-be-learned material was presented. Recall was better when subjects were in the same mood as during learning than when they were in the opposite mood.

The phenomenon of state-dependent retrieval and the effects of manipulating the external context are both consistent with the encoding specificity principle put forward by Tulving. According to Tulving (1979), "The probability of successful retrieval of the target item is a monotonically increasing function of informational overlap between the information present at retrieval and the information stored in memory [p. 408]." The external and internal contexts both affect the amount of "informational overlap"; this overlap is greater when the context at learning and at recall is the same than when it is different.

Prior Knowledge

We have seen that memory traces often contain contextual information in addition to the to-be-learned information. There are many other cases in which what is "remembered" differs even more from the information explicitly presented for learning and actually includes information that was never presented. One of the first systematic investigations of this phenomenon was carried out by Bartlett (1932). In essence, he argued that memory was affected not only by the presented information but also by the subject's store of relevant information or prior knowledge. According to Bartlett (1932): "Remembering is not the re-excitation of innumerable fixed, lifeless and fragmentary traces. It is an imaginative reconstruction, or construction, built out of the relation of our attitude towards a whole active mass of organised past reactions or experience [p. 213]." In other words, memory is interactively determined by the presented information and by prior knowledge.

How can we demonstrate the impact of prior knowledge on memory? Bartlett (1932) had the ingenious idea of asking people to learn material that induced a conflict between what was presented and the reconstructive processes based on knowledge of the world. If, for example, people read a story taken from a culture different from their own, then prior knowledge might produce distortions in the remembered version of the story, rendering it more conventional and acceptable from the standpoint of their own cultural background.

In his best-known experiment, Bartlett asked English subjects to read "The War of the Ghosts," which is a tale belonging to the North American Indian culture. The subjects then attempted to recall as much of the story as possible on a number of occasions; their recall showed a marked tendency to distort the content and style of the original story, and these distortions increased over successive reproductions. A substantial proportion of the recall errors were in the direction of making the story read more like a conventional English story; Bartlett used the term "rationalisation" to refer to this type of error. Rationalisation was involved when a subject recalled that a dying Indian "foamed at the mouth," whereas the original story stated that, "something black came out of his mouth." In addition to rationalisation, there were other kinds of distortion in recall, including flattening (i.e., failure to recall unfamiliar details) and sharpening (i.e., elaboration of certain details).

There are at least four problems with Bartlett's classic work. Firstly, Bartlett did not give very specific instructions to his subjects ("I thought it best, for the purposes of these experiments, to try to influence the subjects' procedure as little as possible [p. 78]"). As a consequence, it is possible that some of the distortions observed by Bartlett were due to conscious guessing and confabulation rather than pure memorial malfunctioning. There is some force in this criticism, because instructions stressing the need for accurate recall have been found to eliminate almost half of the errors usually obtained (Gauld & Stephenson, 1967).

Secondly, Bartlett appears to have assumed that memorial distortions occurred largely as a result of reconstructive processes operating at the time of retrieval on the schema or schemata (defined by Bartlett, 1932, as "an active organisation of past reactions, or of past experience"). In fact, it is likely that most distortions occur because prior knowledge influences the way in which stimulus material is comprehended and stored in memory. It is unfortunate that the paradigm used by Bartlett does not enable us to decide whether distortions are due to processes occurring at study or at recall.

Thirdly, Bartlett's theoretical orientation was rather amorphous. It is not clear exactly what a schema is, nor is it possible to predict accurately the nature of any obtained memorial distortions. A step in the right direction was taken by Schank (1976), with his concept of a "script":

> A script is a giant causal chain of conceptualisations that have been known to occur in that order many times before. . . . What a script does is to set up expectations about events that are likely to follow in a given situation. These scripts can be predicted because they have occurred in precisely this fashion before [pp. 180–181].

The notion of a script was made more concrete by Bower, Black and Turner (1979), who asked students to list activities they associated with events such as going to a restaurant or attending a lecture. There was much agreement across subjects. For example, when describing attending a lecture, most students listed entering the room, finding a seat, sitting down, taking out a notebook, listening to the lecturer, taking notes, checking the time, and leaving. When Bower *et al.* presented stories eliciting specific underlying scripts, they found that unstated script actions were often recalled or falsely recognised.

Fourthly, it could be argued that Bartlett discovered an interesting phenomenon, but one that is rather esoteric and of limited generality. If prior knowledge produces systematic errors in memory only under the unusual circumstances of hearing or reading a story taken from an unfamiliar culture, then the phenomenon has little practical relevance. However, important work carried out by Bransford and his associates in the 1970s (see Bransford, 1979, for a review) has shown that some of Bartlett's ideas have a wider relevance than had been thought previously.

Consider a sentence such as, "Three turtles rested on a floating log, and a fish swam beneath them." When we read that sentence, our knowledge of spatial relationships allows us to infer that the fish must have swum beneath the log as well as the three turtles. Bransford, Barclay and Franks (1972) argued that most people asked to try to understand sentences store away information not only about the sentences themselves but also about any obvious inferences suggested by the sentences. As a consequence, subjects might mistakenly believe that information about the inference had actually been presented.

Bransford *et al.* (1972) tested these ideas by means of an unexpected recognition test. Subjects were presented with a list of "acquisition" sentences (such as "Three turtles. . ."). Later they were presented with a test sentence, and asked if they recognised it. Subjects were confident that they had heard the test sentence before when it corresponded exactly to one of the acquisition sentences. However, a more striking finding was that subjects were equally confident that they had previously heard test sentences that involved inferences from an acquisition sentence (e.g., "Three turtles rested on a floating log, and a fish swam beneath it"), even though these sentences had not, in fact, been presented at acquisition. This finding seems to provide strong evidence that spontaneous spatial inferences are made. However, it could be argued that the inference sentences were only recognised erroneously because of their overall similarity to the original sentences. This possibility was investigated by having a non-inference condition, in which acquisition sentences (e.g., "Three turtles rested beside a floating log, and a fish swam beneath them") were well recognised at test, but similar, non-inference test sentences (e.g., "Three turtles rested beside a floating log, and a fish swam beneath it") were correctly identified as not having been presented before.

Bransford has found in other studies that many different kinds of inferences are formed when people are trying to comprehend sentences or short prose passages, and this inference formation leads to systematic distortions in memory. The most important implication of these findings for Bartlett's (1932) theory is that prior knowledge influences our memory of experienced events in a far more pervasive way than seemed likely on the basis of Bartlett's own experimentation.

An important issue to which reference has already been made is whether prior knowledge affects retention by modifying the initial encoding or comprehension of presented information, or by influencing the retrieval process. The former alternative was favoured by Bransford (1979). According to his constructive hypothesis, comprehension involves the construction of meanings and inferences that may differ in various ways from the presented message, and memorial distortions then occur because learners remember their own constructions rather than what was actually presented. On the other hand, Bartlett's (1932) reconstructive hypothesis appears to emphasise the role played by prior knowledge at the time of retrieval; more specifically, reconstruction is the process of inferring the past rather than merely reproducing stored information.

It has been established that both hypotheses are partially correct. The role played by knowledge or background information in affecting initial comprehension was shown clearly by Bransford and Johnson (1972), who presented the following passage to their subjects:

> The procedure is actually quite simple. First you arrange items into different groups. Of course one pile may be sufficient depending on how much there is to do. If you have to go somewhere else due to lack of facilities that is the next

step; otherwise, you are pretty well set. It is important not to overdo things. That is, it is better to do too few things at once than too many. In the short run this may not seem important but complications can easily arise. A mistake can be expensive as well. At first, the whole procedure will seem complicated. Soon, however, it will become just another facet of life. It is difficult to foresee any end to the necessity for this task in the immediate future, but then, one never can tell. After the procedure is completed one arranges the materials into their appropriate places. Eventually, they will be used once more and the whole cycle will then have to be repeated. However, that is part of life [p. 722].

Subjects who heard this passage in the absence of a title rated it as incomprehensible and recalled an average of only 2.8 idea units, whereas those supplied beforehand with the title "Washing clothes" found the passage easy to understand and recalled more than twice as much (5.8 idea units). This effect of relevant knowledge on memory did not occur simply because the title acted as a retrieval cue that facilitated reconstructive processes at recall, because further subjects who received the title after hearing the passage, but before making comprehension ratings and attempting recall, showed poor comprehension and a low level of recall (2.6 idea units). The only plausible interpretation of the data is that relevant knowledge in the form of a title affected comprehension of the passage and thus its stored representation, but did not influence reconstruction.

One of the major implications of the reconstructive hypothesis is that new information that is relevant to a previously experienced event can affect recollection of that event by providing a different basis for reconstruction. In other words, all of the available information about an event is used to reconstruct the details of that event on the basis of "what must have been true."

This process of reconstruction of the memory of an event in the light of fresh information did not, of course, seem to happen in the study by Bransford and Johnson (1972), perhaps because the incomprehensibility of the untitled passage meant that the subjects did not possess any coherent information that could be re-interpreted subsequently. A more appropriate way of testing the reconstructive hypothesis is to present information that is comprehensible, but can be restructured on the basis of subsequent information.

Such research has been carried out by Elizabeth Loftus and her associates. She has been especially concerned about the possibility that eyewitness testimony relating to crimes and accidents might be systematically distorted by events occurring subsequently. If eyewitness testimony can be as easily manipulated by new information as is implied by the reconstructive hypothesis, then there are important social and legal issues that need to be resolved.

The fragility of memory was convincingly demonstrated by Loftus and Palmer (1974), who were able to show that the wording of a question can influence what observers report about an event they have witnessed. The film of a multiple car accident was presented, after which the subjects described in their own words what had happened and then answered a number of specific questions. Some of the subjects were asked, "About how fast were the cars going when they smashed into each other?," whereas for other subjects the verb "hit" was substituted for "smashed into." Control subjects were not asked a question about car speed. The estimated speed was affected by the verb used in the question, averaging 10.5 mph when the verb "smashed" was used versus 8.0 mph when "hit" was used. This suggests that the information implicit in the question affected the way in which the multiple car accident was remembered.

One week later, all of the subjects were asked the following question: "Did you see any broken glass?" In spite of the fact that there was actually no broken glass in the accident, 32% of the subjects who had been asked previously about speed using the verb "smashed" said they saw broken glass. In contrast, only 14% of the subjects asked using the verb "hit" said they saw broken glass, and the figure was 12% for the control subjects who had not been asked a question about speed. Apparently the reconstructive hypothesis is correct, and eyewitness testimony can be easily distorted by information that becomes available subsequently, even to the extent of leading eyewitnesses to "remember" things that did not happen.

However, there is another explanation. Perhaps the subjects in the "smashed" condition did not actually remember seeing any broken glass, but simply argued to themselves that cars smashing into each other would probably produce some broken glass. In other words, they may have simply conformed to the demands of the experimental situation. This alternative explanation was convincingly refuted by Loftus, Miller and Burns (1978).

It is a truism that eyewitness testimony is unreliable. The work of Loftus is revealing because it demonstrates some of the ways in which such evidence can become unreliable. Recollection of an event seems to be more fragile and susceptible to modification than might have been expected, and this discovery lends weight to attempts by the police and by lawyers to make as little use as possible of leading questions (i.e., questions suggesting to the witness the desired answer).

PRACTICAL APPLICATIONS: EFFICIENT LEARNING TECHNIQUES

Introduction

Much of the research discussed in this chapter is of relevance to the practical issue of increasing the efficiency of human learning. In general terms, processing that produces deep, elaborate, and distinctive encodings will usually be effective in leading to successful long-term retention. The use of imagery, especially interactive imagery that serves to integrate information from different sources, also seems to enhance learning. Prior knowledge undoubtedly helps memory in that it facilitates the organisation and elaboration of to-be-learned information, but it has the associated disadvantage that it can affect the nature of the stored memory traces to such an extent that memory becomes inaccurate.

In everyday life, memory failures often appear to be due to a retrieval problem rather than to inadequate storage of information. For example, I attended a conference shortly before Christmas, and had the intention of delivering a present to a friend of mine for his son. I completely forgot to take the present with me, but realised with a sinking feeling that I had failed to do so just before I arrived at the conference. While this looks like a pure case of retrieval failure, closer examination indicates that matters are actually more complicated. What I had failed to do was to store the kind of information that would have provided me with an adequate retrieval cue. If I had associated my brief-case with the present, then I might well have remembered the present when I put my papers into the brief-case before leaving for the conference. Alternatively, an external memory aid in the form of a humble knotted handkerchief might have also done the trick.

The moral of this example is that when one is learning something, it is important to envisage the circumstances under which the information will need to be retrieved. As students discovered long ago, the best learning and revision strategies are not necessarily the same when preparing for an essay-type examination as for a multiple-choice test. A major practical implication is that the search for a single, optimal learning strategy may well prove elusive for the simple reason that no strategy will be optimal across all possible retrieval environments.

One method of attempting to discover the principles involved in efficient human learning is to study individuals possessing exceptionally good memories. The best-known mnemonist is S., whose amazing powers were investigated by the Russian neuropsychologist Luria (1968). After only 3 minutes' study, S. learned a matrix of 50 digits perfectly, and was able to recall them effortlessly in any direction. More strikingly, he appeared to show almost perfect retention over periods of time extending to several years. S. made great use of synesthesia, which is the tendency for one sense modality to evoke another. His usual strategy was to encode all kinds of material in vivid visual terms. For example (Luria, 1968), he once said to the psychologist Vygotsky, "What a crumbly yellow voice you have [p. 24]."

It may make you feel envious to think of someone having such extraordinary memory ability, but there is another side to the story. He was sometimes so overwhelmed by specific images that he could not see the wood for the trees, as when attempting to comprehend a prose passage: "Each word calls up images; they collide with one another, and the result is chaos. I can't make anything out of this. And then there's also your voice . . . another blur . . . then everything's muddle [p. 65]." The next time you feel like complaining about your poor memory, just consider the potential problems involved in remembering absolutely everything!

Mnemonic Techniques

One of the difficulties involved in discussing efficient learning techniques is that the most effective technique or strategy varies as a function of the particular learning task. It makes a tremendous difference whether meaningful or meaningless material is to be remembered; whether the order in which information is presented has to be retained; whether facts or intentions need to be remembered; and so on. Psychologists have tended to concentrate on memory for facts rather than for intentions, but in everyday life it is often extremely important to remember future actions.

What have psychologists discovered about memory that is relevant to everyday life? In the opinion of many, the answer is disappointingly little. This pessimistic conclusion was expressed trenchantly by Neisser (1978):

> The results of a hundred years of the psychological study of memory are somewhat discouraging. We have established firm empirical generalisations, but most of them are so obvious that every ten-year-old knows them anyway. We have made discoveries, but they are only marginally about memory; in many cases we don't know what to do with them, and wear them out with endless experimental variations. We have an intellectually impressive group of theories, but history offers little confidence that they will provide any meaningful insight into natural behaviour [pp. 12–13].

Neisser may have been more pessimistic than is warranted. There is no doubt that the use of psychological principles in the development of mnemonic techniques can greatly improve learning in certain everyday situations. A key notion is the usefulness of relevant previous knowledge in permitting the efficient organisation and retention of new information, a notion that has received overwhelming support. It has been found that excellent chess players can remember the positions of approximately 24 chess pieces without great difficulty, provided that the configuration of the pieces represents a feasible game position. In contrast, unskilled amateur players can only remember the positions of about ten pieces. These findings reflect differences in knowledge of the game rather than storage capacity *per se*, because experts and beginners do not differ in their ability to remember the positions of randomly placed pieces. In similar vein, it has been found that knowledge of football or soccer correlates +0.81 with the ability to remember football scores (Morris, Gruneberg, Sykes & Merrick, 1981).

Suppose you were given the task of remembering 40 or 50 words in the correct order. On the face of it, this is an extremely difficult and demanding task, especially since you probably have little in the way of relevant previous knowledge to assist you. Mnemonic techniques can supply this missing knowledge in various ways. The ancient method of loci does so by means of a three-step approach: (1) a series of locations is memorised (e.g., places along a familiar route); (2) mental imagery is used to associate each of the to-be-remembered items with the locations; and (3) the learner performs a 'mental walk', moving from location to location and recalling what is stored at each one.

Greek and Roman orators often used this technique when preparing their speeches; they typically associated the key ideas in their speeches with specific mental locations. The effectiveness of the method of loci was demonstrated by Ross and Lawrence (1968). They discovered that people using the method of loci were able to recall more than 95% of a list of 40 or 50 items after a single study trial. Bower (1973) compared recall of five lists of 20 nouns for groups of subjects using or not using the method of loci. The former group recalled 72% of the nouns on average, against only 28% for the control subjects.

The method of loci is one type of peg system, in which the to-be-remembered items are attached to easily memorised items or pegs. Locations are useful pegs, but if you want to be able to recall rapidly a particular item in the series (e.g., the seventh), then a peg system including a method of numbering the pegs is essential. The most popular of such systems is the "one is a bun" mnemonic, which is based on the rhyme, "one is a bun, two is a shoe, three is a tree, four is a door, five is a hive, six is sticks, seven is heaven, eight is a gate, nine is a mine, ten is a hen." One mental image is formed associating the first-to-be-remembered item with a bun, a second mental image links a shoe with the second item, and so. The seventh item can subsequently be retrieved by thinking of the image based on heaven. The "one is a bun" mnemonic has been found to double recall (Morris & Reid, 1970).

Of course, the various peg systems all suffer from limitations, and are only really useful when long lists of separate items need to be remembered. Furthermore, the fact that these systems rely on visual imagery can pose problems when it comes to memorising abstract words. If the same pegs are used twice with different to-be-remembered items, then this corresponds to the A–B, A–C design that should lead to interference (see p. 162). However, informal evidence suggests that the same pegs can be used repeatedly without reducing the effectiveness of learning.

One obvious reason for the success of peg systems is the way in which they provide an organisational framework for unorganised learning material. However, they also supply effective and specific retrieval cues, and their use of interactive images is also important. In a study by Morris and Stevens (1974), it was found that learners instructed to form interactive images recalled 47% more than those told to form a separate image of each word. It would be of theoretical interest to discover the relative importance of each of these factors in producing the memorial advantage enjoyed by peg systems.

The basic strategy of imposing organisation and meaning on unorganised and relatively meaningless stimulus material can be applied to the difficult task of remembering people's names when you see them. A popular strategy starts with the search for an imageable substitute for the person's name (e.g., Eysenck becomes "ice sink"). Then some prominent feature of the person's face is selected, and the image is linked with that feature. The nose might be regarded as a tap over the sink. Brief training in this method has been found to improve recall of names to faces by almost 80% (Morris, Jones & Hampton, 1978), but it is a technique than can lead to some embarrassing mistakes.

An extremely effective strategy for remembering a number of unrelated words is to provide meaningful links between them by incorporating them into a narrative story. Bower and Clark (1969) asked learners to recall 12 lists of ten nouns each, in order, when given the first words of each list as cues. Those who had constructed narrative stories recalled 93% of the words, against only 13% for control subjects.

A final example of a mnemonic technique is the keyword method that has been applied to the task of acquiring vocabulary in a foreign language. The basic strategy starts with the formation of an association between each spoken foreign word and an English word or phrase that sounds like it (i.e., the keyword). It is important that the keyword is easily imaged. Then a mental image is created in which the keyword and the English translation are interacting. In other words, the keyword acts as a link between the foreign word and its English equivalent. For example, the Russian word "zvonok" is pronounced "zvahn-oak" and means bell. This can be learned by using "oak" as the keyword, and forming an image of an oak tree festooned with bells.

The keyword method seems to be more effective when the keywords are provided than when the learners must form their own. In one study (Atkinson & Raugh, 1975), 120 Russian words and their English equivalents were presented. Shortly after learning them, those provided with keywords recalled 72% of the translations compared with 46% for the control subjects. Six weeks later, recall was 43% and 28%, respectively.

It is clear that mnemonic techniques greatly facilitate the acquisition of several different kinds of information, but it has often been argued that such techniques are of little practical use. It is important to note that what is useful for one person may not be so for someone else. Most people may not need to memorise dozens of names, but this may be an essential skill for teachers.

Mnemonic techniques have also been criticised because they are applicable only to rote memory tasks, and do not facilitate higher-level skills such as understanding and reasoning. There is an element of truth in this criticism, but it is somewhat unfair to blame these techniques for failing to achieve purposes they were not designed to accomplish. In any case, it could be claimed that efficient learning of important facts enables the processing system to devote more time to complex cognitive activities.

What about strategies for learning complex, integrated material? Morris (1979) has discussed a valuable method of study known as SQ3R, which stands for Survey, Question, Read, Recite, Review. The initial Survey stage involves skimming through the material, endeavouring to construct a framework that will facilitate comprehension. In the Question stage the learner asks himself questions based on the various headings in the material; the idea here is to make reading purposeful. The material is read thoroughly at the Read stage, keeping the questions from the previous stage in mind. The material is re-read at the Recite stage, with the learner describing the essence of each section to himself after it has been read. Finally, the learner reviews what has been acquired from the stimulus material. Part of the rationale for this study method is that the Survey stage activates previous knowledge, with the subsequent stages involving active, goal-directed processes designed to integrate that knowledge with the stimulus material.

A major issue concerns the relationship between learning and understanding. While it has often been assumed that efficient learning is associated with superior understanding, there are circumstances in which they are negatively related. For example, Nitsch (1977) examined the learning of six new concepts (e.g., "Crinch: To make someone angry by performing an inappropriate act"; "Minge: To gang up on a person or thing"). The participants were given all the concepts and their definitions, and then attempted to identify examples of each concept (e.g., "The striking waitresses angrily approached the restaurant manager" is an example of "minge"). For the same-context subjects, all of the examples for each concept related to a particular context (e.g., "minge" involved cowboys), whereas a number of different contexts were used for varied-context subjects.

If learning proficiency is measured in terms of the ability to name the appropriate concepts when presented with examples of them, then the same-context subjects learned much better than the varied-context subjects. However, on a subsequent transfer test with examples involving completely new contexts, the varied-context subjects identified the concept correctly more often than the same-context subjects (84% versus 67%, respectively). The lesson of this study is that there can be a large difference between learning and understanding: The varied-context subjects learned more slowly than the same-context subjects, but their enhanced understanding of the concepts made it easier for them to transfer their knowledge to a new situation. Psychologists have usually focused on the effects of different learning techniques on retention, but for most practical purposes the ability to apply what one has learned to novel situations is far more important and merits further investigation.

6 Remembering and Forgetting

Everyone is fairly knowledgeable about their own memory abilities. We know that it tends to become progressively more difficult to remember an event with the passage of time, and that there are many things that we can recognise but cannot recall (e.g., an acquaintance's name). Of particular interest, we often seem to be sure that we know something even when we cannot call the desired information to mind. This happens, for example, in the, so-called tip-of-the-tongue phenomenon. Related to this phenomenon are those cases in which we cannot immediately recall the answer to a question, and are almost certain that the answer would not occur to us even with a great deal of thought (e.g., "What is the name of the sixth President of the United States of America?" for English people).

Memory theorists have put forward numerous theories of retrieval and forgetting designed to elucidate these, and other, phenomena. They have been especially concerned with the ways in which the probability of retrieval is affected by the precise form of retention test that is used. While it is true that there is usually less evidence of forgetting in recognition than in recall, there are a number of exceptions. It has been common to assume that any particular kind of retention test always leads subjects to use an invariant set of processing operations, but it is probable that reality is actually much more complex. The point was well expressed by Reitman (1970):

> To what extent can we lump together what goes on when you try to recall: (1) your name; (2) how you kick a football; and (3) the present location of your car keys? If we use introspective evidence as a guide, the first seems an immediate automatic response. The second may require constructive internal replay prior to our being able to produce a verbal description. The third . . . quite likely involves complex operational responses under the control of some general strategy system. Is any unitary search process, with a single set of characteristics and input–output relations, likely to cover all these cases? [p. 485].

As becomes clear during the course of this chapter, no entirely satisfactory theory of forgetting has been put forward. However, it has been established

137

that several different factors play a part in determining forgetting, and we do now have a reasonable understanding of phenomena such as the typical superiority of recognition memory over recall, and of the requisite conditions for producing the reverse effect. Such progress is encouraging given that systematic research into retrieval processes started under 20 years ago.

PERMANENT MEMORY

Theoretical Background

A fundamental issue is whether forgotten information is permanently stored but inaccessible, or whether it has simply been lost from the memory system. Sometimes it is relatively straightforward to demonstrate that forgotten information is still stored, as when a failure to recall some item of information is followed by successful recognition. However, if information is neither recalled nor recognised, and other retention tests also fail to produce memory for the information, then matters are much more conjectural. Complete forgetting is logically consistent with both loss of information and inaccessibility of permanently stored information.

In spite of these uncertainties, many prominent psychologists from Freud to Tulving have favoured the hypothesis of permanent storage. Loftus and Loftus (1980) were interested in the opinions of psychologists on this issue, and so they asked 75 of them to select from the two statements they were given whichever more accurately reflected their views:

1. Everything we learn is permanently stored in the mind, although sometimes particular details are not accessible. With hypnosis, or other special techniques, these inaccessible details could eventually be recovered.
2. Some details that we learn may be permanently lost from memory. Such details would never be able to be recovered by hypnosis, or any other special technique, because these details are simply no longer there [p. 410].

Eighty-four percent of the psychologists endorsed the first statement, thus supporting the permanent memory hypothesis. Loftus and Loftus (1980) asked the same question of 94 non-psychologists, of whom 69% chose the first statement. If it were possible to settle scientific issues in the same way as political elections are decided, then the permanent memory hypothesis is a clear winner. Among the reasons given for adherence to that hypothesis were personal experiences of remembering long-forgotten events, the work of Wilder Penfield, and the powers of hypnosis and psycho-analysis to recover forgotten memories. The obvious strategy is to evaluate these various kinds of evidence, to see whether or not they provide strong support for the permanent memory hypothesis.

Psychologists who believe in permanent memory frequently cite the work of Penfield. He operated on numerous epileptic patients, and he often stimulated the surface of the brain with a weak electric current in an attempt to identify the area of the brain involved in producing epileptic attacks. He discovered that the stimulating electrode sometimes appeared to cause the patient to re-experience events from his or her past with great vividness. Penfield (1969) argued that his findings indicated permanent storage of information:

> It is clear that the neuronal action that accompanies each succeeding state of consciousness leaves its permanent imprint on the brain. The imprint, or record, is a trail of facilitation of neuronal connections that can be followed again by an electric current many years later with no loss of detail, as though a tape recorder had been receiving it all [p. 165].

Close examination of Penfield's data indicates that his conclusions are erroneous. Electrical stimulation was applied to the cortex of the temporal lobe in 520 epileptic patients, and only 40 of them (7.7%) showed any evidence of recovery of long-lost memories. Many of these apparent memories were probably reconstructions rather than genuine recollections. For example, one patient claimed that she saw herself as she had appeared in childhood, and that she felt as if she were actually reliving the experience. Penfield emphasised the vividness and the detail of the patients' remembered experiences, but in most cases the recollections were rather vague and limited to a single sense modality (visual or auditory). From a scientific point of view, it is unfortunate that Penfield did not have any independent verification of the events which his patients claimed to remember during electrical stimulation.

One of Penfield's main contentions was that the precise nature of the reported recollections of the patients was determined by the locus of electrical stimulation. A rather different (and more plausible) conclusion was reached by Mahl, Rothenberg, Delgado, and Hamlin (1964). They argued that a major determinant of the reported memories of a 27-year-old housewife who received brain stimulation was, "the patient's 'mental content' at the time of stimulation [p. 358]."

The evidence from studies of hypnosis also provides much less support for the notion of permanent memory than is commonly believed. While it is true that the Israeli National Police Force and many other police forces have used hypnosis in their attempts to collect relevant evidence from eyewitnesses about matters such as car number plates and the physical characteristics of wanted criminals, it is not certain that the hypnotic method is efficacious in retrieving previously forgotten information. What seems to happen is that the hypnotised individual is less cautious than normal in his or her reported memories, and thus produces numerous recollections, many of which are entirely erroneous. It has been found, for example, that people under hypnosis will quite confidently "recall' events from the future!

In an interesting attempt to discover the ability of hypnosis to improve memory, Putnam (1979) showed people a videotape of an accident involving a car and a bicycle. They were then asked a series of questions, some of which contained misleading information. Some of the subjects were asked these questions while in a hypnotised state, having been told that they would be able to see the entire accident very clearly under hypnosis. In fact, the hypnotised subjects made *more* errors in their answers than did the non-hypnotised subjects, and this was especially true with the misleading questions. These findings led Putnam to conclude that subjects are "more suggestible in the hypnotic state and are, therefore, more easily influenced by the leading questions [p. 444]."

A final source of evidence relevant to the notion of permanent storage concerns the Freudian concept of repression. Freud (1943) argued that most forgetting is due to repression, with the original traces stored permanently in the unconscious, which "knows no time limit [p. 174]." It is usually assumed that repression means motivated forgetting, but Freud attached somewhat different meanings to the concept at different times (Madison, 1956). For example, he sometimes used the term "repression" to refer to the inhibition of the capacity for emotional experience. According to this definition, repression can occur even when there is conscious awareness of ideas, provided that these ideas are lacking their emotional content.

Experimental attempts to demonstrate the existence of repression have usually involved creating anxiety in order to produce forgetting (repression), followed by removal of the anxiety in order to show that the repressed information is still stored ("return of the repressed"). In practical terms, anxiety has usually been produced by providing failure feedback to subjects performing a task, and anxiety has then been reduced either by reassuring the subjects that the failure feedback was not genuine or by providing success feedback on the task previously associated with failure.

Apparent evidence of repression and the return of the repressed has been obtained in several studies (see Eysenck, 1977, and Holmes, 1974, for reviews). However, the interpretation of the findings is controversial. It is possible that people show poor recall after a failure experience simply because they are thinking about their failure rather than devoting all their attention to the recall test. Holmes (1972) found that ego-enhancing feedback reduced recall to the same extent as ego-threatening feedback, and it is plausible to assume that ego enhancement caused a relative lack of attention to the recall task. However, it seems improbable that it would produce repression.

An alternative interpretation is based on the notion of state-dependent retrieval discussed in Chapter 5. Since learning took place in a state of low anxiety, it might be expected that retention would be better in a similar state (i.e., low anxiety) than in a dissimilar state (i.e., high anxiety). The data are in accord with these expectations. All in all, the ambiguous nature of the findings on experimental repression means that they provide inconclusive support for the permanent memory hypothesis.

We have seen that much of the evidence usually cited as favouring the notion of permanent memory for all learned information is weak or inconsistent. The other approach to this issue is to consider whether there is any evidence that contradicts the permanent memory hypothesis. If, for example, information stored in the memory system is sometimes replaced by information that is subsequently made available, then this would imply that at least some stored information is considerably more fragile and susceptible to change than is suggested by the permanent memory hypothesis. The research of Elizabeth Loftus on eyewitness testimony that was described in Chapter 5 is relevant here. In essence, she discovered that misleading questions could distort an eyewitness's recollection of an accident to such an extent that it appeared that accurrate information about the accident had been completely lost. Therefore, it would seem that it may be a relatively rare occurrence for people to remember their earlier experiences with the degree of accuracy of a tape or video recorder; as we saw in the previous chapter, memory for events may be determined to an important extent by current attitudes and knowledge.

In sum, a detailed examination of the evidence indicates that the wide-spread acceptance of the permanent memory hypothesis is unwarranted. Part of the reason for its popularity is probably that it is unfalsifiable: Information may be stored somewhere in long-term memory even if there is no evidence at all that it can be retrieved. While this point must be conceded, it is important to note that no compelling evidence in support of permanent memory has ever been obtained, and this fact, together with its unfalsifiability, indicate that the permanent memory hypothesis should be rejected.

RETRIEVAL FROM SHORT-TERM MEMORY

Since it has typically been assumed that information in the short-term store or working memory is currently being attended to and processed, the obvious expectation is that such information can always be retrieved. However, there is little direct evidence to support these assumptions. The basic paradigm was introduced by Sternberg (1969). On each trial the subject memorises a short set of items (usually between one and six); this is known as the memory set. The memory set is followed almost immediately by a probe item, and the subject must decide as rapidly as possible whether it matches one of the memory-set items.

The basic data from the Sternberg paradigm consist of reaction times of positive and negative responses as a function of the number of items in the memory set. If subjects compare the probe item against all of the memory-set items at the same time, i.e., processing is parallel, then the simplest prediction is that response time will be unaffected by the size of the memory set. However, if the processing rate of each item is affected by the number of items being processed in parallel, then virtually any prediction is possible. If serial scanning occurs, the probe is compared to the memory-set items one at a time. Such a scan might be self-terminating, i.e., it continues only until a match is obtained. With a self-terminating search process, approximately half of the memory-set items would be examined on average on positive ("yes" decision) trials, whereas all of the items would have to be searched through on negative ("no" decision) trials. As a consequence, response times would increase as a function of memory-set size, but the rate of increase should be approximately twice as great on negative trials as on positive trials.

An alternative version of a serial scanning hypothesis is that the search is exhaustive, i.e., the probe is compared against each of the memory-set items even on positive trials. According to this hypothesis, reaction times are directly affected by the size of the memory set, and the rate of increase should be the same on both positive and negative trials.

The typical finding is that the positive and negative functions are both linear and parallel. Sternberg (1969) proposed a serial exhaustive model in which the probe is compared against the memory-set items at a rate of approximately 25–30 items per second. It may seem intuitively more likely that the search process would be self-terminating, but the high speed of scanning may make it very difficult to stop the search at some intermediate point.

In terms of Sternberg's (1969) complete model, which was discussed in Chapter 1 on p. 8, the number of items in the memory set affects the serial exhaustive comparison stage of processing, which is Stage 2 of four stages. The other factors determining reaction time are the time required to process the probe (Stage 1); response decision (Stage 3); and response selection and evocation (Stage 4). According to Sternberg, the times taken to perform Stages 1, 3, and 4 are usually unaffected by the size of the memory set, and thus all effects of memory-set size on reaction time reflect the duration of Stage 2.

Sternberg's serial exhaustive model has not been without its critics (e.g., Corballis, 1975). The model predicts that response time should not be affected by the serial position of the item in the memory set that matches the probe. In fact, there is often a recency effect, with faster response latencies for the last item or two in the memory set, and sometimes there is a small primacy effect (see Eysenck, 1978, for a review). However, Sternberg's model can be modified to account for such effects by assuming that Stage 1 or Stage 3 is affected by the serial position of the probe item (Sternberg, 1975).

Baddeley and Ecob (1973) found that reaction times were faster for items that were repeated in the memory set than for non-repeated items, whereas the most natural assumption from Sternberg's original model is that repetition should have no effect. However, while repetition presumably does not affect the serial comparison processing stage, it may reduce stimulus encoding time or response decision time.

One of the implausible characteristics of Sternberg's model is its assumption that there is only a single strategy that can be used to perform the recognition task. This undue rigidity of the serial exhaustive search model can be seen in connection with the simple finding of speed-accuracy trade-off, i.e., subjects can either respond accurately but slowly or rapidly and less accurately (Banks & Atkinson, 1974). It is actually quite difficult to account for this flexibility in terms of a scan that must run its course before usable information is available.

Perhaps there is no search at all through the memory set, with the speed of response being determined by the strength or familiarity of stored information about the probe (strength theory). This could explain why repeated items and recent items are responded to more rapidly than other items. The basic relationship between the size of the memory set and the reaction time may occur because increasing the number of memorised items reduces the average familiarity of the items in the memory set. However, while strength theories can account for many of the findings, they can only explain in a rather arbitrary way why the relationship between memory-set size and reaction time is linear.

Atkinson and Juola (1974) made out a persuasive case for a theory incorporating elements from the Sternberg and strength models. They assumed that subjects establish a low criterion and a high criterion at two points along a familiarity continuum (see Fig. 6.1). If the probe item's familiarity is below the low criterion, the subject makes a rapid "no" response. If the probe's familiarity exceeds the high criterion, the subject quickly responds "yes." In contrast, if the probe item has an intermediate familiarity value, and is thus in the area of uncertainty between the two criteria, a more extensive search through the memorised list is undertaken. Serial and parallel search processes are often mathematically indistinguishable, and so Atkinson and Juola (1974) were not dogmatic about the nature of this search process. The key assumption was simply that responding would be slower whenever there was a list search.

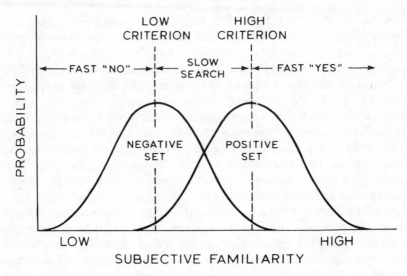

FIG. 6.1   Recognition-memory decision making as a function of the subjective familiarity of
the probe. Adapted from Atkinson and Juola (1973).

This model provides a straightforward account of the effects of instructions emphasising speed or accuracy. If the instructions emphasise
speed, then the two criteria will be placed closer together, and decisions will
mostly be made on the basis of probe familiarity. This leads to a number
of errors, because the familiarity of positive probes will sometimes fall below
the low criterion, and that of negative probes will on occasion exceed the
high criterion. If accuracy is emphasised, then the criteria will be placed
further apart, and the subject will make more use of the slower memory
search. This reduces the average speed of responding, but use of the list
search improves the accuracy of the subject's responses.

All of these predictions were confirmed by Banks and Atkinson (1974).
A more stringent test of the model is also possible. Since the increase in
reaction time as a function of memory-set size is said to be due entirely to
the search process, it follows that the effect of set size on response time
should be greater when the instructions lead the subject to make frequent
use of the search process (i.e., accuracy instructions). In fact, Banks and
Atkinson found that the slope relating size of the memory set to response
time was considerably steeper with accuracy instructions than it was with
speed instructions.

In sum, it is difficult to account for all of the findings in terms of a serial
exhaustive search model or of a strength hypothesis. A theory representing
an amalgam of those two approaches seems more promising, and is more
plausible in view of the flexibility of human processing.

RECALL AND RECOGNITION

Introduction

One of the most obvious facts about memory is that it is usually much easier to remember previous events or experiences when memory is tested by recognition rather than by recall. The simplest explanation of the typical superiority of recognition to recall is strength or threshold theory (Kintsch, 1970). The basic idea is that memory traces vary in strength, and that the trace strength necessary for recall is greater than that required for recognition. This theory assumes that recall and recognition differ only quantitatively, i.e., in terms of the requisite trace strength for memory. Such a theory is troubled by the plentiful evidence that various manipulations have *opposite* effects on recall and recognition. For example, rare words are nearly always better recognised than common words; according to strength or threshold theory, this means that the memory traces of rare words tend to be stronger than those of common words, and so recall should also be higher for rare words. In fact, rare words are usually less well recalled than common words (Kintsch, 1970), and the differential effects of word frequency on recall and recognition cannot readily be accounted for by strength theory.

It is clear that strength or threshold theory is too simple to account for the complex effects of various factors on recall and recognition. As a result, this traditional theoretical approach has been superseded by alternative hypotheses, some of which are now discussed.

Two-process Theory

Some of the difficulties associated with strength theory are obviated by various forms of two-process theory (Anderson & Bower, 1972; Kintsch, 1970). The quintessence of two-process theory is that recall involves a search or retrieval process, followed by a decision or recognition process based on the apparent appropriateness of the retrieved information. Recognition involves only the second of these two processes. More specifically, it is assumed that the knowledge system contains a large number of nodes, each of which corresponds to a concept; many of these nodes are labelled as words. When a word is encountered during learning, the relevant node is accessed automatically, and an occurrence tag is attached to that node. As a result of processing activities, such as rehearsal, associative links or pathways are formed among the nodes. The retrieval stage of recall involves using these associative pathways to generate candidate nodes for the subsequent decision stage. The decision or recognition process involves attempting to locate the appropriate occurrence tags attached to the nodes generated by the retrieval process (recall test) or to the nodes corresponding to the presented test items (recognition).

Two-process theory can readily account for the superiority of recognition to recall: recall involves two fallible stages, whereas recognition has only a single fallible stage. It can also explain the puzzling finding that some variables have the same effect on both recall and recognition, whereas others have different effects. Those variables having comparable effects on both kinds of retention test are assumed to affect the decision or recognition process, whereas variables having different effects are thought to affect the search or retrieval process.

This line of reasoning can be applied to the effects of word frequency. Rare words may have an advantage over common words during the decision or recognition process because the nodes corresponding to rare words have fewer irrelevant occurrence tags associated with them. In contrast, rare words have been encountered in fewer situations than common words, and so such words may have fewer associative links with other words than is the case with common words; this would reduce the likelihood of rare words being retrieved during the initial stage of recall. These theoretical assumptions certainly provide an explanation of the opposite effects of word frequency on recall and recognition, but the whole argument is somewhat *post hoc*.

According to the two-process theory, an item is recalled only when it is both retrieved and recognised. It is thus assumed that the probability of recall is determined by the probability of retrieval multiplied by the probability of recognition. This prediction was tested by Bahrick (1970) in a test of cued recall. Bahrick used the probability of the cue producing the to-be-remembered (TBR) word in free association as an estimate of the retrievability of the TBR word, and ascertained the probability of recognition by means of a standard recognition test. The level of cued recall was predicted reasonably well by multiplying those two probabilities together.

Two-process theory, then, has some successes to its credit, and it provides a reasonable explanation of many recall phenomena. However, it is now generally agreed that the assumption that recognition memory provides a direct measure of the information available in memory is erroneous, as is the related supposition that there is no retrieval problem in recognition memory. These assumptions have been tested by using two groups of subjects who study the to-be-remembered words under the same conditions, thus equating the degree of learning and the establishment of occurrence tags. Both groups are then tested for recognition memory, one group with the test context matching the study context, and the other group with different study and test contexts. Context is usually in the form of additional words presented along with the to-be-remembered words. Recognition memory is typically higher when the study and test contexts are the same than when the two contexts differ (e.g., Tulving & Thomson, 1971). The fact that recognition memory is susceptible to context effects suggests that there can be a retrieval problem in recognition, which is clearly contrary to the spirit of two-process theory.

Advocates of two-process theory (e.g., Anderson & Bower, 1974) have pointed out that it is embarrassed by context effects in recognition memory only when the assumption is made that each word is represented in the memory system by a single node. This assumption may be erroneous. For example, common sense suggests that homographs (i.e., words having two or more totally distinct meanings) are represented by more than one node. Thus, "JAM", in the sense of something to spread on bread and butter, forms one node, and "JAM", in the sense of congested traffic conditions, forms a second node. Multi-node theorists such as Anderson and Bower (1974) have proposed that there is a separate node for each meaning or sense of a word; since most words have a variety of meanings, it may be the rule rather than the exception for words to have multiple nodes.

Multi-node theory assumes that the node to which access is gained when a word is encountered depends on the perceived meaning of the word, which in turn is determined by the prevailing context. As a consequence, a change of context between study and test can impair recognition because a recognition decision is made about a different node from the one tagged on the study trial.

Multi-node theory can account for at least some context effects in recognition memory, but a high price is paid for this achievement. In particular, two-process theory loses much of its predictive power. It is not clear how many nodes any particular word has, and it seems probable that the number and nature of the nodes will vary from individual to individual. Moreover, the initially clear distinction between the processes involved in recall and recognition becomes blurred as soon as it is suggested that retrieving the appropriate node can be a problem in recognition memory as well as recall.

A further difficulty for multi-node theory is that it is equipped to account for only some of the context effects in recognition memory, i.e., those involving a shift in the semantic context of words between study and test. It has been found that changing the context between study and test in a non-semantic fashion can also reduce recognition performance. This happens when there is simply a change in the mode of presentation from a male to a female voice or from upper- to lower-case type.

The fact that recognition memory is susceptible to context effects has been used in other ways to discomfort two-process theory. It is possible to devise circumstances in which recall is considerably higher than recognition, provided that the context is altered substantially between study and recognition test. In a study by Watkins (1973), subjects learned paired associates, such as, "EXPLO–RE" and "SPANI–EL", and were then given tests of recognition (e.g., "RE" and "EL") or of cued recall (e.g., "EXPLO–?" and

HCP–F

"SPANI–?"). Recall was dramatically higher than recognition (67% versus 9%). Since two-process theory predicts that recognition is superior to recall, it can explain such findings only by considerably complicating the original theory.

Why is the two-process theory inadequate? The fatal flaw is the assumption that all that happens when a familiar word is encountered is that a new occurrence tag is added to a pre-existing node. The emphasis is on the similarities between the ways in which a word is encoded on different occasions. Since the specific environmental context affects word processing, any given word may be encoded in radically different ways in different contexts. Any theory of memory that lays stress on invariant mental representations such as nodes is destined to have problems in accounting for the variety of experience.

Encoding Specificity

A theoretical approach that differs considerably from that of two-process theory has been put forward by Tulving (1982, 1983). He assumes that there are basic similarities between recall and recognition, although he has increasingly admitted that there are some major differences. He also assumes that contextual factors are important, and that what is stored in memory represents an amalgam of information from the to-be-learned stimulus and from the context.

Tulving has incorporated these ideas into his encoding specificity principle, which was expressed in the following terms by Wiseman and Tulving (1976): "A to-be-remembered (TBR) item is encoded with respect to the context in which it is studied, producing a unique trace which incorporates information from both target and context. For the TBR item to be retrieved, the cue information must appropriately match the trace of the item-in-context [p. 349]." A few years later, Tulving (1979) put forward a somewhat simpler and more precise formulation of the encoding specificity principle: "The probability of successful retrieval of the target item is a monotonically increasing function of informational overlap between the information present at retrieval and the information stored in memory [p. 408]."

Flexser and Tulving (1978) spelled out in some detail what might be involved in informational overlap. They assumed that both memory traces or engrams and retrieval cues consist of bundles of features. The amount of informational overlap is determined by the number of features in the engram that match features in the retrieval cue.

It will be noticed that the encoding specificity principle does not refer explicitly to either recall or recognition. The reason is that it is intended to apply equally to both forms of retention test. There have been numerous attempts to test the notion of encoding specificity, but what is common to virtually all of them is that there are at least two encoding conditions and at least two retrieval conditions. Suppose that a cross-over interaction is found, i.e., one encoding condition leads to better memory performance than the other encoding condition in one retrieval condition, but the opposite occurs in the other retrieval condition. This indicates (as the encoding specificity principle claims) that memory depends on both memory-trace information and retrieval-environment information.

A concrete example of this research strategy in actions comes in a study by Thomson and Tulving (1970). They presented pairs of words in which the first word was the cue and the second word was the to-be-remembered word. The cues were either weakly associated to the list words (e.g., "Train–BLACK") or were strongly associated (e.g., "White–BLACK"). On the subsequent recall test, some of the to-be-remembered items were tested by weak cues (e.g., "Train–?"), whereas others were tested by strong cues (e.g., "White–?"). The results are shown in Fig. 6.2. As would be expected on the encoding specificity principle, recall performance was best when the cues provided at recall were the same as those provided at input. Any change in the cues lowered recall, even when the shift was from weak cues at input to strong cues at recall.

It has usually been assumed that these results can be accounted for straightforwardly by the encoding specificity principle, i.e., recall cues are

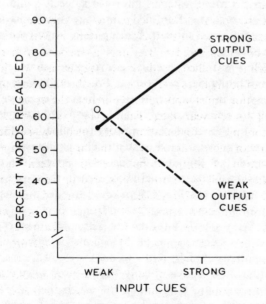

FIG. 6.2 Mean word recall as a function of input cues (strong or weak) and output cues (strong or weak). Data from Thomson and Tulving (1970).

effective only to the extent that they contain information that was directly stored in the relevant memory traces at the time of learning. However, on this line of reasoning it is a little difficult to see why recall was so high when weak input cues were followed by strong recall cues. A more plausible notion is that recall can occur in two rather different ways: (1) the recall cue permits direct accessing of the target information; or (2) the cue leads to recall by an indirect route involving the making of inferences and the generation of possible responses. The direct route is more likely to be used when the input and recall cues match than when they do not, whereas the indirect route is more successful when the recall cue is strongly associated to the to-be-remembered item than when it is weakly associated. Thomson and Tulving (1970) emphasised the importance of the direct route and of the similarity of input and output cues, but the fact that strong recall cues were significantly more effective than weak ones suggests that the indirect route was used fairly frequently.

The distinction between two recall routes was confirmed by Jones (1982). Subjects were shown a list of apparently unrelated cue-target pairs (e.g., "regal–BEER"), followed by cued recall (e.g., "regal–?"). Some of the subjects were told prior to recall that reversing the letters of each cue word would produce a new word that was related to the target word (e.g., "regal" produced "lager," which suggests "BEER"). It was assumed that those subjects who were not informed of the peculiar nature of the recall cues used only the direct recall route, whereas informed subjects could use both the direct and the indirect routes. Informed subjects recalled more than twice as many words as uninformed subjects, bearing testimony to the usefulness of the indirect recall route.

Tulving (1982, 1983) has recently incorporated some of his earlier theoretical notions into a General Abstract Processing System (see Fig. 6.3). There are 13 elements in the model, seven of which are elements of encoding and six of which are elements of retrieval. So far as encoding is concerned, the assumption is that an engram or memory trace is formed as a result of encoding processes applied to environmental events, although it is possible that the nature of the engram may be modified by the encoding of subsequent events. So far as retrieval is concerned, the process of ecphory is of pivotal importance. As Fig. 6.3 makes clear, the process of ecphory combines information from the engram and from the retrieval environment, and converts it into ecphoric information. The phenomenon of encoding specificity occurs as a consequence of the process of ecphory. Recollective experience, as the term implies, refers to conscious awareness of ecphoric information. Finally, the process of conversion is used when either recollective experience or ecphoric information, of which the individual has no recollective experience, is converted into overt behaviour. For present purposes, the key feature of conversion is that recall and recognition have

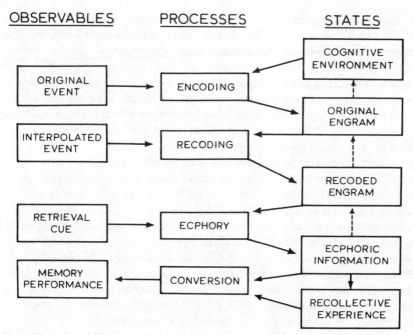

FIG. 6.3   The General Abstract Processing System. Each arrow indicates "influences" or "brings about", and broken arrows refer to effects that do not influence a current act of remembering, but may affect subsequent ones. Adapted from Tulving (1983).

different conversion thresholds. More specifically, more ecphoric information is needed for recall than for recognition, because recall requires naming of a previous event whereas recognition only requires a judgement of familiarity. The details of the conversion process are spelled out by Tulving (1982, 1983) within the context of his Synergistic Ecphory Model of Retrieval.

What are the implications of these theoretical notions for the issue of the relationship between recall and recognition? Recall and recognition are similar with respect to the process of ecphory, i.e., they both involve an amalgam of trace or engram information and retrieval information. However, as we have just seen, recall and recognition differ with respect to the amount of ecphoric information required for memory performance.

Since recall and recognition are both subject to the encoding specificity principle, it follows that both forms of retention test are affected by the contexts in which learning and testing occur. This emphasis on the importance of context enabled Tulving to specify the conditions under which the rather surprising finding of recall being better than recognition might be obtained. The fundamental idea is that the study and test contexts are the same when recall is assessed in order to maximise retention (cf., Thomson & Tulving, 1970), but the two contexts are made as dissimilar as possible for recognition, because this reduces recognition performance.

This approach was adopted in a classic study by Tulving and Thomson (1973). Subjects learned lists of paired associates in which there was a weak semantic relationship between the members of each pair (e.g., "Glue–CHAIR"). On the initial lists, subjects were simply given a test of cued recall (e.g., "Glue–?"). On the final list, however, they were asked to generate free associations to strong associates of the response members of the paired associates (e.g., "Table"), followed by recognition of any list words that were among the items produced on the free association test (e.g., "CHAIR CLOTH DESK DINNER"). Finally, the subjects were given a conventional test of cued recall (e.g., "Glue–?").

Rather similar results were obtained in all three experiments reported by Tulving and Thomson (1973). In their first experiment, recall as measured by the final cued-recall test was 63%, whereas only 24% of the list words produced on the free association test were recognised. At the simplest level, the explanation of these findings is that crucial aspects of the study context (i.e., the stimulus members of each paired associate) were absent during the recognition test, but were re-instated for the recall test.

Why has Tulving (1982, 1983) felt it necessary to add the notion of different conversion thresholds for recall and recognition to his earlier theoretical position? The key empirical evidence was reported by Tulving (1983). Two groups of subjects were presented with the same list of words under the same conditions, and were then given the same retrieval cues. The only difference between the two groups of subjects concerned the conversion requirements: One group had to produce the list words (recall group) to the retrieval cues, whereas the other group made recognition decisions to the same cues.

According to Tulving (1983), the ecphoric information available to any given kind of retrieval cue should be the same for both groups, since both the encoding conditions and the retrieval cues were held constant. However, when the retrieval cues consisted of actual list words, recognition performance was significantly better than recall performance, suggesting that some process in addition to ecphory was determining performance. This additional process was identified as conversion. More striking evidence was obtained from an analysis of memory performance on retrieval cues that were strong associates of list words. It is plausible to assume that those associative cues that are most successful in leading to recall should be the ones producing the most ecphoric information, and, if so, the same cues should also be most likely to lead to erroneous recognition responses. In fact, the opposite result was obtained, and the implication again is that some process over and above ecphory must be involved.

It is not altogether clear to me that these findings provide strong support for an extra conversion process to the process of ecphory. As Tulving (1983) admits, it is possible that the differences in task requirements caused the ecphoric process to be different for the two groups. While Tulving tends to dismiss this interpretation, it seems entirely feasible that the use made of the retrieval cues would depend greatly on the goal of the retrieval process.

What is the importance of Tulving's contribution? One of the valuable features of his theoretical approach is the emphasis on the notion that memory is determined interactively by the nature of the stored trace or engram and by the information available in the retrieval environment. This makes it clear that assertions about the universal memorial superiority of certain encodings to others (e.g., deep ones to shallow ones) or about the greater sensitivity of one kind of retention test to another (e.g., recognition to recall) are inaccurate and subject to numerous qualifications.

One of the most refreshing aspects of Tulving's contribution is the way he has consistently attempted to make extremely general theoretical statements. Reference back to Fig. 6.3 will reveal that the General Abstract Processing System makes no reference (whether explicit or implicit) to particular encoding or retrieval situations, and so is inended to have universal applicability. The same is also true of the encoding specificity principle.

Criticism of Tulving's views has focused largely on his notion of encoding specificity. While several of the standard criticisms seem well wide of the mark, Solso (1974) identified a genuine difficulty:

> If a cue was effective in memory retrieval, then one could infer it was encoded; if a cue was not effective, then it was not encoded. The logic of this theorization is "heads I win, tails you lose" and is of dubious worth in the history of psychology. We might ask how long scientists will puzzle over questions with no answers [p. 28].

It is certainly true that there is a danger of circularity in applying the encoding specificity principle. Memory is said to depend on "information overlap" and, in the absence of any direct measure of that overlap, it is tempting to infer the amount of informational overlap on the basis of retention-test performance. However, we can manipulate the encoding conditions at the time of learning so as to produce systematic and predictable effects on the memory trace. In this way we are not totally reliant on information about the success or otherwise of differential retrieval cues to infer the nature of the memory trace. As a result, it is possible to escape some of the dangers of circularity of reasoning.

Eysenck (in preparation) has pointed to another serious problem. As Fig. 6.3 makes clear, different kinds of stimuli are allegedly treated in very different ways by the processing system. Those stimuli presented at the time of learning (i.e., original events) are liable to be processed in a huge variety of ways, whereas stimuli presented at the time of retrieval (i.e., retrieval cues) are apparently processed in such a straightforward manner that they enter directly into the process of ecphory without any intervening process.

The problem with this approach is that it leads Tulving to de-emphasize the potential variety of retrieval strategies that can be instigated by any given retrieval cue. For example, Tulving (1983) discusses studies (e.g., Kochevar & Fox, 1980) in which retention occurred apparently in contradiction to the encoding specificity principle. These data could be explained away either by arguing that the learning material was encoded in ways that had not been foreseen, or that the retrieval cues were used in more complex ways than evisaged to produce retention. For reasons that are quite obscure, Tulving focuses only on the former possibility.

The de-emphasis on retrieval strategies has also led Tulving to utilise retention tests (e.g., cued recall, recognition) where diverse retrieval strategies are unlikely to be used, and to avoid retention tests (e.g, free recall, interrogations of memory such as, "What did you do last Wednesday?") that might lead to the available retrieval cues being used in several quite different ways.

Recent Views on Recognition

As Mandler (1972) pointed out, our everyday experience suggests that recognition can occur in two rather different ways. Fairly recently, I walked past a man in Wimbledon, and felt immediately that I recognised him. However, I was somewhat puzzled because it was difficult to think of the situation or situations that I had seen him in previously. After a fair amount of thought about it (this is the kind of thing that academic psychologists do think about!), I realised that the man was a ticket-office clerk at Wimbledon railway station, and this greatly strengthened my conviction that my initial feeling of recognition was correct.

Mandler (1980) has developed a theory of recognition memory based on the notion that recognition can involve two distinct mechanisms. Sometimes recognition memory occurs on the basis of the familiarity of the stimulus. Familiarity is determined by the amount of intra-item organisation, which in turn depends on the degree of integration of the sensory and perceptual elements of the stimulus. If the level of stimulus familiarity is high, then the subject rapidly decides that he or she recognises the stimulus. If the level of familiarity is intermediate, then recognition may occur via identification, which involves a retrieval process. This retrieval process makes use of the organised nature of long-term memory, and involves the recovery of relevant contextual information about the stimulus (e.g., its relationship to other concepts, the contexts in which it has usually been encountered, or its functional significance). According to Mandler, the familiarity and retrieval processes operate in parallel, but the familiarity process is completed more rapidly than the retrieval process.

It is clear that the familiarity process cannot be based purely on the absolute value of stimulus familiarity. If it were, then common words would be recognised more often than rare words. In fact, recognition memory is inversely related to word frequency (Gregg, 1976). The relative increment in familiarity produced by presenting a list of words would be greater for rare than for common words, and so it may be that the familiarity process is responsive to this relative increment in familiarity rather than to the absolute level.

How can this two-process model of recognition memory be tested? One relatively straightforward prediction is possible on the basis of Mandler's further assumption that familiarity decays more rapidly over time than do the organisational or structural effects involved in the retrieval process. As a consequence, recognition decisions at long retention intervals should be more likely to involve the retrieval process than those at short retention intervals. Mandler (1967) asked people to sort a fairly long list of unrelated words into between two and seven categories. On a subsequent unexpected test of free recall, there was a remarkably strong relationship between the number of categories used in sorting and the number of words recalled: Each additional category added approximately four words to the total words recalled. Presumably the information was organised more efficiently in long-term memory with the larger numbers of categories, and this facilitated retrieval.

In other words, the extent to which retention-test performance reflects the organisation of the list provides a measure of the involvement of the retrieval process. Mandler, Pearlstone, and Koopmans (1969) used the same sorting task as that utilised by Mandler (1967), and tested recall and recognition at three different retention intervals (immediate, 2 weeks, and 5 weeks). Organisation in terms of the number of categories used in sorting (and so, putatively, the retrieval process) became an increasingly important determinant of recognition-test performance.

Recognition performance following a sorting task was explored further by Mandler and Boeck (1974). They argued that relatively fast recognition decisions should primarily reflect the familiarity process, whereas relatively slow decisions should be based to a greater extent on the retrieval process. As a result, the organisational factor of the number of categories used in sorting should affect slower responses more than faster responses. This prediction was supported by the evidence.

One of the key assumptions of Mandler's (1980) theory is that recognition-memory performance usually depends heavily on stimulus familiarity, whereas familiarity is no more than indirectly relevant to recall. Fairly primitive processing operations are thought to affect stimulus familiarity without any discernible effect on the retrieval process involved in recall. Glenberg, Smith, and Green (1977) manipulated the length of time for which words were rehearsed repeatedly in the same rote fashion. They discovered that a ninefold increase in rehearsal time only produced a negligible 1.5% increase in recall, but a substantial improvement in recognition memory.

Recent research into amnesia (reviewed later in this chapter) provides further support for the theoretical distinction between the familiarity and retrieval processes. It is probably somewhat of an over-simplification, but it is still largely true that the extremely poor long-term memory of amnesics is attributable to deficiencies in the retrieval process rather than in the familiarity process. When successful recognition of pictures required the retrieval of appropriate contextual information, amnesics performed extremely poorly (Huppert & Piercy, 1976). However, amnesics had few problems in answering the question, "Have you seen this picture before?," presumably because only information about familiarity was required. Subsequently, Huppert and Piercy (1978) confirmed that the recognition performance of amnesics is based primarily on stimulus familiarity or strength.

What are the problems associated with Mandler's (1980) two-process theory of recognition memory? The major difficulty is the imprecise specification of the familiarity and retrieval processes, combined with uncertainty about the relative roles played by the two processes in most situations. There is, for example, very little evidence to indicate that the familiarity and retrieval processes operate in parallel rather than seriatim, i.e., with the retrieval process following the inconclusive termination of the familiarity process.

The assumption that familiarity judgements depend on sensory and perceptual features of the recognition-test stimulus rather than its semantic features may be in error. In an unpublished study of mine, subjects learned sentences containing homographs, followed by a recognition test in which either the same or a different meaning of each homograph was used. Subjects were instructed to decide as rapidly as possible if each homograph on the recognition test had been presented in an acquisition sentence, and whether or not the same meaning was presented at learning and at test. The key finding was that subjects presented with a different semantic context at test than at acquisition fairly frequently made a rapid "no" response, followed shortly by a slower "yes" response correcting their mistake. This suggests that the initial familiarity process can be sensitive to the semantic similarity of the acquisition and test encodings, and thus that semantic features can be made use of in the initial judgement of familiarity.

Recent Views on Recall

While many theories of recall assume that recall always occurs in a particular way, introspective evidence gainsays this notion. It is true that, as the two-process theory suggests, we sometimes attempt to recall information (e.g., the name of an acquaintance, or an item on a shopping list) by generating plausible alternatives and selecting one of them, but it seems implausible that this is what normally happens. If, for example, someone asks you for the name of your wife (or husband, live-in companion, or even meaningful other), it is unlikely that you generate a number of possible names before producing your answer.

The distinction between two types of recall has been expressed in various terms by different theorists. Bahrick (1979) distinguished between effortful and effortless recall, whereas Jones (1978, 1979) argued that recall could be based on either extrinsic or intrinsic knowledge. In essence, intrinsic knowledge is information that is provided explicitly for retention (e.g., the cue in cued recall), and extrinsic knowledge is additional information that may also assist in the retention process. For example, suppose someone is presented with "flower–TULIP," and is then given "flower" as the retrieval cue for "TULIP." The cue "flower" may provide *direct* access to the target word "TULIP" if the relevant intrinsic knowledge is available. Failing that, extrinsic knowledge may provide *indirect* access to the target word if it is used to generate words related to "flower" until the appropriate word is generated and recognised. In other words, the two-process theory describes one of the ways in which recall can occur, but generation-recognition is by no means the only way in which recall is possible.

One of the ways of testing this conceptualisation of recall is to use two recall tests in succession. The first is a test of free recall, and it is assumed that those items that are directly accessible or can be recalled effortlessly will be recalled on this test. It then follows that any items subsequently recalled must be recalled by means of the generation-recognition mechanism. This prediction was tested by Bahrick (1970). He provided recall cues that were related more or less strongly to those target words that could not be free recalled. From association norms, he knew the probability that each cue word would generate the appropriate list word, and he also assessed the recognition probability of each list word when presented together with related distractor words. The two-process theory predicts that the probability of successful cued recall should equal the probability of correct generation multiplied by the probability of recognition, and Bahrick's results were very much in line with this prediction.

An alternative approach was adopted by Rabinowitz, Mandler and Patterson (1977). They compared recall of a categorised word list under standard instructions, and under instructions to generate as many words as possible from the list categories saying aloud those they thought had actually been presented in the list. When there was a short retention interval, subjects given the latter generation-recognition instructions recalled 23% more words than those given standard recall instructions. However, the generation-recognition instructions had a negligible effect on recall when recall was only tested after a 1 week retention interval.

It thus appears that generation-recognition can be a useful secondary strategy in free recall, at least at relatively short retention intervals. This conclusion was further supported by Rabinowitz, Mandler and Barsalou (1979), who also fleshed in some of the details of the generation-recognition process. As the two-process theory predicts, both the generation and recognition stages of recall were fallible. Considering the actual list words produced during the generation stage by subjects given generation-recognition instructions: 17% of them were incorrectly rejected by the recognition process.

Does the recognition process used in the generation-recognition recall strategy resemble that used on standard recognition tests? It appears so, because recognition performance was very similar whether the words involved in the recognition-memory decisions were subject-generated (recall based on generation-recognition instructions) or experimenter-generated (standard recognition memory) (Rabinowitz et al., 1979).

We have seen that, at least in free recall, it is possible for extrinsic knowledge to lead to successful recall via the generation-recognition strategy. What about the role played by intrinsic knowledge in recall? A specific set of assumptions was presented by Jones (1976) in his fragmentation hypothesis. According to this hypothesis, the memory trace comprises a fragment of the original stimulus situation, and typically contains a combination of attributes (e.g., colour, shape, location). Recall of the memory trace is all-or-none; if any attribute contained in the stored fragment is used as a retrieval cue, it gives access to the remainder of the fragment. It follows from this theoretical analysis that there should be cue symmetry (e.g., the probability of recalling Attribute B when given Attribute A as a retrieval cue is the same as the probability of recalling Attribute A when given Attribute B as a retrieval cue).

In his original study, Jones (1976) presented naturalistic pictures, each of which incorporated four elements (i.e., object type, location, colour, and sequential position). There were subsequent tests of cued recall in which one or more attributes of each item were presented. With the sole exception of findings involving the attribute of sequential position, there was quite good evidence for cue symmetry. However, one of the limitations of the stimulus materials used by Jones was the relative independence of the trace attributes or components. When the trace elements interact together to form a Gestalt-like memory trace, cueing asymmetry seems to be frequent. Salzberg

(1976) discovered that the more concrete member of a paired associate was the more effective retrieval cue in providing access to the entire paired associate. According to him, if each pair of words is stored as an integrated image, then it is only to be expected that the word that is the more salient part of that image will provide the more reliable access to it.

In sum, there is reasonable evidence that recall can be based on at least two different kinds of processes: direct access and generation-recognition. While there is little doubt that the generation-recognition process postulated by two-process theory actually exists, it is not clear that it plays a major role in recall. Recall based on direct access and utilising intrinsic knowledge is certainly common, but the precise mechanisms involved remain undiscovered.

Recognition and Recall Compared

One of the oldest conundrums in memory research is whether recognition and recall tasks involve basically the same or substantially different processes. At the most general level, it can be claimed that all forms of remembering depend on retrieval cues. As with so many other theoretical issues, William James (1890) adumbrated contemporary wisdom with respect to the importance of cueing:

> Suppose I am silent for a moment, and then say, in commanding accents: "Remember! Remember!" Does your faculty of memory obey the order and reproduce any definite image from your past? Certainly not. It stands staring into vacancy, and asking, "What kind of a thing do you wish me to remember?" It needs, in short, a *cue* [pp. 117–118].

While there is widespread acceptance for the view that cues are an integral part of both recall and recognition, it can reasonably be argued that the kinds of cues available in the two retention tests are rather different. This point of view was expressed by Broadbent and Broadbent (1975) in the form of a rhetorical question:

> Can we not say that both processes (i.e., recall and recognition) involve the presentation of event A and the retrieval of event B; But in recall, B is the to-be-remembered item and A is a cue for recall, whereas in recognition, A is the item and B the circumstances in which it was last experienced? [p. 589].

There is a certain logic to this theoretical position, but it suffers from the problem of glossing over the fact that cues may produce recall or recognition either directly or indirectly. In other words, neither recall nor recognition invariably proceeds in a particular way.

In spite of this caveat, it still seems likely that the precise information required for recall often differs from that needed for recognition. Another important difference between recall and recognition concerns the role played by organisation of the to-be-remembered material in long-term memory. While there are some exceptions (e.g., Mandler *et al.*, 1969), it is usually found that organisation of the material affects recall more than recognition, presumably because complex retrieval processes are more likely to be required for recall than for recognition. In an early study, Kintsch (1968) presented either a highly semantically organised or a poorly organised list, followed by recall or recognition. Recall was approximately 50% higher from the organised than the disorganised list, but recognition memory was unaffected by list organisation. In similar fashion, preventing subjects from organising list items via rehearsal produced a substantial decrement in recall, but had no effect on recognition (Schwartz & Humphries, 1974).

One method of obtaining further evidence about the relationship between recall and recognition is to consider how readily items that cannot be recognised can be recalled. Different theories make different predictions: Two-process theory seems to assume that if an item cannot be recognised, then it cannot be recalled, whereas the encoding specificity principle (Tulving, 1979) allows for the possibility of recognition failure of recallable words. The findings are rather equivocal. Watkins and Todres (1978) found practically no evidence for recognition failure of recallable words, in sharp contrast to several other studies reviewed by Flexser and Tulving (1978). In general terms, recognition failure of recallable words is most prevalent when each to-be-remembered word is studied in a different context; the contexts then being re-presented as the recall cues.

The variability of the findings on recognition failure of recallable words reminds us that sweeping generalisations about the relationship between recall and recognition are usually in error. However, some progress can be made if we take account of the fact that there are at least two recall processes and at least two recognition processes. Recognition failure of recallable words tends to occur when recall involves the direct-access route based on intrinsic knowledge, and recognition requires retrieval of context. On the other hand, recallable words can nearly always be recognized if recall is based largely on generation-recognition, and recognition depends on the familiarity process. In a nutshell, the question of the similarity between recall and recognition has no definite answer; rather, it depends on the relative importance of direct access and generation-recognition on the recall task, and on the relative influence of the familiarity and retrieval processes on the recognition task. Failure to consider these various processes can only lead to chaos.

INTERFERENCE THEORY

Introduction

For a period of 30 years or more, interference theory provided the dominant explanation for "forgetting", and interference is still regarded as one of the major factors involved in forgetting from short-term memory (see Chapter 4, pp. 89–90). The origins of interference theory go back to the nineteenth century and to a student of Wilhelm Wundt called Hugo Munsterberg. He had been used to carrying his watch in one particular pocket; when he shifted it to another pocket, he noticed that thereafter there was a certain amount of delay and fumbling on his part when he was asked for the time.

At the simplest level this anecdote illustrates the way in which old habits can interfere with new ones. In the terms of interference theory, Munsterberg initially learned an association between the stimulus "What time is it?" and the response of removing the watch from his pocket. Subsequently, the stimulus remained the same but a different response was associated with it (i.e., the watch had to be removed from a different pocket). Interference appears to be maximal when two different responses become attached to the same stimulus.

Munsterberg was subject to proactive interference, i.e., forgetting produced by previously learned information. This can be compared with retroactive interference, which refers to forgetting produced by events occurring after learning but before a retention test. The basic paradigms used to measure proactive and retroactive interference are shown in Table 6.1. In each case, learning involves associating a stimulus (A) with a response (B or C). Paired-associated learning is often used in these paradigms, so that an example of an A–B, A–C design would be "Cat-Tree," "Cat-Dirt." In the related A–B, A–Br design the stimuli and responses remain the same on both learning tasks, but each stimulus is re-paired with a different response on the second task. The control subjects are usually given some unrelated learning activity during the time that the experimental subjects are learning the interfering material. In the case of the retroactive interference paradigm this is necessary in order to prevent the control subjects from rehearsing the A–B material throughout the retention interval.

Data and theory

A classic early investigation that apparently provides strong evidence for interference theory was carried out by Jenkins and Dallenbach (1924). They asked two Cornell University students to learn lists of nonsense syllables either early in the day or just before going to bed. Retention was then tested after 1, 2, 4, or 8 hours of normal daily routine or of sleep. The results were

TABLE 6.1.
Basic Paradigms for Proactive and Retroactive Inter-
ference (Group 1 = Experimental Group of Subjects:
Group 2 = Control Group)

| | Proactive Interference | | |
	Learn	*Learn*	Retention *Test*
Group 1	A–B*	A–C	A–C
Group 2	$\dfrac{2}{M}$	A–C	A–C
Group 1	A–B*	A–Br	A–Br
Group 2	$\dfrac{2}{M}$	A–Br	A–Br

| | Retroactive Interference | | |
	Learn	*Learn*	Retention *Test*
Group 1	A–B	A–C*	A–B
Group 2	A–B	$\dfrac{2}{M}$	A–B
Group 1	A–B	A–C*	A–B
Group 2	A–B	C–D*	A–B
Group 1	A–B	A–Br*	A–B
Group 2	A–B	$\dfrac{2}{M}$	A–B

r = re-pairing of the stimuli and responses from the first
learning list.

$\dfrac{2}{M}$ = unrelated learning activity.

* = interference learning activity.

very striking: after 8 hours awake only 9% of the stimulus material could
be recalled, but the figure was 56% when the 8 hours were spent asleep.
Jenkins and Dallenbach attributed this six-fold advantage of sleeping during
the retention interval to the lower incidence of interfering activities while
asleep than awake.

Although this study continues to be cited with approval by many
authorities, it is seriously flawed. The sleep condition always involved
learning late in the evening and the awake condition involved learning in the
morning, there was, therefore, complete confusion between sleep conditions
and time of day. When these two factors are sorted out, it becomes obvious
that the rate of forgetting depends far more on the time of day than on

whether or not the learner is asleep during the retention interval (Hockey, Davies & Gray, 1972). There was considerably less forgetting when the five-hour retention interval occurred between 11 p.m. and 4 a.m. than when it was 6.30 a.m. to 11.30 a.m. (29% forgetting versus 45%), irrespective of whether the retention interval was spent awake or asleep. Thus, a proper interpretation of the data obtained by Jenkins and Dallenbach is more likely to be based on circadian rhythms than on the effects of sleep on interfering activities.

In spite of interpretative difficulties with the study of Jenkins and Dallenbach (1924), there is overwhelming evidence that both proactive and retroactive interference occur (see Postman, 1976, for a review). However, attributing forgetting to either form of interference is descriptive rather than explanatory unless the mechanism or mechanisms responsible for producing interference can be identified. It was originally argued by McGeoch (1932) that forgetting was primarily due to retroactive interference, which was produced by response competition from the interpolated learning. For example, in the A–B, A–C design, subjects who are re-tested on the A–B associations sometimes erroneously produce C responses, and researchers assumed that the number of second-list intrusions during first-list recall provided a measure of the degree of response competition.

It became apparent fairly quickly that response competition was unable to account for more than a small proportion of retroactive interference. Melton and Irwin (1940) required subjects to learn two lists of nonsense syllables, but more learning trials were given to the second list. They found that retroactive interference increased with increasing learning trials on the second list. On the response-competition hypothesis, the number of second-list intrusions during recall of the first list should have increased because of more interpolated learning and should therefore have been in line with the amount of retroactive interference. In fact, response competition increased up to a point and then decreased as a function of the number of trials on the second list. It therefore became necessary to postulate some factor over and above response competition to account for retroactive interference, and this additional factor was assumed to be unlearning of the first-list associations as a result of second-list learning.

Unequivocal evidence of unlearning (which is sometimes likened to extinction in conditioning studies) seems to require the use of a situation in which response competition is minimal. This was achieved by Barnes and Underwood (1959) in a study in which subjects learned two lists of paired associates in an A–B, A–C design, and the number of learning trials on the second list was manipulated. Retention was measured by means of modified modified free recall: Subjects were presented with each A item and asked to recall both the first- and second-list responses (i.e., B and C). It was argued that the requirement to produce both responses reduced the role played by response competition. With increasing amounts of second-list learning, recall of first-list responses decreased progressively, suggesting that un-learning of the stimulus–response associations of the first list had occurred.

Subsequent research by Postman and Stark (1969) made it seem rather unlikely that the interfered-with associations had actually been unlearned. They used the A–B, A–C paradigm and tested for retroactive interference by using an associative matching task after the second list had been learned. The associative matching task involved giving the subjects the stimuli and responses from the first list and asking them to match them as they had appeared during learning. In contrast to the usual recall findings, there was no evidence of retroactive interference on the associative matching task (i.e., there was no loss of the first-list associations). However, the more usual finding is some retroactive interference in the A–B, A–C paradigm when using the associative task, especially when the associative matching task includes the specific competing responses from the second list among the response alternatives (Anderson & Watts, 1971).

Some more evidence that retroactive interference can occur in the virtual absence of unlearning was obtained by Tulving and Psotka (1971). Their subjects learned between one and six categorised word lists, with each list comprising four words belonging to each of six conceptual categories. After the subjects had been presented with their last list, they were asked to provide free recall of the words from all of the lists they had seen. Approximately 65% of the words from the first list were recalled when there were no other lists, but this figure declined to 30% when five further lists had been presented and learnt. This is a typical example of retroactive inter-ference, with forgetting being determined by the number of interfering events.

Did learning the subsequent lists produce unlearning of the first list, or did it simply make the information less accessible? Tulving and Psotka favoured the latter interpretation because there was practically no evidence of retroactive interference on a subsequent test of cued recall, on which the names of all the categories used in all the lists were presented as cues. Indeed, performance on cued recall was remarkably similar to the level of original learning that was measured by free recall tests given immediately after each list was presented.

Some of these findings suggest that retroactive interference occurs because subjects find it difficult to generate the response terms of the first list. When the responses are made available, as in the associative matching task, there is sometimes no retroactive interference. This idea was given formal expression by Postman; he proposed the notion of response-set interference, i.e., there is response competition between all the B terms of the first list and the C terms of the second list, rather than between individual responses.

One of the strange implications of response-set suppression from the perspective of contemporary cognitive psychology is that the subject apparently has remarkably little control over his or her retrieval processes. In addition, if we emphasise intereference at the level of entire response sets, we are in danger of ignoring the existence of stimulus-specific retroactive interference. This more specific form of interference is shown by the fact that there is more retroactive interference in the A–B A–C paradigm than in the A–B, C–D paradigm.

There are other theoretical ideas put forward by interference theorists. For example, there is rather more to the unlearning hypothesis than has been suggested so far. A–B associations are allegedly unlearned or extinguished during A–C learning, and, in line with the conditioning analogy, it is assumed that there is spontaneous recovery of the B responses during the retention interval. There are various studies using the A–B, A–C paradigm and measuring retention by means of the modified modified free recall test. The prediction is that there should be an increase in the number of B responses produced at longer retention intervals, but there is only slight supporting evidence (see Postman, 1976).

It was believed for many years that retroactive interference was the major determinant of forgetting. The position changed, however, with the publication of an extremely influential article by Underwood (1957). He reviewed the research dealing with the forgetting of a list of items over a 24-hour retention interval, and discovered that approximately 80% of the original learning was forgotten in a day if the subject had previously learned 15 or more other lists in the same experiment, against only 20–25% if no earlier lists had been learned. These findings suggested that proactive interference can have a massive influence on forgetting.

There is a methodological problem with many of the demonstrations of proactive interference that is often ignored. While the learning of each successive list is equated in the sense that all lists are learned to a specified criterion (e.g., all items correctly recalled on a single test), subjects tend to reach the criterion more rapidly with the later learning lists. As a consequence, subjects have less exposure to the later lists than to the earlier ones, and this may account for at least some of the apparent evidence for proactive interference. Warr (1964) equated the amount of exposure to the learning material on all lists, and found that the forgetting rate was relatively unaffected by the number of lists previously learned. However, Underwood and Ekstrand (1967) obtained substantial proactive interference in a study in which the learning rate did not increase over lists, so the issue is still open.

The major mechanism by which proactive interference is assumed to occur is response competition based on the spontaneous recovery of first-list responses over time. As has already been mentioned, there is little direct evidence of such spontaneous recovery. When recovery of first-list responses has been observed, it has often occurred some 25 minutes after learning. Unfortunately for interference theory, this corresponds to a retention interval at which very little proactive interference is usually obtained!

As was the case with retroactive interference, advances in thinking about proactive interference occurred when it was discovered that some kinds of retention test show no evidence of proactive interference. Underwood, Broder and Zimmerman (1973) used the associative matching test (i.e., all the stimulus and response members of the learned paired associates had to be matched appropriately), and found that the rate of forgetting was unaffected by the number of lists learned previously. This suggests that proactive interference may involve response-set competition, but subsequent work (e.g., Postman & Keppel, 1977) has failed to provide any strong support for this.

A further factor that is involved in producing proactive interference is increasing difficulty of list differentiation as the number of lists learned increases (Postman & Keppel, 1977). Striking evidence of the potential importance of list differentiation has been obtained in studies of part-whole transfer. Experimental subjects learn two lists of words, the second of which consists of all the words from the first list, together with an equal number of new words. Control subjects also learn two lists, but there are no overlapping words. The usual findings are counter-intuitive, with the experimental subjects learning the second list more slowly than the controls, in spite of having already spent some time learning half of the words. The problem experienced by the experimental subjects appears to be mainly one of list differentiation; they can recall the list two words that also appeared in list one, but are not sure which list they came from (Sternberg & Bower, 1974).

It is obvious that proactive and retroactive interference both occur under the appropriate circumstances, and the mechanisms put forward by interference theorists (e.g., unlearning, response competition, and response-set competition) undoubtedly play a part in producing forgetting. However, there is a suspicion that some at least of these mechanisms (e.g., unlearning) are descriptive rather than explanatory. It is also rather doubtful whether interference theory can account for forgetting outside of the narrow range of paradigms of the A–B, A–C type.

The most fundamental limitation of interference theory is its failure to take proper account of internal processing operations. This is explicable in view of its origins as a simple stimulus–response theory, but it poses various problems. For example, one of the basic assumptions is that the amount of interference depends on stimulus similarity, with maximal interference occurring when the stimuli on two learning tasks are the same (i.e., A–B, A–C). However, the amount of interference produced by, say, phonemic similarity depends on the extent to which the stimulus materials are processed phonemically.

METAMEMORY

Retrieval failures can cause inconvenience and embarrassment, as when we forget someone's name or vital information on an examination. Given the inevitable imperfection of memory, are there any ways to alleviate the problem? One useful asset would be some internal system that was able to tell us reasonably accurately whether we would be able to retrieve a desired item of information if we made a concerted effort, because clearly there is no point in spending valuable time trying to retrieve the irretrievable. As is explained shortly, there is in fact evidence that we are fairly successful in deciding whether or not we possess certain information that cannot be recalled. This ability to monitor the contents of memory forms part of the larger area of metamemory, the knowledge that we have about the workings of our own memory systems.

Seminal work on memory monitoring was carried out by Hart (1965). He asked college students to try to answer a series of general knowledge questions (e.g., "What sea does West Pakistan border?"). If the subjects were unable to recall the answer, they were asked to decide the extent to which they believed that they knew the answer on a six-point scale. Finally, the subjects were given a four-alternative recognition test (e.g., (a) Arabian Sea; (b) Caspian Sea; (c) Red Sea; and (d) Black Sea). When subjects expressed a very strong feeling of not knowing the answer, only 30% of the answers were correctly recognized, against a chance level of 25%. This figure of 30% should be compared with the corresponding figure of 75% when subjects felt very strongly that they did know the answer. In other words, people can estimate fairly accurately what information is potentially accessible.

At first glance, it seems paradoxical that people can know that they know something even though they are quite unable to recall it. However, the paradox disappears when we remember that knowledge is not necessarily all-or-none: It is entirely possible to be unsure which sea West Pakistan borders while nevertheless being able to recall some relevant information (e.g., the approximate geographical location of West Pakistan). The simplest hypothesis is that judgements of feeling-of-knowing are based on the amount of partial knowledge that can be retrieved (see Blake, 1973).

This hypothesis was investigated by Brown and McNeill (1966). They read out dictionary definitions of rare words, and their subjects attempted to identify the words defined. If they were unable to do so, but felt that the answer was on the tip of their tongue, then they guessed the initial letter, number of syllables, and so on, of the missing word. It was clear that those in the tip-of-the-tongue state often had access to many of the features of the word they were trying to recall. For example, subjects in that state were correct 57% of the time when guessing the word's initial letter.

One of the limitations of the paradigm devised by Brown and McNeill (1966) is that it does not permit any assessment of partial knowledge of semantic features, because those features are provided in the definition. Accordingly, Eysenck (1979c) reversed the task used by Brown and McNeill by giving subjects rare words and asking them to provide definitions. When subjects could not provide an accurate definition of the word, they were still able to predict the extent to which they would be able to recognise words semantically related to the word that could not be defined.

An important aspect of metamemory concerns our awareness of when retrieval from memory has been successful: How good are we at discriminating between answers that are definitely correct and those that may be in error? This issue was addressed by Lichtenstein and Fischhoff (1977), who asked their subjects general information questions, and gave them two answers to choose between (e.g., "Bile pigments accumulate as a result of a condition known as: (a) gangrene, (b) jaundice"). Confidence in the accuracy of their choices was related to the actual accuracy, but there was a tendency for undergraduate students to exaggerate their degree of accuracy. For example, when they were totally confident that they had selected the correct answer, they were actually in error approximately 15% of the time.

PRACTICAL APPLICATIONS: AMNESIA

Some of the theoretical notions about learning and forgetting that we have explored in this and previous chapters seem potentially relevant to an understanding of amnesia. Amnesics include cases of accidental brain damage, epileptics, and sufferers from Korsakoff's syndrome (i.e., advanced alcoholism, including nutritional deficiency). All of these different kinds of amnesics are usually considered as a single group for research purposes, the main reason being that they exhibit a similar patterning of memorial deficiencies. In essence, amnesics have reasonable normal short-term retention, exemplified by their ability to engage successfully in casual conversation, but they are severely impaired in their long-term retention of freshly acquired information.

What is responsible for the poor long-term retention of amnesic patients? At the risk of over-simplification, it is possible to distinguish between encoding deficit hypotheses (which focus on problems of information storage) and retrieval deficit hypotheses (which claim that amnesics only show inferior memory performance under certain retrieval conditions).

Cermak's (1979) encoding deficit hypothesis can most readily be considered in the context of the levels-of-processing approach of Craik and Lockhart (1972). According to Craik and Lockhart, deep or semantic processing leads to better long-term memory than shallow or non-semantic processing. Cermak simply claimed that amnesic patients do not encode semantic information adequately, and cited a number of studies supportive of this hypothesis. Cermak and Moreines (1976) read out a list of words and asked their subjects to indicate when a word was repeated, or when a word rhymed with a previous word, or when a word belonged to the same category as an earlier word. The Korsakoff patients were reasonably good at detecting repetitions, but rather poor at the category task that necessitated semantic processing. They were able to detect rhymes if no more than two words intervened between the two rhyming words, but their performance was extremely poor with four intervening items.

These findings are representative of those obtained by Cermak and his associates. That is to say, amnesics do show clear evidence of impaired semantic processing, but it appears that their processing deficiencies extend beyond the semantic level. Indeed, it is likely that amnesics are less proficient than normals at virtually all forms of verbal processing, and the same appears to be true of non-verbal haptic processing (i.e., based on touch) (Strauss & Butler, 1978).

If a major factor in the poor memory performance of amnesics is impoverished semantic processing, then it might be possible to decrease their memory impairment by using techniques that require amnesics to process semantically. This strategy has been used a number of times with extremely modest success. In one study (Cermak & Reale, 1978), subjects were asked questions about words necessitating shallow, orthographic processing (e.g., "Is it written in upper-case letters?"), or phonemic processing (e.g., "Does the word rhyme with . . . ?"), or deep, semantic processing (e.g., "Does the word fit in the sentence: . . . . ?"). Amnesics responded to these questions without error and almost as rapidly as control subjects, thus indicating that they were carrying out the requisite forms of processing.

On the subsequent unexpected recognition test, the control subjects showed the usual pattern of much better retention of semantic than orthographic encodings, with phonemic encodings intermediate. The amnesics, however, showed very poor recognition memory, and recognised no more semantically or phonemically analysed words than orthographically analysed words. It thus seems unlikely that more than a small fraction of the memory impairment of amnesics can reasonably by attributed to an inability or unwillingness to process information semantically.

All in all, the processing and memorial deficiencies of amnesics are too pervasive to be explicable in terms of Cermak's encoding deficit hypothesis. Moreover, while it is true that amnesics do frequently manifest both semantic processing deficits and a profound long-term memory impairment, there is little concrete evidence of a direct causal link between thest two deficiencies.

A very different theoretical approach was favoured by Weiskrantz and Warrington (1970). They assumed that amnesic subjects acquired information normally, and that their primary difficulty is one of retrieval. If the amnesic's problem is not centred mainly at the time of storage, then it should be possible to find retention tests on which amnesics perform almost as well as normals. Weiskrantz and Warrington measured memory for words by means of tests of free recall, recognition, and identification of the list words when presented in fragmentary form. The typical memorial inferiority of amnesics was obtained with free recall and recognition, but they did not show any retention deficit with the fragmentary word test.

What is going on here? One explanation is that the amnesics' defective control over stored information causes them to retrieve too much information. As a consequence, amnesics usually experience great difficulty in coping with interference from irrelevant material at the time of retrieval. On this account, amnesics perform well with fragmented words because the number of response alternatives that need to be considered is severely limited. Further support for this interpretation was obtained by Warrington and Weiskrantz (1974). They varied the extent to which a recall cue restricted the number of possible response alternatives. Amnesics benefitted more than controls when the cues could apply to only a few words.

Rather more direct evidence that amnesics are susceptible to interference was produced by Winocur and Weiskrantz (1976), who considered the interference effects of one list on the learning of a second list. Amnesics and controls learned an initial list of paired associates, consisting of pairs of related words, almost equally well. This was followed by a second paired associate list in which the stimulus words from the first list were paired with new related words. Amnesics showed little learning of this second list, and intrusions from the first list constituted a much higher percentage of the total errors made by amnesics than by the control subjects.

The retrieval deficit hypothesis favoured by Weiskrantz and Warrington accounts for part of the memorial problem experienced by amnesics. However, they have been unable to provide any convincing evidence that amnesics store information as efficiently as normals. In fact, it is becoming increasingly clear that amnesics experience problems at both storage and retrieval. Stern (1981) and others have argued persuasively for a context encoding deficit theory, according to which amnesics encode the to-be-remembered information fairly adequately, but fail to store much information about the immediate context. As a result, they often know they have seen a particular stimulus item before, but they cannot remember under what circumstances. According to this theory, amnesics show good memory when tested with fragmented words because very little contextual information is required to mediate recall.

One of the appealing features of the context encoding deficit theory is that it encompasses various other theoretical approaches. Thus, it claims that amnesics suffer from a partial encoding deficit which may or may not impair memory performance, depending on whether contextual information is essential for retention. Deficient encoding of context by amnesics was demonstrated by Huppert and Piercy (1976). Having familiarised their subjects with a set of 80 pictures on one day, they presented 40 of these now familiar pictures together with 40 unfamiliar pictures the following day. This was followed by a recognition-memory test for the pictures presented on the second day. Control subjects correctly recognised 89% of the presented pictures and falsely recognised 3% of the familiar non-presented pictures, whereas amnesics correctly recognised only 70% of the presented pictures and falsely recognised 51% of the familiar distractors.

The relatively poor performance of the amnesic patients might reflect either simply a massive memory deficit or an inability to discriminate between the pictures on the basis of their temporal presentation context. However, another finding reported by Huppert and Piercy (1976) seems to favour decisively the latter interpretation. When amnesics were asked the question, "Have you seen this picture before?," they made very few errors, presumably because contextual information was not required for accurate memory performance. It might still be argued that the partial ability of the amnesics to discriminate between presented pictures and familiar distractors suggests that amnesics do store some contextual information. However, it seems that this apparent discrimination occurred because amnesics based their judgements mainly on trace strength rather than stored contextual information (Huppert & Piercy, 1978).

A related theoretical approach has been increasingly popular in recent years. If we draw a distinction between retention tests that require conscious recollection and those that test memory indirectly by asking the subject to perform tasks the success of which depends upon previously acquired information, then amnesics appear to be at more of a disadvantage on the former retention tests than on the latter. This phenomenon was first demonstrated by Clarapède (1911) who concealed a pin in his hand while shaking hands with an amnesic patient. The patient was reluctant to shake hands with Clarapède the next day, but could not explain his reluctance.

There are several recent studies (e.g., Jacoby & Witherspoon, 1982; Meudell & Mayes, 1982) in which amnesics showed clear evidence of learning despite a virtual absence of conscious recollection. Jacoby and Witherspoon asked their subjects various questions (e.g., "What is the part of the clarinet that vibrates?"), the answers to which consisted of homophones (e.g., "reed" which is homophonic with "read"). The amnesics were subsequently extremely poor at recognizing the words they had generated in the question-and-answer phase of the experiment. The subjects were then simply asked to spell various words, with no mention being made of the previous task. The spelling of homophones tended to be in line with the answers given earlier (e.g., "reed" rather than "read"), and this tendency was as marked in amnesics as it was in control subjects.

Is it only amnesic patients who exhibit learning in the absence of conscious remembering? Definitely not. Meudell and Mayes (1981) asked amnesics and normals to search cartoons for specified objects. Seven weeks later, the amnesics showed evidence of retention by their rapid rate of search, in spite of their inability to recognise the actual cartoons. The normal subjects showed precisely the same dissociation between learning and awareness when they were tested after an interval of 17 months. It may thus be that learning without conscious awareness may simply reflect rather limited information storage.

In sum, the history of research into amnesia is very much a success story. The initial supposition that amnesics possess no ability to establish new information in long-term memory has been discredited, and some understanding of the kinds of learning that amnesics are capable of and of the appropriate ways of assessing what has been learned has been achieved. As Baddeley (1982) has pointed out, there is a strong possibility that applied research into amnesia and other memory impairments will ultimately influence theoretical developments within memory research. For example, the traditional distinction between recall and recognition may prove to be less important than that between retention based on conscious recollection and retention without awareness.

7 Imagery and Visual Memory

The concept of "imagery" has had a rather chequered history. Over 2000 years ago, Aristotle regarded imagery as the major medium of thought, and many of the mnemonic systems devised by the ancient Greeks involved imagery in some form (see Yates, 1966). More recently, Galton (1883) revived interest in mental imagery. He asked several people to imagine their breakfast table that morning, and to decide how clearly they could visualise it. There were substantial individual differences, with some people reporting that they had no conscious mental imagery at all.

Everything changed in the early years of the twentieth century. The Behaviourists were determined to make psychology "objective," and to this end they put a stop to any serious investigation of mental phenomena such as imagery for a period of some 40 years. Interest in mental imagery has increased considerably in recent years, and indeed imagery occupies a position of pivotal importance in many theories of cognitive psychology. It has been claimed that imagery plays an important role in perception (Neisser, 1976), that it facilitates learning (Paivio, 1971), and that it is involved in problem solving (Sternberg, 1980). Since we are consciously aware of words and of images, it makes intuitive sense to emphasise the importance of both verbal and imaginal processing to cognitive functioning.

The concept of "imagery" has been defined in several rather different ways in recent years, but a point of agreement among most of the definitions is that they refer to a close, if unclear, relationship between imagery and perception. One of the more pellucid definitions was offered by Neisser (1972): "A subject is imaging whenever he employs some of the same cognitive processes that he would use in perceiving, but when the stimulus input that would normally give rise to such perception is absent [p. 245]."

In view of the continuing controversy about the usefulness of "imagery" as a theoretical construct, we consider the relevant issues in the next section. When some clarification of these issues has been achieved, we then discuss the relevance of imagery to some of the major areas of cognitive psychology.

IS "IMAGERY" A VIABLE CONSTRUCT?

In spite of overwhelming introspective evidence of mental imagery, its theoretical status remains equivocal. There are many philosophers and psychologists who argue that our experience of imagery is merely an epiphenomenon, or by-product, of other processes of which we may not be aware. There are several other criticisms that have been levelled at the concept of "imagery" over the years, and we consider these in turn.

Critics of imagery theory (e.g., Pylyshyn, 1973) have attacked the notion that the visual images stored in memory resemble mental photographs or pictures. Firstly, this picture metaphor implies that images are perceived in very much the same kind of way as pictures. This is erroneous, because pictures require basic perceptual processing such as figure-ground segregation, whereas images are already highly organised into objects. Secondly, if we forget part of an image, it is not a random fragment that is lost, as would be the case if someone tore off the corner of a picture. Rather, it is a meaningful unit that is lost. Thirdly, if uninterpreted images were stored at random in long-term memory in the same way that holiday photographs are sometimes thrown into a large box, then it would be almost impossible to retrieve a given image when required. In fact, of course, it is usually relatively easy to retrieve desired images.

At a more general level, there are considerations of the various codes involved in information processing. There must be perceptual or visual codes to account for our perceptual abilities, and verbal codes to enable us to transmit and receive verbally encoded messages. According to Pylyshyn (1973), the fact that we can readily translate or exchange information between these two codes (as when we describe a picture) indicates the necessity for postulating some kind of common format or interlingua. The great structural differences between visual and verbal representations preclude a direct translation.

What are the major characteristics of this putative interlingua? Pylyshyn (1973, 1979) and others have argued that the form of representation is propositional. Propositions are abstract, language-like representations that assert facts about the world. They may be more adequate for representing information about the world than are images, because mental pictures do not assert anything, and are thus neither true nor false. If perceptual and verbal information is ultimately translated into this common propositional form, it would apparently be most parsimonious to assume that all information is stored propositionally from the beginning. Thus, it is only necesary to postulate a single form of representation for all information.

A final criticism of the imagery approach was made by Anderson (1978). He argued that it is impossible in principle, to describe unequivocally the form of representation which is actually used to perform a task. He expressed the essence of his position in the following way:

> One must perform tests of the representation in combination with certain assumptions about the processes that use the representation. That is, one must test a representation-process pair. One can show that, given a set of assumptions about an image representation and a set of processes that operate upon it, one can construct an equivalent set of assumptions about a propositional representation and its processes . . . Given any representation-process pair it is possible to construct other pairs with different representations whose behaviour is equivalent to it. These pairs make up for differences in representation by assuming compensating differences in the processes [p. 263].

Since it is always possible to produce a propositional theory that mimics exactly the predictions of a theory that assumes image representations, it follows that there is no compelling reason to propose an imagery theory.

There are several valid counter-arguments that can be made against these criticisms, some of which are put forward by Kosslyn (1980, 1981). The criticisms of the picture-metaphor theory of imagery are essentially attacks on a straw man, because no one subscribes to such a simplistic viewpoint. What most imagery theorists believe is that image representations resemble those that underlie the experience of seeing something, but in the case of imagery these representations are retrieved from long-term memory and do not stem from sensory stimulation. In other words, images are similar to percepts, and thus images share the highly organised structure of most percepts. As a consequence, it is well wide of the mark to berate imagery theorists for postulating the existence of uninterpreted images.

If images are the stored by-products of previous perceptual experiences, and so have an internal organisation, then it is not necessarily true that it would be extremely difficult to access a required image. Words are also meaningful units of information stored in long-term memory, and there is almost complete agreement that they are stored in a highly organised way that facilitates retrieval. There seems to be no good reason why the same should not be true of images.

What about the argument that knowledge can be represented in the form of propositions but not in images? It cannot be argued that the mere possession of propositions in long-term memory constitutes knowledge, otherwise it would be necessary to claim that books are knowledgeable. Whether we are speaking of propositions or images, some processes must operate on them for us to have knowledge. If knowledge is regarded as involving active processes performed on stored representations, then it is not obvious that postulating propositional rather than imaginal representations is of much use. Knowledge can be derived from perceptual experiences, and it can also be derived in similar fashion from mental images.

One of the key criticisms of imagery theory is the notion that the translation between perceptual and verbal codes necessitates an intervening code, or interlingua, incorporating propositional representations. There is a massive difficulty with this argument, as Anderson (1978) pointed out. If all translation between codes requires an intervening code, then we are left with an infinite regress. The translation between the visual or perceptual code and the propositional code requires yet another code (say code X), and the translation between the perceptual code and code X necessitates a further code, and so on *ad infinitum*.

The greatest challenge to imagery theories in recent years has come from propositional theories. It has to be admitted that the notion that there is a single form of internal representation (i.e., propositions) is an intuitively appealing one, since it appears to offer important gains in terms of elegance and parsimony over imagery theory. Moreover, it is indisputably the case that virtually any information can be represented in propositional form, and also that most (or even all) imagery phenomena can be accounted for by means of a formulation postulating only propositional representations.

However, the fact that all empirical findings could potentially be explained by a propositional theory does not, of course, mean that such a theory is necessarily correct. Amongst other problems, current propositional theories lack any strong inherent constraints, and thus often do no more than offer a *post hoc* "explanation" of empirical findings. As a consequence, propositional theories (unlike imagery theories) rarely make interesting predictions about imagery phenomena.

Some of the difficulties with propositional theories can be seen clearly if we consider a concrete example. A visual stimulus (e.g., a letter) is presented at various orientations in its normal or reversed form, and the subject's task is to decide as rapidly as possible whether the stimulus is in its normal or reversed form. The standard finding (see Shepard, 1978, for a review) is that the decision time is a linear function of the extent to which the orientation of the stimulus deviates from the upright. Within an imagery theory, it seems natural to assume that the process operating on the image is time-consuming, and that it gradually changes the orientation of the image until the upright position is reached. A propositional theory could also account for the basic finding by assuming that the stimulus is encoded as one or more propositions, and that a series of small changes is produced in these propositional representations until propositions describing a normal, or a reversed, letter are attained. However, such a theory seems relatively implausible and *post hoc*. It is not clear how the visual stimulus would be represented propositionally, or why rotation is gradual. As Kosslyn and Pomerantz (1977) pointed out, rotation of 180° should be very easy within a propositional account, because the propositions can readily be altered in the appropriate way (e.g., "top" becomes "bottom"; "left" becomes "right"). In fact, 180° rotation produces the longest decision time of all.

There are many other cases in which a propositional theory account seems far less plausible and parsimonious than one stemming from imagery theory. If, for example, verbal and visual stimuli are both stored in the same propositional format, there seems to be no strong reason for assuming that propositions encoding verbal information are stored primarily in the left hemisphere of the brain, whereas propositions encoding visual information are stored mainly in the right hemisphere. In fact, this kind of difference in functioning of the two hemispheres has been found (Cohen, 1977), and is more consistent with the notion of two quite separate forms of processing (i.e., verbal and imaginal).

The two major protagonists in the controversy concerning the theoretical status of imagery (i.e., Kosslyn and Pyslyshyn) both seem to have fallen into the trap of regarding images and propositions as the only possible sorts of representation. This may well be erroneous, but the lack of systematic attempts to identify other forms of representation means that our discussion has necessarily focused on images and propositions.

In sum, attempts to discredit imagery have proved unsuccessful, and it must therefore be concluded that imagery is very much a viable construct. Propositional theories provide the main alternative to imagery theories, but they have by no means demonstrated their superiority. Indeed, explanations of many phenomena in terms of imagery are clearly more adequate than explanations that do not invoke imagery.

IMAGERY AND PERCEPTION

Introduction

The most popular view about imagery is that the process of imaging closely resembles the process of perception. This has the definite advantage that it suggests several testable predictions about imagery, but it poses at least one difficulty that has sometimes gone unrecognised. If, as Neisser (1972) and others have claimed, a visual image is very much like a percept that has been formed in the absence of the appropriate stimulus, why do we not confuse images and percepts? Of course, it is true that we are occasionally confused, as happens in the case of hallucinations, but anyone suffering from many hallucinations is unlikely to remain at liberty for long!

We are still left with the problem of explaining why images and percepts are rarely confused. Part of the reason may be that percepts are usually more detailed and vivid than images. In addition, since percepts depend heavily upon the current stimulus situation, they are typically less susceptible to internal control by the individual than are images. Manipulations such as walking, altering the direction of gaze, or turning the light on, are all likely to affect the quality and content of percepts more than images, and thus provide further ways of distinguishing between percepts and images.

Equivalence

There are various ways of assessing the similarity between perception and imagery. Perhaps the most obvious method is to ask some people to perform a task under perceptual conditions while others do the same task under imagery conditions. A comparison of performance can provide some indication of the functional equivalence of perception and imagery.

A relatively straightforward example of this experimental approach was reported by Finke and Kosslyn (1980). Subjects were initially presented with dots 6, 12, or 18 millimetres apart, and instructed to indicate how far out into the visual periphery the dots could move until it was no longer possible to tell that the dots were separate. This task was performed either by perception or in the imagination. Two fields of vision were tested, the vertical and the horizontal.

The results are shown in Fig. 7.1. Under both perception and imagery conditions, the fields of resolution increased at less than a constant rate as the distance separating the two dots increased. Furthermore, subjects having

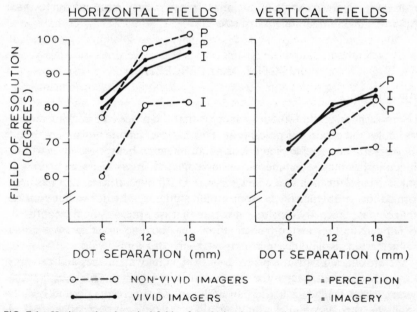

FIG. 7.1   Horizontal and vertical fields of resolution in perception and imagery as a function of dot separation and vividness of imagery. Data from Finke and Kosslyn (1980).

vivid imagery produced fields of resolution in imagery that were remarkably similar in size to the fields of resolution obtained in perception, whereas non-vivid imagers produced fields of resolution in imagery that were somewhat smaller than those obtained in perceptual conditions. Perhaps the most remarkable finding was the overall similarity of the fields of resolution in imagery and in perception: In both cases the fields were elongated along the horizontal axis, and the upper half of the field was larger than the lower half.

On the face of it, these findings indicate a considerable degree of functional equivalence of perception and imagery. However, it is possible that subjects in the imagery condition merely made plausible guesses about the fields of resolution, and did not actually rely on imagery at all. This alternative explanation seems less tenable as a result of further work by Finke (1980) using the same experimental approach of the spaced dots. Subjects were asked to make guesses about the characteristics of the various fields of resolution in imagery conditions. They made several errors, arguing for example that field size would increase in direct proportion to increasing dot separation. They were not aware that perceptual fields of resolution are asymmetrical along the vertical axis. Most of the subjects did guess correctly that the fields would be elliptical in shape, but they greatly exaggerated the actual amount of field eccentricity.

The very different patterns of responses produced by imagery subjects as opposed to those subjects instructed to guess the various fields of resolution in imagery conditons, make it improbable that subjects responding in the imagery condition were merely responding on the basis of guess-work or plausible inferences. This conclusion is strengthened by the fact that there are several other studies in which functional equivalence between perception and imagery has been demonstrated, despite the great complexity of the performance data obtained in perceptual conditions (see Finke, 1980, for a review).

It is a matter of some theoretical significance to distinguish between those situations in which equivalence occurs and those in which it does not. An interesting first step in this direction was reported by Finke (1980). It concerns the McCollough effect, which is produced by asking subjects to view horizontal black bars on a background of one colour in alternation with vertical black bars on a second colour. After this alternation has been viewed for an extended period of time, horizontal and vertical bars presented in the absence of a coloured background appear to be faintly tinged with colours complementary to those observed previously: This is the so-called McCollough effect.

Attempts were made to obtain the McCollough effect in two rather different imagery conditions. When subjects observed the colours but imagined the bar patterns, the normal McCollough effect was obtained.

However, when the bar patterns were presented visually and subjects imagined the colours, there was no McCollough effect. The behavioural differences between the two imagery groups tend to eliminate an explanation in terms of expectation or guessing, and many subjects apparently predicted that the effect would be the opposite of the actual McCollough effect.

The major conclusion drawn by Finke (1980) on the basis of his findings was as follows: "While mental images and physical objects can be functionally equivalent at levels of the visual system where pattern information is processed, such equivalences do not extend to levels where colour information is processed [p. 120]." Colour information is processed at very low levels of the visual system, whereas pattern orientation is processed at higher visual levels. The important implication is that imaginal processes operate at a central level and thus are able to mimic relatively high-level perceptual processes but not more peripheral ones.

Selective Interference

If we asked people to perform a perceptual task and an imagery task at the same time, what would we expect to happen? If, as is commonly assumed, perception and imagery use some of the same processes, then there would be competition for common processing resources leading to interference between the two tasks. Systematic investigation of the amount of interference obtained with different combinations of tasks can even be used to identify the precise combination of processing resources necessitated by any given task (Navon & Gopher, 1979).

The prediction of interference between perceptual and imagery tasks has been supported numerous times. In one of the earliest studies, Segal and Fusella (1970) asked their subjects to perform a visual or auditory detection task after forming a visual or auditory image. They discovered that auditory images interfered more with the detection of auditory signals than with the detection of visual signals, whereas visual images interfered more with the detection of visual signals. Since there was some interference in all conditions, it seems reasonable to conclude that there is a generalised effect of mental imagery upon perceptual sensitivity in addition to a relatively large modality-specific effect.

While the existence of significant interference effects between concurrent perceptual and imagery tasks clearly indicates that the two tasks involve some common processes, it is not always easy to identify these processes. Consider, for example, the task of hearing the locations of digits within a matrix described by means of an auditory message that is either easily visualised or is rather difficult to visualise, and then trying to reproduce the matrix accurately. When this task is combined with pursuit rotor (i.e., tracking a light moving along a circular track), it turns out that performance on the easily visualised messages is greatly impaired, but there is no adverse effect of tracking on the non-visualisable message (Baddeley, Grant, Wight & Thomson, 1975).

Perhaps the most obvious interpretation of these findings is that the pursuit rotor involves visual perception, and it is for this reason that it interferes with performance on the visualisable message. However, further research has revealed that this account is erroneous. The pursuit-rotor task involves both visual and spatial processing, and it seems that the spatial component is the critical one. Baddeley and Lieberman (1980) found that a specifically visual concurrent task (brightness judgements) actually disrupted performance more on the non-visualisable message than the visualisable one. However, the results were very different when a spatial concurrent task with no visual input was used; this involved subjects attempting to point at a moving pendulum while blindfolded, with auditory feedback provided. This auditory tracking task produced a substantial reduction in recall of the visualisable messages, but had little effect on the non-visualisable messages. It thus appears that recall of visualisable messages of the kind used by Baddeley et al. (1975) and by Baddeley and Lieberman (1980) is interfered with by spatial tasks rather than by visual tasks, implying that processing of the visualisable messages relies on spatial rather than visual coding.

The distinction between spatial coding and visual coding is probably of major theoretical significance. Consider the well-known work on mental rotation carried out by Shepard and his colleagues (reviewed by Shepard, 1978). In a typical study (Cooper & Shepard, 1973), alphanumeric characters were presented either in their normal form (e.g., "F") or in reversed, mirror-image form (e.g., "Ⅎ"). The stimulus was presented at various degrees of rotation from the upright, and the task was to decide whether it was normal or reversed. As is shown in Fig. 7.2, the time taken to make a decision was a linear function of the degree of rotation from the upright position of the presented stimulus.

Does this mental rotation involve mainly visually-based coding or spatial processing? Evidence that there is not necessarily a visual component in mental rotation was obtained by Carpenter and Eisenberg (1978). They discovered that blind children who touched a single letter presented in a normal or mirror-image form experienced no particular difficulty in performing the mental rotation task. Furthermore, these children, who had never seen letters, claimed that they twisted the letters around in their minds. Carpenter and Eisenberg concluded that, "mental rotation is an operation that requires a representation with spatial components rather than specifically visual components [p. 124]."

The emphasis in the literature has been very much on the existence of interference effects between perceptual and imagery tasks which occur as a

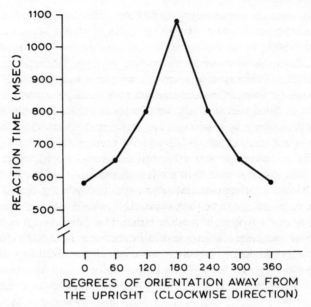

FIG. 7.2   Mean time to decide whether a visual stimulus was in its normal or mirror-image version as a function of orientation. Data from Cooper and Shepard (1973).

result of competition for limited resources which are specific to each sensory modality, e.g. vision, hearing. It is true that the magnitude of the observed interference effect does sometimes depend upon the modality of the inter-fering task (e.g., Segal & Fusella, 1970), but it seems improbable that this is the only relevant factor. In particular, it is plausible to assume that complex perceptual tasks disrupt most imagery tasks to a greater extent than do easy perceptual tasks.

Modality and complexity of the interfering perceptual task were both manipulated by Phillips and Christie (1977). Their subjects had to remember random visual block patterns for a few seconds, a task that apparently involves quasi-visual or imaginal processes. Various tasks were performed during the retention interval. The key finding was that pattern retention was much higher following the reading of a series of visually presented digits than it was after an addition task involving visual or auditory digits. The disruptive effect of the addition task was unaffected by the presentation modality of the digits to be added. In other words, the amount of interference was determined far more by the processing demands of the interpolated task (i.e., reading versus adding) than by stimulus modality (i.e., visual versus auditory).

Phillips and Christie (1977) concluded that imagery and perceptual tasks compete for limited general purpose resources, such as attention or the central executive component of working memory. This certainly accounts for the powerful interfering effect of adding auditory digits on retention of random visual patterns, a finding that is difficult to explain in terms of special modality-specific resources. However, it is premature to argue, as they do, that there is no specific visuo-spatial processing system.

In sum, the selective interference paradigm provides a potentially informative approach to the question of the similarities and dissimilarities between perception and imagery. In practice, it has often proved difficult to interpret the resulting interference effects. It has still not been established whether the effects are due to competition for general resources or for specific ones, although the likelihood is that both kinds of competition occur. Even when it seems likely that a perceptual and an imagery task are competing for the same specific resource, it can be problematical to identify that resource (e.g., visual versus spatial). In spite of these interpretative difficulties, however, the broad sweep of the evidence on selective interference is entirely consistent with the notion that similar cognitive processes are involved in perception and in imagery.

Selective Facilitation

The message that emerges clearly from work on selective interference is that perceptual and imaginal processes can have mutually disruptive effects on each other. Such effects make one wonder about the usefulness of imagery in everyday life: If a major result of imagining is to impair perception, then it might well be more of a hindrance than a help. However, the selective interference studies lack ecological validity—or applicability to real life—in at least one crucially important way, in that the concurrent perceptual and imagery tasks are usually entirely different from each other. In everyday life, the contents of concurrent perceptual and imaginal activities are likely to be very similar to each other, and the consequence is mutual facilitation rather than interference.

How does imagery facilitate perception? According to Neisser (1976), an especially useful form of imagery is the cognitive map, which permits the individual to anticipate the locations of places and objects which have not yet come into view. It is the anticipatory nature of imagery that serves to facilitate perceptual processes; in the words of Neisser (1976):

Imagining is not perceiving, but images are indeed derivatives of perceptual activity. In particular, they are the *anticipatory phases* of that activity, schemata that the perceiver has detached from the perceptual cycle for other purposes ... The experience of having an image is just the inner aspect of a readiness to perceive the imagined object [pp. 130–131].

In Neisser's theoretical conceptualisation there is a very close relationship between perception and imagery. Indeed, perception depends on the interactive effects of information from the external environment and previous knowledge in the form of imagery. This line of reasoning is plausible, and has the great merit of demonstrating that imaginal processing may be far more relevant to everyday cognition than has usually been recognised. However, it would obviously be reassuring if facilitatory effects of imagery on perception could be demonstrated in the laboratory. There are, in fact, numerous studies on perceptual set that illustrate the advantages of forming images that anticipate perceptual information. A simple example concerns the Posner task, in which subjects are presented with two letters one after the other, and must decide whether they are both the same letter of the alphabet. On positive trials the decision time is faster when the second letter is the same size as the imaged letter than when a size discrepancy exists (Hayes, 1973). Presumably when the letters are the same size the image of the first letter provides a more precise and accurate anticipation of the second letter, and this facilitates processing of the second letter.

Kosslyn's Computational Theory

Until fairly recently, most imagery theorists have contented themselves with relatively vague generalisations, such as the assumption that the process of imaging closely resembles the process of perceiving. However, this state of affairs has been remedied somewhat by the recent theorising of Kosslyn (1980, 1981). He has proposed a computational theory of imagery that attempts to spell out in some detail exactly how the process of imagery occurs. Indeed, his theory is sufficiently precise for it to be implemented by means of a computer-simulation model.

At a very general level, what Kosslyn has done is to make use of common ideas about the mind's eye and its ability to inspect mentally visualised scenes. His attempt to produce a comprehensive theory of imagery on this basis is too complex to describe fully here (for that, see Kosslyn, 1980, 1981), but an outline can at least be given. Images are alleged to have two main components: One is the surface representation (a quasi-pictorial representation that occurs in a visual buffer), and the other is the deep representation, which is the information stored in long-term memory that is utilised in the generation of the surface representation.

Our conscious experience of imagery depends on the surface representation. This surface representation occurs in a visual buffer that has only a limited extent (Finke & Kosslyn, 1980), and so can include information from only a limited visual arc. The resolution of the buffer is greatest in the centre, and decreases progressively as the periphery of the buffer is approached

(Finke & Kosslyn, 1980). A further characteristic of the visual buffer is that surface representations within it last for rather short periods of time, and indeed start to decay immediately after they are activated. In attempting to conceptualise the nature of the visual buffer, it may be useful to bear in mind that Kosslyn originally made use of a metaphor in which images were claimed to resemble spatial displays on a cathode ray tube screen. As this metaphor suggests, the basic idea is that surface images preserve the relative positions and distances of all parts of the objects or scenes being imaged.

There are two kinds of deep representations in long-term memory that can form the basis for surface images: literal and propositional. Literal representations provide information about how something looked, rather than what it looked like. These representations are stored in the computer model as lists of co-ordinates that indicate where points should be placed in the visual buffer to form appropriate images of objects or scenes. In contrast, propositional representations consist of lists of abstract propositions that together serve to describe some object or scene.

So far some of the key aspects of Kosslyn's computational theory have been described, but no indication has been given of the processes involved in transforming a deep representation into an appropriate surface image. According to Kosslyn (1981), four processes are involved. The PICTURE process converts the deep literal representation into a surface image within the visual buffer. The FIND process searches the visual buffer looking for a particular object or part of an object. The PUT process "performs a variety of functions necessary to image a part at the correct location on an image [p. 52]." Finally, the IMAGE process is responsible for co-ordinating the activities of the other three processes.

Additional processes need to be invoked if a surface image must be inspected in order to answer some question (e.g., "Which is longer, the distance between a cat's eyes or one end of its mouth and the other?"). The LOOKFOR process makes use of the RESOLUTION process to determine if the surface image is appropriately scaled, adjusts the scale if necessary by means of either the ZOOM process or the PAN process, and then scans to the appropriate location by means of the SCAN process, which moves information through the visual buffer so as to change what is most sharply in focus.

Image transformation typically seems to occur incrementally, and involves the SCAN process. The ZOOM and PAN processes are sometimes used to transform the surface image, and an additional process that serves to alter the orientation of the image is the ROTATE process. It is, of course, this last process that allegedly accounts for the mental rotation findings of Shepard and his colleagues (Shepard, 1978). While incremental image transformation is the norm, it appears that blink transformations are also possible. Blink transformations are discontinuous rather than incremental, and involve letting one image fade and then replacing it with a different image of the same object or scene.

Kosslyn's computational theory has also been used to account for the finding that imagery is sometimes (but not always) used when people are asked question about the visible properties of objects or scenes (Kosslyn & Jolicoeur, 1980). The theory assumes that image encodings are accessed in parallel with propositional ones. If the appropriate propositional encoding is located before the process of imaging is complete, then imagery will not influence the decision process. It follows that imagery will most frequently be used when relevant propositional information is either missing from long-term memory or inaccessible. This agrees with the anecdotal observation that questions referring to things that have not been explicitly learned (e.g., "how many windows are there in your living room?"; "Is a hamster smaller than a mouse?") are answered via the use of imagery, whereas questions with overlearned answers (e.g., "Is a hamster small?") are not.

Kosslyn's computational theory is rather difficult to evaluate because it is virtually the only theory that attempts to provide a comprehensive explanation of imagery phenomena. However, doubts have been expressed about the ways in which conscious experience of imagery is used in the theory. The properties of the visual buffer may correspond to those commonly attributed to the "internal eye," and thus the theory is congruent with our conscious experience. However, it seems probable that the visual buffer merely contains information about the products of prior cognitive processes, and it is not at all clear that introspective evidence can ever shed much light on those cognitive processes and operations. In other words, there is a strong suspicion that Kosslyn's computational theory omits many of the factors underlying image formation, and thus fails to provide a completely explanatory theory of image phenomena.

On the positive side, there is no doubt that Kosslyn's theory, deficient as it is in some respects, provides a more adequate account than any other theory of many findings. For example, the findings on mental rotation reported by Shepard (1978) seem most readily explicable in terms of a manipulable image that can be rotated, and other explanations in contrast seem rather forced and arbitrary. In addition, some of the findings take the notion of a resemblance between perception and imagery, and develop it in exciting ways that have great theoretical significance. For example, the work on fields of resolution by Finke and Kosslyn (1980) demonstrated a great similarity between perception and imagery, and also provided important evidence about the limits of the visual buffer. All in all, Kosslyn's computational theory constitutes a useful first step in the construction of a complete theory of imagery.

Conclusions

The evidence discussed in this chapter seems to demonstrate unequivocally that there is an intimate relationship between perceptual and imaginal processes. However, it should be noted that various interpretations of the data are possible. As Anderson (1978) pointed out, any theory in this area must postulate a form of representation together with processes operating upon that representation. It is possible to explain the similarities between perceptual and "imaginal" processes by assuming that there is a propositional representation in both cases.

Some of the major findings are actually not too difficult to account for in propositional terms. For example, consider modality-specific selective interference effects between a perceptual and an imagery task. These interference effects may result from the greater similarity of the sets of propositions generated by the two concurrent tasks in the same-modality conditions than in the different-modality conditions.

Since imagery and propositional theories can both handle the similarities between perception and imagery that have been discovered, it is obvious that the contrasting theoretical viewpoints must be evaluated on other criteria. As was pointed out earlier in the chapter, matters become rather clearer when theoretical parsimony and plausibility are considered. In terms of those criteria, imagery theories provide more satisfactory explanations of many of the findings than do propositional theories, and so are to be preferred.

PROBLEM SOLVING

Introduction

There is considerable anecdotal evidence that imagery is extensively used in problem solving, but rather few rigorous experimental demonstrations. Many people report that they make use of imagery while performing mental arithmetic calculations, especially when retaining sub-stage results. Skilful chess players often report using visual imagery in considering projected moves. Chess masters are much better than novice players at recalling actual board positions, which suggests superior powers of imagery, but their visual memory for randomly arranged pieces is no better than that of novices (de Groot, 1966). Thus, the expert player may simply rely on a mental library of overall visual patterns of chess positions which facilitate chunking of actual positions, but are of little use with random board positions.

Other kinds of problems almost invariably lead to the reported use of imagery. For example, consider a cube-dicing problem in which a cube, which is painted red on the sides and blue on the top and bottom faces, is

HCP–G*

turned into 27 mini-cubes as a result of two vertical and two horizontal slices; the task is to determine how many of these small cubes have both red and blue faces. Although it seems subjectively obvious that pictorial images are constructed in order to solve this problem, it is difficult to be sure that structural descriptions or propositional representations are not used instead. The same objection can be raised to the claim that working out the number of windows in your house necessarily involves imaginal processes.

In spite of the generally inadequate state of knowledge, there are some problems that have been relatively thoroughly investigated, and in which the role played by imaginal processing has been reasonably well established. Two such problems (syllogistic reasoning and the sentence-picture verification task) are discussed here in some detail.

Syllogistic Reasoning

The role played by imagery in solving various kinds of problems has been a matter of some controversy. The theoretical issues involved can be illustrated with reference to the cognitive processes that are required for transitive inference. This issue has most frequently been investigated in studies of syllogistic reasoning. Syllogistic reasoning is concerned with the conclusions that follow logically from a set of premises or assumptions. Much research on syllogistic reasoning has involved three-term series problems. Two statements and an associated question are presented to the subject (e.g., "Tom is taller than Dick. Harry is taller than Tom. Who is the tallest?"), and the subject has to answer the question as rapidly as possible. According to Huttenlocher (1968), such problems are solved by forming an image of a spatial array which contains the terms of the problem. Thus, in the example given, Tom might be represented by a longer vertical column than Dick, and Harry by an even longer column. The answer can then be "read off" the imaged array.

Huttenlocher's (1968) theory further assumes that the difficulty of any particular three-term series problem depends on the order of the premises. The easiest form of the problem is one in which the first term presented is an end term (e.g., the tallest or shortest individual), and the order of presentation allows the terms to be entered consecutively into the imaged array in a preferred direction (to the right or downwards). In other words, task difficulty is determined primarily by the ease with which an image of the spatial array can be constructed.

In contrast, Clark (1969) proposed a linguistic model to account for performance on three-term series problems. This model incorporated three main principles. Firstly, a premise, such as, "Tom is taller than Dick," is transformed into two internal representations, "Tom is tall" and "Dick is tall," and there is some weighting of the terms so that the information in the premise can be retrieved subsequently. Secondly, the model assumes that the solution is reached more rapidly when there is congruence between the premises and the question. For example, if the premises are "Tom is taller than Dick; Harry is taller than Tom," the question "Who is the tallest?" is congruent, whereas the question "Who is the shortest?" is incongruent. Thirdly, an unmarked comparative adjective is more readily processed than a marked one. Unmarked adjectives, such as, high, deep, and tall, convey only relative position on a scale, whereas marked adjectives (e.g., low, shallow, short) also imply absolute information. For example, "How short is Fred?" contains the implicit assumption that Fred is short, whereas "How tall is Fred?" is appropriate regardless of Fred's actual height.

The evidence is more favourable to the linguistic model than to the imagery theory. The linguistic theory correctly predicts that the presence or absence of congruence between the premises and the question should affect speed of solution. In contrast, the imagery theory cannot account for the congruence effect, because the same imaginal representation is constructed regardless of the form of the premises. According to the imagery account, the premise "Harry is not as tall as Tom" should take longer to process than the premise "Tom is not as short as Harry" because the image has to be constructed in the non-preferred leftward direction. Clark's (1969) linguistic model predicts that the latter premise should be more difficult to process because its comparative adjective is marked. The results usually favour the linguistic model's prediction.

Of course, the fact that the data tend to favour Clark's linguistic model rather than Huttenlocher's imagery model by no means proves that syllogistic reasoning involves linguistic rather than imaginal processing. Alternative versions of the imagery theory can be, and have been, put forward, and predict the data reasonably well. Another interesting possibility is that syllogistic reasoning involves a combination of linguistic and imaginal processes; this suggestion was made by Sternberg (1980), who went on to propose a linguistic-spatial mixed model of transitive inference. According to this model, subjects initially engage in linguistic processing of the verbal information presented in the premises. This is followed by a recoding of the premise information into a mentally-generated spatial array. Further linguistic processes follow during the reading of the question and the preparation of the response.

Sternberg (1980) attempted to decide what kind of processing was occurring by correlating the speed of performance on the various components of the three-term series problem with measures of verbal and spatial ability. There was a correlation of only +.20 between these two abilities, but both correlated with time to solution; the correlations were −.35 and −.49 for verbal ability and spatial ability, respectively. These correlations are consistent with the notion that verbal and spatial-imaginal processes both play a part in syllogistic reasoning.

According to the mixed model, the formation of a spatial array is the major processing operation involving imagery; in line with this assumption, spatial ability correlated more strongly than verbal ability with encoding time (-0.51 and -0.25, respectively). In contrast, the response time was claimed to include several linguistic processes, such as, reading of the question and encoding of relationships expressed by unmarked adjectives; response time correlated -0.30 with verbal ability, but only -0.09 with spatial ability.

The mixed model was further evaluated by comparing its predictive accuracy to that of the linguistic model and of the spatial-imaginal theory. In each of several experiments the mixed model was significantly more accurate than the other two theories (Sternberg, 1980). In an extension of this work, Sternberg and Weil (1980) assigned subjects to linguistic, spatial, or mixed groups on the basis of the theory which best predicted each particular individual's performance. Solution speed correlated with verbal ability but not spatial ability for those subjects whose performance was best predicted by the linguistic model, whereas speed correlated only with spatial ability for subjects in the spatial group. Finally, speed in the mixed group correlated with both verbal and spatial ability. The implication is that there are various processing strategies that can be applied to three-term series problems, and that individuals may differ in the relative importance of verbal-linguistic and spatial-imaginal processes in their preferred strategy.

Sentence-picture Verification Task

The notion that there can be considerable flexibility in the strategies applied to a particular problem is also relevant to the sentence-picture verification task. A simple sentence (e.g., "Plus is above star") is followed by a simple picture (e.g., $\ast$), and the subject's task is to decide whether or not the picture is described by the sentence. It is possible that a verbal strategy is used in which the sentence is retained in memory in verbal form, the pictorial information is transformed into a verbal description, and then the two verbal descriptions are compared. An alternative possibility is that a visual image is formed on the basis of the presented sentence, and this image is then compared with the picture. It should be noted that because there are only two possible pictures (i.e., $\ast$ and $\ast$), a sentence such as "Star is not below plus" can be represented imaginally as $\ast$.

Various verbal and propositional theories have been put forward, all of which agree that the greater linguistic complexity of negative sentences over affirmative sentences means that there is an extra time-consuming processing operation during verification for negative sentences. In contrast, the time to perform the comparison once an image has been produced (i.e., from picture onset to responding) should not be affected by the linguistic structure of the sentence according to the pictorial-spatial theory, because this information is removed from the internal representation when the image is constructed. Thus, verbal-linguistic theories assume that most of the complex processing operations occur at the comparison or verification stage, whereas the major processing requirement in the imagery theory occurs during sentence comprehension (i.e., transforming the sentential information into an imaginal representation).

MacLeod, Hunt, and Mathews (1978) applied the linguistic model of Carpenter and Just (1975) to the data of their subjects. They discovered that the model accounted well for the performance of 43 subjects, but provided a poor fit to the data of a further 16 subjects. The pattern of performance was radically different in the two groups. In particular, the large difference between affirmative and negative sentences in the well-fit group totally disappeared in the poor-fit group.

MacLeod et al. (1978) argued that the insensitivity of the poor-fit subjects' performance to linguistic factors suggested that they had used a pictorial or imagery strategy. Furthermore, the poor-fit subjects carried out the actual comparison between the sentence and the picture much more rapidly than the well-fit subjects, presumably because they did not have to convert the visual information of the picture into a propositional form. In contrast, the poor-fit subjects took almost a second longer than the well-fit subjects to process the sentence, presumably because they had to convert the sentence information into an imaginal representation.

Is it not rather speculative to assume that the well-fit subjects made use of a verbal-linguistic strategy and the poor-fit subjects used a pictorial-imagery strategy? Additional support for these assumptions was reported by MacLeod et al. (1978). When verification times were correlated with verbal ability, with spatial ability held constant statistically, the correlation was a highly significant $-.44$ for the well-fit group but a trivial $-.05$ for the poor-fit group. On the other hand, when verification times were correlated with spatial ability, and verbal ability was held constant, the correlation was $-.64$ for the poor-fit group compared to only $+.07$ for the well-fit group.

A further method of testing the idea that quite separate verbal-linguistic and pictorial-imagery strategies are used by the well-fit and poor-fit subjects was introduced by Mathews, Hunt, and MacLeod (1980). They explicitly instructed their subjects to use either a pictorial or a linguistic strategy, and discovered that the performance pattern of those told to use the pictorial strategy closely resembled that of the poor-fit subjects, whereas the performance pattern of the subjects instructed to use the linguistic strategy approximated to that of the well-fit subjects.

In sum, there is impressive evidence that the sentence-picture verification task can be performed by means of at least two qualitatively different processing strategies. It seems probable that one of these strategies involves verbal-linguistic-propositional processing, whereas the other relies heavily on pictorial or imaginal processing. If two radically different strategies can be used to solve a task presented under highly controlled laboratory conditions, then it is likely that flexibility of processing is the rule rather than the exception under the less controlled circumstances of everyday life.

MEMORY

Eidetic Imagery

Some individuals appear to experience a particularly vivid form of visual imagery that closely resembles perceptual experience. It is known popularly as photographic memory, but the technical term is eidetic imagery. In some of the early studies there was evidence that the incidence of eidetic imagery decreased during childhood, perhaps because it reflects an early stage of development in which perception and imagery are not distinct processes. There were also early suggestions from cross-cultural research that a higher proportion of people from primitive than from advanced societies demonstrate eidetic imagery. This difference was originally believed to reflect the replacement of eidetic imagery by language and abstract modes of thought in western societies. Later work revealed that the apparent incidence of eidetic imagery depends critically on the criteria used to define it, and the extremely variable findings from different studies are not indicative of any clear links between eidetic imagery and age or cultural sophistication (Gray & Gummerman, 1975).

The most common method of investigating eidetic imagery involves presenting a picture for inspection, removing the picture, and then eliciting a verbal description of the picture. It has been claimed that there are various consistent features of the descriptions given by eidetikers. These include reporting that the picture can still be seen; a high degree of confidence in the report; use of the present tense; considerable accuracy; and a pattern of eye movements corresponding to the features being reported. People classified as eidetikers often fail to fulfil all of these criteria, and it has sometimes been reported that there is no correlation between accuracy and the presence of the other indicators of eidetic ability (Leask, Haber, & Haber, 1969). When reasonably stringent criteria are used, the incidence of eidetic imagery is approximately 5% in normal children, and probably lower in adults.

The method described above is not beyond reproach. Certain aspects of subjects' reports (e.g., the use of the present or past tense) can obviously be influenced by the precise nature of the questions posed by the experimenter, and it is an unsatisfactory method because there are no necessary and sufficient criteria for eidetic imagery. A more objective approach is to construct two stimuli in such a way that the fusion of one stimulus with the image of the other produces a configuration not predictable from knowledge of either stimulus on its own. This superimposition method was used with dramatic effect by Stromeyer and Psotka (1970). They made use of computer-generated Julesz patterns, consisting of pairs of patterns constructed by blackening cells of 100×100 matrices so that simultaneous binocular viewing produced perception of a single random-dot figure with a square floating in front of the background. The complexity of these patterns precludes ascertaining the identity of the floating figure with binocular fusion.

Stromeyer and Psotka (1970) discovered a 23-year-old teacher called Elizabeth who could fuse two 100×100 matrices even when there was an interval of 24 hours between the presentation of the two stimuli. This finding implies that she must have retained nearly all of the information in the complex and virtually meaningless pattern that was presented first. In further experiments, patterns made up of one million dots were used, and these too could be fused at intervals of up to four hours.

Elizabeth's performance is certainly striking, but it appears to be unique. When the superimposition method has been used with gifted mnemonists, apparent eidetikers, or normal samples, the findings have nearly always been negative. This is the case even though much simpler patterns than those of Stromeyer and Psotka (1970) have generally been used, and the interval between the two stimuli has been considerably shorter.

In sum, research on eidetic imagery has proved somewhat disappointing. The indications are that the original notion that eidetic imagery is qualitatively different from other forms of imagery is erroneous. It is far more likely that eidetic imagery is the same as the imagery normally involved in picture memory, perhaps differing only in vividness. This conclusion is supported by the virtual failure of the superimposition method to reveal any eidetic imagery, and by the lack of any criteria for performance on the picture-description task that are unique to eidetic imagery.

Visual Memory

There have been numerous studies of the long-term retention of visual stimuli, such as pictures. A major issue has been whether or not visual memory differs from verbal memory in important ways. Evidence to suggest that there may be significant differences comes from a comparison of the levels of long-term memory performance: Pictures seem to be much better remembered than words. For example, when 2560 pictures were presented over a number of days, approximately 90% of them were identified correctly on a subsequent test of memory (Standing, Conezio, & Haber, 1970).

Two rather different interpretations of the superiority of pictures over words in long-term memory have been advanced by Paivio (1971). According to the image-superiority hypothesis, imaginal processing is inherently more memorable than verbal processing, and pictures are more likely than words to be processed imaginally. One of the possible reasons for the superiority of imaginal processing is the wealth of detail available in pictures but absent from words. However, Nelson, Metzler, and Reed (1974) found no differences between photographs and unembellished line drawings of the main themes of the photographs in recognition memory. In contrast, the dual-coding or coding-redundancy hypothesis argues that pictures are better remembered than words because they are more likely to be processed both verbally and imaginally. As a consequence, pictorial information can be retrieved either via the verbal code or the imaginal code, and the loss of one code during the retention interval does not necessarily preclude retrieval.

The two hypotheses often make the same predictions, but they do differ with respect to the predicted level of retention when pictures cannot be processed satisfactorily at the verbal level. The image-superiority hypothesis appears to predict that pictures will still be well remembered, whereas the dual-coding hypothesis predicts a relatively low level of retention. Most of the available evidence conforms to the prediction of the dual-coding hypothesis. When concrete words and pictures are presented so rapidly that the pictures cannot be named or labelled, and the concrete words cannot produce imagery, there is no difference in either free recall or recognition memory between the two kinds of stimulus material (Paivio & Csapo, 1969).

In a study by Wiseman and Neisser (1974), subjects were presented with Mooney pictures, which consist of relatively unstructured arrays formed by deleting the contours of a naturalistic scene. These pictures were recognised only when they were interpreted at the time of the original presentation and then evoked the same interpretation during the recognition test. In other words, pictorial stimuli are only well remembered under certain circumstances, suggesting that there is not necessarily any intrinsic memorial superiority associated with the use of imagery.

The dual-coding hypothesis is also supported by studies reviewed by Richardson (1980) in which memory for pictures was compared under conditions where subjects were or were not explicitly instructed to name the objects represented in the pictures. Labelling instructions typically enhanced both recall and recognition, indicating that a combination of imaginal and verbal processing improves subsequent long-term retention.

Perhaps the most crucial assumption of the dual-coding hypothesis is that there is functional independence of the verbal and imaginal codes operating in human memory. It is rather difficult to obtain definitive evidence for or against such a general assumption, but an interesting attempt to do so was reported by Paivio and Csapo (1973). Words and pictures were presented, and some of them were repeated. In the condition of greatest interest, items were presented once as words and once as pictures. If words and pictures are stored as entirely independent codes, then the probability (P) of recalling items presented in both verbal ((w) and pictorial (p) form can be calculated from the recall data for once-presented items, using the following formula: $P_{pw} = P_p + P_w - P_p P_w$. As predicted by this independence hypothesis, repetitions which pictured previously named objects or which named previously pictured objects were additive in their effects (actual recall = 57%; predicted recall from formula = 59%). In contrast, picture-picture and word-word repetitions produced lower recall performance than would be expected on the basis of independent effects.

Paivio and Csapo (1973) reported a further experiment in which steps were taken to limit the processing of pictures to imaginal coding and that of words to verbal coding. Recall of pictures was almost twice as high as that of words (16% versus 9%). Overall, then, the findings of Paivio and Csapo support both the dual-coding and image-superiority hypotheses, and they suggest (Paivio & Csapo, 1973) that it would be wrong to regard the two hypotheses as mutually exclusive: "Picture superiority under standard free recall conditions can best be explained in terms of an additive contribution of imaginal and verbal memory codes, with the contribution of the former being decidedly greater than that of the latter [p. 200]."

In sum, there is reasonable evidence that verbal and visual or imaginal memory codes can be distinguished in studies of long-term memory. However, it is disappointing that more penetrating questions have not been investigated systematically. We know relatively little about these memory codes, other than the fact that they differ, and it is surely desirable in future to attempt to delineate their characteristics in some detail.

8 Language

Language plays a central role in all our lives. Without language, there would be no conversations, no books, no newspapers, and no radio. There are many who also argue that thought itself would be improverished in the absence of language. Language is also of great cultural significance, because it is largely through language that knowledge is recorded and subsequently transmitted from one generation to the next.

Language is vitally involved in various psychological processes ranging from reading and listening to writing and speaking. It is manifestly impossible to deal with all of the aspects of language within the compass of this book, and so what is covered in this chapter consists of some of the most interesting topics in the broad field of language. Additional aspects of language are dealt with in other chapters: the role of the articulatory loop in reading (Chapter 4); learning from prose (Chapter 5); language acquisition in children (Chapter 9); and retarded reading development in children (Chapter 9). Fuller discussions of the psychology of language can be found elsewhere in various places, including the following: Arbib, Caplan and Marshall (1982); Clark and Clark (1977); and Paivio and Begg (1981).

In view of the enormous significance of language to human behaviour, it is very puzzling that it was almost totally neglected as a topic for study during the first half century or more of experimental psychology. Indeed, it was only as a result of the activities of non-psychologists that psychologists began to address themselves seriously to the systematic investigation of language. How can we account for the earlier neglect? Part of the reason was probably because the Behaviourist and neo-Behaviourist approach that held sway for so long was ill-suited to the task of explaining language phenomena. This can be seen if we consider the most thorough attempt to provide a Behaviourist theory of language, that of Skinner (1957). In essence, he tried to explain the acquisition of language primarily in terms of reinforcement principles. Those utterances of the young child that are rewarded or reinforced become progressively stronger. Skinner also emphasised the notion of stimulus control, with utterances increasingly being produced in appropriate situations only.

Chomsky (1959) showed decisively what a threadbare theory of language acquisition Skinner had proposed. In real life, it is often extremely difficult or even impossible to identify the reinforcing events allegedly producing language learning. At the age of three, my daughter Fleur would lie in bed early in the morning singing or talking to herself, and she in common with her brother William babbled a lot when very young. In order to account for such phenomena, Skinner was forced to rely heavily on the notion of "automatic self-reinforcement." This can account for these phenomena in a *post hoc* manner, but lacks explanatory power. Skinner's emphasis on the individual's reinforcement history seems to imply that an individual would not reply appropriately to the challenge, "Your money or your life," unless he had experienced a past history of being killed (and thus been negatively reinforced)!

Detailed analysis of the language behaviour of young children provides further damaging evidence against a reinforcement theory of language acquisition. For example, Brown, Cazden and Bellugi (1969) observed the interactions between middle-class American parents and their young children. Their key finding was that parents reinforce the speech of their children on the basis of its accuracy or truth rather than the grammar used. According to Skinner, this training should produce adults whose speech is very truthful but ungrammatical; in fact, as we all know to our cost, the speech of most adults is grammatical but not notably truthful.

Nineteen fifty-seven was a landmark year for students of language. In addition to Skinner's work, a very different approach to language by Chomsky saw the light of day. Chomsky (1957, 1965) proposed a theory of language from the perspective of a linguist. Only some of the theory's highlights will be presented here (Greene, 1972, has written an excellent account of Chomsky's ideas). Chomsky, like most linguists, was intrigued by the fact that an infinite number of utterances is possible in any language, but that these utterances are nevertheless systematic and organised in various ways. It is an important aim of linguistics to produce a set of rules that will simultaneously take account of the productivity and the regularity of language. Such a set of rules is commonly referred to as a grammar, and, ideally, a grammar should be able to generate all of the permissible sentences in a given language, while at the same time rejecting all of the unacceptable sentences.

Chomsky's (1957, 1965) attempts to wrestle with these problems culminated in his transformational grammar. As with many other linguistic systems, this grammar distinguished between the syntax, the phonology, and the semantics of language. Syntax is concerned with the rules specifying what strings of words are structurally and propositionally well formed. Phonology deals with rules for moving from the phrases comprising a sentence to the appropriate sounds. Finally, semantics refers to the rules that determine how meaning is assigned to well-formed sentences.

A further important distinction emphasised by Chomsky was that between the surface structure and the deep structure of a sentence. The surface structure involves a hierarchical division of a sentence into units usually known as phrases. A surface analysis can be used to clarify certain ambiguities. For the ambiguous sentence, "They are cooking apples," there are two possible surface-structure representations, in one of which "cooking" is part of the same phrase as "apples," and in the other of which "cooking" is part of the verb. However, such analyses do not serve to resolve ambiguities in other sentences. In the sentence, "Visiting relatives can be boring," "visiting" modifies "relatives" irrespective of whether the meaning is that it is sometimes tedious to go to see relatives or that relatives who come on a visit can be boring. However, the two meanings of this and other sentences are distinguished in the deep structure. Whereas the surface structure involves the actual phrases used in a sentence, deep structure refers to the phrases in an underlying hypothetical word string. According to Chomsky, the deep structure reflects the meaning of a sentence more directly than does the surface structure. Different deep structures can be changed into the same surface structure by means of transformation rules that specify how surface structures are to be derived from deep structures.

The value of postulating a deep structure in addition to a surface structure can be seen if we consider the following two sentences: "The man wrote the book," and "The book was written by the man." The meaning of those two sentences is obviously very similar, but the surface-structure representations of the sentences do not accurately reflect that fact. In contrast, the similarity of meaning is made manifest in the deep-structure representations.

Chomsky's ideas were greeted enthusiastically by many psychologists at first, but there has been a marked waning of interest in recent years. Why should this be so? Firstly, Chomsky was primarily concerned with linguistic competence, i.e., the abstract knowledge that people possess about a language, rather than with linguistic performance. In real life, people often speak ungrammatically, and they sometimes totally misinterpret linguistic communications. Psychologists are naturally eager to explore these deficiencies, but Chomsky's lack of interest in linguistic performance means that his theoretical ideas are of little value in this connection.

Secondly, the emphasis in the transformational grammar is on syntax rather than semantics. The deep structure is at the centre of Chomsky's theoretical formulation, with both meaning and sound deriving from it. The deep structure itself forms part of the syntax, with meaning being assigned to it only after the deep structure has been generated. Of course, psychologists recognise the importance of syntax in language comprehension and production, but they feel that meaning is even more important. The starting point in language production is presumably some meaning that the language user wishes to convey, and the goal of comprehension is to understand the meaning of what has just been listened to or read.

Thirdly, there is an increasing realisation that the psycholinguistic tradition of considering the sentence in isolation from the context in which it is spoken or read is far too limited. When attempting to understand a speaker's sentence, we make use of any relevant stored knowledge, the previous utterances of the speaker, our assessment of his character, and so on. For example, the sentence, "I am not a crook," may well be interpreted differently if spoken by the Archbishop of Canterbury rather than by Ex-President Richard Nixon. Contextualist notions of this kind have been proposed by Jenkins (1974) and by Bransford (1979), and are considered at greater length later in the chapter.

Nowadays there are several theories of language, none of which is held in the universal esteem that was once given to Chomsky's views. Some contemporary theories of language are discussed in the pages that follow, but a recent influential approach that contrasts vividly with that of Chomsky will be mentioned briefly at this point. A number of theorists, such as Wanner, Winograd, Minsky and Johnson-Laird, have argued that artificial intelligence can make a significant contribution to our understanding of the psychology of language. In essence, the claim is that aspects of computer functioning closely resemble aspects of the human use of language. More specifically, it has been suggested (e.g., Johnson-Laird, 1977) that someone listening to a spoken message typically does the equivalent of compiling a corresponding program in his or her own internal language. In other words, the process of comprehension of language by humans can, at least in principle, be mimicked by the construction or compilation of a computer program. Sometimes, as in the case of Johnson-Laird's (1977) semantic transition network, the computer system is designed to produce sentences as well as to understand them.

The most obvious advantage (from a psychologist's point of view) of the computational approach over the Chomskian one is that the emphasis is strongly on the processes involved in language comprehension and production. Although Chomsky has had very little to say about linguistic processes, it is imperative for the computational theorist to have explicit and precise assumptions about such processes when constructing his or her programs. However, virtually all of the existing programs in this area deal with a very limited universe of discourse. For example, the computer program of Steedman and Johnson-Laird (1977) was equipped only to answer questions about "particles" moving to and fro. It remains unclear whether it will be possible for the computational approach to match the generality of application that was a key feature of Chomsky's theorising.

Trenchant criticisms of the entire artificial intelligence approach to language were levelled by Dresher and Hornstein (1977). They argued that it was unscientific, because it failed to produce any general theoretical principles. According to them:

> The purported explanations being advanced are not really explanations at all. More specifically, in practically every case, the accounts given are, at best, based on programmes or plans for programmes which simply presuppose the very phenomena which they are meant to explain. Thus, at the very heart of these programmes lie the most idiosyncratic facts concerning the limited domains dealt with.... Lacking general principles, this work cannot contribute to the articulation of a scientific theory of language [pp. 379–380].

I think that Dresher and Hornstein (1977) are no more than partially correct in their criticisms. They are right to point out that workers in artificial intelligence have been relatively unconcerned about general linguistic principles. However, it seems probable that the attempt to construct programs that will mimic human language processes will ultimately produce substantial dividends in terms of clarifying issues and resolving theoretical controversies.

Our discussion of the theories of Skinner, Chomsky, and artificial intelligence researchers has highlighted the diversity of theoretical approaches to language. This diversity will become more apparent during the rest of this chapter when we consider linguistic processing from various different angles.

IS LANGUAGE UNIQUE TO MAN?

A comparison of humans and other species indicates that one of the most important differences lies in the power and adaptability of the natural communication systems available to us but denied to all other species. The fact that other species do not possess language does not necessarily mean that they are incapable of acquiring it, and several researchers have endeavoured in recent years to teach apes the rudiments of language. This attempt has some theoretical interest. According to Skinner (1957), spoken language is learned in very much the same way as other responses, i.e., only those utterances that are rewarded or reinforced tend to be strengthened. As a consequence, there is nothing special about language, and thus there is no reason why language should not be learned by other species.

In contrast, Chomsky (1957, 1965) has claimed that language is a unique system. It cannot be acquired by other species, because language learning can only occur in organisms possessing various innate linguistic mechanisms. Man is the only species to have such innate mechanisms, according to

Chomsky, and they form a part of the so-called "language-acquisition device."

We can only decide whether or not apes have succeeded in acquiring language if we have some criteria for defining language. Hockett (1960) proposed a large number of such criteria. One criterion was semanticity, i.e., the units or words of a language must have meaning. Another criterion was arbitrariness, i.e., there must be an arbitrary connection between the form or sound of the units or words and their meaning. Two further important criteria were displacement, which means that language is produced in the absence of any direct controlling stimuli, and prevarication, which refers to the ability to tell lies and jokes. Finally, there are the crucial criteria of productivity, iteration, and recursion. Productivity means that an infinite number of different expressions is possible within the language. Iteration refers to the possibility of adding units or words to the ends of sentences to create new sentences (e.g., "He wrote a book"; "He wrote a book to earn some money"; "He wrote a book to earn some money to go on holiday"; "He wrote a book to earn some money to go on holiday in Provence"). Recursion is the capacity to embed one phrase or sentence within a second phrase or sentence (e.g., "He wrote his book"; "He wrote a letter before starting on his book"; "He wrote a letter explaining why he had made that decision before starting on his book").

Most of Hockett's criteria seem sensible, but some anomalies appear if these criteria are applied stringently. For example, written human language does not qualify as a language, because it fails three of the criteria that we have not mentioned so far: broadcast transmission and directional reception; rapid fading; and use of a vocal-auditory channel. It would obviously be ludicrous to argue that someone who loses the use of his or her vocal chords through illness has thereby lost the ability to use language.

Let us turn to the success (or otherwise) of attempts to provide apes (mainly chimpanzees) with language. The earliest efforts were rather farcical. They involved trying to persuade apes to talk as we do. Countless hours of patient teaching produced the meagre outcome of three or four barely recognisable English words. The human's vocal apparatus is specifically designed to permit speech, whereas that of the ape is not; therefore the almost total lack of success of this approach should come as no surprise.

The big breakthrough came in 1966 when the Gardners began teaching American Sign Language to a 1-year-old female chimpanzee. They called her Washoe after the name of the county in Nevada where they lived. After 4 years of fairly intensive training, Washoe had acquired a vocabulary of 132 signs, she was able to produce novel combinations of as many as five signs, and she was also able to initiate conversation. Furthermore, she combined some signs in a consistent order (e.g., she was more likely to sign "baby mine" than "mine baby" and "tickle me" than "me tickle"), which has been taken as evidence that Washoe had learned some of the rudiments of grammar.

Washoe had other achievements to her credit. She apparently showed semantic generalisation in her application of signs to new examples. Thus, she originally acquired the sign "open" with reference to a door, but she then used the sign in the presence of cupboards, drawers, and boxes. Young human children often over-generalise, and will, for example, embarrass their parents by calling the milkman and the postman "Daddy." Washoe showed the same tendency. She learned the sign "hurt" when looking at a scratch, but subsequently used it when she saw a tattoo mark and her teacher's navel.

There was modest evidence of displacement in Washoe's signing. She did on occasion refer to objects even when they were not physically present (e.g., "Allgone cup"; "More milk"). The best-known anecdote concerning Washoe's mastery of language apparently demonstrates that she possessed the additional ability to create new meanings by recombining the signs she had learned. She was asked, "What that?", in the presence of a swan, and replied "water bird."

Washoe's accomplishments have convinced many people that she has acquired language. Is this a reasonable conclusion? Not necessarily, and there are several reasons for caution. Firstly, there is the danger of anthropomorphising, i.e., of interpreting the behaviour of Washoe in human terms. Even if Washoe produced some of the same signs as a deaf person who has been taught American Sign Language, it would still be hazardous to assume that the signs had the same significance or meaning for ape and man. Secondly, many of Washoe's signs are the same as gestures and behaviour patterns which are observed to occur naturally in apes. These include "tickle" (signed by tickling), "hug" (signed by hugging), "pick" (signed by picking a part of the anatomy), and "scratch" (signed by scratching). A comparison between the gestural repertoire of Washoe and untrained apes would undoubtedly reveal that Washoe's achievement is less striking than is commonly assumed. Thirdly, it is highly misleading to claim that Washoe even partially mastered American Sign Language. Signs in American Sign Language are defined in terms of four parameters (hand configuration, movement, orientation, and location), but the Gardners consistently focused only on hand configurations.

What about Washoe's apparent grasp of syntax as revealed by her consistent ordering of combinations of signs? A very simple explanation of this pattern of behaviour was offered by Terrace, Petitto, Sanders and Bever (1979), who carried out a detailed analysis of the behaviour displayed by Washoe in the film "Teaching Sign Language to the Chimpanzee: Washoe." Washoe produced a total of 35 multi-sign sequences; all of them were preceded by a similar utterance or a prompt from the teacher, so that her consistent ordering of signs may be an indication of imitative behaviour rather than mastery of grammar.

The most scientific attempt to teach sign language to an ape was made by Terrace (1979). He and his co-workers tried to teach American Sign Language to a chimpanzee called Nim Chimpsky (a rather feeble pun on Noam Chomsky). Between 18 and 35 months, Nim was observed by his teachers signing over 19,000 utterances consisting of two or more signs, and within this huge total there were 5235 different combinations. Analysis of the two-sign combinations consisting of a transitive verb and "me" or "Nim" showed that Nim chose the verb-first order 83% of the time (e.g., "tickle Nim" rather than "Nim tickle").

The above finding suggests that there was a definite structure to Nim's utterances, just as there is with children's expressions. There was another similarity between Nim's utterances and those of children. When children are starting to produce two-word combinations, approximately 80% of their utterances belong to eight semantic categories. Two of these categories are action + object (e.g., "eat grape") and object + beneficiary (e.g., "food Nim"). Terrace discovered that 84% of Nim's two-sign combinations fitted these eight semantic categories.

Thus far, it looks as if Nim's expressions were strikingly similar to those of young children. However, closer examination suggests a very different conclusion. Children initially produce utterances containing about one and a half words on average, but this rapidly escalates to an average of four words or more per utterance. In contrast, the average length of Nim's utterances remained remarkably constant at approximately one and a half signs throughout the period between 26 and 46 months. Children's longer expressions typically convey much more information than their shorter ones, but those of Nim did not. Most of Nim's three-sign combinations simply added emphasis to what he might sign in a two-sign combination. This can be seen very clearly if we consider Nim's most frequent three-sign combinations, which were as follows: "play me Nim," "eat me Nim," "eat Nim eat," and "tickle me Nim." Precisely the same uninformativeness characterised Nim's most popular four-sign combinations: "eat drink eat drink," "eat Nim eat Nim," "banana Nim banana Nim," and "drink Nim drink Nim." Shakespeare it isn't!

Videotapes of interactions between Nim and his teachers revealed other differences between the language behaviour of Nim and human children. Seventy-one percent of Nim's utterances began while his teacher was still signing, so that Nim interrupted his teachers much more frequently than most children interrupt their parents. This suggests that Nim was not really interested in having a genuine conversation with his teachers. Among children just starting to talk, under 20% of their utterances consist of imitations of their parents' expressions, and approximately 30% of their utterances are spontaneous and not merely a response to an adult. The corresponding figures for Nim were very different. Some 40% of his signings were imitations of what his teacher had just signed, and only 10% of his signings were spontaneous. It must be concluded that Nim used language in a significantly less creative and innovative manner than even very young human children.

The findings from studies of apes taught sign language have usually been over-interpreted. Several of the criteria for language (e.g., iteration, recursion, productivity, and displacement) have either not been demonstrated, or the evidence for their existence is weak. At the most general level, much of what appears to be the strongest evidence that apes' signings reflect a partial mastery of language is amenable to simpler, non-linguistic explanations. It is hard to disagree with the conclusions drawn by Seidenberg and Petitto (1979):

> What is required in the ape signing literature . . . is evidence that the apes' production is not merely imitative, that they can produce or comprehend signs in non-stereotypic situations, that sign production or comprehension is not exclusively a function of cuing by non-linguistic aspects of the environment, or the teacher's behaviour, or the structure of a particular test, and that their behaviour is not merely the routinised, inflexible, over-learned product of intensive and specific training [p. 207].

There have been other attempts to teach language to apes which have not involved sign language. The best known was that of Premack (1976), who developed an artificial language in which the words consisted of coloured plastic shapes that could be attached to a magnetic board. This artificial language was taught to an ape called Sarah. She made significant progress, but the fact that she was raised in rather unnatural laboratory conditions meant that she did not use language in spontaneous social situations in the way that Washoe and Nim sometimes did.

One of the advantages of Premack's method of teaching language over that based on signing is that it reduces the short-term memory load associated with relatively long utterances. Perhaps as a result, Sarah showed evidence of having developed language to a greater extent than Washoe. For example, Sarah had some understanding of the relationship between the symbols she manipulated and the objects they represented. When she was asked to indicate the attributes of the blue chip (which was the symbol for an apple), Sarah selected "red" and "round," which were the same attributes she assigned to the fruit itself. Sarah also appeared to understand the significance of word order in expressions such as, "Red on Green" and "Green on Red", when they were used to describe the relative positions of two coloured cards. She was able to arrange the cards to correspond to a sentence, and to construct a sentence describing the arrangement of the cards.

Among Sarah's other accomplishments were the ability to replace the question mark in sentences of the form "A same as A?" with the symbol for "Yes", and to replace it with "No" in sentences such as "A not same as A?" In a sentence such as "A is ? to B," she inserted the "not same as" symbol in place of the question mark. Furthermore, she exhibited a success rate of approximately 80% when presented with further sentences of the same basic form but incorporating new lexical items. Finally, she responded appropriately to sentences such as "If Sarah take apple then Mary give chocolate" and "If Sarah take apple then Mary not give chocolate," and she then transferred this lexical format successfully to different sentences of the same form.

It is clear that Sarah has acquired a set of relatively complex skills, but it is arguable whether these should be regarded as language acquisition. In striking contrast to the young child, Sarah's use of "language" almost totally lacks inventiveness, and she never acquired a new syntactic form without receiving considerable training. Thus, there was no real evidence of the productivity, iteration, and recursion which Hockett (1960) regarded as important criteria for defining language.

If someone taught a chimpanzee to arrange coloured chips in the order red, blue, yellow, and green to obtain food, few people would regard that as indicative of language acquisition. If the teacher argued that red was the symbol for "please," blue was the symbol for "give," yellow for "me," and green for "food," then one might feel tempted to regard that as evidence that the chimpanzee had mastered some elements of language. However, it is not really clear in either case that the chimpanzee is using language. The overall impression from Sarah's behaviour is that it resembles that of the hypothetical chimpanzee described above; in other words, Sarah has become reasonably adapt at playing a relatively complicated board game, but she has signally failed to develop langue as a medium of communication and thought.

In sum, it seems probable that there is less here than meets the eye. There is much evidence consistent with the notion that apes have acquired language, but that evidence can be explained more simply. Even those who believe that apes have been able to acquire language must admit that there is little or no evidence of linguistic criteria such as productivity, displacement, iteration, and recursion in the behaviour of any of the specially trained apes, and thus they cannot be said to have learned a fully-fledged language. Of course, human children typically require several years of language training to master all of the properties of language, and so it could be argued that any linguistic deficiencies in the utterances of the trained chimpanzees could have been eliminated with further training. However, this argument is much weakened by the fact that Nim showed remarkably little language development during the last two years of intensive language training he received. As of now, the safest conclusion must be that language in its complete form is unique to man.

LANGUAGE AND THOUGHT

One of the most intriguing puzzles in cognitive psychology concerns the relationship between language and thought. There is reasonable agreement that language and thought are closely related in most adults, but there has been much controversy as to whether thought determines language, or language determines thought.

The Behaviourists, as might have been expected, came up with an engagingly simple answer to the problem of the relationship between language and thought. They tended to equate the two, and Watson even claimed that thinking was merely sub-vocal speech. It is true that there are often signs of sub-vocal speech when someone is attempting to solve a problem, but it was always implausible to assume that thinking is nothing but sub-vocal speech. As the philosopher Herbert Feigl pertinently remarked, Watson "made up his windpipe that he had no mind." If evidence were required to refute Watson's position, it was provided in a rather dangerous study carried out by Smith, Brown, Toman and Goodman (1947). Smith was given a curare derivative that paralysed his entire musculature, and he had to be kept alive by means of an artificial respirator. This temporary paralysis prevented him from engaging in sub-vocal speech or any other bodily movement, and so should have rendered him incapable of thought. In fact, he reported later that he had been able to observe what was going on around him, to comprehend other people's speech, and to think about these events while in the paralysed state.

The best-known theory about the interrelationship of language and thought was put forward by Benjamin Lee Whorf (1956). He was a fire prevention engineer for an insurance company who spent his spare time working in linguistics. According to his hypothesis of linguistic relativity, language determines or strongly influences thinking. To begin with, there are significant differences among the world's languages. The Hanuxoo people in the Philippines have 92 names for different varieties of rice, the Eskimoes have dozens of words to describe different snow and ice conditions, and there are hundreds of camel-related words in Arabic. It is possible, but unlikely, that these differences influence thought. A more plausible explanation is that different environmental conditions affect the things that people think about, and these come to be reflected in linguistic usage.

It is natural to suppose that one's native language is free of peculiarities, but that is not true. English, in common with several other European languages, makes use of a subject-predicate structure, and this leads its speakers to objectify abstractions. For example, we say that "It is raining" or "It is sunny," but what does the "it" refer to? In numerous other languages, such meanings would be expressed as "raining now" or "sunny now." Of course, the crucial question (and the one that is difficult to answer) is whether this feature of the English language actually affects the way in which we think.

It is extremely difficult to submit the Whorfian hypothesis to direct experimental test. However, one of the implications of the hypothesis is that any group of people whose language development is retarded should show evidence of impaired thought. The deaf, for the most part, constitute a group with retarded language, although they do differ considerably in the extent of the retardation. As the result of much research, Furth (1966) concluded that the deaf perform at a lower level than the hearing on cognitive tasks which normally involve language, but that there is no effect of deafness on those basic intellectual abilities not dependent on language (e.g., conceptual thinking, abstraction, and generalisation). These conclusions are rather inconsistent with the Whorfian hypothesis. However, it appears that Furth has overstated his conclusions, since deaf children do show inferior performance on most tasks lacking a major language component. For example, deaf children attain conservation of quantity and of liquids approximately five years later than normal children.

The major interpretative problem with regard to the low level of performance of deaf children on cognitive tasks is that deaf children differ from normal children in a number of ways. In addition to their poor language development, deaf children may also suffer from cultural deprivation, lack of education, and emotional disturbance, and it is difficult to determine which of these factors is primarily responsible for their cognitive limitations.

It is possible to identify a number of hypotheses concerning the impact of language on behaviour. Miller and McNeill (1969) distinguished between strong, weak, and the weakest hypotheses. According to the strong hypothesis, language determines thinking. The weak hypothesis states that language affects perception. The weakest hypothesis claims only that language affects memory, i.e., information that is easily encoded linguistically will be better remembered than information that is less readily encoded. In practice, it is the weakest hypothesis that has been tested most frequently, and it is to such research that we now turn.

Some apparent support for the weakest form of the Whorfian hypothesis was obtained by Brown and Lenneberg (1954), in a study on colour codability and memory. Codability was defined on the basis of the time taken to name each colour chip, the amount of agreement on its name, and the length of the name itself. Recognition memory was better for the more codable chips, even with a very short retention interval of 7 seconds. In related work, Lenneberg and Roberts (1956) discovered that Zuni speakers made more errors than English speakers did in recognising yellows and oranges. The relevance of this finding is that there is only one word in the Zuni language to refer to yellows and oranges.

While the findings of Lenneberg and Roberts (1956) suggest that language affects memory, later studies brought this conclusion into doubt. Heider (1972) made use of the fact that there are 11 basic colour words in English, and that each of these words has one generally agreed upon best colour, known as a focal colour. The typical finding is that English speakers find it easier to remember focal than non-focal colours, and Heider wondered whether the same would be true of the Dani. The Dani are a Stone Age agricultural people living in Indonesian New Guinea, and their language has only two basic colour terms: "mola" for bright, warm hues and "mili" for dark, cold hues. In spite of the substantial linguistic differences between English speakers and the Dani, both groups of people showed better recognition memory for focal colours.

Heider subsequently changed her name to Rosch, and carried out further work with the Dani. In one study (Rosch, 1973), the ability of the Dani and of English speakers to learn nonsense names for focal and non-focal colours was assessed. Both groups found it easier to learn nonsense names for focal than for non-focal colours, despite the fact that the Dani have no words to describe focal colours accurately.

What does research on memory for colours tell us about the relationship between language and thought? The basic finding is that the similarities between cultures regarding which colours are remembered most easily are far more pronounced than the dissimilarities, despite considerable differences from one language to the next in the terms available to describe colours. The natural interpretation of this finding is that language does not dictate the way in which colours are perceived and remembered. Indeed, the evidence is more consistent with the notion that thought affects language. Numerous languages have words for the same 11 focal colours, and it appears from work on the physiology of colour vision (de Valois & Jacobs, 1968) that these colours are processed specially by the visual system.

It may be too sweeping to argue that language has no effect on thought. At the very least, each language may affect certain habits of thought, even if it does not restrict cognitive functioning to a major extent. Ervin-Tripp (1964) investigated the thinking of Japanese-American bilinguals. When these subjects were given sentence-completion or word-association tests, their performance resembled that of Japanese monolinguals when they responded in Japanese, but it was like that of American monolinguals when they responded in English.

A number of theorists who have argued that language determines thought have assumed, whether explicitly or implicitly, that thinking necessitates the use of language. A more defensible viewpoint is that thinking can make use of language, imagery, or propositions. Some of the evidence in favour of an imagery system was presented in Chapter 7, but it is worth noting here that many factor-analytic studies of intelligence have uncovered separate verbal and spatial ability factors. Furthermore, some problem-solving tasks could scarcely be solved by the use of language alone. Consider a three-inch cube which is painted blue. It is cut up into 27 one-inch cubes by making two parallel cuts along each of the three dimensions. The problem is to determine how many of these smaller cubes have paint on three faces, and on two faces, and on no faces. Virtually everyone who solves this problem reports using imagery, and task performance correlates with other measures of spatial ability, but not with measures of verbal ability.

Is the structure of language influenced by thought? Thinking certainly begins at an earlier developmental stage than language in the human child, and it seems reasonable to follow Piaget in arguing that language in the young child builds on the cognitive abilities which have developed during the pre-language sensori-motor period. According to this viewpoint, language is shaped, at least in part, by the thoughts it must communicate. It seems intuitively plausible to assume that language is the servant of thought rather than its master.

The evidence is actually rather equivocal. While some findings, which are the next to be cited, support the notion that thought may influence language, other findings do not. Several of these negative findings have emerged from developmental studies, and are discussed in Chapter 9. Some of the evidence cited by Whorf (1956) in support of his hypothesis of linguistic relativity seems more consistent with the opposite point of view, that thought influences language. The fact that Eskimoes have many words to describe snow and Arabs have several terms to refer to camels suggests that language users develop highly differentiated terms to describe aspects of their environment as and when such differentiation is relevant to their life experience. This is also suggested by the way in which people who discover a new interest (e.g., sailing, photography) quickly start learning the appropriate technical terms.

Every language appears to have a preferred word order for expressing the subject, verb, and object within sentences. There are six possible orderings, two of which (object–verb–subject and object–subject–verb) are not found among the large sample of the world's languages analysed by Greenberg (1963). The most popular order is subject–object–verb (44% of languages), followed by the subject–verb–object order found in English (35% of languages). The most striking finding is that the subject nearly always precedes the object; this is the case in 98% of languages. It is not absolutely clear what this consistent ordering means, but it does seem natural to think about the initiator of action before considering the recipient of that action.

The notion that thought influences language receives further support in some studies with Piagetian tasks. For example, Sinclair-de-Zwart (1969) identified conservers and non-conservers on the standard Piagetian task in which children have to decide whether there is more liquid in a tall, thin container or a short, wide container (in fact, there is the same amount of liquid in each). She also administered tests of linguistic competence relevant to the conservation task, such as, use of comparatives and co-ordination (e.g., "This is tall but it's thin; this is short but it's wide"). There was a marked superiority of conservers over non-conservers on these tests of language skills, indicating some relationship between language and the cognitive skills required for conservation. The key finding was that only approximately 10% of the non-conserving children who were taught the conservation-relevant language showed evidence of conservation as a result. Thus, acquisition of the appropriate linguistic skills did not facilitate thought, suggesting that the link between linguistic competence and ability to conserve is due to the fact that mastery of the cognitive skills involved in conservation facilitates learning the relevant linguistic terms.

In sum, it is probable that thought influences language, but it is doubtful whether language has more than a marginal biasing effect on thought. This generalisation applies only to older children and adults in whom thought and language combine in an interactive relationship. In young children, language and thought are virtually independent and this may be a major factor limiting their ability to act effectively in many situations. However, it is only sensible to be rather cautious when drawing conclusions about the relationship between language and thought. In those cases where certain linguistic features and forms of cognition are associated, it is important to bear in mind that this is correlational evidence. In consequence, it is often speculative to assume that there is a causal link, and even riskier to make a judgement about the direction of causation.

COMPREHENSION

Introduction

When listeners or readers pay attention to the verbal material presented to them, they usually attain some level of understanding of the information conveyed by that material. Such understanding or grasp of the meaning is the most crucial component of comprehension. However, it is obvious that several different processes are involved. These include letter identification and iconic processing when reading, and speech perception and echoic processing when listening, followed by parsing and the determination of word classes, and concluding with extraction of the meaning of the presented information in the light of contextual information. This is merely a sketch-map of the processes involved in comprehension, and processes probably overlap in time rather than following one another in an orderly fashion.

One of the problems with the study of comprehension is the great flexibility of the processes involved, and the fact that there are various levels of comprehension. Consider, for example, the sentence, "The man said that he was not a crook." It is a relatively easy sentence to understand, and yet only limited comprehension is possible in the absence of any information about "the man" referred to in the sentence. If you were told that the sentence concerned Richard Nixon, then a more complete understanding would be possible.

It is often assumed that one of the early processes involved in comprehension is to divide a sentence into its constituents (i.e., basic phrases or units), as a prelude to arriving at a semantic interpretation of each constituent. The psychological reality of the constituent was established by Graf and Torrey (1966), who presented sentences visually a line at a time, and divided up each sentence so that every line either consisted of a constituent or parts of two constituents. For example, sentence (1) was presented in conformity with its constituents, whereas sentence (2) was not:

1   During Word War II,
    even fantastic schemes
    received consideration
    if they gave promise
    of shortening the conflict.

2   During World War
    II, even fantastic
    schemes received
    consideration if they gave
    promise of shortening the
    conflict.

The basic finding was that comprehension was better when the constituent structure of each sentneces was preserved in the visual display.

Rather more direct evidence that sentence processing proceeds constituent by constituent was obtained by Caplan (1972). Subjects heard a sentence followed by a probe word, and had to decide as rapidly as possible whether the probe word had appeared in the sentence. A certain amount of ingenuity produced pairs of sentences in which the only significant difference was whether or not the probe word occurred in the last constituent of the sentence. As an illustration, consider the following sentences that were both probed with the word "oil":

1 Now that artists are working fewer hours oil prints are rare.
2 Now that artists are working in oil prints are rare.

In the first sentence, "oil" is part of the last constituent, whereas it is part of the first constituent in the second sentence. The key result was that the probe word was recognised more rapidly if it had occurred in the last constituent, presumably because information in the last constituent had just been processed.

Of course, the constituent structure of a sentence is not the only relevant factor in determining comprehension. Several theorists have emphasised the importance of the propositional structure of sentences. The role of the number of propositions in affecting reading or comprehension time for sentences was studied by Kintsch and Keenan (1973). They manipulated the number of propositions in sentences and paragraphs, but controlled the number of words. An example of a sentence with four propositions is "Romulus, the legendary founder of Rome, took the women of the Sabine by force," whereas the following sentence contains eight propositions: "Cleopatra's downfall lay in her foolish trust of the fickle political figures of the Roman world." The reading time increased by approximately one second for each additional proposition.

Several of the factors and processes involved in comprehension have been discussed, but important issues relating to the order in which these processes are carried out have virtually been ignored. Several theories have addressed the issue of the ordering of processes, but it is perhaps fair to argue that the crucial theoretical distinction is between serial and interactive models, a distinction which we consider in terms of the comprehension of spoken language. Serial models (e.g., that of Forster, 1979), which have been popular until fairly recently, typically assume that the flow of information within the processing system occurs in one direction only, from the bottom up. Such models often assume that language comprehension requires analysis of the input at the phonological, lexical, syntactic, and semantic levels, and that processing occurs sequentially, level by level.

This serial model can be contrasted with interactive models (e.g., Marslen-Wilson & Tyler, 1980), in which it is assumed that the processing system is more flexibly structured. According to interactive models, various knowledge sources (e.g., lexical, syntactic, semantic) interact with each other in complex ways to produce efficient analysis of spoken language. Thus, a crucial distinction between serial and interactive models is that the former models assume that spoken language is processed in a relatively fixed and invariant series of processing stages, whereas the latter models allow for much greater variety in terms of the pattern of processing activities involved in comprehension.

Some of the points raised so far can be clarified if we consider a specific version of an interactive model, that proposed by Marslen-Wilson and Tyler (1980). According to their cohort model, early in the auditory presentation of a word, various recognition elements become active. These elements consist of words known to the listener that conform to the sound sequence that has been heard so far. This collection of potential candidates for the presented word is termed by them the "word-initial cohort." Words belonging to this cohort are then eliminated either because they cease to match the bottom-up processing of the input word as this proceeds, or they are inconsistent with the semantic or other context. Processing of the auditory word only needs to continue until the information available from the context and from the word itself is sufficient to eliminate all but one of the words in the word-initial cohort.

Marslen-Wilson and Tyler (1980) tested some of these theoretical notions in a word-monitoring task, in which subjects had to identify pre-specified target words presented within spoken sentences. The sentences were either normal sentences, or syntactic sentences (i.e., grammatically correct but meaningless), or random sentences (i.e., unrelated words), and the target looked for was a member of a given category, or a word that rhymed with a given word, or a word that was identical to a given word. The dependent variable of interest was the speed with which the target could be detected.

In general terms, the results conformed much more closely to the predictions of an interactive model than of a serial model. For example, the interactive model predicts that sensory information from the target word and contextual information from the rest of the sentence combine inter-actively in word recognition, whereas serial models predict that sensory information is extracted prior to the use of contextual information. As an interactive model would lead one to expect, there was an interaction between the spoken duration of the target word (an aspect of sensory information) and the type of sentence it was embedded in (contextual information). Response times were longer for words of greater spoken duration. This tendency was much the greatest when the sentential context (the context provided by the remainder of the sentence) contained no useful syntactic or semantic information (i.e., random word order), and was least when the target word was presented in normal prose. This indicates a kind of trade-off between sensory and contextual information: if there is adequate contextual information, then complete sensory analysis is not necessary.

Further support for the interactive approach comes from a consideration of the great speed of word recognition in a normal sentence context. In that context, subjects initiated their responses approximately 200 msec. after the onset of the target word when it was identical to the given word. This figure should be compared against the mean spoken duration of the target words used in this study which was 369 msec. The first 200 msec. of a word typically correspond to the first two phonemes of a word, and there are usually numerous English words consistent with those two phonemes. Therefore, contextual information must be used extremely early in processing, which is asssumed by interactive models but seems rather inconsistent with serial models in which contextual information is used only after several other processes have occurred.

Interactive models are attractive because they describe a very efficient way in which initial comprehension may occur. The efficiency stems from the fact that all relevant sources of information are used concurrently to provide rapid word identification. In contrast, serial models will often produce rather inefficient and slow performance. However, there are obvious limitations with the approach of Marslen-Wilson and Tyler (1980). Firstly, it may be wondered whether the rather artificial tasks they used led their subjects to process sentences in ways quite different to those normally used when listening for comprehension. Secondly, their model (and most others) is relevant only to word recognition, which is but one aspect of sentence comprehension, and it remains to be seen whether interactive models can be applied successfully to larger units of spoken speech.

Context Effects

We saw in the previous section that the speed of word recognition can be affected quite substantially by the sentential context in which a word is presented. However, there are even more important effects of context on comprehension. As was pointed out in Chapter 5, the meanings that are assigned to sentences, and to words within sentences, are affected substantially by the context in which they are experienced. Much confusion has occurred because the term "context" has become rather amorphous, and is increasingly used to refer to several different things. For present purposes, we largely limit our use of the term to *verbal* context.

In the case of words within sentences, the other words in the sentence constitute much of the verbal context. As a result, the precise interpretation given to a particular word can be shown to be affected by its immediate sentential context. Let us consider at this point a study by Halff, Ortony and Anderson (1976). They made use of several sentences containing the word "red," presenting them two at a time to their subjects. The task was to decide whether the red object in one sentence was definitely redder than the red object in the other sentence, or whether the two objects could be equally red. The major finding was that the degree of redness associated with the word "red" varied considerably as a function of the sentence context. Furthermore, the word "red" was thought to cover a range of reds in most sentences, with the exact range varying from sentence to sentence. Thus, "red" in the sentence "The boy with red hair stood out in the crowd" covered a wider range of the redness continuum than the same word in the sentence "As the sun set the sky turned red." The implication is that the sentential context surrounding a word determines its possible representations.

A more dramatic illustration of the way in which the meaning assigned to a word can be influenced by sentential context was provided by Barclay,

Bransford, Franks, McCarrell and Nitsch (1974). Various sentences were presented (e.g., "The student picked up the ink" or "The student spilled the ink"), and were followed by phrases as cues to prompt recall of the object nouns. The phrase "Something in a bottle" was a better cue for the former than the latter sentence, whereas "Something that can be messy" was a more effective cue for the latter sentence. If it is assumed that the effectiveness of a retrieval cue depends upon the way in which the to-be-remembered information is comprehended, then context can dictate which semantic features of a word will be processed.

In the examples of context effects considered so far, we have regarded each sentence as a separate entity. In reality, of course, comprehension of a sentence is usually affected by the sentence or sentences that preceded it. Anyone who doubts that will probably be convinced if they think back to snatches of conversation that they have overheard. Ignorance of the earlier part of such conversations greatly hinders the comprehension process.

One of the normal characteristics of discourse is that information is presented gradually. Each sentence builds on the foundation established by previous sentences, and also adds some fresh information. Clark and Haviland (1977) argued that a speaker will usually attempt to achieve this gradual presentation of information by adhering to the given-new contract, which is based on a distinction between information which the speaker believes the listener already knows and accepts as true (i.e., given information) and information which the speaker feels the listener does not yet know (i.e., new information). They described the given-new contract in the following terms: "Try to construct the given and the new information of each utterance in context: (a) so that the listener is able to compute from memory the unique antecedent that was intended for the given information, and (b) so that he will not already have the new information attached to that antecedent [p. 9]."

For his part, the listener initially identifies the given and the new information in the current sentence, and then searches through memory for previous information that precisely matches the given information. The listener's task is made somewhat easier by the fact that given information usually occurs earlier in a sentence than new information. In addition, focal stress (i.e., the strongest stress and highest pitch in the sentence) typically falls on that part of the sentence containing new information.

Perhaps the most obvious prediction from Clark and Haviland's (1977) given-new theory is that violations of the given-new contract should slow down the speed of comprehension. For example, consider the following pairs of sentences:

1   Ed was given an alligator for his birthday.
     The alligator was his favourite present.

2 Ed wanted an alligator for his birthday.
   The alligator was his favourite present.

The second sentence in each pair can only be readily comprehended when the first sentence provides all of the necessary contextual information. This is true of the first sentence in pair (1), but in pair (2) it is necessary to draw the inference that Ed was given an alligator for his birthday in order to understand the second sentence fully. The expectation that it would take time to draw this inference and so comprehension would take longer was confirmed by Haviland and Clark (1974).

Further evidence in favour of the psychological validity of the given-new contract was presented by Clark and Haviland (1977). The given-new contract is an important example of the fundamental notion that the comprehender is attempting to work out what the speaker or writer intended him or her to understand rather than merely determining the propositional content of what is expressed.

Inferences

There are numerous cases in which the reader or listener has to be actively involved in the comprehension process in order to fill in gaps in the presented information. In general, it is remarkable how successful we are in drawing inferences to make sense of what we hear and read. Try your hand at understanding what is going on in the following story taken from Rumelhart and Ortony (1977):

1 Mary heard the ice cream man coming.
2 She remembered the pocket money.
3 She rushed into the house.

You probably made various assumptions or inferences while reading the story, perhaps including the following: Mary wanted to buy some ice cream; buying ice cream costs money; Mary had some pocket money in the house; and Mary had only a limited amount of time to get hold of some money before the ice cream man arrived. The important point to note is that none of these assumptions is explicitly stated in the three sentences that were presented. It is so natural for us to draw inferences in order to facilitate understanding that we are not always aware that we are doing so.

We are more likely to attempt to draw inferences if a sentence does not appear to fit the current context. Under such circumstances, we tend to generate backward inferences in an attempt to locate an earlier context that is appropriate. Thorndyke (1976) investigated backward inferencing in a study on story memory. In one story, the sentence, "The hamburger chain owner was afraid his love for french fries would ruin his marriage," was followed a few sentences later by the final sentence, "The hamburger chain owner decided to join weight-watchers in order to save his marriage." In connecting these sentences, it is appropriate to infer that the hamburger chain owner was fat and his wife did not like obesity, but it is inappropriate to infer that the hamburger chain owner's wife did not like french fries.

Thorndyke (1976) tested to see whether subjects had been more likely to draw the appropriate inference than the inappropriate inference by using a recognition test on which subjects had to decide whether various sentences had been presented in the story. Actual story sentences were correctly recognised 85% of the time, appropriate inferences were incorrectly recognised as having been presented 58% of the time, but only 6% of the subjects falsely recognised inappropriate inferences. Of course, these findings merely indicate that the appropriate inferences were drawn, but do not show unequivocally that these inferences were drawn at the actual time the story was comprehended. However, the use of more sensitive techniques has shown that many inferences are drawn as part of the comprehension process (e.g., McKoon & Ratcliff, 1981).

There are other circumstances in which inferences must be drawn. If the literal meaning of a sentence seems appropriate to the context, then that is assumed to be the intended meaning. However, if the literal meaning does not seem to be appropriate, then the listener goes beyond the literal meaning to discover the conversationally implied meaning. If a wife says to her husband, "Would you mind opening the window, dear?", he is asking for trouble if he only takes account of the literal meaning of the question, and responds "yes" or "no." Other cases in which the literal meaning is not the intended meaning include such rhetorical devices as irony, sarcasm, and understatement.

Clark and Lucy (1975) discovered that statements with both literal and intended meanings were nearly always interpreted in terms of their intended meaning. However, they also found evidence that the literal meaning was worked out. The sentences "I'll be very happy if you make the circle blue" and "I'll be very sad unless you make the circle blue" both have the same intended meaning, and yet the latter sentence took a lot longer to comprehend. Since negative sentences typically take longer to understand than positive sentences, this result is probably due to a difference in the literal meanings of the two sentences, with "unless" having the inherent negative meaning "if not."

One of the most common circumstances in which inferences tend to be drawn is when a statement strongly implies something that is not explicitly stated. Such statements are said to contain a pragmatic implication. This can be contrasted with a logical implication, in which some information is necessarily implied by an utterance. The distinction can be clarified by one or two examples. The statement, "Tess forced Stephen to rob the bank," logically implies "Stephen robbed the bank." In contrast, the statement, "The dangerous fugitive was able to leave the country," only pragmatically implies "The fugitive left the country." Pragmatic implication was also involved in ex-President Nixon's statement, "And I just feel that I have to be in a position to be clean and to be forthcoming." This implies that Nixon is, in fact, clean and forthcoming, but is also compatible with the statement, "I am not actually clean and forthcoming."

Strong evidence that people do typically make the predicted inferences from sentences containing pragmatic implications was obtained by Brewer (1974). He presented sentences such as "The angry rioter threw a rock at the window" (implying that the rock went through the window) and "Dennis the Menace sat in Santa's chair and asked for an elephant" (implying that Dennis the Menace sat on Santa's lap). In a subsequent test of cued recall, subjects recalled the pragmatic implications of the sentences more frequently than the sentences they had actually heard.

Are pragmatic inferences made at the time of comprehension and storage, or are they constructed at retrieval? Most of the available evidence suggests that they are usually made during the process of comprehension. For example, Monaco (1976) discovered that telling subjects before presenting a passage that they would receive a multiple-choice retention test led them to draw fewer inferences from the passage than they did when told they would be given an essay test. These instructions could have affected inference drawing at either input or retrieval. However, the same instructions had no differential effect on inference drawing when given only *after* the passage had been presented, presumably because they could not influence passage comprehension.

The ability to make inferences obviously depends on possession of appropriate knowledge about the world. For example, we infer that a rock thrown at a window will go through that window on the basis of our knowledge about the weight of rocks and the fragility of windows. Very often, our knowledge relates to complex sequences of events, and is organised in the form of scripts, frames, or schemata (discussed further in Chapter 11). For example, most people can be said to possess a restaurant script, in that they have clearly defined expectations of the events likely to occur in a restaurant setting. These include entering the restaurant, being shown to a table, receiving a menu, ordering from it, a waiter or waitress bringing the food, eating the food, receiving the bill, leaving a tip, and paying the waiter, waitress or cashier.

The existence of such scripts has been claimed to be responsible for our ability to make sense of relatively fragmentary information, with the relevant script helping to "fill in the gaps" (Schank, 1976). The obvious difficulty is that such conceptualisations tend to be rather vague. A step in the right

HCP-H*

direction was taken by Bower, Black and Turner (1979). They asked students to indicate the activities they associated with various events, and found a reasonable level of consensus. Most students agreed that attending a lecture involved entering the room, finding a seat, taking out a notebook, taking notes, and so on. This suggests that scripts really do exist. Bower *et al.* also found that story memory often incorporated unstated script actions, indicating that scripts are activated appropriately.

Evaluation of Contextualism

Several convincing demonstrations of the notion that comprehension is affected by context in the form of other words in the sentence, previous sentences, and world knowledge of various kinds have been discussed. It has thus been established beyond peradventure that the comprehension process often makes considerable use of information over and above that explicitly contained in the sentence currently being processed by the listener or reader. However, some doubts about the value of the contextualist approach remain. One difficulty lies in the concept of "context" itself. A term that is used in an extremely broad sense is in danger of meaning practically nothing. "Context" sometimes refers only to verbal context, but a number of theorists no longer use it in that sense alone. Bransford (1979), for example, equated context with "appropriately activated knowledge," but he unfortunately failed to specify what knowledge is "appropriately activated."

Clark and Carlson (1981) attempted to clarify matters by proposing a distinction between intrinsic and incidental context. Intrinsic context is that part of the context that is potentially necessary for a process to be carried out, and incidental context is all of the remaining context. With reference to the process of comprehension, they offered the following definition of intrinsic context: *"The intrinsic context for a listener trying to understand what a speaker means on a particular occasion is the common ground that the listener believes holds at that moment between the speaker and the listeners he or she is speaking to* [p. 319]." The "common ground" between two people consists of their mutual suppositions, beliefs, and knowledge. An important part of the common ground from the listener's perspective (and the speaker's as well) is the earlier part of the conversation. If the speaker and the listener both belong to a given community (e.g., they are both psychologists), then the common ground will include scripts relating to membership in that community.

One of the major implications of this theoretical approach is that it emphasises the flexibility of the intrinsic context. As two people interact more with each other, the common ground between them increases, and so does the intrinsic context. In fact, almost anything could potentially become part of the intrinsic context. Clark and Carlson (1981) gave the hypothetical example of two people (Ed and Joe) who have a mutual friend called Max. Max carries a teapot around with him, and occasionally rubs the backs of someone's legs with it. Since this information is known to both Ed and Joe, it constitutes part of the common ground between them, and thus belongs to the intrinsic context. As a result, there is no confusion when Ed says to Joe, "'Well, Max did it this time. He tried to teapot a policeman' [p. 327]."

Apart from problems with the definition of "context," the contextualist theory is also plagued by a lack of testability. At present, evidence that context has affected comprehension is taken as support for the theory, but failure of context to influence the process of comprehension is not usually regarded as disproving the theory. Instead, it is argued that the context in question was "inappropriate," not attended to, or forgotten.

What is needed is a theory that specifies the precise circumstances in which any particular aspect of the context will influence comprehension. Clark and Carlson's (1981) emphasis on the common ground between speaker and listener may prove useful here. Another factor that needs systematic investigation is the goal of the listener or reader. An extremely large number of inferences can be drawn from most linguistic communications, it is therefore likely that the reader or listener draws mainly those inferences relevant to his or her present purposes. This hypothesis was investigated by Black (1981), who asked some subjects to rate two passages for comprehensibility, while other subjects were asked to read the same passages for a subsequent essay test of memory. The former subjects made fewer inferences than the latter subjects, presumably reflecting the difference in reading purpose.

In sum, the contextualist approach has produced several striking experimental demonstrations but a dearth of adequate explanations. The present position can be encapsulated by modifying slightly the title of one of Pirandello's plays: six phenomena in search of a theory.

LANGUAGE PRODUCTION

We know rather more about language comprehension than we do about language production. An important part of the reason for this is because it is fairly straightforward to exercise experimental control over the material to be comprehended, but extremely difficult to manipulate an individual's production of language. A further problem in accounting for language production is that one really needs more than simply a theory of language. This is because language production is basically a goal-directed activity; people speak in order to influence other people, to be sociable, to impart information, to express concern, and so on. If it is at all complicated to attain the desired goal then various non-linguistic cognitive and reasoning processes are involved in producing language.

If two people are to have a satisfactory conversation, then it is necessary for the person speaking at any given moment to adhere to certain conventions. Grice (1967) argued that the key to successful communication lies in the Cooperative Principle, according to which both speakers and listeners must attempt to be cooperative. Grice proposed a total of four maxims that the speaker should adhere to: quantity, quality, relation, and manner. According to the maxim of quantity, the speaker should be as informative as necessary, but not more so. The speaker should be truthful, according to the maxim of quality. The maxim of relation requires the speaker to say things that are relevant to the conversation, and the maxim of manner exhorts the speaker to make his contribution easy to understand.

Some evidence that speakers do, indeed, take account of the maxim of quantity was obtained by Olson (1970). He pointed out that what needs to be said depends on the context. For example, one cannot account for what someone says simply by focusing on the referent that the speaker wishes to describe. One must also know the objects from which the referent needs to be differentiated. It is sufficient to say, "The boy is good at football," if the other players in a football game are all men, but not if the other players are also boys. In the latter case, it is necessary to be more specific (e.g., "The boy with red hair is good at football").

In applying the maxim of quantity, the speaker also has to take account of the listener's knowledge of a topic. If the speaker and the listener have several friends in common, then it may be reasonable for the speaker to say, "Bill bought Tom's old Beetle." However, if the listener does not know who Tom is, and only knows Bill as Dr. Smith, then the speaker will typically convey the information in a rather different fashion: "Dr. Smith bought the orange car parked outside your office." The key point is that the process of language production often involves deciding on the factual information to be expressed, and then deciding exactly how this information should be expressed in the light of such factors as the environmental context and the available knowledge of the listener.

Several theories of the stages involved in speech production have been proposed. As a fairly representative example of such theories, we can consider the views of Garrett (1976). He argued that a speaker initially decides on a message he or she wants to communicate. Then the speaker decides on a syntactic outline (i.e., slots to put words in), selects appropriate content words (e.g., verbs, nouns), chooses affixes and function words, and finally produces speech.

At the most general level, Garrett's theory (as well as many others) claims that there is pre-production planning. In other words, the speaker engages in fairly detailed planning of an utterance before beginning to speak. How do we know that the mind is operating in advance of the mouth? One kind of evidence relates to the kinds of errors that people make while speaking. If it can be shown that sounds or words from the later parts of a sentence intrude into the earlier part of a spoken sentence, then this suggests that the speaker must have thought ahead.

One of the best-known errors of this type is the Spoonerism, in which the initial letter or letters of two or more words are transposed. The Rev. W. A. Spooner, after whom the Spoonerism was named, is credited with several memorable Spoonerisms. These include, "You have hissed all my mystery lectures" and "The Lord is a shoving leopard to his flock." There is a strong suspicion that many of the Rev. Spooner's gems were not produced spontaneously, but were the result of much painstaking work.

Another kind of speech error is known as the stranded morpheme (e.g., "He has already trunked two packs"). With such errors, the functional morphemes (e.g., "–ed," "–s") typically remain in the appropriate positions, whereas the content morphemes (e.g., "trunk," "pack") are transposed. This suggests that Garrett (1976) may have been right to assume that a speaker decides on a syntactic outline before filling it with the appropriate words.

According to Garrett (1976), the speech plan for words is calculated prior to the plan for precise pronunciations. There is some indirect evidence for this contention. If words are interchanged, the distance between them is typically longer than the distance between interchanged sounds. For example, Spoonerisms tend to occur within a single constituent rather than across constituents.

Of course, the number and nature of speech errors are both much affected by the precise conditions under which the speaker is operating. Deese (1978) drew a distinction between spontaneous speech and prepared speech. Spontaneous speech occurs when people answer unexpected questions, whereas the prepared speech studied by Deese covered situations such as seminar presentations in which the content but not the wording is prepared in advance. There were many fewer grammatical and stylistic mistakes with prepared speech than with spontaneous speech. This finding presumably reflects the speaker's limited capacity: When much of the available processing capacity must be devoted to the task of deciding on the meaning to be communicated, there is insufficient capacity remaining to transform the meaning consistently into an acceptable linguistic form.

We saw earlier that there is considerable evidence that speech utterances are pre-planned to some extent. It is of some practical and theoretical interest to discover precisely how far ahead of current speech any pre-planning actually extends. An indication that pre-planning extends over several words was obtained by Cooper and Ehrlich (1981). They asked their subjects to memorise two phrases, each of which contained three nouns. After the phrases had been committed to memory, the speed of speech production was measured from the presentation of a cue for one phrase to the onset of speech. The two phrases were sometimes identical, or they differed in one, two, or all three nouns. Speed of speech onset was inversely related to the number of words that differed between the two phrases, suggesting that there was some pre-planning. Of more interest, the speed of speech onset for phrases differing in only one noun was unaffected by the location within the phrase of that noun. This implies that pre-planning of speech extended over the entire phrase.

It has often been assumed that pauses or hesitations in speech are made use of by speakers in order to enable them to plan ahead. Although this suggests that an analysis of where in speech these pauses occur would shed light on the issue of pre-planning, pauses in speech are sometimes related to the speaker's task, or emotional and motivational states, which complicates any interpretation. However, it has been found that pauses in spontaneous speech typically occur more often at grammatical junctures than elsewhere. Boomer (1965) also discovered that such pauses lasted longer on average than those at other locations (1.03 seconds versus 0.75 seconds, respectively). Pauses that coincide with phrase boundaries differ in another way from pauses occurring within a phrase: The former tend to be filled with sounds such as "um," "er," or "ah," whereas the latter are typically silent (Maclay & Osgood, 1959).

The data on pauses are consistent with other evidence in suggesting that language production occurs one constituent at a time. Maclay and Osgood (1959) obtained support for this notion in their analysis of repetitions occurring in spontaneous speech. When speakers repeated themselves, they tended to repeat or correct an entire constituent (e.g., "Turn on the stove—the heater switch").

We have now considered some of the psychological processes involved in speech. What about the processes involved in writing, which is the other major form of language production? According to Hayes and Flower (1980), writing consists of three main processes: PLANNING, TRANSLATING, and REVIEWING. Within each of these processes, various sub-processes can be identified. Thus, the PLANNING process makes use of three sub-processes: *generating*, *organising*, and *goal-setting*. In general terms, the function of the PLANNING process is to make use of information from both the task environment and long-term memory in order to set goals. When the goals have been established, a writing plan is formulated to produce written text that conforms to those goals. More specifically, the *generation* process retrieves information from long-term memory, and each item of information that is retrieved is used as a cue to retrieve the next item of information. In this way, a retrieval chain is created, which continues to grow until an irrelevant item of information is retrieved. The *organising* process selects the most relevant information retrieved by the *generation* process, and organises it into a coherent writing plan. The *goal-setting* process stores away useful rules (e.g., "Keep it simple") for subsequent use by the *editing* process.

The TRANSLATING process operates in the service of the overall writing plan to produce language that conforms in meaning to information retrieved from the writer's long-term memory. This process is needed, because information in long-term memory may often be stored in propositional form rather than directly as language. Finally, the REVIEWING process consists of the two sub-processes of *reading* and *editing*. Its function is basically to improve the quality of the text produced by the TRANSLATING process. These improvements may be quite varied, ranging from corrections of spelling and grammar to changes in the text to make it conform better to the writing plan.

Hayes and Flower (1980) assumed that the order in which these processes and sub-processes were used was quite flexible, but the natural sequence is clearly PLANNING, then TRANSLATING, and finally REVIEWING. This orderly progression can be altered, however, because both the *editing* and *generating* processes can interrupt other processes. It was assumed that the *editing* process would be used whenever deficiencies in the text were detected. Of course, individual differences also affect the ordering of the processes. Some writers prefer to produce a rapid first draft before reviewing the text, whereas others edit frequently as they write and attempt to produce a perfect first draft.

How do we know that the processes postulated by Hayes and Flower (1980) are actually used in writing ? Their main evidence was based on protocol analysis, in which writers attempted to verbalise their mental activities during writing tasks. In particular, they used the protocol of a writer who appeared to be especially aware of his ongoing writing processes. He produced 1 page of completed text, together with 14 pages based on thinking aloud and 5 pages of notes.

It appeared from his protocol that he had started with the *generating* process, followed by the *organising* process, and then the TRANSLATING process. Analysis of what he wrote confirmed this impression, since there was a definite progression over time from unorganised fragments to more structured items, and then to complete sentences. The protocol analysis also revealed that the *generating* process was more persistent during the first, or *generating*, stage than the subsequent *organising* and TRANSLATING processes. The mean length of the retrieval chain was 6.4 ideas during the *generating* stage, against only 2.0 thereafter. Finally, as expected, the flow of processing was frequently interrupted by the *editing* and *generating* processes.

There are various potential problems with protocol analysis (see Chapter 1). It is likely that the necessity to provide a verbal protocol affects the composition and writing processes, perhaps because the writer thinks more analytically than he or she usually would. It is also possible that the task of providing a protocol interferes with the composition process, especially for those writers who find composing text a rather difficult task even in the absence of any distraction. In spite of these difficulties, it appears that Hayes and Flower (1980) have made a promising start to the task of uncovering the key processes underlying writing performance.

Collins and Gentner (1980) were rather more specific about some of the goals in writing. They argued that there are at least four general objectives: making the text comprehensible; making it enticing; making it persuasive; and making it rememberable. Various devices can be used to achieve these goals. Some devices are structural, such as moving from the general to the particular or using the argument form (e.g., evidence for a position followed by evidence against). Others are stylistic devices (e.g., metaphor, humour, rhetorical questions), and still others are content devices (e.g., tangibility).

In sum, writing consists of several complex processes that probably operate concurrently. This suggests that some aspects of the writing process become automatic, presumably as a result of much practice. It may be relevant that many famous authors attribute their writing skill to an almost daily preoccupation with writing.

A major issue when considering language production is to evaluate the equivalence (or non-equivalence) of different ways of producing language. People speak approximately five or six times faster than they can write, and it might be thought that this rate differential would have important implications for linguistic production. In fact, it appears that the mode of response output has surprisingly little impact on language production. For example, Gould (1978) discovered that people became as competent at dictating letters as at writing them after less than one day's practice at dictation. Nevertheless, many of the participants in this study reported that they did not feel confident about dictation, perhaps because of the lack of a readily available external record of what they had said up to that point. In view of the much greater speed with which sentences can be spoken than written, one might anticipate that dictating would be much faster than writing among those whose dictating skills have been acquired over a number of years. Once again, the differences were modest. Dictation rarely becomes much more than 35% faster than writing (Gould, 1979).

Gould (1980) has divided the time taken to dictate and to write letters into various component times. His subjects were videotaped while composing letters, and the generating, reviewing, accessing, editing, and planning times were calculated. Planning, which was assumed to be occurring during pauses not obviously devoted to other strategies, accounted for a greater proportion of the total time than any other process. Of particular interest, planning time represented approximately two-thirds of composition time for both dictated and written letters.

Even if the quality of the finished product is comparable within different response modes, there might still be substantial individual differences, with some people excelling at writing, others at speaking, and still others at dictating. Gould (1978) compared people's quality of letter writing across these three response modes, and found that there were generally high inter-correlations. Thus, a good letter writer is a good letter writer irrespective of output modality. What are important in language production are the internal mechanisms responsible for composition. Composition is the fundamental skill, and the method of composition is merely a component of that skill that is related to the nature of the task environment. Indeed, the great similarities that appear to exist between writing and speech almost tempt one to believe that writing often resembles speaking to oneself.

PRACTICAL APPLICATIONS

One of the major themes of this chapter has been the way in which comprehension frequently encompasses more than the information explicitly presented. This can have serious consequences in many real-life situations. Of special concern is the tendency for that which is only pragmatically implied to be functionally equivalent in its effects to that which is directly asserted. This tendency can be very important when eyewitness testimony is being evaluated in a court of law. There is, of course, awareness of some of the potential problems on the part of the legal profession. For example, lawyers are not usually allowed to ask leading questions of someone giving evidence. The notion of a "leading question" is somewhat vague; however, Black (1951) defined leading questions as those:

> ...which suggest to the witness the answer desired, or which embody a material fact, and may be answered by a mere negative or affirmative, or which involve an answer bearing immediately upon the merits of the case, and indicating to the witness a representation which will best accord with the interests of the party propounding them [p. 1034].

It is clearly desirable in the interests of justice that leading questions are not allowed. However, it is striking that apparently trivial differences in the way in which a question is asked can have a marked effect on the answers elicited. Loftus and Zanni (1975) showed people a short film of a car accident, and then asked them various questions about the accident. Some of the eyewitnesses were asked, "Did you see a broken headlight?," whereas others were asked, "Did you see the broken headlight?" In fact, there was no broken headlight in the film, but the latter question implies that there was. Only 7% of those asked about a broken headlight said that they had seen it, against 17% of those asked about the broken headlight.

There are other cases in which the way in which questions are worded has influenced the memory of eyewitnesses. Loftus, Altman and Geballe (1975) showed people a film of a classroom protest demonstration and afterwards asked them either aggressively or passively worded questions about the incident. The eyewitnesses were then asked a week later for their recollections of the demonstration. Those who had been asked aggressively worded questions previously, rated the protest as being noisier and more violent, the demonstrators as more belligerent, and the students in the classroom as more antagonistic than did those who had been questioned with passively worded questions.

We have seen that evidence can be distorted if eyewitnesses are asked questions containing various subtle kinds of bias. Evidence can also be deliberately distorted by the witness. A witness must swear to tell the truth, the whole truth, and nothing but the truth, but he does not have to swear that he will *imply* only the truth. The potential importance of this distinction was shown by Harris, Teske and Ginns (1975). They discovered that people who heard the statement, "I didn't steal the money" or "I wasn't forced into stealing the money" were equally likely to assume in later questioning that the witness did not steal the money. This is in spite of the fact that the first statement is a direct assertion whereas the second one is not. Someone who uttered the second statement might really have been thinking, "I wasn't forced into stealing the money, but I took it anyway."

Harris (1978) considered two ways in which simulated jurors might be better able to distinguish between direct assertions and pragmatic implications. The first way was to increase the number of people involved in deciding on the truth or falsehood of the statements of a witness, on the grounds that this would enhance the probability that at least one of the jurors would detect when a statement merely contained a pragmatic implication rather than a direct assertion. The second way was to warn some of the simulated jurors about the importance of distinguishing between assertions and implications, and they were also given several relevant examples.

The simulated jurors heard part of a hypothetical trial testimony revolving around the evidence of a Mr. Ranson. He was an investment broker at a securities firm, and he had discovered an apparent burglary upon returning to work one evening after dinner. Many of his statements were expressed either as assertions or implications (e.g., "I rang the burglar alarm in the hall" or "I ran up to the burglar alarm in the hall"; "I walked away without taking any money" or "I was able to walk away without taking any money"). There was a tendency for the simulated jurors to assign a higher truth value to assertions than to implications, but implications were judged to be true 64% of the time. Neither the size of the group making decisions about the truth of Mr. Ranson's statements, nor the inclusion of explicit warnings, had any effect on decision making. This suggests that it may be rather difficult to prevent people from treating pragmatic implications as statements of fact.

The distinction between direct assertions and pragmatic implications also has practical application in the area of advertising. There are sanctions both in Britain and in the United States of America (and many other countries as well) against advertisers who make false assertions about a product, but it is more difficult to eliminate false implications. However, the Federal Trade Commission in America has moved towards a definition of deception based on the impression that the consumer receives as a result of an advertisement rather than on the intentions of the advertiser.

A relevant example concerns the case brought against Warner-Lambert, the makers of a mouthwash called Listerine Antiseptic. The lower courts in the United States of America ruled against Warner-Lambert for producing advertising that created a "lingering false belief." Part of the commercial in question went like this:

> "Wouldn't it be great," asks the mother, "if you could make him coldproof?" Well, you can't. Nothing can do that (boy sneezes). But there is something you can do that may help. Have him gargle with Listerine Antiseptic. Listerine can't promise to keep him cold-free, but it may help him fight off colds. During the cold-catching season, have him gargle twice a day with full-strength Listerine. Watch his diet, see he gets plenty of sleep, and there's a good chance he'll have fewer colds, milder colds this year [Harris & Monaco, 1978, p. 18].

On the face of it, this commercial seems reasonable, since all of its major assertions are hedged with qualifications. However, when Harris (1977) presented this commercial to 15 subjects, merely changing the name of the product to "Gargoil," he found that all of them subsequently regarded the statement "Gargling with Gargoil Antiseptic helps prevent colds" as true. Thus, people hearing this commercial drew certain inferences from it that were not explicitly stated.

Of course, advertisers make use of several different kinds of tricks to persuade people to draw false inferences. One trick is to present an incomplete statement incorporating a comparative adjective (e.g., "X washes whiter"). The hope is that consumers will assume that X washes whiter than other washing powders, but the advertisers could claim that they meant only that X washes whiter than coal dust. Another device is to ask a negative question in such a way as to imply an affirmative answer (e.g., "Isn't it time you treated yourself to a Y?"). It is common for car advertisements to create a misleading impression by reporting several different pieces of information (e.g., "The new Z has more front-seat headroom than an A, more rear-seat hiproom than a B, and a larger boot than a C"). This suggests that the Z is amazingly capacious, but it is, in fact, entirely possible that the new Z is more cramped overall than A, B, and C.

Harris, Dubitsky, Perch, Ellerman and Larson (1980) investigated the ability of consumers to discriminate between assertions and implications in advertisements. They asked people to watch the evening news on CBS on a particular day, and then to turn up the following day to answer some questions about the programme. During the news programme there were commercials for Old Spice after-shave, Mazola margarine, Bayer aspirin, Eveready batteries, Roman Meal bread, Miller High Life beer, Wheat Thins crackers, and Ford cars. Questioning on the following day revealed that the subjects were as confident of the truth of implied claims as they were of asserted claims.

Can anything be done to prevent people from treating mere implications as if they were assertions? Bruno (1980) attempted to do so by means of a training programme. Training consisted of emphasising the distinction between assertions and implications, giving a short test, and then discussing the accuracy of the answers produced with the subjects. This training did have some effect, but unfortunately it was not exactly the desired effect. What happened was that the trained subjects became generally more cautious about deciding that any statement was true, but they were no better than untrained subjects at discriminating between assertions and implications.

The unwanted influence of pragmatic implication may extend beyond courts of law and commercial advertising. It is possible, for example, that doctors may sometimes unwittingly influence their patients' thought processes. Such a possibility was suggested by an intriguing study reported by Loftus (1975). Various people were asked either, "Do you get headaches frequently, and, if so, how often?" or, "Do you get headaches occasionally, and, if so, how often?" Those who were asked the former question reported a mean of 2.2 headaches a week, against only 0.7 for those who were asked the latter question.

All in all, the effects of pragmatic implication are more pervasive than one would have imagined. People are not only prone to draw inferences, but also seem to store these inferences in the same way as direct assertions. A potentially worrying aspect of the research evidence is that active training programmes designed specifically to enable people to distinguish between assertions and implications are largely ineffective. It is not simply a matter of forewarned is forearmed; rather, more in the way of remedial education is called for to reduce people's gullibility.

9 Cognitive Development

For many years, the Behaviourists argued that learning was essentially a matter of forming stimulus–response connections. Within the context of that theoretical orientation, the Behaviourists attempted to minimise the differences between rats and humans, and they naturally regarded cognition in the child as basically similar to that in the adult, albeit at a rather simpler level. As a consequence, they had no special interest in exploring cognitive development. Several later theorists, including Piaget, disputed the Behaviourist contentions, and argued that really profound changes occurred during the course of cognitive development.

This more recent approach has played a major role in increasing experimental and theoretical interest in the problems and issues of cognitive development. It is now generally recognised that, apart from the intrinsic interest and value of investigating cognitive development, it also facilitates our understanding of adult cognition to consider its antecedents. Of course, cognition in the child covers very much the same wide range of topics as cognition in the adult, and there is insufficient space in one chapter to provide a comprehensive survey. What has been done instead is to focus on five major topics: (1) the development of thinking and intelligence as described by Piaget; (2) the course of perceptual development; (3) the changes in memorial functioning during the years of childhood; (4) the acquisition of language; and (5) the practical problem of reading retardation.

PIAGETIAN THEORY

Introduction

Far and away the most influential theorist in the area of cognitive development has been Jean Piaget. He and his colleagues in Geneva have put forward the most thorough account ever offered of the ways in which children's thinking develops. Indeed, such is the richness of his theoretical contribution that only the sketchiest account can be provided here.

At the most general level, Piaget argued that the development of intelligence is the highest form of adaptation of an individual to his or her environment. Adaptation involves an interaction between the individual's knowledge and the external environment, and two basic processes can be identified in this interaction: assimilation and accommodation. Assimilation occurs when there is some kind of cognitive structuring of an external object or event in accordance with the individual's pre-existing cognitive organisation. In contrast, accommodation occurs when this cognitive organisation is modified by the need to deal accurately with the requirements of environmental events. In other words, adaptation involves both an assimilation of the external environment *to* cognitive structure and an accommodation *of* cognitive structure to the external environment. The distinction between assimilation and accommodation resembles that between top-down and bottom-up processing discussed at some length in Chapters 1 and 2.

According to Piaget, proper adaptation requires a balance or equilibrium between assimilation and accommodation. However, there are occasions on which behaviour is primarily a function of only one of those processes. Perhaps the clearest example of the primacy of assimilation over accommodation is play, in which reality is interpreted in accordance with the whim of the individual. Dominance of accommodation over assimilation is seen in imitation.

We have concentrated so far on extremely general theoretical conceptions. At a slightly more specific level, we can distinguish between two kinds of theorists. One group argues that cognitive development involves merely changes in the amount of knowledge available to the child, and the efficiency with which that knowledge is used in thinking. According to such theorists, the thought processes of children and adults differ only quantitatively, i.e., there are no fundamental differences in cognition during development. The second group of theorists claims that there are dramatic qualitative changes in thinking during the years of childhood, and that the modes of thinking characteristic of adolescence are radically different from those of early childhood. Piaget can appropriately be regarded as the foremost member of the second group.

Piaget's belief in the existence of profound changes in thought processes during cognitive development led him to postulate a number of stages through which children pass. His stage-dependent explanations of cognitive development are discussed in detail in the next section, but it is pertinent at this point to consider some of the major assumptions of a stage analysis. Firstly, there must be sufficient discontinuities in cognitive development to permit the identification of qualitatively different cognitive stages. Secondly, while the ages at which different children attain any particular stage can vary, the sequence of stages should remain invariant. Thirdly, the cognitive operations and structures defining a stage should constitute an integrated whole. Fourthly, a stage has an initial period of preparation involving a transition from the preceding stage, followed by a final period of achievement. Thus within any given stage there is a shift from structural disequilibrium to equilibrium.

There has been much controversy about the advantages and disadvantages of stage theories of cognitive development. A potential merit of such theories is that they reduce the complexities of developmental changes in behaviour to manageable proportions. On the other hand, there is the obvious danger with stage theories of over-estimating the differences between stages while at the same time under-estimating the variations within a given stage. Piaget was well aware that children in a particular stage of development do not invariably adopt the mode of thought characteristic of that stage across all tasks and situations, and that it often happens that a child can successfully apply a cognitive structure to task A rather earlier in development than to task B. He coined the term "horizontal décalage" to refer to this state of affairs, and these horizontal décalages introduce a certain degree of intra-stage heterogeneity where only homogeneity might have been anticipated.

The Stages of Cognitive Development

According to Piaget, there are four major stages of cognitive development. The first of these is the sensori-motor period, which lasts from birth to approximately 2 years of age. The second stage is that of pre-operational thought, spanning the years between 2 and 7. Then comes the stage of concrete operations, which typically occurs between the ages of 7 and 11 or 12 years, and the fourth, and final, stage of formal operations immediately follows the stage of concrete operations.

In a general way, the reason for postulating these stages is Piaget's feeling that children's modes of thinking show various developmental changes. Initially, the young child deals with the environment by manipulation of objects; thus, sensori-motor development is quintessentially intelligence in action. After that, thinking becomes dominated by perception during the stage of pre-operational thought. From 7 years onwards, thinking is increasingly influenced by logico-mathematical considerations. During the stage of concrete operations, logical reasoning can be applied only to what is real or perceptually accessible; during the subsequent stage of formal operations, the older child or adult can think logically about potential events or even abstract propositions.

What is it that provides the impetus for these cognitive developments? According to Piaget's equilibration hypothesis, children are likely to experience a state of disequilibrium when they encounter cognitive conflict. This disequilibrium is resolved when new cognitive structures develop that serve to re-establish equilibrium.

1. The Sensori-motor Period. The sensori-motor period is divided into six separate stages of development. The most important accomplishment of this period is the gradual attainment of the concept of the permanent object, which permits the child to be aware of the existence of objects and of their locations even when they are not in view. During the first three stages of the sensori-motor period, the child simply ceases to be aware of the continued existence of objects when they disappear from view (it is literally a case of "out of sight, out of mind"). Thus, for example, the child at the third stage (roughly between 4 and 8 months) will not search for an object that is completely covered, even if the child has just been playing with it.

There is some notion of object permanence during the fourth and fifth stages of the sensori-motor period, but it is apparently too closely anchored to perception and to the child's own motor activities. In the fourth stage, the child will search for completely hidden objects. However, if the child is allowed to find an object hidden in one location, and the child then sees the object being hidden in a second location, it will often look for the object at the first location. The apparent implication of such perseverative search is that, from the child's point of view, the identity of an object is bound up with the actions that have been made to it at the first location.

There is some progress in the development of the object concept during the fifth stage from approximately 12 to 18 months. The child now searches only at the location in which the object was seen to be hidden, and does not make the mistake of searching at the locations of earlier successful recoveries. However, the child is still deficient in its thinking about hidden objects. If an adult hides an object in his hand, and then puts his hand in his pocket, the child at this stage will look for the hidden object only in the adult's hand. The child obviously fails to realise that the object could have been left in the pocket.

During the sixth and final stage of the sensori-motor period, the child is able to represent objects and actions internally. The ability to do this helps to free the child from some of the limitations of perception and action. In a nutshell, the child's object concept has finally evolved to the point at which objects are regarded as having an existence that is independent of the child.

So far, we have presented Piaget's views on cognitive development during the sensori-motor period in a non-evaluative way. However, there is a growing feeling that Piaget has under-estimated the abilities of young children. Consider, for example, the fact that children in stage three do not search for objects that are completely covered. While Piaget claimed that this demonstrated that such children lacked an object concept, it is possible that young children have some awareness that the object still exists, but do not fully understand spatial relations, such as "in" or "behind."

How can we distinguish between these rival interpretations of the data? One way is to make the object disappear in a simple way that places less emphasis on spatial relations. When an object was made to disappear by removing all light from it, infra-red television cameras revealed that very young children rapidly reached out in the correct direction (Bower & Wishart, 1972). This indicates some semblance of object permanence, as does a further study by Bower (1973). Suppose that an interesting object was presented to a stage three child, and then covered, and finally the cover was removed and the object had disappeared. Piaget's theory leads to the prediction that the child should not take any special notice of this unexpected event, because the object had ceased to exist for him or her as soon as the object was covered. In fact, the disappearance of the object produced signs of surprise when the cover was removed, showing that hidden objects do not simply cease to exist for the young child. Why then do young children fail to search for covered objects? Perhaps the real reason is that they find it difficult to remember unfamiliar combinations of objects: They do not know what it looks like when one object is placed inside another, and so they often experience problems in recalling that there is something underneath or inside the cover. When the cover is removed, however, the child does remember the previously seen combination of objects and is surprised that the desired object is no longer there.

Further difficulties with Piaget's theoretical analysis of the sensori-motor period arise in connection with his views on perseverative search, i.e., the tendency for the child to search for an object at a location where it has previously been obtained, in spite of the fact that he has just seen it hidden at a second location. Piaget explained perseverative search as reflecting the child's belief that an object's existence depends upon his own actions, and thus in some sense "exists" only at the initial location. Butterworth (1974) was unable to replicate Piaget's findings, discovering that only about half of his stage four children consistently searched at the first location, with the other half searching at the second location. Moreover, basically the same results were obtained when there was only passive observation of the object in its first location, indicating, contrary to Piaget's views, that the child's own actions cannot be used to explain perseverative search.

What then determines whether or not perseverative search occurs? Not surprisingly, the amount of relevant spatial information in the visual environment is an important factor. Young children usually search correctly at the second location when the covers at the two locations provide distinctive cues, and there is a stable background (Butterworth, Jarrett & Hicks, 1982). In contrast, when there is no immediate background at the initial location, perseverative search at the first location is the norm (Butterworth & Jarrett, 1982).

In sum, it now seems doubtful that the evolution of the concept of object permanence is quite as slow as Piaget claimed. Piaget seems to have used conditions that made it maximally difficult for young children to provide evidence of object permanence. Under more favourable conditions, even young children in stages three and four can demonstrate a reasonable grasp of the concept of object permanence.

2. The Pre-operational Stage. In spite of the achievements of the sensori-motor period, the child at the conclusion of that period is allegedly still not capable of "true" thought. The reason is that sensori-motor intelligence is concerned with actual objects and events in the external environment, and thus lacks the flexibility that characterises "true" thought. According to Piaget, considerable progress at a cognitive level is achieved during the pre-operational stage that lasts approximately between the ages of 2 and 7 years. Whereas the sensori-motor child operates largely at the level of direct action, the pre-operational child becomes increasingly capable of symbolic functioning. Of course, the acquisition of language plays an important part in the cognitive advances of pre-operational children, but Piaget tended to regard language as one of the manifestations of the symbolic function rather than as an independent determinant of the development of thinking. In other words, language development was seen as largely a reflection of some more fundamental cognitive change.

Despite the achievements of the pre-operational stage, Piaget devoted most of his attention to chronicling the deficiencies of thought found in this stage of development. One of the major limitations of the pre-operational child is his egocentrism, i.e., his tendency to take it for granted that his way of thinking about things is the only possible way. This egocentrism is reduced through social interaction, in which the existence of arguments and disagreements forces the child to take account of alternative viewpoints.

Egocentrism results in a lack of differentiation between the self and the world, and this in turn makes the child unable to distinguish clearly between psychological and physical events. As a consequence, the child's thinking is characterised by realism (the tendency to regard psychological events as having a physical existence); animism (the tendency to endow physical objects and events with psychological qualities); and artificialism (the tendency to consider that physical objects and events were created by people).

Piaget (1967) provided numerous examples of each of these kinds of egocentric thinking. Realism was revealed by the way in which pre-operational children seemed to believe that dreams were events in the real world:

Engl ($8\frac{1}{2}$):   Where do dreams come from?—I don't know.—Say what you think.—From the sky.—How? Where do they come?—To the house.—Where is the dream whilst you are dreaming?—Beside me.—Are your eyes shut when you dream?—Yes.—Where is the dream?—Over there [p. 95].

Children show animism when they claim that the wind feels it when it blows against a mountain, or that a button feels it when it is pulled off a shirt. While young children often attribute consciousness to all things, they gradually restrict consciousness to those things that can move, and then to things which appear to be spontaneously active (e.g., clouds).

An example of artificialism concerns my daughter Fleur at the age of 3 years. We were on Wimbledon Common, and I told her that the sun would come out when I had counted to ten. When it did so, she was entirely confident that Daddy had the power to control the sun, and often begged me to make the sun appear on gloomy and cold days!

At least some of the apparent egocentricity shown by pre-operational children may simply reflect the application of rational thinking to impoverished data. Even intelligent adults can be confused when asked a question on a topic of which they possess little knowledge. We have a remote control for our television set, and I have asked several friends to explain how it works. The answers have been weird and wonderful and completely inaccurate, and many of them would probably have been classified as egocentric by Piaget.

Evidence that the amount of relevant knowledge possessed by the child affects the apparent egocentricity of what he says was obtained by Berzonsky (1971). When children were asked about remote events (e.g., "Why does the moon change shape?"), predominantly egocentric answers were elicited, but sensible mechanical explanations were fairly common when they were asked about familiar events, such as, the flying of kites or the flattening of a tyre.

The major criticism that we have made so far about Piaget's views on egocentrism is that some of the available data may have been misinterpreted. It is also possible that the data themselves are inadequate and misleading. In the well-known mountains task, children look at a model of mountains and then have to decide which of several pictures represents the view that someone would have viewing the display from a different angle. Children younger than 8 years old nearly always select the photograph of the scene as they themselves see it, which was attributed by Piaget to their inability to escape from an egocentric perspective.

An alternative view is that poor performance on the mountains task occurs in large measure because the task is alien to the child's experience of the world in that it fails to relate to normal human purposes. Hughes (1975) attempted to remedy this defect by using a task requiring children to hide a doll so that two policemen looking from different perspectives to the child could not see it. In this task, the intentions of the characters are immediately obvious to young children. Ninety percent of children aged between $3\frac{1}{2}$ and 5 years solved the problem, and thus successfully avoided an entirely egocentric perspective.

The pre-operational child's thinking is not only limited by egocentrism in Piagetian theory. This child tends to be dominated by her own perception, and pays attention to only one aspect of the total situation (this is called "centration" by Piaget). The way in which centration produces errors is shown by experiments on various kinds of conservation. Conservation is the term used to refer to the recognition that certain properties of a display do not vary despite changes in other properties of the display. In his classic studies on conservation of quantity, Piaget presented the child with two glasses of the same size and shape containing the same quantity of liquid. When the child has agreed that there is the same quantity of liquid in both glasses, all of the liquid from one of the glasses is poured into a different glass that is taller and thinner. The child is then asked if the two glasses (the original one and the new one) contain the same amount to drink, or if one contains more. Pre-operational children fail to show conservation, arguing either that there is more liquid in the new container ("because it's higher") or that there is more in the original glass ("because it's wider"). In either case, according to Piaget, the child centres or focuses on only one dimension (height or width), and uses it as the basis for her decision.

The pre-operational child fails on conservation tasks partly because of centration, but also partly because she lacks crucial internalised, concrete operations. In particular, she lacks the logico-mathematical operation of reversibility, which involves the ability to undo, or reverse, mentally some operation that one has previously carried out. In the case of the classic conservation experiment, reversibility permits the realisation that the effect of pouring the liquid from one container into another could be negated precisely by the inverse action of pouring the liquid back into its original container. The pre-operational child also fails to conserve because she does not think in terms of compensation (i.e., the increase in the height of the liquid in the new container is offset by the accompanying decrease in width).

The conservation task is almost certainly the best known of the Piagetian tasks, and it allegedly supports a number of Piaget's theoretical notions. The failure of children up to the age of approximately 7 years to perform this apparently simple task with success seems to indicate that pre-operational children are overly influenced by certain aspects of their immediate perceptual environment (centration), and that they lack important logical tools.

These conclusions have been hotly disputed. It has been argued that children often fail the conservation task simply because of their inability to understand the question rather than because they do not understand the concept of conservation. An appropriate method of testing this notion is to assess conservation in such a way that the role of language is minimised. Wheldall and Poborca (1980) devised a non-verbal paradigm based on operant discrimination learning. Whereas only 28% of their 6-year-old and 7-year-old subjects showed conservation when tested in the normal verbal fashion, 50% did so when tested non-verbally. These data suggest that linguistic misunderstanding is one factor involved in non-conservation, but the fact that one-half of the subjects were non-conservers, even with the non-verbal assessment procedure, indicates that other factors must be considered.

It is possible that many pre-operational children are capable of demonstrating conservation, but usually fail to do so because they are influenced too much by the altered appearance of the visual display. This line of reasoning led Bruner, Olver, and Greenfield (1966) to arrange matters so that children could conceptualise the changed situation before seeing it. They achieved this by placing two beakers of different shapes behind a screen with only the tops of the beakers visible. Then water was poured from one beaker into the other behind the screen. When asked whether there was the same amount of water in the second beaker as there had been in the first, children of all ages between 4 and 7 years showed much more evidence of conservation than they had in the standard form of the conservation task. Among 5-year-olds, for example, approximately 80% were correct with the screen in place against only 20% under standard conditions. Subsequent removal of the screen reduced conservation judgements considerably in 4-year-olds, but had little effect on older children. Finally, the children were given the standard conservation task for a second time, and the percentage of 5-year-olds showing conservation had more than trebled from 20% on the first test under standard conditions to approximately 70% on the second test.

Bruner et al. (1966) were not content with merely demonstrating that young children's ability to conserve had been under-estimated in previous research. They also argued that Piaget's contention that conservation depends on reversibility and/or compensation was erroneous, and suggested that a sense of identity was of fundamental importance. In other words, the child must realise that the water poured from one beaker to another remains the same in spite of the move. Some support for these notions was obtained by questioning the children about the reasons for their judgements on the conservation task. Children who nearly always achieved conservation claimed that the water was the same, suggesting that a sense of identity is a necessary (if not sufficient) prerequisite for conservation. In addition, sensitising children to the issue of identity by asking the question, "Is it still the same water?," led to a marked increase in the number of children able to conserve.

A rather different attack on Piaget's interpretation of findings with the conservation task was mounted by Donaldson (1978, 1982). She argued that children tend to be influenced in their interpretation of language by the particular context in which they hear it. In the conservation task, the experimenter produces a deliberate and apparently important change in one of the quantities, and this may lead the child to think about the experimenter's intentions. This emphasis on change may bias the child towards non-conservation, especially if pre-operational children answer the subsequent conservation question on the basis of what they think the experimenter means rather than what he actually says.

These ideas were first tested by McGarrigle and Donaldson (1974). They substituted an apparently accidental transformation of the stimulus array by a "naughty teddy bear" for the usual deliberate transformation by the experimenter. Many more children achieved conservation under these conditions than in the standard task. However, while these results seem to support the notion that the apparent reason for transforming the array is important, a simpler explanation is also possible. It may be that the children paid less attention to the transformed array when the transformation was produced accidentally.

Very striking findings based on a similar approach to that of McGarrigle and Donaldson (1974) were reported by Light, Buckingham and Robbins (1979). They tested 5- and 6-year-olds in pairs, with both members of each pair being given glass beakers of the same size and containing the same number of small pasta shells. They were told that the shells would be used to play a competitive game, and so it was essential that both players started with an equal number. Then the experimenter pretended to notice that one of the beakers had a badly chipped rim and might therefore be dangerous to handle. The shells were accordingly transferred to another beaker of a different shape, and the children were asked whether there was still the same quantity of shells in each beaker.

Conservation was shown by 70% of the children in this incidental transformation condition, against only 5% in a standard intentional transformation conditions. Why was there this large difference? It may have been that the change seemed less important when the transformation was regarded as merely incidental. Alternatively, the children exposed to the incidental transformation may have paid relatively little attention to the transformation, and thus were unaffected by it.

Piaget's views of the pre-operational child as one who is unable to understand and use logical rules, and who cannot combine separate perceptual inputs, led him to the conclusion that the child would be incapable of solving even the simplest syllogism. Consider, for example, transitivity problems, in which the child makes length judgements about three sticks. According to Piaget, the pre-operational child cannot reason that if stick A is longer than stick B, and stick B is longer than stick C, then it must follow that stick A is longer than stick C.

Bryant and Trabasso (1971) argued that the pre-operational child's difficulty with transitivity problems might stem from poor memory rather than deficiencies in logical inference. They gave children between the ages of 4 and 6 years extensive training on the relative lengths of five different sticks, and found that these young children were reasonably successful at making transitive inferences. They argued that the amount of previous training reduced the memory problem, and it is noteworthy that children who failed to solve the transitivity problems were usually unable to recall what they had learned during the initial training.

What can be concluded about Piaget's theoretical analysis of the thinking of the pre-operational child? Firstly, Piaget tended to consider only one possible reason for the errors that such children make on a particular task. As we have seen, inaccurate performance is not always attributable to egocentricity or lack of the appropriate logico-mathematical operations. Several other factors, such as, lack of knowledge, poor memory, lack of familiarity with task materials, and details of the way in which the task is presented must all be considered.

Secondly, there is a growing feeling that Piaget under-estimated the cognitive skills of pre-operational children. This is supported by the typical finding that the version of a task preferred by Piaget often produces considerably inferior performance to that obtained on other, logically equivalent versions of the same task. Piaget tended to select tasks that were rather abstract and lacking in meaning for the child, and which required attention to subtle nuances of language for their solution. Such tasks are not well designed to demonstrate the true capacities of young children, as was eloquently described by Donaldson (1978):

> By the time they come to school, all normal children can show skill as thinkers and language-users to a degree which must compel respect, so long as they are dealing with "real-life" meaningful situations in which they have purposes and intentions and in which they can recognise and respond to similar purposes and intentions in others.... He uses his skills to serve his compelling immedi-ate purposes. But he does not notice how he uses them, and so he cannot call them into service deliberately when the compelling purpose has gone [p. 121].

3. The Period of Concrete Operations.   According to Piaget, the age of 7 years typically represents the demarcation between the period of pre-operational thought and that of concrete operations. A child of this age demonstrates a variety of new intellectual achievements indicating that a higher level of intellectual development has been attained. For the first time, evidence of conservation is shown, the child has become less egocentric (e.g., he or she realises that a person of another nationality regards him as a foreigner), and awareness of class relationships is shown (e.g., in a display of roses and carnations, he or she knows there are more flowers than roses).

How can this cognitive advance be characterised? Piaget claimed that the transition from pre-operational to concrete-operational thinking represents an increasing independence of thought from perception. Underlying this is the development of various logico-mathematical operations, which consist of cognitive actions organised into a strong structure. Examples of such operations include the actions implied in common mathematical symbols, such as, $+$, $-$, $\div$, $\times$, $>$, $<$, and $=$. The most important of such operations is reversibility, which involves the ability to cancel out the effects of a perceptual change by imagining the inverse change.

Until the age of 11 or so, the logical operations used by the child are not independent of the immediate situation; in other words, the child's thinking is effective only to the extent that it is concerned with a particular concrete situation. This inability of the concrete-operational child to free his or her thinking from the immediate situation may explain why, for example, conservation of quantity is attained approximately 2 years earlier than conservation of weight, despite the fact that both forms of conservation involve the same logical operations.

One of the points stressed by Piaget is that cognitive operations are usually combined or organised into a system or structure. An operation, such as, "greater than," cannot really be considered independently from the operation "less than," because an individual has failed to grasp the meaning of "A is greater than B" unless he or she appreciates that this statement means that "B is less than A." Piaget coined the term "grouping" to refer to logical systems resembling, but not identical to, logical groups. A group consists of a set of elements and an operation bearing on those elements such that the properties of combinativity, associativity, identity, and inversion hold true (e.g., the system of positive and negative numbers.)

In sum, Piaget claimed that the concrete-operational child has developed a relatively coherent and well-integrated cognitive system which is used to organise and manipulate the environment. More specifically, certain logico-mathematical structures are regarded as excellent models of the actual organisation of cognition during the years between 7 and 11. This is a bold and intriguing hypothesis, but it suffers from some fairly obvious inadequacies. In particular, it seems to be primarily a competence model, describing the kinds of knowledge needed to solve various kinds of problem, rather than a performance model. A child may fail to solve a conservation problem because the necessary logical knowledge has not been acquired, but also because of the complexity of the task, poor motivation, momentary inattention, or because of lack of verbal skills. In other words, what is largely missing from Piaget's account is a detailed analysis of the psychological processes which determine the extent to which the child's knowledge is actually made use of in any particular situation.

At the empirical level the difficulty for Piagetian theory is the frequent tendency for concrete-operational children to appear to demonstrate a grasp of some logico-mathematical structures in one situation but to fail to do so in other similar situations. Such behavioural inconsistency reveals that the possession of certain kinds of knowledge is no guarantee of successful performance on tasks requiring the utilisation of that knowledge.

4. *The Period of Formal Operations.* According to Piaget, the child of 11 or 12 years of age experiences a reorientation to reality that leads him or her to move from the stage of concrete operations into the final developmental stage, that of formal operations. What are the major characteristics of this reorientation? Perhaps the single most important general property of formal-operational thought is the ability to think in terms of many possible eventualities or states of the world; this permits an escape from the limitations of immediate reality, and helps to promote hypothetico-deductive thinking. Closely related to this ability is that of combinatorial analysis, in which the formal-operational adolescent is able to tackle a problem by systematically considering all of the factors in the problem, together with all of the possible combinations of factors. The formal operations that are such a vital aspect of adult thought are actually operations that are performed upon propositions which are the results of previous concrete operations; as a consequence, Piaget referred to formal operations as "second-degree operations" or "operations to the second power."

It is not always easy in practice to decide whether a particular child is actually making use formal operations when trying to solve a problem. However, Inhelder and Piaget (1958) provided the following suggestions for distinguishing between problem solvers using formal operations and those relying solely on concrete operations:

> Analyse the proofs employed by the subject. If they do not go beyond observation of empirical correspondences, they can be fully explained in terms of concrete operations, and nothing would warrant our assuming that more complex thought mechanisms are operating. If, on the other hand, the subject interprets a given correspondence as the result of any one of several possible combinations, and this leads him to verify his hypotheses by observing their consequences, we know that propositional operations are involved [p. 279].

Our description of formal-operational thought has been rather abstract, and may benefit from the inclusion here of an illustration of the kind of empirical study carried out to investigate the thought processes of older children and adolescents. The subject is supplied with a set of weights and a string that can be lengthened or shortened, and his or her task is to work out what determines the frequency of the oscillations of a pendulum formed by suspending a weight on a string from a pole. The factors that are likely to be considered include the length of the string, the weight of the suspended object, the force of the subject's push, and the position from which the pendulum is pushed. In fact, only the length of the string is relevant.

When pre-operational children are confronted with this problem, they typically provide inconsistent explanations; however, they tend to claim that the strength of the impetus they give to the pendulum is the crucial factor. Concrete-operational children often observe that the frequency of oscillation is affected by the length of the string, but they are unable to isolate this variable from all of the others. In contrast, many formal-operational children manage to solve the problem successfully. According the Piaget, the ability to solve the pendulum problem presupposes the understanding of a complicated combinatorial system combined with hypothetico-deductive thinking.

Piaget has attempted to characterise much of formal-operational thinking in terms of the logico-mathematical structures allegedly involved. More specifically, he has argued that there is an integrated lattice-group structure underlying adolescent thinking. A lattice is formed from the set of all possible combinations in a particular problem situation, and the group that Piaget has emphasised is a four group consisting of four different trans-formations (i.e., identity, negation, reciprocal, and correlative). Further details of Piaget's use of logical principles to explain formal-operational thought can be found in a book by Flavell (1963).

How adequate is the Piagetian analysis of adolescent thought? In the first place, the notion that adolescents typically operate at the level of complex logical thought is one more likely to evoke a wry smile than a nod of agreement from harassed schoolteachers. Secondly, it seems probable that Piaget has greatly exaggerated the role played by logico-mathematical structures in adolescent and adult intelligence. Although it is, of course, entirely possible to devise problems requiring the use of logical principles for their solution, it is equally possible to think of problems that do not necessitate the application of logic. Indeed, adults in their everyday lives typically deal with problems that have no single perfect solution, and that cannot be solved simply by the rigorous use of logic. Consider, for example, Guilford's (1971) distinction between convergent and divergent thinking. Convergent thinking is of primary importance when the presented informa-tion is sufficient to determine a unique answer. It could be argued that Piaget has been concerned with convergent thinking, because logical deduction or compelling inference is involved. However, divergent thinking, which relates to fluency and flexibility of thought, and is involved when several different answers are required to a problem (e.g., "List the possible uses of a brick"), has been largely ignored by Piaget.

In spite of these omissions, it is still true that Piaget has made a valuable contribution to our understanding of adolescent thought. It seems clear that the development of cognition during the years of childhood involves an increased ability to think in an abstract, logical fashion despite the distractions of the immediate environment. In a sense, Piaget's achievement is that he has taken this fundamental idea and used it as the basis for a more detailed account of adolescent thought than had been proposed previously.

An Evaluation

A number of the limitations of Piaget's approach to cognitive development have already been discussed. In particular, he tended to over-interpret his findings, claiming that children lack cognitive and logical principles of broad significance merely because they fail to solve a particular problem involving those principles. This ignores the possibility that the way in which the problem is presented, or the child's unfamiliarity with the task materials, may be responsible. We have encountered numerous examples of young children being successful when given a problem presented in a slightly different manner. While Piaget's theory can account for such apparent behavioural inconsistency in general terms (via the notion of horizontal décalage), it almost totally lacks the specific theoretical formulations needed to provide a complete explanation.

At the risk of over-simplification, we could encapsulate Piagetian theory as claiming that cognitive development involves a shift from the irrational and the illogical to the rational and the logical. As we have seen, the assumption that young children think in an illogical fashion is no more than partially true. When confronted by meaningful and naturalistic problems, young children often reason in a rational and coherent way. The assumption that adults think logically is also only a half-truth, as is made abundantly clear in Chapter 10, which contains numerous examples of illogical and incoherent thinking in intelligent adults. Another example with a Piagetian flavour to it concerns transitive inference. Piaget has described how concrete-operational children master the logical principles underlying transitive inference, so that they are able to realise that if, for example, A is longer than B, and B is longer than C, then A must be longer than C. However, even intelligent adults do not appear to understand these logical principles fully. In an informal study, the author asked various well-educated people whether it followed necessarily from the fact that tennis player A usually beats player B, and that player B usually beats player C, that player A usually beats player C. There was fairly general agreement that the conclusion is a necessary one. In fact, while transitivity always holds when the problem involves a single dimension such as length or height, it does not necessarily hold with multi-dimensional concepts, such as, tennis-playing ability. In the example above, tennis player A may be an excellent player generally, but vulnerable against left-handed players such as C.

Another major problem with Piaget's approach concerns his preferred research strategy, which basically involved assessing the ability of children of different ages to solve certain problems. This approach can provide a reasonably accurate description of major developmental changes, but it makes it difficult to uncover the causal determinants of those changes. This is not to argue that Piaget was uninterested in the factors producing cognitive development. According to his equilibration hypothesis (Piaget, 1970), the existence of a conflict between different interpretations of a situation, or between a child's expectations concerning the outcome of an action and the actual outcome, produces a state of disequilibrium. This disequilibrium in turn leads in a rather obscure fashion to the development of new cognitive structures that restore equilibrium.

Two of the ways in which disequilibrium can occur are as a result of a disagreement between one child and another (inter-individual conflict) or by simply presenting the child with two conflicting interpretations (intra-individual conflict). Piaget argued that conflict with peers was especially important in reducing egocentrism and leading to decentring, and Doise and Mugny (1979) reported that socially induced conflict was more effective than intra-individual conflict in promoting advances in thinking. However, Emler and Valiant (1982) discovered that both forms of conflict were equally effective, suggesting that the important factor is simply the existence of conflict.

The notion that conflict leads to cognitive development may seem plausible, but is in some ways remarkably vague. If there are two conflicting interpretations of a situation, then one or other of the interpretations is wrong, or both interpretations are wrong. How is the child to decide which is the correct interpretation? A very different approach was offered by Bryant (1982), who suggested that it is agreement between interpretations or strategies that leads to intellectual development. In other words, the value of a particular interpretation or strategy is perceived when it reliably leads to the same answer as a different strategy.

Bryant (1982) pitted conflict theory against his own in a task that involved deciding whether two blocks of wood were equally tall. The decision could be made in a simple way by means of visual comparison or in a more sophisticated way by using a measuring rod. During a series of demonstration trials, both kinds of decision had to be made. When the two blocks were at different levels, the two decisions were often in conflict, whereas the decisions were nearly always in agreement when the blocks were side by side at the same level. The key issue was what would happen after the demonstration trials when the children were free to use whichever measurement technique they favoured. The results were clearcut: conflict did not cause any increase in the use of the better measurement technique (i.e., the measuring rod), but agreement did lead to greater use of the measuring rod.

It is possible, of course, that both agreement and conflict can produce cognitive advances at different times and under different circumstances. However, reliance on agreement seems sensible because it will usually be the case that if two different strategies produce the same solution, then that solution is correct. In contrast, Piaget's equilibration hypothesis needs to be expanded to explain how it is that the child moves from cognitive conflict to the correct solution.

The merits of the Piagetian approach can be seen if we consider a continuum going from theoretical specificity to generality. Highly specific theoretical approaches (e.g., early Behaviourism) focus on fine-grained analyses of developmental changes in response patterns, and so make it difficult to see the wood for the trees. Within the confines of such approaches, cognitive development tends to appear as the rather haphazard achievement of a myriad of specific skills. In contrast, Piaget adopted an approach of considerable generality, which allows one to see certain coherent trends in cognitive development. For example, it seems logical and inevitable that the second-order operations (i.e., operations upon operations) characteristic of formal-operational thought come into existence at a later developmental stage than first-order operations. Piaget's approach also makes cognitive development appear coherent in a slightly different way. The fact that children at around the age of 7 years old rapidly gain the ability to solve a wide range of cognitive tasks is understandable in the light of Piaget's contention that all that is necessary is the acquisition of a limited number of cognitive structures and operations (e.g., reversibility). However, it seems probable that Piaget has exaggerated the importance of general cognitive structures and operations; while it is true that children develop some fairly general logical reasoning skills, much of their intellectual development involves the acquisition of more specific knowledge, a fact strangely neglected by Piaget.

PERCEPTUAL DEVELOPMENT

For a long time it was believed that William James (1890) was correct when he described the perceptual experience of the newborn infant as a "booming, buzzing confusion." This view is no longer prevalent, but there do appear to be a number of conspicuous deficiencies in some of the basic visual mechanisms of infants during the first month of two of life. Firstly, very young infants show very imperfect visual accommodation, i.e., the lens of the eye does not change its shape (accommodate) reflexly when objects are presented at different distances. Secondly, the two eyes of the infant do not always move together and and fixate on the same object. In more technical language this is known as inadequate binocular convergence. Finally, infants in the first 2 months of life have relatively poor visual acuity.

In view of the deficiencies mentioned above, together with the fact that infants do not typically seem to behave as if they had reasonably adequate perceptual skills, it is perhaps not surprising that the infant's actual perceptual achievements have been ignored until fairly recently. Historically, the work of Fantz (1961) was important in changing the climate of opinion. She was faced by the problem that the limited behavioural repertoire of the infant makes it difficult to assess what he perceives. Her solution to this problem was to use a preference paradigm in which a number of visual stimuli were presented at the same time. She argued that if an infant looked at one stimulus more than at the others, this selectivity implied that he or she could discriminate perceptually between them.

In a classic experiment by Fantz (1961), infants between 4 days and 5 months of age were shown three head-shaped discs, one of which was painted black where the hair might have been with the rest left blank, one had a face painted on it, and the third disc consisted of a scrambled face. The infants looked most at the realistic face and least at the blank face at all age levels. Such findings led Fantz (1966) to the following controversial conclusions:

> The findings have tended to destroy . . . myths—that the world of the neonate [newly born baby] is a big booming confusion, that his visual field is a form of blur, that his mind is a blank state, that his brain is decorticate, and that his behaviour is limited to reflexes or undirected mass movements. The infant sees a patterned and organised world which he explores discriminatingly within the limited means at his command [pp. 171–172].

These conclusions may be largely true, but there have been criticisms of the evidence upon which Fantz relied. In particular, the difference in preference between the real and scrambled faces obtained by Fantz (1961) was slight, and other researchers have not always been able to replicate this finding. Even if the difference is a genuine one, it is still possible that infants were simply responding to the symmetry of the real face.

Further early evidence that infants possess considerable perceptual skills was obtained by Gibson and Walk (1960) in their studies on the "visual cliff." The apparatus they used consisted of a glass-top table with a checked pattern immediately underneath half of the glass ("shallow" side), whereas below the rest of the glass the checked pattern was on the floor ("deep" side). The impression created was of a drop between the two halves. The infant was placed on the shallow side of the table, and an attempt was made to persuade him to crawl over the edge of the "visual cliff" by offering him toys or having his mother call him. Most of the infants, who were aged between

$6\frac{1}{2}$ and 12 months, refused to do this, suggesting that they possessed at least the rudiments of depth perception.

It has sometimes been assumed that this work on the visual cliff indicates that crucial aspects of space perception are innate. However, this assumption is dubious, since infants who are old enough to crawl could obviously have learned about depth perception as a result of their experience. There is some evidence for developmental changes in the perception of depth. When 9-month-old infants were placed on the shallow side of the visual cliff apparatus they showed heart-rate deceleration, but the same infants showed heart-rate acceleration when placed on the deep side, perhaps indicative of fear. The most interesting finding was that the heart rate of 2-month-old babies did not correspond to this "natural" pattern; instead, they actually showed greater heart-rate deceleration in the visual cliff situation on the deep side than on the shallow side. This suggests that full depth perception does not develop during the first 2 months of life.

Rather more convincing evidence that at least some perceptual skills do not depend upon learning has been obtained by other researchers. In one notable study, Wertheimer (1962) investigated auditory perception in a new-born baby who was under 10 minutes old. The baby was presented with a series of sounds to his left and to his right, and he looked in the appropriate direction each time. Thus some of the elements of auditory perception are available at birth, as is a degree of motor co-ordination and control.

In the visual modality, it has long been known that infants gradually seem to lose interest and stop looking at an object if it is shown several times in one position, but they resume looking at it when the object's distance from the infant is changed. Does this indicate that infants are actually able to perceive distance, or is it simply that they respond to the alteration in apparent size? Bower, Broughton and Moore (1970) tried to provide an answer to this question. They showed infants of under 2 weeks two objects, the first of which was small and approached to within 8 centimetres of the infant's face, and the second of which was large and approached to within 20 centimetres. The objects and distances were selected so that the two objects would appear to be the same size at their closest point to the infant. In spite of this equivalence of apparent size, the object which approached closer elicited more defensive reactions from the infants. The implication is that even very young babies possess the rudiments of depth perception.

One of the major features of adults' visual perception is the existence of several kinds of constancy (e.g., size, shape). In the case of size constancy, we perceive an object as having a particular size irrespective of its distance from us, in spite of the fact that the retinal image of that object is considerably smaller when the object is far away than when it is close at hand. Bower (1964) tested for the presence of size constancy in infants aged between 75 and 85 days. They were initially trained to turn their heads towards a 30-centimetre cube placed nearly 1 metre from their eyes by being rewarded by the experimenter popping up and saying "peek-a-boo" every time they made the appropriate head turn. Bower then observed the amount of head turning to the same stimulus placed 3 metres from the infant (same real size as the training stimulus but much smaller retinal image) and to a 90-centimetre cube placed 3 metres from the infant (much larger real size than the training stimulus but the same retinal size). There were almost three times as many responses to the former stimulus than to the latter. The fact that responding depended more on real size than on retinal size indicates at least some size constancy; however, it was not complete, since there were more responses when the 30-centimetre cube was presented at its original distance of 1 metre than when it was 3 metres away.

Similar kinds of experiments have been carried out on shape constancy (e.g., Bower, 1965). It appears that the position is similar to that reported for size constancy, namely, that children as young as 2 months of age show some shape constancy, but complete constancy is lacking. The existence of these, and other, constancies in very young babies, together with a partial ability to perceive depth, suggests that spatial-perceptual competence is present much earlier in development than had previously been supposed. Furthermore, while some of these perceptual achievements may involve learning, it is difficult to believe that learning plays a major role. The reason is that the kinds of exploratory and reaching behaviour that might enable the infant to develop his spatial-perceptual abilities are not typically displayed before 3 months of age.

In sum, very young infants seem to possess some of the main skills involved in visual space perception. However, it is abundantly clear that their visual perception is deficient in several respects. Infants are adept at locating objects within the visual field, but they are unable to analyse those objects perceptually in a precise and fine-grained fashion. When the visual fixation patterns of 1- and 2-month-old infants looking at various stimuli were compared (Salapatek, 1975), some interesting differences were detected. The younger infants tended to look only at a limited part of the external contour of a compound stimulus (e.g., a small square inside a large square), whereas the older infants were more inclined to fixate on the internal features of such stimuli.

Additional deficiencies in the looking patterns of young infants are revealed when several visual stimuli are presented at the same time (e.g., Tronick & Clanton, 1971). Infants as young as 20 days of age are reasonably adept at co-ordinating head and eye movements in order to maintain attention to a particular stimulus, or to shift attention to a new stimulus. However, these infants are less adept than older infants in exploring the visual environment, and they look at fewer locations.

What can be concluded about the development of perceptual skills?

Firstly, it is becoming increasingly clear that much of the basic machinery and many of the mechanisms of perception are available shortly after birth. Secondly, there is a considerable increase in the precision and refinement of perceptual skills during the first few months of life. Thirdly, since certain perceptual skills (such as those involved in the interpretation of environmental stimuli) can only be acquired when prerequisite memorial and cognitive developments have occurred, the attainment of adult-like perception is a lengthy process.

MEMORY

There is overwhelming evidence that the ability to retain virtually every kind of information increases considerably during the years of childhood. In terms of possible explanations for this state of affairs, the theorist is faced with an *embarras de richesses*. In essence, the cognitive functioning of older children is so much more advanced than that of younger children that there are developmental changes in practically all of the processing activities relevant to learning and memory.

One of the processing activities that has attracted much interest is rehearsal. The first obvious issue is whether there are developmental changes in the likelihood that rehearsal will be used to facilitate learning. This issue was investigated by Flavell, Beach and Chinsky (1966), who showed pictures for subsequent recall to 5-, 7-, and 10-year-olds, and determined the amount of rehearsal by using lip-reading evidence. Their main finding was that the percentage of children who rehearsed increased from 10% among 5-year-olds to 60% among 7-year-olds, and to 85% among 10-year-olds. Since recall performance also increased with age, it is tempting to conclude that a failure to rehearse reduced retention among the younger children.

A rather more interesting issue is whether age has any effect on the nature of rehearsal activity. When children aged 7 years old and above were asked to rehearse out loud while learning several lists, the overall amount of rehearsal was similar in all age groups, but there were differences in what was rehearsed (Cuvo, 1975). Young children's rehearsal was frequently limited to repetition of a single word, whereas older children and adults tended to rehearse a number of different words concurrently. Other studies have shown that rehearsal is more likely to reflect the semantic structure of a list of words in older children, with words related by meaning being rehearsed together.

Of course, rehearsal is basically a verbal mnemonic, and part of the reason why young children do not rehearse may be because of their limited language development. If that were the case, then even very young children might show evidence of rehearsal-like activity provided that language was not involved. This notion was tested by Wellman, Ritter and Flavell (1975), who told 3-year-olds a story about a dog. A toy dog was placed under one of four identical cups at that point in the story at which the dog was put in the doghouse. Each child was told to remember the location of the dog while the experimenter went to fetch some more props. Behaviour resembling rehearsal was shown by the children, who looked at and touched the cup hiding the dog more often than any of the other cups.

Perhaps the most fundamental issue in this area is how to account for the failure of young children to use effective mnemonic techniques such as rehearsal. Flavell (1977) argued that there are two major alternative explanations that need to be considered. Firstly, there may be a production deficiency, i.e., the child may not make spontaneous use of a particular learning technique for reasons other than his inability to use the technique effectively. Secondly, there may be a mediational deficiency, i.e., the child is simply unable to use the particular learning strategy at all, or uses it so ineffectively that it does not enhance retention. This distinction between production deficiency and mediational deficiency appears to be of value, provided that we realise that it is not always easy to determine which kind of deficiency a child is suffering from. Part of the problem here is that there is no pure measure of spontaneous production of a learning technique: The presence or absence of any given technique depends heavily on the nature of the learning task and the stimulus materials.

How can we attempt to distinguish empirically between these two kinds of deficiency? In practice, a child's failure to use some learning strategy is classified as a production deficiency if suitable training or instructions enable the child to use that strategy effectively. A good example of this approach is provided in a study by Keeney, Cannizzo and Flavell (1967). Children of 6 and 7 years old who rehearsed spontaneously had better recall on a serial learning task than children of the same age who did not rehearse (see Fig. 9.1). The non-rehearsers seem to have suffered from a production deficiency because minimal instruction and demonstration by the experimenter was sufficient to induce them to rehearse, and improved their memory performance up to the level of the spontaneous rehearsers.

In general terms, the evidence indicates that very young children have mediational deficiencies, whereas children between the ages of approximately 5 and 8 years often have production deficiencies. Why do some children fail to utilise mnemonic strategies that they are capable of using, and that would enhance their retention? It appears that they often have a very limited awareness of the potential value of such strategies, as is shown by their replies to direct questioning. This lack of awareness presumably underlies a further finding from the study by Keeney et al. (1967). The children whose retention had benefited from training in rehearsal often stopped rehearsing when they were told that it was optional.

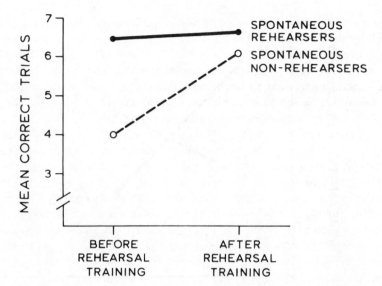

FIG. 9.1   Mean number of correct trials (max. = 10) on a non-verbal serial recall task for children (mean age = 6 years 10 months), who were spontaneous rehearsers and non-rehearsers, before and after training in rehearsal. Data from Keeney *et al.* (1967).

One of the most obvious differences between children of different ages is the amount of knowledge that they possess. This is of importance to memory, because full comprehension of learning material is greatly facilitated by appropriate background information. Ann Brown has used the term "head-fitting" to refer to the fit between the information to be remembered and the child's knowledge base. If the amount of relevant knowledge possessed by the learner is of major significance, then we might discover that a well-informed child can remember some things better than an ill-informed adult. This prediction was tested by Chi (1978) who looked at digit recall and reproduction of chess positions in children of approximately 10 years of age, who were skilled chess players, and in adults knowing little about chess. As can be seen in Fig. 9.2, the usual memorial superiority of adults over children was obtained for digit recall, but the children's recall of chess positions exceeded that of adults by more than 50%.

The possession of stimulus-relevant knowledge not only facilitates comprehension, it also increases the ability of the learner to embellish, or elaborate on, the stimulus material in various ways. The relevance of this to memory is that there is considerable evidence that long-term memory is better when there has been a great deal of elaboration rather than when there has been only a little (see Chapter 5). A common form of elaboration is inference drawing, which can be illustrated by a sentence such as "John shot

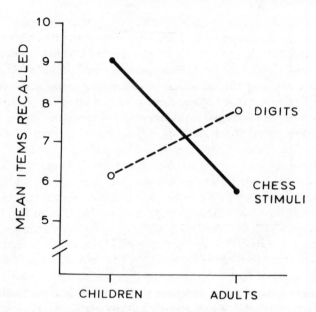

FIG. 9.2   Immediate recall of chess positions and digits in children (mean age = 10 years 6 months) with expert knowledge of chess and in adults with limited knowledge of chess. Adapted from Chi (1978).

Mary." Although it is not explicitly stated, most adults reading that sentence would draw the inference that John had a gun.

Paris and Lindauer (1976) investigated children's ability to make inferences. They made use of sentences describing an action performed by an individual (e.g., "Her friend swept the kitchen floor *with a broom*"). Half of the sentences included the instrument usually used to perform the activity (i.e., the italicised part of the example sentence), but the remaining sentences did not. Memory was then tested by providing the instruments as retrieval cues for the sentences. These cues were much more effective for 7-year-olds and 9-year-olds when the instrument had been presented at the time of learning than when it had not, but the memory performance of 11-year-olds was relatively unaffected by the nature of presentation. These findings suggest that only the oldest children routinely inferred the instruments during sentence presentation.

We have seen that, as children grow older, they are more likely to rehearse; to rehearse in an effective way; to possess relevant knowledge; and to draw inferences from what they read or hear. There is also some evidence (e.g., Kobasigawa, 1974) that young children use less effective and systematic retrieval strategies than older children. In addition, there is developmental growth in metamemory, i.e., intuitive knowledge about memory. Young children seem to have a very primitive understanding of the major factors and strategies involved in enhancing memory. For example, children aged 6 or 7 years old have been found to be equally likely to select previously recalled and unrecalled items for further study in a multi-trial learning task, apparently not realising the advantage of allocating extra study time to information they have as yet been unable to recall. Flavell (1977) described several such examples of apparent deficiencies of metamemory in young children. It is tempting to argue that memory performance is causally determined by metamemory, but this would be simplistic. A better formulation is that metamnemonic knowledge is necessary, but not sufficient, to produce certain beneficial effects on learning techniques.

Some interesting evidence concerning the potential value of metamemory training was obtained by Lodico, Ghatala, Levin, Pressley and Bell (1983). They gave some of their 7-year-old subjects metamemory training in the form of general principles of strategy monitoring designed to encourage them to evaluate the success of any given strategy. Thereafter, they and other children were exposed to two learning strategies in a memory task. Those children who had received the metamemory training were more likely to select the more effective learning strategy subsequently.

A rather different approach to the development of memory has been taken by Piaget. His key assumption is that the ways in which children tackle learning tasks reflect their current state of intellectual development. Piaget and Inhelder (1973) spelt out some of the implications of this theoretical position:

> The mnemonic code, far from being fixed and unchangeable, is structured and restructured along with general development. Such a restructuring of the code takes place in close dependence on the schemes of intelligence. The clearest indication of this is the observation of different types of memory organisation in accordance with the age level of a child so that a longer interval of retention without any new presentation, far from causing a deterioration of memory, may actually improve it [p. 361].

Piaget and Inhelder (1973) reported a number of experiments designed to test this hypothesis, one of which involved the concept of seriation. The attainment of this concept can be measured by giving a child a set of sticks of varying lengths, and asking him to place them in an ordered way from shortest to longest. Children of 4 and 5 years old cannot do this task, but those of 6 usually can. In the memory experiment, children between the ages of 3 and 8 years were shown ten sticks ordered from shortest to longest, and were asked to study them for a memory test. When retention was measured a week later, the children's attempts to draw the sticks reflected their level of understanding of seriation. The same children were asked to draw the sticks again several months later; amazingly, almost 75% of them produced drawings that were more accurate (i.e., more seriated) than their earlier attempt! Even more strikingly, if only those children (5- to 8-year-olds) who theoretically were in the process of acquiring the concept of seriation were considered, then 90% showed improvement. According to Piaget and Inhelder (1973), this improvement in memory reflected a development of the cognitive structures relevant to seriation.

There are two potential problems with this kind of study. Firstly, it is difficult to be sure whether we are dealing with actual memory of the stimulus or simply with a plausible reconstruction of what might have been presented. Secondly, while it is reasonable to attribute the improvement in memory over time to an increased understanding of the seriation concept, it is still possible that other developmental changes are involved. Liben (1975) attempted to resolve the second problem. Children aged 8 years old were shown a picture of a crane on a steep slope. There was a vertical wire with a heavy ball on the end of it hanging from the crane. The children were asked to draw the crane from memory two weeks after seeing it. The relevant concept here is verticality because it requires an understanding of verticality to realise that the wire orients with reference to the true vertical rather than with the surface of the hill. Approximately 3 months after seeing the crane, half of the children were given training on the verticality concept, and 2 months after that everyone was given a second memory test. Forty percent of those children given the special training drew the wire closer to the true vertical on this test than on the initial one, against only 14% of the untrained children. This finding supports Piaget's contention that memory is strongly influenced by the state of development of the relevant cognitive structures.

In sum, the major problem when investigating developmental changes in memorial functioning is that age is such a powerful variable. You can take almost any process involved in the storage and retrieval of information and there will be a systematic improvement in the utilisation of that process during the years of childhood. It is still not clear which developmental changes are the most consequential for memory, but the most fruitful approach is probably to regard the processes of memory as interdependent.

LANGUAGE ACQUISITION

Introduction

Of all the cognitive achievements of young children, none is more impressive than the acquisition of language. What is especially striking about language acquisition is the speed with which it typically occurs, almost irrespective of the general intellectual competence of the child. In addition, and something that continues to puzzle many psychologists, is the fact that children successfully acquire the grammar of their native language, in spite of its complex and abstract nature and the inability of most parents to state the relevant grammatical principles.

There has been considerable theoretical interest in the factors that permit language acquisition to proceed so swiftly. In essence, we can look for the answer either in the child or in the environment. It is possible, as Chomsky (1965, 1980) and others have claimed, that all human languages conform to universal structural principles, and that children are innately provided with many of the prerequisites for language acquisition. In other words, we possess some kind of language acquisition device. While such a device could obviously account for the speed of language acquisition, it is unclear that we really are so richly endowed (see Chapter 8 for a discussion). It is also a matter of controversy whether all languages actually conform to a limited set of universal principles.

The emphasis in recent years has shifted increasingly to environmental factors that might facilitate language acquisition. Firstly, interactions between the young child and its mother or caretaker in the first few months of life may enable the child to develop cognitively in ways that are relevant to language acquisition (Bruner, 1974). Secondly, the nature of the conversations between the child and mother or caretaker at later ages may be such as to encourage language development. For example, the mother may use simple, repetitive, language, and ask questions and supply answers so as to provide an optimal linguistic environment (e.g., Snow, 1977). These recent developments will form our main focus.

Cognitive Prerequisites for Language

There has been a growing awareness that language develops in an interpersonal context in which the mother or caretaker plays the central role. Whatever else language is, it is quintessentially an effective means of communication, and thus represents a natural development of the child's earliest forms of communication. As Bruner (1974) has pointed out, very young infants are extremely good at communicating demands. During the course of their first year, infants' pre-verbal communication patterns evolve and become sensitive to the communications of their mothers. For their part, mothers generally respond to their infants' spontaneous behaviour with interest, and in ways designed to encourage the infants to continue the interaction (Schaffer, 1977). As a result, the infant learns that communication involves turn taking, is rewarding, and can be used to affect the behaviour of others. These discoveries help to set the scene for subsequent verbal interactions.

Bruner (1975) has proposed more specific hypotheses about some of the ways in which language development may be aided by the mother. He argued that all natural languages display topic-comment structure, which is represented grammatically as subject-predicate. The structure allegedly reflects the structure of action as it occurs within mother-child interactions. According to videotape evidence collected by Bruner on children between the ages of 7 and 13 months, the mother usually waits until both she and her child are attending to the same object before acting upon it or commenting on it. This pattern seems to resemble the topic-comment structure of language.

Bruner (1975) also suggested that language typically follows an order of agent–action–object–recipient (e.g., "Mary gave an apple to the teacher"), and that the acquisition of this word order is facilitated by the action sequences observed by the child that conform to this order. Videotape evidence indicated that the mother was initially the agent of most actions, with the child the recipient. When the child was a little older, the mother often attempted to shift attention from the agent (i.e., herself) to the act by dramatising it in some way.

These observations led Bruner (1975) to the following conclusions:

> The structures of action and attention provide bench-marks for interpreting the order-rules in initial grammar: that a concept of agent–action–object–recipient at the pre-linguistic level aids the child in grasping the linguistic meaning of appropriately ordered utterances involving such case categories as agentive, action, object, indirect object, and so forth [p. 17].

This theory, while it has been influential, seems deficient in a number of respects. It is not really clear how children are supposed to recognise the resemblance between action sequences and verbal sequences. The emphasis on the universality of certain patterns of action implies that there are "natural" word orders, and that languages deviating from them should be difficult to acquire. This is not, in fact, the case. The implication that word order in early speech should be subject before object is not always upheld. For example, among young Turkish children 27% of their utterances had the object preceding the subject (Slobin, 1982). In other words, there is less consistency in early language than expected by Bruner (1975).

The theoretical position adopted by Bruner (1975) is a specific example of a more general approach to language that was proposed by Cromer (1974). According to him: "we are able to understand and productively to use particular linguistic structures only when our cognitive abilities enable us to do so [p. 246]." This cognition hypothesis is intuitively appealing. It suggests that it is the rapid development of general cognitive skills during the early years of life that accounts for the speed of language acquisition.

Piaget was a prominent supporter of the cognition hypothesis, arguing that the development of language depends on the development of thought. Of particular importance, he claimed that language can only start properly when the concept of object permanence is fully developed during the sixth stage of the sensori-motor period. One of the implications of this theoretical position is that there ought to be a correlation between the development of object permanence and language production. Corrigan (1978) reported such a correlation, but the correlation became totally trivial when the effects of age were eliminated by means of partial correlation.

Some of the problems with the cognition hypothesis were spelled out by Harris (1982). He pointed out that the notion that the development of language is determined by the emergence of cognitive skills seems to imply that language comprehension and language production should develop together. In fact, most of the evidence suggests that comprehension precedes production, and this difference is unexplained by the cognition hypothesis.

A final telling point against simple versions of the cognition hypothesis concerns second language acquisition. Since second language acquisition typically occurs much later in development than first language acquisition, there is usually a considerable increase in cognitive abilities between first and second language acquisition. As a consequence, the sequence for language acquisition should differ substantially between first and second languages. In fact, the available evidence indicates that language acquisition for first and second languages is very similar (McLaughlin, 1978).

In sum, the notion that the course of language acquisition is dictated by the development of appropriate cognitive abilities has received surprisingly little empirical support. Perhaps instead of claiming that the cognitive prerequisites are both necessary and sufficient for language acquisition, it would be more accurate to argue merely that they are necessary for language acquisition. In other words, language acquisition depends on a variety of factors, of which the existence of the appropriate cognitive abilities is but one. At the very least, the child has to learn the precise relationships between his cognitive abilities and the speech he or she hears, and the relationships between ideas and words may sometimes be difficult to determine.

The Linguistic Environment

It is highly probable that much of interest about language acquisition can be learned from an analysis of the child's linguistic environment. As we have already mentioned, it has often been assumed that the mother or caretaker structures her linguistic and non-linguistic communications to the child in such a way as to facilitate language acquisition. At the linguistic level, this may involve the use of simple language that is spoken slowly and clearly, that is repetitive, and that refers to the immediate environment. At the non-linguistic level, the mother's actions and gestures may help the child to comprehend her concurrent speech.

These theoretical notions have immediate intuitive appeal, but have by no means been demonstrated conclusively to be correct. One problem concerns the alleged advantages of the limited linguistic input of the mother to her child. While there may indeed be certain advantages, there are also clear disadvantages. It is, in principle, impossible to infer the grammatical structure of a language on the basis of a limited and unrepresentative sample of permissible sentences in that language. In terms of an analogy, it is as if someone attempting to work out all of the rules of chess were permitted to watch only the first few moves of any chess game. No knowledge about the rules relating to, for example, castling and queening could possibly be obtained.

At least two kinds of evidence are needed to support the hypothesis that the mother's communication patterns aid language. Firstly, her linguistic and non-linguistic communication patterns must conform to those deemed facilitatory of language. Even if they do, it does not necessarily follow that those communication patterns have a substantial impact on the course of language acquisition. Therefore, the second kind of evidence that is required is that the communication patterns of the mother have a direct, causal influence on the child's development of language.

Most (if not all) theories of syntax regard active, declarative sentences as the simplest grammatically, and so a reasonable prediction is that this form of sentence would be used very frequently by the mother when talking to her young child. In fact, while such sentences are fairly common, mothers also typically produce numerous interjections and sentence fragments (see Gleitman and Wanner, 1982, for a review). More detailed evidence about sentence complexity was obtained by Shatz (1982) who videotaped interactions between mothers and their young children aged between 18 and 34 months. When she analysed the questions asked by the mothers, Shatz discovered that these questions served 11 different functions, and were expressed in various different forms. Unsophisticated children (two-word speakers or less) and sophisticated children (average utterance length of three or four words) were exposed to most of the possible variations, and thus could hardly be said to have received a very simple linguistic input. However, mothers did tend to favour certain kinds of questions over others, and this tendency was more marked among the mothers of unsophisticated children. It may be that the mothers of the unsophisticated children were attempting to simplify their language for the benefit of their children.

Shatz (1982) performed additional analyses on her videotaped conversations. She argued that if mothers are instrumental in facilitating language development, then it might be expected that they would often repeat previous utterances in a slightly different form in order to increase their children's comprehension of language. Such reformulations represented only 4% of maternal utterances, and often incorporated more than one change from the original utterance, which must have made them hard to comprehend. She also discovered that there was practically no correlation between the frequency with which the mother reformulated earlier utterances and the linguistic level of the child.

As a result of these findings, Shatz (1982) was rather dismissive of the hypothesis that the mother's linguistic communications serve to facilitate language development in the child. However, her pessimism may prove unfounded, since other research points to a different conclusion. Ellis and Wells (1980) discovered that children having the most rapid language development tended to receive more directives and questions than children whose language development was slower. Harris, Jones, and Grant (in press) videotaped interactions between mothers and children between the ages of 6 and 10 months. The mother's speech usually referred to an object within the immediate environment that the child was attending to. While this link between what is seen and what is heard may facilitate language comprehension, the child still has the problem of deciding exactly which aspects of the environment are being referred to in the mother's speech.

There may be other important aspects of maternal speech that have usually been ignored. It is known, for example, that mothers usually speak to their young children rather slowly and with exaggerated stress patterns. As Gleitman and Wanner (1982) pointed out, children's early speech consists primarily of words or parts of words that are normally stressed in adult speech. This is supported by the fact that words are often pronounced at first with the unstressed parts missing (e.g., my daughter Fleur initially said "nana" instead of "banana"). Most importantly, early speech tends to be "telegramic," with many words that would normally be present in a sentence simply being omitted. The usual argument is that it is the semantically unimportant words that are omitted, but this hardly accounts for all of the omissions. It seems more likely that it is the unstressed words that are omitted. Thus young children are sensitive to stress patterns in speech, and mothers seem to be responsive to this sensitivity in their speech patterns.

While we have focused so far on the mother's linguistic patterns, it may be that accompanying non-linguistic actions, such as gesture, also help to facilitate language comprehension. However, systematic analyses of videotaped mother-child interactions by Shatz (1982) failed to provide much support for this contention. Firstly, she found that there was relatively little consistency about the relationship between different kinds of sentences and the accompanying gestures. As a result, gestural information alone was insufficient to indicate whether the mother was asking a question, or producing an imperative or declarative sentence. Secondly, gestures did not provide much guide to meaning, because any particular meaning was accompanied by quite different gestures on different occasions. Thirdly, gestures were no more likely to accompany requests for difficult actions than for easy ones.

However, less discouraging evidence was obtained from a comparison of reference cycles (i.e., the mother talking about the names of objects or their attributes) and action cycles (i.e., the mother talking about actions or objects). The gestures accompanying these cycles were highly regular for each mother (though different from one mother to another), so that the child could have decided fairly accurately whether his or her mother was talking about reference or action on the basis of gestural information. In addition, the youngest children responded more successfully on gestured than un-gestured reference cycles.

Common sense indicates that the multitude of linguistic and non-linguistic communications that the mother directs at her child must have a major influence on the child's acquisition of language. However, it has proved surprisingly difficult to obtain more than modest evidence for this common-sensical notion. One possible reason for this is that the researcher who videotapes mother-child interactions has available an enormous amount of information, and it is difficult to distinguish between important and unimportant maternal communications. Another possible reason is that what is important in the mother's speech or action depends heavily on those cognitive skills that the child has available. Thus, for example, a certain aspect of maternal speech may have little effect on children of, say, 9 months, because they are not equipped to respond to that aspect, but it may have a profound effect 3 months later when the relevant cognitive prerequisites have been acquired. In other words, more attention needs to be paid to possible interactions between the nature of maternal linguistic and non-linguistic communications and the developmental status of the child.

Conclusions

The ease with which the overwhelming majority of young children acquire language remains in many ways a profound mystery. However, it is obvious that we will need to consider both the cognitive capacities of the child (both innately endowed and acquired during development) and the nature of the linguistic and non-linguistic environment. While some of the relevant cognitive capacities may be provided innately in some kind of language acquisition device, it is probably more fruitful to focus on the child's experiences of manipulating the environment and participating in social interactions. These pre-linguistic learning experiences then equip the young child to acquire language under the appropriate circumstances, and most mothers or caretakers seem to provide such circumstances. In other words, language acquisition depends on a contribution from the child in the form of relevant cognitive abilities, and from the environment in the form of comprehensible linguistic and non-linguistic inputs, and it is the child-environment interaction that holds the key to the acquisition of language.

PRACTICAL APPLICATIONS: READING RETARDATION

Introduction

Probably the greatest cognitive accomplishment of childhood is the mastery of language in its various forms, including comprehension of both spoken and written language and the production of fluent speech. Of these skills, the one that is most likely to cause problems is that of the comprehension of written language (i.e., reading). It is particularly noteworthy that reading retardation often occurs in children who otherwise display reasonable general ability, and it is with such cases of specific reading retardation that we are concerned here. General reading retardation, in which poor reading is part and parcel of generally inadequate cognitive skills, appears, on the other hand, to be a less mysterious problem, and is not discussed.

Of course, there are numerous reasons for the occurrence of specific reading retardation. However, we are not concerned here with reading retardation caused by brain damage, instead the emphasis is on general trends that apply to many cases of children with specific reading retardation. There are many possible approaches that could be used in the attempt to further our understanding of specific reading retardation. However, the one discussed here is based on the notion that it is worthwhile to try to identify one or more cognitive mechanisms that may be deficient in the case of retarded readers. As Jorm (1983) pointed out in an excellent review of the relevant research, a reasonable starting point is the working memory system originally proposed by Baddeley and Hitch (1974), and developed subsequently by Baddeley and Lieberman (1980), Hitch (1980), and others (see Chapter 4 for details). Working memory consists of a modality-free central executive, a visuo-spatial scratch pad, and an articulatory loop. The central executive has limited capacity and is rather similar to attention, whereas the articulatory loop and the visuo-spatial scratch pad are slave systems. The articulatory loop uses a phonological code and is utilised during verbal rehearsal, whereas the visuo-spatial scratch pad handles visual and/or spatial information. Reading requires attention, involves a visual input, and sometimes requires phonological coding. There are, therefore, good reasons for exploring the relationship between reading retardation and the functioning of the components of working memory.

This line of reasoning was strongly supported by Daneman and Carpenter (1980), who devised a new measure of working memory capacity. They argued that better readers should process sentences more efficiently than poorer readers, and thus should have more of the limited capacity of working memory available for storage. They tested this notion by presenting their subjects with a number of sentences for comprehension, followed by attempted recall of the last word in each sentence. The measure of working memory capacity was the reading span, which was defined as the maximum number of sentences that could be read with perfect recall of the last words. Reading span correlated substantially with separate measures of reading comprehension (many of the correlations were approximately +.7), indicating the close relationship between reading ability and working memory functioning.

The Involvement of Working Memory

As Jorm (1983) pointed out, the typical research strategy has involved selecting two groups of children differing markedly with respect to reading achievement but matched for both I.Q. and age. Both groups of children are then given a memory task involving some component of working memory. The existence of a significant deficit for retarded readers helps to clarify the nature of their impairment, and may be of use when planning remedial instruction.

Of the various components of working memory, it is probably the articulatory loop that has received the most attention. The essence of the articulatory loop is that it holds a limited amount of verbal information in the correct sequence in a phonological code. If retarded readers have a deficient articulatory loop, then this should become manifest on tasks necessitating serial recall of verbal items (e.g., memory span). A review of 11 studies in which retarded and normal readers equated for I.Q. had been tested for digit span revealed that the retarded readers were significantly inferior in six of the studies (Rugel, 1974).

There are various possible reasons why retarded readers might show a deficit in memory span, and some of them were explored by Torgesen and Houck (1980). They compared the memory-span performance of retarded readers who did or did not have inferior digit span. Two pieces of evidence suggested that inefficient use of strategies was not the problem. Extremely rapid presentation rates of up to four items per second presumably eliminated the use of strategies, but did not reduce the size of the memory-span deficit. Attempts by the experimenter to group or chunk the stimulus material also failed to reduce the difference in memory span between the two groups. However, Torgesen and Houck did manage to eliminate memory-span differences when the input items were nonsense syllables. This suggests that the problem may lie in accessing information about familiar items in long-term memory.

The usual finding from supra-span serial learning tasks is that retarded readers usually perform worse than non-retarded readers. This is consistent in a general way with the notion of impaired functioning of the articulatory loop. However, it is typically unclear whether the poor level of performance is actually due to inability to remember the order of the stimulus items (which would probably reflect some inefficiency of the articulatory loop) or to forgetting of the items themselves (which might well be due to other factors). The evidence is rather mixed, but there is usually little support for the notion that retarded readers have impaired serial order retention when item and order retention are assessed separately (e.g., Hulme, 1981).

If retarded readers make less use than normal readers of the articulatory loop when engaged in serial recall tasks, then it can be predicted that they should be less adversely affected by phonologically similar stimulus items. The reason is that phonological coding is largely or exclusively a function of the articulatory loop. The usual finding is that normal readers are more affected than retarded readers by phonological similarity (e.g., Shankweiler, Liberman, Mark, Fowler & Fischer, 1979). While the findings are reasonably consistent, it is by no means clear exactly why retarded readers show reduced use of the articulatory loop.

There are a few studies looking at possible effects of reading retardation on visuo-spatial short-term memory. A central difficulty is to discover tasks for which subjects make use of only visuo-spatial coding and do not engage in verbal recording and rehearsal. Jorm (1983) reviewed the relevant research and it is clear that there are practically no differences between retarded and normal readers with respect to visuo-spatial coding.

Thus, the picture that emerges from studies of short-term memory is one in which retarded readers experience problems in coding information phonologically in the articulatory loop, but code visuo-spatial information adequately. The same pattern manifests itself in studies of long-term memory. Retarded readers are usually not at a disadvantage in studies of non-verbal long-term memory or studies of verbal long-term memory that rely heavily on retention of semantic information. However, retarded readers perform poorly on long-term memory tasks where phonological coding is necessary, such as paired-associate learning of aurally presented nonsense words (e.g., Vellutino, Steger, Harding & Phillips, 1975). Vellutino et al. analysed the errors that were made, and found that those of normal readers tended to be based on phonological information, whereas those of retarded readers were based on semantic information.

Other studies have reported evidence that retarded readers have difficulties in accessing phonological information in long-term memory. For example, retarded readers are slower than normal readers at naming various kinds of stimuli (e.g., colours, digits) (Spring & Capps, 1974). Ellis and Miles (1978) used the Posner paradigm, in which subjects have to make physical-identity judgements (e.g., "AA") or name-identity judgements (e.g. "Aa") for pairs of letters. There was no effect of reading retardation on the speed of physical-identity judgements, but retarded readers were slower in making name-identity judgements. These findings imply that retarded readers take longer than normal readers to access, and make use of, phonological codes.

What conclusions can be drawn from the evidence? A severe limitation of most of the findings is that they are essentially correlational in nature. That is to say, we know that those children with poor reading skills tend also to show deficiencies on those memory tasks depending heavily on the articulatory loop. Such correlational evidence cannot, of course, establish causality. An inefficient articulatory loop may cause reading retardation, or lack of practice and/or skill in reading may cause deficiencies in reading-related mechanisms (e.g., the articulatory loop). One way of attempting to resolve this issue is to see whether a deficiency in phonological coding at one age is predictive of poor reading performance at a later date. This approach was adopted by Liberman and Mann (1981), who discovered that kindergarten children who were least affected by phonological similarity on a short-term memory task tended to have the worst reading performance a year later.

We may tentatively conclude that a major problem with many (but not all) retarded readers is deficient use of phonological information. The potential importance of this deficiency in explaining reading retardation is as follows. It is possible in reading to proceed either directly from print to meaning or indirectly via phonological recoding. It appears that phonological recoding is more likely to occur among beginning readers than among older children (e.g., Doctor & Coltheart, 1980). Evidence that retarded readers take a long time to produce phonological representations was obtained by Jorm (1981), who found large differences between retarded and normal readers in the time taken to pronounce printed, nonsense words.

In other words, retarded readers may find reading difficult because their attempts to access the meanings of printed words via phonological representations are hindered so much by their slow retrieval of phonological information. There are other ways in which phonological coding problems might interfere with reading comprehension. For example, the articulatory loop may "hold" information about the first words in a sentence while the later words are processed (especially with beginning readers), and this may facilitate comprehension of the sentence as a whole. However, the task of integrating the different parts of a sentence may be more difficult for retarded readers with deficient articulatory loops. Some indirect evidence in support of this position was obtained by Perfetti and Lesgold (1977), who discovered that retention of the wording of clauses that had just been read was poorer in retarded than in normal readers.

In sum, we have seen that cognitive psychology can aid our understanding of a very practical problem in cognitive development. While there are some inconsistencies in the evidence, it appears to be the case that retarded readers often have difficulty in phonological coding and efficient use of the articulatory loop. Such identification of the deficient cognitive processes and mechanisms is an essential prerequisite to successful techniques of remedying retardation of reading.

10 Problem Solving and Reasoning

Research on and theorising about the higher mental processes are characterised by a rather unsatisfactory fragmentation into relatively specific areas. Thus, there are those who investigate problem solving, others who study reasoning, and still others are concerned with the structure and nature of intelligence. Until quite recently, there was remarkably little liaison between these three groups of workers. How can we account for this state of affairs? One obvious answer is that the interests of researchers in the three areas are rather different: Reasoning research often makes use of problems in logic, the logicality or otherwise of the subjects' performance being of prime significance, whereas problem-solving research is broader in scope, while research into intelligence has traditionally focused on individual differences and on the number and nature of the factors comprising intelligence.

Even though it is possible to understand how these schisms arose, it still seems somewhat strange that they persist. In particular, consider the related areas of problem solving and deductive reasoning. There appear to be three main criteria for deciding that an individual is engaging in problem-solving activities (Anderson, 1980):

1. The activities must be goal directed, i.e., the individual attempts to attain a particular end state.
2. The attainment of the goal or solution must involve a *sequence* of mental processes rather than just one. Thus, being asked what time it is and supplying the answer simply by looking at your watch would not qualify as problem solving.
3. The processes involved should be discernibly cognitive. This is a difficult criterion to apply in practice, but is intended to rule out such mundane activities as dealing a pack of cards.

Let us apply these three criteria to a typical deductive reasoning task in which the subject is asked to decide whether or not the conclusion follows logically from the premises:

Premises
If Crystal Palace win, I will be happy.
I will not be happy.
Conclusion
Therefore, Crystal Palace are not going to win.

It seems obvious that the behaviour of anyone tackling this task is goal directed, and that task solution requires a number of intervening cognitive processes. It could still be argued that deductive reasoning tasks involve logic, whereas most problems do not. This argument is not acceptable, however, when we draw a distinction between the requirements of a task and the mental processes actually used by someone attempting to solve it. In fact, logical reasoning tasks are very frequently tackled in an alarmingly illogical way. It thus appears that deductive reasoning is a special case of problem solving, and that the theoretical concepts applicable to problem solving should also be applicable to deductive reasoning, and vice versa.

Newell (1980) has argued forcefully for unification of these areas of psychological study. As a start in that direction, he proposed the problem space as the fundamental organisational unit of all human, goal-directed, symbolic activity, including both problem solving and reasoning. The notion of a problem space was defined in the following way by Newell (1980): "[It] consists of a set of symbolic structures (the *states* of the space) and a set of *operators* over the space. Each operator takes a state as input and produces a state as output, although there may be other inputs and outputs as well [p. 697]." In other words, all kinds of problem solving make similar demands on the subject: The appropriate operator-state combinations must be selected from an *ensemble* of possibilities. It is also true of all problems, according to Newell, that problem-space operators can only be used seriatim, and that there is always a limited set of states that could potentially become the current state.

It seems probable that in the future textbooks will provide a unified account of problem solving and reasoning. This is not feasible at present, however, because reasoning has only recently come to be regarded as an example of problem solving, and the necessary empirical and theoretical links do not exist as yet. Accordingly, the traditional separation of problem solving and reasoning will be maintained in this chapter.

PROBLEM SOLVING

Early Research

One of the first of the major theoretical approaches to problem solving was that of the Gestaltists in the earlier part of this century. They argued that the process of problem solution necessitated reorganising the elements of the problem situation in such a way as to provide a solution. This reorganization involves a sudden flash of insight (sometimes referred to as the "aha" experience). An example was provided by Wolfgang Köhler (1925), who watched apes in a cage attempting to obtain bananas hanging from the ceiling out of reach. The solution required the apes to place crates on top of each other in order to form a staircase to the bananas. Task solutions were typically preceded by a period of intense thinking by the ape, followed by an apparent flash of insight.

This theoretical analysis of problem solving is in stark contrast to that offered earlier by Thorndike (1898). His observations led him to argue that problem solving often occurs by trial and error, i.e., responses are made at random until one of them proves successful. In a famous experiment, Thorndike (1898) placed a cat in a puzzle box, and it had to make some arbitrary response (e.g., clawing at a loop of string or a lever) in order for a trap door to open and allow it to escape and eat food. The animal hardly appeared to think at all; rather, it squeezed the bars, clawed at loose objects, or jumped on things in the box until the appropriate response was made accidentally. After a fair amount of practice, the cat tended to eliminate the unsuccessful responses and to escape more quickly from the puzzle box.

The theoretical accounts put forward by Thorndike and by the Gestaltists could hardly be more different. Thorndike argued that problem solving in animals was a painfully slow process almost devoid of thought, whereas the Gestaltists claimed that problem solution occurred suddenly and as a result of much active thinking. This theoretical controversy seems rather sterile with the benefit of hindsight. Tasks obviously differ in terms of the likelihood of insight occurring: even Einstein would not have been able to show insight if placed in the puzzle-box apparatus! In order for insight to occur, there must at the very least be a meaningful relationship between the animal's responses and their effects on the environment. Furthermore, both theoretical positions are erroneous. Thorndike was wrong, to assume that the process of problem solving is typically random rather than purposive, and the Gestaltists were wrong to assume that insight (a rather amorphous notion) is a frequent occurrence.

One of the more serious weaknesses of the earliest theoretical approaches was that they failed to provide a detailed analysis of the processes involved in problem solution. A partial exception is the hypothesis put forward by Wallas (1926). He argued that the thinking process could be divided into four stages: (1) there is *preparation*, in which information is gathered, and preliminary attempts at solution are made; (2) there is the stage of *incubation*, when the problem is put aside for a period of time; (3) there is *illumination*, in which the key to the solution appears in a flash of insight; (4) there is the stage of *verification*, in which the solution is checked.

The most interesting notion proposed by Wallas (1926) was that of the importance of allowing incubation to occur. There is some support for this idea in the experiences of various famous creative people. For example, Ghiseli (1952) reported this quotation from the French mathematician Poincaré:

> The changes of travel made me forget my mathematical work. Having reached Coutances, we entered an omnibus to go some place or other. At the moment when I put my foot on the step the idea came to me, without anything in my former thoughts seeming to have paved the way for it, that the transformations I had used to define the Fuchsian functions were identical with those of non-Euclidean geometry [p. 37].

This is, of course, only anecdotal evidence. Empirical support for the notion of incubation was obtained by Silveira (1971), who gave her subjects the cheap necklace problem. Initially, there are four separate pieces of chain, each of which comprises three links, and all of the links within each piece of chain are closed. It costs two cents to open a link, and three cents to close a link. The task is to join all 12 links of chain to form a single circular chain at a total cost of no more than 15 cents. She found that 55% of those who worked uninterruptedly at the task solved it within 30 minutes. If there was a half-hour break during task solution, then 64% solved the problem, and this rose to 85% among those having a 4-hour break. Since the interrupted subjects did not come back to the problem with their solutions completely worked out, this study provides reasonable evidence of incubation. It is not clear *why* incubation was successful, but it may have worked because it prevented subjects fixating on inappropriate methods of solving the problem.

Some of the readers of this book are undoubtedly in suspense as to the solution of the necklace problem. What needs to be done is to open all three of the links in one chain at a cost of six cents; these three open links are then used to join together the other three pieces of chain, at an additional cost of nine cents. It may well be relevant that the solution to this problem depends on a single crucial insight. Problems that can be solved in a straightforward manner would probably not benefit from a period of incubation.

Effects of Past Experience

One of the most obvious facts about problem solving is that the speed and accuracy with which most problems can be solved increase dramatically during the years of childhood. In a general sense, this illustrates the marked beneficial effect that previous learning and experience can have on the processes involved in solving problems; technically, this is known as a positive transfer effect. Consider, for example, the case of someone who only uses one particular car while learning to drive, and who then switches to a different car. While we might expect there to be some initial difficulties in adjusting to the slightly different feel and layout of the new car, the usual finding is that there is a rapid adjustment to the requirements of driving it; in other words, there is positive transfer of training.

While it is very straightforward to see that previous learning can facilitate problem solving by supplying well-practised skills and strategies, it is perhaps less obvious that knowledge acquired in the past can sometimes seriously disrupt, and interfere with, subsequent attempts to solve problems. Such disruption, which is often referred to as a negative transfer effect, has been demonstrated many times in the laboratory. For example, we tend to regard any particular object as suitable for a strictly limited range of purposes, and often experience difficulty in realising that the object can be used in other ways. This phenomenon is known as functional fixedness, and was investigated in a classic study by Maier (1931). The task was to tie together two strings hanging from the ceiling. The strings were so far apart that the subject could not grasp both at once. There were various objects in the room, including a chair and a pair of pliers. Most of the subjects tried various solutions involving the chair, but these were unsuccessful. In the correct solution, the pliers are tied to one string, that string is set swinging like a pendulum, and the second string is held in the centre of the room until the first string swings close enough to grasp. Only 39% of Maier's subjects saw this solution within 10 minutes, presumably because of the difficulty of perceiving that pliers can be used as a weight on the end of a pendulum in addition to their more conventional use.

Rather more direct evidence of functional fixedness was obtained by Duncker (1945). He used a problem in which a candle had to be mounted on a vertical screen, and among the objects available were a book of matches and a box of drawing pins. Since a box is usually regarded primarily as a container, most people find it hard to think of using the box as a platform for the candle. This functional fixedness is more pronounced when the box is initially full of drawing pins than when it is empty, presumably because in the former case the normal use of a box as a container is emphasised.

Another problem on which the assumptions stemming from past experience are erroneous is the well-known nine-dot problem (see Fig. 10.1). The subject's task is to join up all of the dots with four connected straight lines without lifting his or her pencil from the paper. The problem can only be solved by going outside the perimeter of the square, but practically no subjects do this spontaneously (Weisberg & Alba, 1981). Once again, past experience limits and constrains thinking rather than facilitating it.

So far, we have considered cases in which knowledge acquired outside the laboratory appears to disrupt the solution of some problem within that

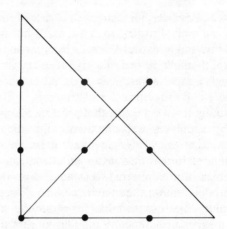

FIG. 10.1   The solution to the nine-dot problem.

situation. The obvious limitation of such studies is that we can only speculate on the nature of the subjects' pre-experimental experiences. A potentially superior approach is to provide people with certain kinds of experience during the course of an experimental session, and then investigate the consequences for problem solution. Perhaps the best-known example of this approach is the work done on water-jar problems by Luchins (1942). Each problem involved three water jars, each of which had a different capacity, and the task was to imagine pouring liquid from one jar to another in order to finish up with a designated amount of liquid in one of the jars.

In one of Luchins' (1942) studies, the key problem was as follows: *Jar A* has a capacity of 28 quarts, *Jar B* of 76 quarts, and *Jar C* of 3 quarts, and the task is to finish up with 25 quarts in one of the jars. This problem is, of course, laughably easy: *Jar A* is filled, and then *Jar C* is filled from it, leaving 25 quarts in *Jar A*. As might be expected, 95% of the control subjects, who had received minimal previous training, solved this problem. However, only 36% of the subjects in a different condition were successful on this problem. The reason is that these subjects had previously received seven other water-jar problems, each of which could be solved by filling *Jar B*, and using the contents to fill *Jar C* twice and *Jar A* once (i.e., $B - 2C - A$). Because the first seven problems all had the same relatively complicated three-jar solution, it encouraged the subjects to form a specific mental set or *Einstellung*. It was the attempt to use this solution on the eighth problem that disrupted performance.

Another finding from this study concerned some of the later problems in the series, which could be solved either by means of the complex method applicable to the early problems (i.e., $B - 2C - A$) or by a simpler method ($A + C$ or $A - C$ for different problems). Approximately 80% of the subjects who had received the earlier problems continued to use the complex method, against only 1% of subjects who had not.

According to Luchins (1942), these various findings pointed to the following conclusion: "*Einstellung*—habituation—creates a mechanised state of mind, a blind attitude towards problems; one does not look at the problem on its own merits but is led by a mechanical application of a used method [p. 15]." In my opinion, this disparaging view of the effects of *Einstellung*, or set, is far more applicable to the finding that a simple problem could not be solved at all than to the finding that a complex solution was used when a simpler one was available. In the latter case, it was obviously more efficient to continue to use a well-practised solution than to spend time looking for a different, but simpler, solution.

Perhaps the most dramatic example of the mental set occurred in a study by Levine (1971). Subjects were presented with a series of cards, each of which contained two letters (A and B), with one letter on the left and the other on the right. As each card was presented, the subject had to say either "A" or "B", and the experimenter indicated whether the chosen alternative was correct or not. The solutions to the initial problems depended on a position sequence (e.g., the solution involved selecting the letter on the right, then the letter on the left, then the letter on the left, and then the sequence restarted). After the subjects had become accustomed to such sequence problems, they were given a problem of amazing simplicity: selection of the letter "A" was correct, whereas selection of the letter "B" was incorrect. In spite of the apparently trivial nature of the problem, 80% of university students failed to solve it within 100 trials. What is more, when these non-solvers were then asked to select the correct solution from a choice of six possibilities, none of them was successful.

How are we to account for this failure of university students to master a problem that any self-respecting monkey or even rat could solve with ease? According to Levine (1971), subjects use their previous experience with a task to infer the hypothesis set from which the solution to the current problem will come. The notion of a hypothesis set is rather vague, but refers to a class or category of hypotheses. In the experiment just discussed, the relevant hypothesis set would correspond approximately to sequence solutions. When the subject initially selects an erroneous hypothesis set, he exhausts all of the possible hypotheses in that set before deciding to select an alternative hypothesis set. If the first hypothesis set selected is both wrong and infinitely large, as seems likely to happen when a series of sequence problems is followed by a letter problem, then in theory the subjects should never abandon the incorrect hypothesis set. This kind of theory can explain both Levine's findings and those of Luchins.

It is often suggested in textbooks that the negative transfer effects produced by functional fixedness, mental set, and so on, reveal serious deficiencies in adult thought processes. There may be a grain of truth in this suggestion, but there are other factors that need to be considered. In everyday life, it is probable that the most efficient and successful way of tackling most new problems is to make maximal use of previous experience rather than ignoring it. In other words, the application of past experience to problems is usually appropriate but occasionally inappropriate, and it would be misleading to focus on the latter cases at the expense of the former.

Computer Theories: General Problem Solver

The research discussed so far has revealed some of the conditions that determine the speed and accuracy of problem solution. However, it is also important to investigate the details of the mental processes involved in solving problems, and significant advances have been made in this direction. Of particular importance has been the advent of attempts to simulate human problem-solving activities on the computer, an enterprise undertaken most successfully by Newell and Simon (1972) with their General Problem Solver.

The basic strategy followed by Newell and Simon consisted of various stages. The first step was to ask people to solve problems, and to talk aloud while they were working on those problems. The next step was for Newell and Simon to use their subjects' reports as the basis for deciding what the general strategy on the task was. Finally, Newell and Simon tried to specify this strategy in detail so that they could programme it into their General Problem Solver.

One of the aims of the entire project was to evolve a general theoretical approach to problem solving that would be applicable across a range of different problems. This led Ernst and Newell (1969) to make use of the General Problem Solver on 11 very varied problems including letter-series completion, proving theorems, the tower of Hanoi, and missionaries and cannibals. The General Problem Solver was, in fact, able to solve all of the problems, but it did not always seem to do so in the way that people normally solve problems.

Newell and Simon (1972) provided in-depth analyses of the strategies used by people deriving solutions for crypto-arithmetic problems, solving theorems in logic, and playing chess. In order to do this, they represented each problem as a problem space consisting of the initial state of the problem, the goal state of the problem, all possible operations that could be applied to any state to change it into a different state, and all intermediate states of the problem. The problem-solving process is characterised by a series of states of knowledge through which the individual passes between the initial and goal states, and by the set of operators which move him or her from one state to another.

Not surprisingly, Newell and Simon (1972) assumed that people do not wander around randomly within the problem space; rather, there is a goal-directed search through the problem space which makes use of plans and sub-goals. The basic strategy used for searching through the problem space is known as means–ends analysis. It involves the problem solver generating goals and attempting to find operators capable of satisfying each goal. If a particular goal cannot be satisfied directly, then a sub-goal is created. There are three general sub-goals that can be used in means–ends analysis:

1. Transform *state A* into *state B*. In this case, the problem is currently in one state but you would like to change it into some other state. The first step is to compare the two states; if they differ, you must endeavour to specify precisely what that difference is.

2. Reduce difference between *state A* and *state B*. The task here is to find an operator that is appropriate for that difference, and that can be applied to *state A*.

3. Apply operator to *state A*. What happens here is that the operator is compared to *state A*. If they match, then you can apply the operator and produce *state B*. If they do not match, then return to sub-goal (2).

There is a danger that some of this description of the General Problem Solver may have seemed rather like mumbo-jumbo to the reader unfamiliar with computer jargon. Accordingly, here is an illustrative example taken from Newell and Simon (1972) of the kinds of thinking involved in means–ends analysis:

> I want to take my son to nursery school. What's the difference between what I have and what I want? One of distance. What changes distance? My automobile. My automobile won't work. What is needed to make it work? A new battery. What has new batteries? An auto repair shop. I want the repair shop to put in a new battery; but the shop doesn't know I need one. What is the difficulty? One of communication. What allows communication? A telephone . . . and so on [p. 416].

The approach to problem solving put forward by Newell and Simon (1972) argues that there are two major sources of difficulty that may be encountered by the problem solver: (1) inadequate representation of the task environment in the problem space; and (2) the application of inappropriate strategies or operators. It is one of the strengths of their theoretical analyses that they drew such a clear distinction between errors of representation and errors of strategy or process. It seems probable that the main stumbling block in problem solving is usually in the selection of the appropriate strategy, but there are exceptions to this general rule. Anderson (1980) gives the mutilated chessboard problem as an example of the importance of representation. Assume that two diagonally opposite corner squares have been cut out of a chessboard, thus leaving 62 squares. Then assume that you have 31 dominoes, each of which covers exactly two squares on the board. Your task is to decide whether or not it is possible to arrange the dominoes so that they cover all of the 62 squares. If it can be done, you must explain how. If it cannot be done, you must indicate why not.

The correct answer is that the board cannot be covered by the dominoes. The way to arrive at this solution is to include in your initial representation of the problem the fact that, since each domino covers two adjacent squares, it must cover one black and one white square. The appropriate representation encourages us to consider the number of black and white squares remaining after the two corner squares have been removed. Since these two squares are necessarily of the same colour, we are left with 32 squares of one colour and 30 squares of the other colour, and it is for this reason that the dominoes will not all fit on the board.

If we turn to the ways in which inappropriate strategies impair problem solving, it is clear that we frequently rely on heuristics, which are methods that tend to lead to successful solutions, but which are not guaranteed to do so. Heuristics are effectively rules of thumb that have been acquired through experience, and the means–ends analysis incorporated into the General Problem Solver is an example of a heuristic. A common heuristic when solving problems is to make moves on the basis of increasing the degree of similarity between the state of the problem and the goal state. This is usually a reasonable strategy, but some complex problems necessitate departing from that strategy part of the time. For example, consider the so-called missionaries and cannibals problem in which there are three missionaries and three cannibals on one side of a river. The goal is to transport everyone across the river using a boat that can carry two people at a time. A complicating factor is that the cannibals must never be allowed to outnumber the missionaries on either side of the river, because then the cannibals would eat them.

A solution to the problem is shown in Table 10.1. It has been discovered that many people experience special difficulty with the sixth move. The most plausible reason for this is that that move is incompatible with the goal-similarity heuristic: it involves moving two people back to the wrong side of the river, and thus gives the appearance of moving away from the solution.

A detailed analysis of the way in which inappropriate strategy selection can impede performance on the missionaries and cannibals problem was provided by Simon and Reed (1976). They used a slightly more complex version of the problem than the one we have discussed, and discovered that most subjects initially use the strategy of keeping the number of cannibals

Table 10.1
A Correct Solution to the Missionaries and Cannibals Problem. M = missionary, C = cannibal, and b = boat. The horizontal line represents the river.

(1) $\dfrac{\text{MMMCCC \quad b}}{}$ (7) $\dfrac{\text{MMCC \quad b}}{\text{MC}}$

(2) $\dfrac{\text{MMCC}}{\text{MC \quad b}}$ (8) $\dfrac{\text{CC}}{\text{MMMC \quad b}}$

(3) $\dfrac{\text{MMMCC \quad b}}{\text{C}}$ (9) $\dfrac{\text{CCC \quad b}}{\text{MMM}}$

(4) $\dfrac{\text{MMM}}{\text{CCC \quad b}}$ (10) $\dfrac{\text{C}}{\text{MMMCC \quad b}}$

(5) $\dfrac{\text{MMMC \quad b}}{\text{CC}}$ (11) $\dfrac{\text{CC \quad b}}{\text{MMMC}}$

(6) $\dfrac{\text{MC}}{\text{MMCC \quad b}}$ (12) $\dfrac{}{\text{MMMCCC \quad b}}$

and missionaires equal on each side of the river. Only when this fails to solve the problem do they shift to the more adequate means–ends strategy of selecting the move that takes the maximum number of people across the river, or the fewest back to the starting point.

One of the key characteristics of human problem solving is that the strategies applied to a problem tend to change and become more efficient over time. The original version of the General Problem Solver suffered from the limitation that it did not learn from experience in a systematic way. Anzai and Simon (1979) attempted to remedy this deficiency. They devised an adaptive system that started with only general problem-solving procedures, but was able to make use of the knowledge of results obtained during the performance of a task. This adaptive system made various attempts to solve the Tower of Hanoi problem, in which five discs of varying size have to be moved from one peg to another under various constraints. When the system detected a bad outcome of a sequence of moves, its subsequent behaviour was modified to avoid this in future, whereas successful sequences of moves were stored as chunks. This system improved the quality of its problem solving over time in much the same way as a female subject who spent $1\frac{1}{2}$ hours solving the Tower of Hanoi problem in progressively more efficient ways.

How great a contribution has the General Problem Solver made to our understanding of problem solving? It seems probable that the notion that problem solving typically proceeds on the basis of attempting to reduce the differences between the present and desired states is of fundamental importance in most problem-solving activities. It is likely that the notion of multi-level processing, involving a distinction between general executive procedures and relatively task-specific operations, is also of wide applicability. However, the General Problem Solver may be inadequate in other ways. For example, it seems to de-emphasise the importance of forward planning. As Greeno (1974) has pointed out, people trying to solve the missionaries and cannibals problem often use operators larger than a single move, but this differs from the strategy employed by the General Problem Solver.

One of the limitations of the approach adopted by Newell and Simon (1972) is that they concentrated on a particular class of problems in which the initial state, the goal state, and the various permissible moves are all clearly specified. Such problems may be considered to be well-defined, in contrast to ill-defined problems where the problem solver himself or herself actually helps to determine the various aspects of the problem. Problems in the real world are more frequently ill-defined than well-defined, and they also differ from the move problems used by Newell and Simon in that every possible solution has disadvantages as well as advantages associated with it. In addition, problems in real life typically depend far more for their solution on specific knowledge and experience than do those investigated by Newell and Simon. It is a matter for future research to decide whether the essentials of the General Problem Solver can safely be extrapolated outside the limited domain of problems to which they most obviously apply.

DEDUCTIVE REASONING

Introduction

It has often been assumed that, when we study deductive reasoning, we are basically dealing with mental operations that are logical in nature. This assumption is, in fact, erroneous, but it is still true that much of the research on deductive reasoning has had as its main focus the comparison of human reasoning performance with the prescriptions of logic. As a consequence, it will be useful to begin by considering the nature of logic in some detail.

The essence of a logical system is a set of principles or rules of inference; these rules are statements that authorise certain conclusions provided that certain premises are true. Within a logical system, a valid deduction requires that the rules of inference be correctly applied. One of the more important rules of inference is *modus ponens*, which states that given the proposition "If A then B," and also given A, then one may validly infer B. In the following example, given the two premises, then the conclusion is valid.

Premises
If there is a recession, then this book will not sell.
There is a recession.
Conclusion
This book will not sell.

It is important to note that the validity of a logical argument is not affected by whether or not its premises and conclusions are actually true. Thus, in the following example, the argument is valid even though its conclusion is obviously false:

Premises
If she is a woman, then she is Aristotle.
She is a woman.
Conclusion
She is Aristotle.

Most people experience little difficulty in accepting arguments based on *modus ponens*, but sometimes have problems with another rule of interference known as *modus tollens*. This rule states that, if we are given the proposition "If A then B," and we are also given the fact that B is false, then we can infer that A is false. Thus, the following argument is valid:

Premises
If the sun shines then this is Neasden.
This is not Neasden.
Conclusion
The sun is not shining.

Logic may appear to be rather limited in a number of ways. It is tautological, in that it merely states necessary consequences of that which has already been assumed. However, logic plays a major role in the important subject of mathematics. This is illustrated by Euclidean geometry, in which a set of theorems or conclusions is deduced logically from an initial set of axioms or principles.

Deductive logic also appears to be important in the evaluation of scientific theories. It is impossible to verify or prove a theoretical statement such as, "All learning involves reinforcement," no matter how many experiments provide supporting evidence. However, as Popper (1959) has pointed out, it is possible to falsify a theory, and falsification can be achieved by deductive logic. All that needs to be done is to discover a single counter-example (e.g., learning occurring in the absence of reinforcement), and the theory has been disproved.

Syllogistic Reasoning

Syllogistic logic was devised by Aristotle, and syllogisms have frequently been used by psychologists interested in deductive reasoning. The typical paradigm involves the presentation of two premises, with the subject attempting to decide whether a given conclusion follows logically from those premises (a number of examples of syllogisms were given in the previous section).

The key issue has been that of deciding between the logical or rationalist viewpoint, according to which people behave rationally and logically when confronted with problems of logic, and the non-logical viewpoint, which claims that people often attend to aspects of the problem which are irrelevant to its logical structure, and that they are affected by various response biases. It might be supposed that the former perspective predicts extremely high levels of performance on logical reasoning tasks, whereas the latter position predicts poor performance, but this would be simplistic. According to rationalists (e.g., Henle, 1962), many errors occur simply because people misunderstand or misrepresent the problem; after this initial mis-understanding, the reasoning itself is logical. Henle also claimed that errors could occur because of the subject's "failure to accept the logical task," as might happen if they only consider the truth or falsity of the conclusion itself, rather than whether it follows from the premises.

Before evaluating the respective merits of the logical and non-logical viewpoints, it may be worthwhile to consider performance on syllogistic reasoning tasks in some detail. The most striking finding is the relatively poor level of performance exhibited by the intelligent young people used as subjects in much of the research. However, the distribution of errors is by no means random. Rips and Marcus (1977) gave their subjects various syllogisms, and required them to decide whether the stated conclusion was always true, sometimes true, or never true given the premises. There was a large difference in performance between problems involving *modus ponens*, on which virtually no errors were made, and those involving *modus tollens*, where the error rate exceeded 30%. It is not absolutely clear why this should be the case, but it seems probable that the failure to use *modus tollens* is due to our lack of practice in thinking about what is not the case.

One of the earliest theories of performance on syllogistic tasks was proposed by Woodworth and Sells (1935) in their "atmosphere effect" theory. They claimed that people fail to reason logically, and that the nature of the premises created an atmosphere which led people to draw certain conclusions. More specifically, Woodworth and Sells suggested that positive premises lead people to accept a positive conclusion, whereas negative premises are seen as warranting a negative conclusion. If one of the premises is positive and the other is negative, then people incline towards a negative conclusion. They also considered universal statements (e.g., 'All As are Bs') and particular statements (e.g., 'Some As are Bs'). According to the atmosphere effect theory, universal premises predispose people towards accepting a universal conclusion, whereas a particular conclusion is accepted after particular premises. People were said to prefer a particular conclusion when one premise is universal and the other is particular.

The evidence broadly supports this theory. Consider the four categorical syllogisms below:

1. All As are Bs
   All Cs are Bs
   Therefore all As are Cs

2. No As are Bs
   All Cs are Bs
   Therefore No As are Cs

3. No As are Bs
   No Bs are Cs
   Therefore No As are Cs

4. No As are Bs
   No Bs are Cs
   Therefore All As are Cs

Which of these syllogisms do you think are valid? According to atmosphere theory, people should be more likely to accept the conclusions on syllogisms 1 and 3 than on syllogisms 2 and 4, and this generally seems to be true (Evans, 1982). For the benefit of anyone who may be wondering, all four syllogisms are, in fact, invalid. There is also evidence to support the other part of the atmosphere effect theory that relates to universal and particular premises and conclusions.

The atmosphere effect theory does contain a grain of truth, but it by no means tells the whole story. The simple fact that people show a certain amount of ability to distinguish accurately between valid and invalid syllogisms means that they are not entirely at the mercy of the atmosphere created by the premises. More disconfirming evidence was obtained by Johnson-Laird and Steedman (1978). According to the atmosphere effect theory, people should be equally likely to accept the invalid conclusion in each of the following two syllogisms:

1. Some As are Bs
   Some Bs are Cs
   Therefore Some As are Cs

2. Some Bs are As
   Some Cs are Bs
   Therefore Some As are Cs

In fact, people were more likely to accept the invalid conclusion in syllogisms like 1 than in syllogisms like 2. It seemed as if people are more willing to accept a conclusion having A as its subject and C as its conclusion if there is a chain leading from A to B one premise, and from B to C in other.

A further difficulty with the atmosphere hypothesis is that there are alternative explanations of many of the findings. In many cases, the reason why an invalid conclusion is accepted may be because the premises are misinterpreted. According to Chapman and Chapman's (1959) conversion hypothesis, subjects commonly misinterpret universal affirmative propositions to mean that the converse is also true (e.g., "All As are Bs" is taken to mean "All Bs are As"), and the same is true of particular negative statements (e.g., "Some As are not Bs" is taken to mean "Some Bs are not As"). Some of the clearest support for the conversion hypothesis was obtained by Ceraso and Provitera (1971). When the premises were stated less ambiguously (e.g., "All As are Bs" was stated as "All As are Bs, but some Bs are not As"), there was a substantial improvement in performance.

With respect to the issue of whether people think logically or illogically on syllogistic problems, the evidence supporting the atmosphere theory suggests illogical thinking, whereas that favouring the conversion hypothesis is consistent with logical thought applied to misinterpreted premises. Rather more direct support for the idea that thinking is often illogical comes in work on belief bias, which is the tendency to evaluate the conclusion on the basis of personal beliefs rather than with respect to the premises. Evidence of belief bias has been obtained in several studies. For example, Janis and Frick (1943) obtained an interaction between subjects' attitudes to the conclusions of syllogisms and their judgements of the validity or invalidity of those syllogisms. In this interaction, there were more errors when subjects agreed with the conclusions of invalid syllogisms than when they agreed with valid syllogisms, and there were more errors on valid syllogisms when they disagreed with the conclusions.

What can reasonably be concluded about performance on syllogistic reasoning tasks? Firstly, the notion that people basically think logically on such tasks seems rather bizarre in the light of the evidence. It is true that some errors of performance occur when logical reasoning is applied to premises that have been misunderstood, but that by no means accounts for all of the errors that are made. Secondly, it is obvious that there are many different reasons why people experience difficulty in coping with syllogisms. These include misinterpretation of the premises, reliance on the atmosphere created by the premises, belief bias, and ignorance of some of the rules of inference (e.g., *modus tollens*). The interested reader will discover even more reasons discussed in a book by Evans (1982). Thirdly, we can describe much of people's behaviour in the following terms: Syllogisms are treated as problems, and various heuristics or rules of thumb are made use of in the attempt to find the solution. In other words, thinking on syllogistic tasks is fundamentally illogical.

Wason Selection Task

Some of the inadequacies of human reasoning that are revealed by performance on syllogistic tasks are even more clearly manifest on the Wason selection task (Wason, 1966). In particular, as we go on to discuss here, the failure to use *modus tollens* appropriately is instrumental in determining performance on the selection task. The basic paradigm used with the selection task consists of four cards lying on a table; the subject is informed that each card has a letter on one side and a number on the other, and also that a rule applies to each of these four cards (e.g., "If there is an R on one side of the card, then there is a 2 on the other side of the card"). Finally, the instructions indicate that the subject must select only those cards that would need to be turned over in order to decide whether the rule is true or false.

Suppose that the four cards have the following symbols uppermost: R, G, 2, 7. The most popular answer to this problem is to select the R and 2 cards, but this is not the right answer. The key to solving the problem is to realise that the discovery of a single card that does not obey the rule is sufficient to falsify it. If the 7 card had an R on the other side, then that would disprove the rule, whereas the 2 card is irrelevant: if it does not have an R on the other side, then it tells us nothing about the truth of the rule, and if it does have an R on the other side, this merely tells us that the rule may be true. To cut a long story short, the cards that actually need to be selected are R and 7, but in a typical series of experiments on university students it was found that only 4% chose the R and 7 cards (Johnson-Laird & Wason, 1970).

What is the nature of the difficulty with this apparently reasonably straightforward problem? Wason (1966) argued that what was happening was that subjects were mistakenly searching for cards which could verify the rule rather than those which could falsify it. However, Wason (1968) discovered that instructions explicitly asking for selections to prove the rule false or untrue were not very effective in improving performance, and he also found that 'therapeutic' procedures designed to emphasise the falsifying potential of the 7 card were relatively unsuccessful.

An alternative explanation has been offered by Evans (Evans, 1972; Evans & Lynch, 1973). He proposed in essence that subjects have a matching bias, i.e., a bias towards those items mentioned in the rule. Strong support for this notion was obtained by Evans (1972), who asked subjects to name a combination of a letter and a number on a card which in conjunction would violate or falsify a rule, given that each of a set of cards had a letter on one side and a number on the other side. When the rule was, "If the letter is a T then the number is not a 4," most of the subjects produced the correct answer "T and 4." Of more interest, most subjects gave exactly the same answer when the rule was, "If the letter is not a T then the number is a 4"! In this case, of course, the answer is totally wrong, and should consist of a letter other than T with a number other than 4. In other words, matching bias was the norm irrespective of the problem itself.

An alternative explanation of the remarkably poor performance displayed by intelligent adults on the Wason selection task is the rather abstract and unrealistic nature of the problem. An early attempt to remedy this was made by Wason and Shapiro (1971). They used four cards (Manchester, Leeds, car, and train), with the means of transport written on one side and the destination on the other side. The subjects were given the rule, "Every time I go to Manchester I travel by car," and asked to decide which cards needed to be turned over to evaluate the truth or falsity of the rule. The correct answer (Manchester and train) was given by 62% of the subjects, against only 12% when a logically equivalent problem was given in an abstract form.

There are at least two possible kinds of explanation for these findings: Reasoning is facilitated either by the use of concrete and meaningful material, or by using a version of the Wason task that relates directly to the subjects' experience. The former explanation was preferred initially, but the bulk of the more recent evidence tends to support the latter explanation. For example, Griggs and Cox (1982) failed to replicate the findings of Wason and Shapiro (1971) among a group of American students in Florida, presumably because most of them had no direct experience of Manchester or Leeds. They obtained very different results when the rule was, "If a person is drinking beer, then the person must be over 19 years of age," and the four cards were as follows: drinking a beer, drinking a coke, 16 years of age, and 22 years of age. This rule corresponds to the Florida law on drinking and led to 73% of the subjects producing the correct answer (against 0% on an abstract version of the problem).

We have discussed the Wason selection task in some detail because it reveals with clarity some of the major characteristics of adult human thought. In particular, it is striking that the thinking of most intelligent adults can apparently be so illogical. This is shown by the fact that performance on the logic-based Wason task is affected quite substantially by factors such as the realism and truth status of the task content which have nothing to do with logic. Furthermore, the tendency of subjects to show a matching bias indicates a rather primitive level of thought far removed from the incisive rigour of logical thinking. It has also been suggested by Evans (1982) that people are not usually aware of the processes underlying their reasoning performance. If they are asked to explain their card selections, they make use of the available information about the task instructions and their own behavioural responses to construct a rationalisation or justification of their performance on the task. In support of this rationalisation hypothesis, Evans and Wason (1976) gave their subjects the selection task, together with what purported to be the correct solution. In fact, the four groups of subjects were each given a different "solution." Practically none of the subjects disputed the correctness of the alleged solution, and most of them constructed reasonable justifications for the selections involved in the arbitrary solution they had been given, despite the fact that the proffered solution usually differed from that which they would have arrived at unaided. All in all, the notion of *homo sapiens*, the rational and logical being, espoused by Piaget and others, looks rather implausible on the basis of performance on the selection task.

Mental Models

Johnson-Laird (1983a, 1983b) has recently made an impressive contribution to theorising about deductive reasoning. He argued that the first stage in syllogistic reasoning involves constructing an integrated mental model that incorporates information from the premises of the syllogism. This mental model resembles the model that would be produced if the events referred to in the premises were perceived or imagined. The construction of a mental model based on the premises usually suggests some conclusion, the validity of which is assessed by searching for alternative mental models of the premises that would be incompatible with that conclusion. In general terms, valid conclusions are not made on the basis of logical principles, but on the assumption that a conclusion is valid provided there is no way of interpreting the premises so as to invalidate it.

The above processes of reasoning depend on the processing resources of working memory, and so are subject to its limited capacity. As a result, the process of constructing mental models can be a time-consuming business. The limitations of working memory are also relevant to the task of forming the initial integrated model based on the premises, since some premises are not in a form permitting immediate integration, and so further processes making demands on working memory need to be carried out.

Some of these ideas can be clarified if we consider a specific example (Johnson-Laird, 1983b). Ask yourself what (if any) valid conclusion can be drawn from the following premises:

All of the beekeepers are artists.
None of the chemists are beekeepers.

According to Johnson-Laird (1983b), there are three possible mental models of these premises. A relatively obvious model is as follows:

chemist
chemist

....

beekeeper = artist
beekeeper = artist
(artist)
(artist)

The dotted line indicates that beekeepers and chemists are separate categories of people. The model also indicates that every beekeeper is also an artist, and that there may be some additional non-beekeeper artists (indicated by the brackets). This model suggests the invalid conclusion, "None of the chemists are artists," which was drawn by 60% of the subjects in a study reported by Johnson-Laird (1983b). The fact that that conclusion is invalid can be seen if a second mental model is constructed:

$$
\begin{aligned}
&\text{chemist} \\
&\text{chemist} \quad = \text{artist} \\
&\cdots\cdots\cdots\cdots\cdots\cdots\cdots\cdots\cdots\cdots\cdots \\
&\text{beekeeper} = \text{artist} \\
&\text{beekeeper} = \text{artist} \\
&\qquad\qquad\quad (\text{artist})
\end{aligned}
$$

This mental model suggests the conclusion, "Some of the chemists are not artists." This conclusion was drawn by 10% of the subjects, but is also invalid, as the third mental model shows:

$$
\begin{aligned}
&\text{chemist} \quad = \text{artist} \\
&\text{chemist} \quad = \text{artist} \\
&\cdots\cdots\cdots\cdots\cdots\cdots\cdots\cdots\cdots\cdots\cdots \\
&\text{beekeeper} = \text{artist} \\
&\text{beekeeper} = \text{artist}
\end{aligned}
$$

Any subject who successfully constructed all three mental models might feel that there was no valid conclusion that could be drawn from the premises, and 20% of the subjects arrived at that point.

In fact, there is a valid conclusion that can be drawn from the premises: "Some of the artists are not chemists." This relation is common to all three mental models, but would only be likely to be discovered after all three mental models had been constructed. Moreover, it seems more "natural" for one of the left-hand items (i.e., beekeeper or chemist) to form the subject of the conclusion, and so the mental models need to be evaluated in relatively complex ways. In view of these difficulties, it is perhaps not surprising to discover that none of the university students used as subjects drew the valid conclusion.

We have seen that the mental model approach can predict the kinds of errors that occur on deductive reasoning tasks. It also proved successful in predicting the probability of drawing valid conclusions. When performance was averaged across three studies, the percentage valid conclusions drawn from premises yielding only one mental model was 78%, against 29% with two mental models, and 13% with three mental models.

What is the potential value of the mental model approach? Firstly, there is a more detailed specification of the mental processes intervening between problem presentation and the subject's response than has been customary in the past. This precision has enabled Johnson-Laird to construct computer programmes to simulate human performance on a number of problems. Secondly, Johnson-Laird (1983a) has shown convincingly that it is entirely possible for a system to solve logical problems successfully without making use of any of the rules of logic. Rather than arguing that reasoning is logical when it is successful and illogical when it fails, it may be more accurate to distinguish between those situations in which appropriate mental models are or are not constructed. As a result, the entire controversy about the logicality of human thought may need to be considered afresh.

INDUCTIVE REASONING

Introduction

One of the distinguishing characteristics of an inductively valid argument is that the conclusion is highly probable but not necessarily true. It may help to see why if we consider an example of an inductive inference:

Every experiment on learning has found that it depends on reinforcement. Therefore, learning always depends on reinforcement.

The conclusion is not necessarily true, because other experiments carried out in the future may reveal circumstances in which learning occurs in the absence of reinforcement. Of course, it usually makes no practical difference whether a conclusion is certain or only highly probable, but logicians and philosophers have agreed that it is important to distinguish between deductive and inductive reasoning.

Although it is obviously possible to decide whether a task requires deductive or inductive reasoning, it is more difficult to decide whether or not separate mental processes are used by people confronting the two kinds of tasks. We have already seen that people do not follow strictly logical principles when given deductive reasoning tasks, and a similar conclusion applies to inductive reasoning performance. The way in which the distinction between deductive and inductive reasoning is blurred at the psychological level was described in the following terms by Bolton (1972):

Experiments on deductive reasoning show that subjects are influenced sufficiently by their experience for their reasoning to differ from that described by a purely deductive system, whilst experiments on inductive reasoning lead to the view that an understanding of the strategies used by adult subjects in attaining concepts involves reference to higher-order concepts of a logical and deductive nature [p. 154].

Concept learning

One major way in which inductive reasoning has been investigated is by considering the processes involved in concept learning. The typical paradigm involves several stimuli, some of which are identified by the experimenter as positive instances of the concept he or she has in mind, whereas others are identified as negative instances. The subject's task is to utilise the accumulating information from these positive and negative instances to decide what the concept is.

The modern era was ushered in by Bruner, Goodnow, and Austin (1956). In most of their research, they made use of stimuli consisting of rectangular cards containing various objects. These cards varied on four dimensions: number of borders around the edges of the cards (one, two, or three); number of objects in the middle of the cards (one, two, or three); shape of the objects (square, circle, or cross); and colour of the objects (red, black, or green). Bruner et al. typically used conjunctive concepts, in which a number of features had to be present together, in order for an instance to be positive (e.g., "two black circles"). In some studies they used the reception paradigm, in which the experimenter decided on the sequence of positive and negative instances to be presented to the subjects; in other studies they utilised the selection paradigm, in which the subjects had all the cards in front of them, and selected one at a time, being told by the experimenter whether it was positive or negative.

Some of the most interesting data obtained by Bruner et al. (1956) stemmed from work on the selection procedure. The major advantage of this procedure is that it is often possible to infer the problem-solving strategies used by subjects on the basis of their pattern of selections, and also on the basis of the hypotheses that they volunteer during the task. This richness of information about what the subject was thinking and doing prior to attainment of the concept represented a significant improvement on earlier research. According to Bruner et al., subjects mostly made use of a strictly limited number of strategies. One of these strategies was conservative focusing, which proved to be very efficient. It involved focusing on the first positive instance, and selecting another card that differed from it in only one attribute. If this second card was also a positive instance, then the attribute varied must have been irrelevant to the concept. Thus, if one green circle with three borders is a positive instance, and so is one green circle with two borders, then the number of borders is not part of the concept. On the other hand, if the second card was a negative instance, then the attribute varied must have been relevant.

A related strategy used by some of the subjects was focus gambling. As the name implies, it is a rather riskier kind of strategy than conservative focusing. In focus gambling, the subject changes two or more of the attributes of the first positive instance when selecting the next card. If that card is also a positive instance, then a lot of information has been obtained. However, if the next card is a negative instance, then the subject does not know which of the two changed attributes was responsible for the error.

The third major strategy identified by Bruner *et al.* (1956) was successive scanning. This involved starting with a hypothesis, and then selecting cards that yielded information relevant to it. In using this strategy, the subject usually scanned and remembered only those attributes of each card that were relevant to his or her current hypothesis.

In general, focusing proved to be a more successful and efficient strategy than scanning. One of the difficulties with scanning is that the heavy demands on memory that it requires produce what Bruner *et al.* (1956) called "cognitive strain." They demonstrated the importance of this factor by asking subjects to solve two problems with the stimulus array in view and a third problem with it out of sight. Scanners took longer to solve the problem imposing the increased memory load than to solve the first two problems, whereas focusers were unaffected by the increased memory load.

How important is the contribution made by Bruner *et al.* (1956)? On the positive side, their emphasis on detailed data collection and on the internal strategies and hypotheses used by the subject give their work a contemporary feel. Even if many of their specific theoretical formulations are erroneous, their basic approach to concept learning seems reasonable. On the negative side, decisions about the strategies used by individual subjects were not made in a rigorous way: it was often claimed that subjects had followed a particular strategy, even though several of their selections differed from those that would have been expected on that strategy (e.g., making redundant card selections that provided no new information). A more serious criticism concerns the apparent lack of relevance of the findings to everyday life. While focusing was very efficient on a task with a very small number of potentially relevant attribute dimensions, it would typically only enable the individual to eliminate dimensions one by one from an almost infinite set if used in the real world. Furthermore, while the laboratory subject can afford the luxury of suspending judgement about the nature of the concept while focusing on one attribute dimension after another, the same person in the real world may need to decide rapidly whether to approach or avoid another person or an object. Under such circumstances, the appropriate strategy is to act on the basis of the best available hypothesis, as is the case with scanning.

We have concentrated on the results that Bruner *et al.* (1956) obtained with the selection paradigm. However, they also reported some interesting findings with the reception paradigm, in which the experimenter, rather than the subject, controlled the order in which stimuli were presented. In essence, they discovered that most subjects used either the wholist strategy or the partist strategy. In the wholist strategy, all of the features of the first positive instance are taken as the hypothesis. Any of these features that are not present with subsequent positive instances are eliminated from the hypothesis. In contrast, the partist strategy involves taking part of the first positive instance as a hypothesis. After that, the original hypothesis is maintained provided that the subject consistently makes correct decisions about positive and negative instances. As and when a mistake is made, partist subjects attempt to select a new hypothesis that is consistent with the information obtained from previous items.

The wholist strategy was found to be the optimal strategy. In part, this is because it imposes much less of a demand on memory: Wholist subjects only need to remember the current hypothesis, and can ignore information about previous instances. Bruner *et al.* found that approximately twice as many subjects used the wholist strategy as used the partist strategy, but the typical finding in other research has been that subjects use the partist strategy much more often than the wholist strategy. Obviously, the choice of strategy is bound to be affected by many factors, including the cognitive skills of the individual and the complexity of the problem.

Bower and Trabasso (1964) proposed a hypothesis-sampling theory to account for performance on concept-learning tasks based on the reception paradigm. According to this theory, subjects sample or select one of the possible hypotheses at random, and then decide whether each stimulus is a positive or a negative instance on the basis of that hypothesis. When the hypothesis leads to an incorrect prediction, subjects reject it and select another hypothesis that is consistent with the current trial. This clearly resembles the partist strategy described by Bruner *et al.* (1956), with the exception that Bower and Trabasso assumed that subjects did not make use of information from earlier trials when selecting a new hypothesis.

The crucial assumption of the hypothesis-sampling theory is that concept learning is regarded as a discontinuous, all-or-none phenomenon, in which subjects make no progress until they formulate the correct hypothesis. Such a view contrasts with associative theories that regard concept learning as a continuous strengthening of reinforced responses. The latter view seems to find support in the fact that group data do usually show a continuous improvement in performance over trials. However, it is possible that such group data are not representative of individual performance, and that individual discontinuities are being concealed. Bower and Trabasso (1964) investigated this possibility on a concept-learning task, and found that individual performance was very close to chance right up to the trial immediately prior to the one on which they made their last error (i.e., after this point they made no further errors).

A rather different test of hypothesis-sampling theory was made by Bower and Trabasso (1963). If it is true that subjects do not remember and make use of information from previous instances, then their performance should not be harmed by giving them information consistent with one hypothesis for some time, and then surreptitiously giving them feedback consistent with a completely different hypothesis. The data obtained by Bower and Trabasso provided a striking confirmation of this prediction.

The major contentions of hypothesis-sampling theory have usually been supported, especially the "win–stay, lose–shift" notion, i.e., the current hypothesis is maintained as long as it produces accurate predictions, but it is changed when it does not. For example, Levine (1966) found on a concept-learning task that people retained their hypotheses on 95% of the trials on which they guessed correctly whether they had been presented with a positive or a negative instance of the concept, whereas they switched to another hypothesis 98% of the time following an incorrect guess. However, there has been less support for the notion that information from previous trials is not remembered, and Levine (1966) discovered that subjects' performance was somewhat better than would have been expected on the basis of only remembering the last trial.

Our earlier discussion of deductive reasoning showed that many people experience difficulty in making use of negative information, i.e., a statement of what is *not* the case. The same problem appears to plague people who are engaged on inductive reasoning tasks such as concept learning. Part of the reason for this state of affairs is likely to be the fact that we spend our lives experiencing only what is the case. This reluctance or inability to use negative information did not, of course, extend to the great detective Sherlock Holmes. In "The Silver Blaze" (Doyle, 1974), Sherlock Holmes asked Inspector Gregory to consider "the curious incident of the dog in the night-time." The mystified and slow-witted Inspector Gregory replied, "The dog did nothing in the night-time," to which Holmes replied triumphantly, "That *was* the curious incident [p. 33]." Holmes realised that a dog barking at an intruder would have provided little useful evidence, but the dog's failure to bark proved that the intruder was someone the animal knew.

Our greater familiarity with positive than with negative information is undoubtedly one of the main reasons why negative information is not used efficiently. It is also true that negative information is often intrinsically less helpful than positive information. If you are looking for a colleague, and discover that he is not in his room, this does not tell you much about where he is to be found. However, when steps were taken to equate the amount of information available in positive and negative instances, subjects still made better use of the information from positive instances (Hovland & Weiss, 1953).

People are not only unskilled in the use of negative information, they also fail to seek it out when it is essential for successful task performance. In a classic study by Wason (1960), people were told that the three numbers "2 4 6" conformed to a simple relational rule, which was "three numbers in increasing order of magnitude." Their task was to generate sets of three numbers, and to provide reasons for each choice. The experimenter indicated whether each set conformed to the rule. At any time that the subject thought he had discovered the correct rule he was to announce it. What typically happened was that subjects thought of a hypothesis (e.g., the second number is twice the first, and the third number is three times the first), and then generated sets of numbers that were consistent with that hypothesis (e.g., "6 12 18"; "11 22 33"; "47 94 141").

This approach to the problem produced rather poor performance. Only 21% of the subjects were correct with their first attempt to state the rule. The optimal way of testing the correctness of a hypothesis is to look for sets of numbers that will *disconfirm* the hypothesis. Thus any subjects who had entertained the hypothesis that the second number is twice the first and the third is three times the first could have discovered that this hypothesis was erroneous by selecting a series such as "6 10 20". Failure to attempt hypothesis disconfirmation prevented the subjects from replacing their initial hypotheses, which were too narrow and specific, with the correct general rule.

The deep-rooted reluctance to look for disconfirming evidence was shown even more clearly by Wason (1968) in further work on the same task. He asked 16 subjects to indicate, after they had expressed their hypotheses, what they would do in order to determine whether these hypotheses were incorrect. Three of them insisted defiantly that their hypotheses could not possibly be incorrect, and nine more said that they would generate only sets of numbers that were consistent with their hypotheses, waiting until one set was identified as not conforming to the rule. Only one-quarter of the subjects gave the right answer, which is to generate sets of numbers inconsistent with the hypothesis in order to see whether or not they conform to the experimenter's rule.

Intuitive Strategies of Inference

Suppose that you have something wrong with you, and that a medical encyclopaedia indicates that your physical complaint is one of the symptoms of a relatively rare and unpleasant disease. The natural reaction is to think about the chances that you are suffering from that disease. This is an example of the kind of inference that is drawn every day. It has proved of considerable interest to psychologists because of the systematic errors that tend to be involved. In the example quoted, let us assume that two people in 1000 have the disease, that the probability of having the physical complaint if you are suffering from the disease is .7, and that the chances of having the complaint if you do not have the disease are 1 in a 100. Most people in these circumstances would feel that they were probably suffering from the disease. In fact, there is a mathematical formula known as Bayes' theorem that allows us to calculate the actual probability, given the information above about the various component probabilities. It turns out that the true probability that you have the disease is only .123, which is undoubtedly much lower than your estimate would have been.

Why are there such striking inaccuracies in human thinking on this problem and on a host of related problems? It seems likely that people simply decide between alternative possibilities (e.g., having versus not having the disease) on the basis of which one appears more representative of the evidence (e.g., having a physical complaint). This way of thinking is inadequate because it does not take account of the base-rate information, which in this case relates to the numbers of people suffering from, and not suffering from, the disease. The number of non-sufferers is vastly more than the number of sufferers, and it is the failure to make use of this fact that produces wildly inaccurate estimates.

Kahneman and Tversky (1973) referred to the tendency to make judgements on the basis of the extent to which the salient features of an object or person are representative of (or similar to) the features thought to be characteristic of some category. This is known as the "representativeness heuristic," and they documented some of the errors in thinking that follow from the use of this heuristic. For example, subjects were provided with brief descriptions of five people, and told that these descriptions had been chosen at random from a total of 100 descriptions. Half of the subjects were told that the total consisted of descriptions of 70 engineers and 30 lawyers, whereas the other subjects were informed that there were 70 lawyers and 30 engineers. The subjects' task was to decide the probability that the person written about in each description was an engineer (or lawyer).

Let us consider a concrete example. Here is a description (Kahneman & Tversky, 1973) that was designed to be similar to the subjects' engineer stereotype and dissimilar to their lawyer stereotype: "Jack is a 45-year-old man. He is married and has four children. He is generally conservative, careful, and ambitious. He shows no interest in political and social issues and spends most of his free time on his many hobbies which include home carpentry, sailing, and mathematical puzzles [p. 241]." Subjects in both conditions decided that there was approximately a .90 probability that the person was an engineer. This inferential decision obviously reflects use of the representativeness heuristic: Jack's description resembles a typical engineer more than a typical lawyer, and therefore he is probably an engineer. However, once again the base-rate information has been ignored. The probability estimates ought to be affected by whether the description was chosen at random from a set of descriptions composed largely of engineers or one composed mainly of lawyers. In fact, the estimates for this, and the other descriptions took practically no account of the proportions of lawyers and engineers in the total sample.

It should not be concluded that people are unable to use base-rate information. When the subjects were asked to estimate the probability that an individual chosen at random, and about whom they had no information, was an engineer, they estimated likelihoods of either .7 or .3, depending on the base-rate data that had been supplied. Very different results were obtained (Kahneman & Tversky, 1973), however, when given an essentially worthless and uninformative description: "Dick is a 30-year-old man. He is married with no children. A man of high ability and high motivation, he promises to be quite successful in his field. He is well liked by his colleagues [p. 242]." Subjects who read this description typically rated the likelihoods that Dick was an engineer or lawyer as equally likely (.5) irrespective of the underlying base rates. In other words, base-rate data are used when no information is provided, but are totally ignored when worthless information is provided!

Some clarification of the circumstances in which base-rate information will be utilised was obtained by Tversky and Kahneman (1978). They told their subjects that there were two taxi companies in a town; these were the Blue Company and the Green Company. An accident involving a taxi occurred, and the subjects' task was to judge the likelihood that the taxi had been blue. Some subjects were told that 85% of the town's taxis were blue and the remaining 15% were green, and they were also informed about an imperfect eye-witness identification. These subjects relied mainly on the eye-witness evidence in making their judgements, and largely ignored the base-rates. Other subjects were told that the town had an equal number of blue and green taxis, but that 85% of the taxi-related accidents involved blue taxis. In this condition, the subjects relied heavily on base-rate information in assessing the likelihood that the taxi involved in the accident was blue.

The difference in performance between the two conditions seems rather mysterious, because the relevance of the base-rate is the same in each case. It may be that people are more inclined to take account of base-rate information when it seems to be causally relevant. When the base-rate referred to percentages of taxi-related accidents involving blue and green taxis, it was easy to see that careless versus careful driving tendencies causally affect the chances of being involved in an accident.

These findings serve to illustrate the limitations of the theory of represen-tativeness. In a nutshell, the problem is that the theory can account for any findings too readily: Failure to utilise base-rate information is attributed to use of the representativeness heuristic, whereas successful use of base-rate information means that the representativeness heuristic was not used. In order to have a proper predictive theory, we need further information about the exact circumstances in which the representativeness heuristic will, and will not, be used.

Base-rate information may sometimes be ignored or de-emphasised because it appears relatively dull or uninteresting. As the well-known social engineer Joseph Stalin remarked, "The death of a single Russian soldier is a tragedy. A million deaths is a statistic." It has always been recognised by those working in the media that vivid and concrete examples of social injustice are much more effective than quoting Government statistics. Evidence supporting these ideas was obtained by Borgida and Nisbett (1977). Introductory psychology students who planned to specialise in psychology were provided with information about ten advanced psychology courses, either in the form of a statistical summary allegedly based on the reports of the dozens of students who had taken each course the preceding term, or in the form of ratings and brief comments presented in a face-to-face situation by two or three students who had already taken each course. While the abstract statistics were more informative than the face-to-face recommendations, those students who had received information face-to-face were more influenced by their experience, indicating an intention to take more of the highly evaluated courses and fewer of the poorly evaluated courses than did the students who were given the statistical summary.

We have seen some of the errors in inferential thinking that can occur when undue reliance is placed on the representativeness heuristic. Tversky and Kahneman (1974) discussed two further heuristics, one based on the availability of instances and the other involving adjustment from an anchor. When people are attempting to estimate the relative frequency of particular objects or events, they often make use of information about the relative availability of these objects or events in perception or memory. This "availability heuristic" is extremely valuable when availability is highly correlated with objective frequency, but it can be misleading under other circumstances. Suppose that people are asked whether each of five letters (K, L, N, R, V) appears more often in the first or the third position in English words. When this was done, each of the five letters was judged to occur much more frequently in the first than in the third position (Tversky & Kahneman, 1973). In fact, all of these letters appear in the third position in more words than in the first position. The probable reason for inaccurate performance on this task is that it is much easier to generate words beginning with a particular letter than those having a given letter as the third letter.

The other heuristic discussed by Tversky and Kahneman is the "adjustment heuristic". The heuristic of adjustment from an anchor is sometimes used in numerical prediction when a relevant variable is available. Consider the following example taken from Tversky and Kahneman (1974). Subjects were given one of the following problems:

1. $8 \times 7 \times 6 \times 5 \times 4 \times 3 \times 2 \times 1$ or
2. $1 \times 2 \times 3 \times 4 \times 5 \times 6 \times 7 \times 8$

They were asked to estimate the product within 5 seconds, which prevented them from doing the complete calculation. The median estimates were 2250 for the first problem and 512 for the second problem; these estimates are substantially lower than the correct answer, which is 40,320. What probably happened here is that the subjects performed a few steps of the problem, and then adjusted their answers upwards from the totals they had reached. Both here and elsewhere, however, the adjustments are typically insufficient.

We turn now to the key issue that emerges from this work on the heuristics used in inferential reasoning, namely, why is it that people are apparently so prone to large and systematic errors in their thinking? One reason is undoubtedly that people do not usually detect the biases in their judgements of the likelihoods of various eventualities, and so do not realise that certain corrections are needed in their thinking.

One of the most obvious reasons why people use heuristics in their thinking is that they reduce cognitive strain by offering a straightforward way of tackling many diverse problems. A more important reason is that the heuristics very frequently facilitate accurate thinking. For example, in many cases the availability of different classes of events provides a relatively unbiased estimate of their objective frequency. If people were asked to estimate the relative frequencies of words beginning with "L" and with "N," or of words with "L" and "N" in the third position, then it is probable that differences in the relative ease of generation of relevant words would have reflected accurately differences in frequency.

A similar argument is applicable to the representativeness heuristic. This heuristic incorporates the insight that the characteristics of the sample ought to resemble those of the parent population, and often allows us to reach sound conclusions. Indeed, it is important to note that when the representativeness heuristic produces errors, it is usually because other factors are ignored or slighted, rather than that representativeness itself is irrelevant to the particular inferential task.

Analogical Reasoning

One of the commonest forms of reasoning involves the drawing of analogies between the current problem situation and a related one. It has often happened in the history of science that theoretical developments stem from a scientist noticing and making use of an analogy taken from a very different area of knowledge. The computer model of human information processing, the billiard-ball model of gases, and the hydraulic model of the blood circulation system are all examples of scientific theories based on analogies.

Gick and Holyoak (1980) investigated the ease with which people can make use of analogies on a complex task known as Duncker's radiation problem:

> Suppose you are a doctor faced with a patient who has a malignant tumour in his stomach. It is impossible to operate on the patient, but unless the tumour is destroyed the patient will die. There is a kind of ray that can be used to destroy the tumour. If the rays reach the tumour all at once at a sufficiently high intensity, the tumour will be destroyed. Unfortunately, at this intensity the healthy tissue that the rays pass through on the way to the tumour will also be destroyed. At lower intensities the rays are harmless to healthy tissue, but they will not affect the tumour either. What types of procedure might be used to destroy the tumour with the rays, and at the same time avoid destroying the healthy tissue? [pp. 307–308].

The correct solution to this problem is to direct multiple low-intensity rays at the tumour from different directions. In order to help subjects in their discovery of the solution, Gick and Holyoak (1980) preceded this problem by presenting subjects with three stories to be memorised. In one of them, a general wanted to capture a fortress. A full-scale direct attack was impossible, because all of the various roads radiating outwards from the fortress had been mined; as a result, only small groups of men could travel along them safely. The general solved the problem by dividing his army into small groups which converged at the same time on the fortress along different roads. The other two stories to be memorised ("The Wine Merchants" and "The Identical Twins") were irrelevant to the subsequent radiation problem.

Only approximately 10% of those subjects not given the three stories produced the correct solution, against 92% of subjects who received them, and were told that one of them might be relevant to the problem. The finding that nearly all of the subjects were able to make use of the analogy when its potential relevance was pointed out to them means that they were reasonably adept at discovering points of correspondence between a military operation and the radiation problem, despite the large differences in content between the story and the problem. This indicates an ability to ignore irrelevant detail and to focus on the relatively abstract level at which the story about the military operation could be mapped onto the requirements of the radiation problem.

However, it appears that the drawing of appropriate analogies from past experience does not happen effortlessly and automatically. Subjects who memorised the three stories but were not given the hint that one of the stories might facilitate problem solution performed at approximately the level of the control subjects on the radiation problem. In other words, the fact that an appropriate analogy is stored in long-term memory is no guarantee at all that it will actually be used when relevant.

Why do people often fail to notice the relevance of a previously encountered analogy to a current problem? The major reason is probably that transfer of training is typically directly related to the similarity between the previous learning and the present task. When, as in the study by Gick and Holyoak (1980), the potential analogy was presented in a very different context from that in which the problem appeared, it can be very difficult to connect the two bodies of information spontaneously.

One of the rather unusual aspects of much of the work carried out on analogical reasoning by Gick and Holyoak (1980), and by others, is that the crucial problem could be solved with complete success by making use of the appropriate analogy. In real life, matters are often much more complex; the reason for this is that the fit or match between previous knowledge and the current problem is nearly always imprecise. At least in scientific research, analogies often have a great initial impact on thinking, but doubts grow as the implications of the analogy are explored systematically. For example, we discovered in Chapter 4 that an analogy between aspects of human information processing and memory storage on the one hand, and the ways in which a computer functions on the other hand has been extremely popular. However, the consensus of opinion nowdays is that there are indeed some intriguing similarities, but the analogy has appeared increasingly less appealing as more and more differences have been discovered.

PRACTICAL APPLICATIONS

In practical terms, the key issue is whether our knowledge and understanding of problem solving and reasoning can be used to teach people how to solve problems more efficiently. This issue has been discussed at length in various places (e.g., Tuma & Reif, 1980), but there is still some controversy about the feasibility of producing substantial improvements in general problem-solving ability. Of fundamental importance in resolving this issue is the extent to which problem-solving skills are of general applicability or relatively specific to a narrow range of problems. It was thought at one time that children should be taught Latin in order to improve their ability to think logically, but the well-known studies of Thorndike (1924) seem to have invalidated that notion. Subsequent research has tended to indicate that practice on one task will transfer successfully to a second task only provided that very similar skills or knowledge are required by both tasks. Specificity is also indicated by a consideration of the enormous number of specific items of knowledge that must be possessed by many expert problem solvers. For example, it has been estimated that a chess master must have approximately 50,000 chunks of information relating to configurations of pieces during a game stored in long-term memory.

It is clear that the attempt to teach problem-solving skills is doomed if any single skill is relevant to only a tiny fraction of potential problems. However, there are indications that there may be some general skills that are applicable to numerous problem situations. A rather general strategy that was discussed earlier in the chapter is means–ends analysis, that involves establishing the difference between the present position and the goal state, and then attempting to reduce that difference. While Newell and Simon (1972) produced some evidence of the general significance of means–ends analysis, it is not clear from their work whether means–ends analysis is applicable to problems other than well-defined puzzles. There is now evidence that means–ends analysis is used in at least some more naturalistic situations. Simon and Simon (1978) discovered that a beginner solving problems in kinematics seemed to make use of information about the difference between the equations that she had and those that would be required for problem solution, in order to decide on the new equations that would reduce this difference. Of course, means–ends analysis could only have been used in this case provided that the student had sufficient specific knowledge to enable her to make an accurate assessement of the difference between the current position and the goal state. Simon and Simon also discovered that an expert did not rely on means–ends analysis, but instead constructed a "physical representation" that acted as a cue for applying the relevant principles.

Means–ends analysis is not the only general problem-solving strategy. "Mapping" is another general strategy: It involves mapping the given problem situation onto something that is already known, and basically consists of argument by analogy. Yet a further general strategy is "planning," in which the problem as given is transformed into an abstracted version retaining only some of the features of the original problem. This abstracted problem is then solved, and this facilitates solution of the original problem.

The implication of what has been said so far in this section is that problem-solving skills can most readily be improved by focusing on general strategies. A number of the chapters in the book edited by Tuma and Reif (1980) provide some support for that contention. Teaching should emphasise the principles underlying strategies such as means–ends analysis, because otherwise these skills may not be transferred to new problem situations. According to Simon (1980), a valuable way of making problem solvers employ these general strategies is by using worked examples and requiring them to work through various problems in an active way.

There is at least one limitation with respect to the usefulness of teaching general skills such as means–ends analysis. Such evidence as is available (e.g., Simon & Simon, 1978) indicates that general skills become progressively less important as expertise develops. Experts typically possess a very large number of clusters or chunks of information, and can use these chunks to expedite the solution process.

So far we have considered some of the general principles that are of potential value in teaching people how to solve problems more efficiently. At the more specific level of practical hints, we can refer back to some of the research discussed in this chapter. As we have seen, one of the commonest inadequacies is to tackle a problem in ways which are too narrow and over-influenced by certain past experiences (e.g., the effects of set or *Einstellung* studied by Luchins, 1942; the phenomenon of functional fixedness). Simple awareness of the dangers of such mental sets can be quite effective; Luchins (1942) found that the warning, "Don't be blind," greatly reduced his subjects' tendency to affected by an inappropriate set.

A prime necessity in successful problem solving is being extremely flexible in the approach to problems. If the most obvious approach to a problem fails to produce the solution within a reasonable period of time, then it is probably advantageous to change strategies. It is important in this connection to remember that the nature of the stumbling block may lie in the way in which you represent the problem, the sequence of operations applied to that representation, or both.

We have seen that most people have a blind spot about negative information: they tend not to search for such information, and also have great difficulty in using it if it is given to them. The simplest way of improving your ability to handle negative information is probably to reconsider the important work of Wason and his colleagues. They give verbal reports of subjects who failed to make efficient use of negative information, and they analyse in detail the kinds of inappropriate cognitive strategies used by many people when confronted with problems requiring the use of negative information for their solution.

If we turn to inference drawing, then the ways in which people might be encouraged to draw more accurate inferences are relatively obvious. Firstly, rules of thumb such as the representativeness and availability heuristics tend to be over-applied, and so it is always worth considering the adequacy of any rule of thumb used to solve an inferential problem. Secondly, as Nisbett and Ross (1980) have pointed out, it may be of value to make use of some additional rules of thumb or slogans. Among those they suggested were, "It's an empirical question," "Methinks I detect the availability (or representativeness) heuristic at work," "That's a vivid datum all right, but I'll still consult the base rates, thank you," and Lord Cromwell's cry, "I beseech you, in the bowels of Christ, think it possible you may be wrong."

These slogans may help, but it is amazingly difficult to change some entrenched ways of thinking. For example, most psychologists are aware that the interview method is a very inadequate way of selecting people for university courses and academic appointments, and yet nearly all psychology departments still rely heavily on interviews for selection purposes! There seems to be an almost irresistible tendency to attach far more weight to the vivid information provided by face-to-face interaction than it actually merits.

One of the key issues in the whole area of human inference is to decide when it is cost-effective to replace inadequate intuitive strategies with more complex and time-consuming formal strategies of inference. The most relevant criterion would appear to be the importance of the benefits that might result from the use of these strategies: Very simple strategies are appropriate when deciding what biscuit or cake to eat at tea-time, but not when deciding on a career.

The Nature and Structure of Knowledge

Most people possess millions of pieces of information about the world in which they live. We know that it is colder in the winter than in the summer, that $2 + 2 = 4$, that man has landed on the moon, that Leonardo da Vinci was a painter, and that we sit in chairs. We also know that brandy is a kind of liqueur, that Christopher Columbus discovered America, that criminals are sent to prison, that there is a game called Monopoly, and that Elizabeth Taylor has been married several times.

The knowledge we possess is stored in memory in a relatively permanent form. Is our world knowledge contained within the long-term memory store in the same way as the information from most memory experiments? Tulving (1972) argued against this possibility. He proposed a conceptual distinction between semantic memory and episodic memory. According to Tulving, the overwhelming majority of experiments on human memory have been concerned with episodic memory, which consists of an experiential record of events and occurrences. Thus, if an experimental subject is presented with a list of words including the word "chair," and told to learn them for a later test, the subject is in effect being asked to remember that he saw the word "chair" in that particular experimental context. He is emphatically not expected to learn the concept "chair," which the experimenter assumes forms part of his world knowledge.

Episodic memory, then, has an autobiographical flavour about it, and it refers to the storage of specific events or episodes. In contrast, much of our knowledge about the world lacks this autobiographical reference. According to Tulving (1972), most of our world knowledge is stored in semantic memory, which he defined in the following terms:

> It is a mental thesaurus, organized knowledge a person possesses about words and other verbal symbols, their meanings and referents, about relations among them, and about rules, formulas, and algorithms for the manipulation of these symbols, concepts, and relations. Semantic memory does not register perceptible properties of inputs, but rather cognitive referents of input signals [p. 386].

There has been some controversy about the usefulness of this distinction between episodic and semantic memory. On the one hand, it seems intuitively reasonable to draw such a distinction, and it is usually possible to decide whether information is stored in episodic or semantic memory on the basis of whether or not it has an autobiographical flavour associated with it. On the other hand, it is obvious that episodic and semantic memory must be strongly interdependent. For example, episodic memory for prose passages shows very clearly the way in which the interpretation of the passage is influenced by the knowledge contained in semantic memory (see Chapter 5). In addition, if we ask how information usually gets into semantic memory, the answer is that such information initially forms part of episodic memory. I know that two inverted V's on the front of a car indicate that the car is a Citroën, and this information forms part of my semantic memory. However, my daughter Fleur only discovered this fascinating and useful piece of information when I told her about it very recently, and it is presumably stored in her episodic memory. In ways that remain unclear, repeated exposure to certain kinds of information seems to produce a shift from episodic to semantic memory.

Such considerations suggest that there is no precise dividing line between episodic and semantic memory. Perhaps it would be better to regard episodic and semantic memory as end points on a continuum rather than as qualitatively different memory systems. For present purposes, we retain the distinction for its heuristic value, while recognising that it has a somewhat dubious theoretical status.

The other chapters in this book deal with the processes involved in attention, perception, imagery, learning, comprehension, reasoning, and so on. It is impossible to provide an adequate account of these processes without considering the ways in which they involve the individual's knowledge about the world, and there has been some discussion of this earlier in the book. The important point to note is that semantic memory is intimately involved in most cognitive processes, and that this chapter should accordingly be read in conjunction with previous chapters.

In view of the diverse nature of the information stored in semantic memory, there are several different ways in which a chapter on semantic memory could be organised. However, one of the major distinctions between theories of semantic memory concerns the size of the unit with which they are concerned. We can identify a progression in unit size from individual concepts at the lowest end, via event structures (i.e., the relations and functions into which a given concept enters), to frames or scripts (i.e., organised sequences of several concepts and event structures). In general terms, the earlier part of this chapter examines relatively small units in semantic memory, whereas the latter part deals with larger, and more organised, structures.

ORGANISATION OF SEMANTIC MEMORY

The most obvious fact about semantic memory is that it is highly organised. This can be demonstrated very simply. Semantic memory contains literally millions of pieces of information, and yet we can answer most questions about that information extremely quickly. For example, it takes people only 975 msec. on average to decide that a sparrow is a bird (Smith, Shoben & Rips, 1974), they can decide correctly that "rolt" is not an English word in 918 msec. (Rubenstein, Lewis & Rubenstein, 1971), and they can think of the name of a fruit beginning with the letter "P" in 1,170 msec. (Loftus & Suppes, 1972). It seems improbable that people would be able to respond accurately on such tasks with responses latencies of approximately one second unless semantic memory was organised or structured in some way.

The Network Theory of Collins and Quillian

Having established that semantic memory is organised, clearly the next step is to try to discover the nature of its organisational structure. A great landmark here was the seminal work of Collins and Quillian (1969, 1970). They introduced an experimental technique, and also put forward a theory which has served as the point of departure for many later theorists. Some of the basic theoretical ideas of Collins and Quillian are illustrated in Fig. 11.1. They assumed that semantic memory was organised as a network of interconnected concepts arranged hierarchically, and they used nodes to represent concepts. Another key assumption was that of cognitive economy. For example, we know that canaries can fly, that robins can fly, that wrens can fly, and so on. However, according to Collins and Quillian, it would be cognitively uneconomical to have information about being able to fly stored

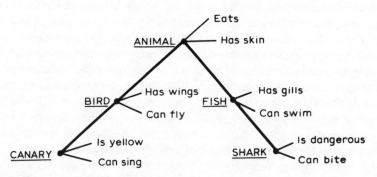

FIG. 11.1   The hierarchical structure of semantic memory in the theory of Collins and Quillian (1969).

with each bird name. Instead, they proposed that properties common to virtually all birds (e.g., can fly; has wings) are stored only at the bird node. Only those properties that distinguish one species of bird from others (e.g., the fact that canaries are yellow) are stored at the lowest level of the hierarchy. At the opposite extreme, properties that are common to virtually all animals (e.g., possession of skin) are stored at the animal node. The general principle is that information is stored as far up the hierarchy as possible, thus minimising the storage of information.

Collins and Quillian (1969, 1970) tested these ideas by means of a speeded verification task. They presented their subjects with sentences, such as, "A canary has wings," "Coca-Cola is blue," and asked them to decide as rapidly as possible whether the sentence was true or false. They focused mainly on response latencies to true sentences, arguing that the greater the separation of subject and predicate in the hierarchy, the slower would be the verification time. The reason is that they assumed that it takes some time to traverse each level in the hierarchy. As predicted, verification times were fastest when the subject and predicate were at the same level in the hierarchy (e.g., "A canary is yellow"), of intermediate speed when the subject and predicate were separated by one level in the hierarchy (e.g., "A canary has wings"), and were slowest when there were two levels separating the subject and predicate (e.g., "A canary has skin").

Some of the theoretical views of Collins and Quillian are eminently sensible. Consider their proposal that we often make use of inferential processes (e.g., we work out that a canary has wings by combining the information that a canary is a bird and that birds have wings). It is clear that such inferential thinking is quite common. Most people would agree that Aristotle had a big toe, but it is improbable that this information is stored directly in semantic memory. What presumably happens is that we know that Aristotle was a man, and that most men have big toes, and so we *infer* that Aristotle must have had a big toe.

In spite of the initial enthusiasm with which Collins and Quillian's theory was greeted, it is no longer regarded as tenable. There are several reasons for this disenchantment. While the various sentences used by Collins and Quillian differed in the hierarchical distance between subject and predicate, they also differed in a number of other salient characteristics. You may have noticed that some of the sentences used by Collins and Quillian seem much more familiar than others (e.g., compare "A canary is yellow" with "A canary has skin"). Conrad (1972) asked people to describe a canary, a bird, an animal, and so on. She then discovered that those properties that were frequently mentioned with a concept were those that subjects verified rapidly. Indeed, when frequency or familiarity was controlled, the number of levels to be traversed in the logically based hierarchy had little effect on verification time. While these data cast grave doubts on the adequacy of the model proposed by Collins and Quillian, they do not (as Conrad assumed) totally discredit the notion of cognitive economy. For example, all of her subjects supplied "has wings" as one of the properties of a bird, but none of them supplied it for "canary," "ostrich," or "owl."

A second complication for the theory concerns the assumption that the hierarchies are organised logically. It follows from this assumption that the hierarchical distance between an animal name, such as, "horse," and the superordinate concept "mammal" should be less than that between "horse" and "animal." In consequence, people should be able to verify "A horse is a mammal" more quickly than "A horse is an animal." In fact, the opposite result has been obtained (Rips, Shoben, & Smith, 1973).

A third difficulty for Collins and Quillian is that their theory seemed to assume that all instances of a category would be verified equally rapidly, provided that they were equidistant from the superordinate category. In fact, verification times tend to be faster for more typical or representative members of a category than for relatively atypical members (e.g., Rips et al., 1973). Thus, for example, people can decide more rapidly that "A robin is a bird" than that "A chicken is a bird."

A final inadequacy with the theoretical position of Collins and Quillian (1969, 1970) concerns the speed with which false sentences can be rejected. The most natural assumption is that falsification times should co-vary with the hierarchical distance between the subject and the predicate. Thus, for example, it should take a long time to decide that "A building is a cat" is untrue. In fact, the usual finding is the exact opposite, with falsification times being inversely related to hierarchical separation of subject and predicate, although there are some exceptions (e.g., Glass & Holyoak, 1975).

Spreading Activation Theory

As a result of these pertinent criticisms of the model put forward by Collins and Quillian (1969, 1970), it was revised by Collins and Loftus (1975) in their spreading activation theory. They abandoned the notion that semantic memory is hierarchically organised, and proposed instead a structure based on semantic relatedness or semantic distance. There are several ways in which semantic relatedness can be measured empirically. One method involves giving subjects pairs of words, and simply asking them to decide how closely related they are. An alternative method is to ask subjects to rate the typicality of different instances of a superordinate category, it being assumed that typicality is inversely related to semantic relatedness. A third method is to ask people to list members of a given category, and the resultant production frequency of an instance provides an indication of how closely related it is to the category.

According to Collins and Loftus (1975), semantic relatedness is reflected in the accessibility or strength of the links connecting concepts. The theory included a number of different kinds of links, including "isa" links to indicate membership of a superordinate category, and "isnota" links. Whenever a person sees, hears, reads, or thinks about a concept, the corresponding node in semantic memory is activated, and activation then spreads from that concept to neighbouring ones. The exact spread of activation is determined by the strength of the initial activation, the proximity to the point of activation, and the amount of time that has passed since the onset of activation.

The final component of the spreading activation model is a set of complicated decision processes. In essence, the decision process evaluates the evidence from intersecting paths of activation, takes account of the nature of the links connecting concepts, and of the total strength of activation at a particular point. The values or strengths of the positive pieces of evidence are summed, and the same is done for negative evidence. "True" and "false" decision criteria are established, and the subject responds when the summed values exceed one of the criteria. The evidence itself can take various forms. For example, when evaluating the sentence "All birds are canaries," the activation of counter-examples (e.g., "robin") can be used as negative evidence. Alternatively, when evaluating, 'Is a mallard a bird?', the activation of superordinate connections between mallard and duck, and between duck and bird, would provide strong positive evidence. If two concepts have a common superordinate with mutually exclusive links to that superordinate, then that can often represent strong negative evidence. Thus, we can answer the question, "Is a mallard an eagle?", by considering activated links that indicate that a mallard is a duck, and that ducks and eagles are mutually exclusive kinds of birds.

The spreading activation model of Collins and Loftus (1975) has an advantage shared by most network models in that it makes clear that the meaning of a word is substantially affected by the relationships between that words and its associated concepts. It also provides a straightforward explanation of one of the basic findings in the literature, namely, that the greater the semantic relatedness of an instance and a category, the faster the decision that the instance is a member of the category.

The spreading activation model also has the merit of assuming that there are various ways in which falsification can occur. This is suggested by some of the apparent contradictions in the evidence. It has often been found that it is easier to decide that an instance is not a member of a category when the semantic relatedness of instance and category is minimal. However, Glass and Holyoak (1975) found that a sentence such as "All birds are dogs" was rapidly rejected, in spite of the fact that the concepts "bird" and "dog" are semantically related. They asked people to supply false completions to sentences of the type "All S are ——." False statements that were produced frequently were subsequently rejected more rapidly than false statements given infrequently. This can be handled by Collins and Loftus (1975): all they need to do is to assume that there is a strong "isnota" link between "bird" and "dog" which provides strong negative evidence.

The spreading activation model is reasonably successful at accounting for the major findings from the speeded verification task. However, this success is achieved at the cost of having a theory of some complexity that makes numerous assumptions. It could, indeed, be argued that the theory lacks parsimony and is unduly complicated.

Some doubts have also been expressed concerning the details of the assumptions about the spread of activation. Collins and Loftus (1975) assumed that the amount of activation arriving at any node was a decreasing function of the number of links (the distance) that the activation has traversed. They also assumed that activation takes a significant amount of time to spread between nodes. These assumptions were examined experimentally by Ratcliff and McKoon (1981). They obtained evidence supporting the first assumption, but the second assumption was found to be erroneous. Activation was present at virtually the same moment at all activated nodes, and so the time required for activation was not a function of distance from the initially activated node.

Feature Theory

The theories of Collins and Quillian (1969, 1970) and Collins and Loftus (1975) are both examples of network models. Concepts are represented in a network, and performance on the speeded verification task is a function of the distances separating concepts. In contrast, Rips et al. (1973) and Smith et al. (1974) proposed a feature theory. They argued that the meaning of a word can be represented as a set of semantic features. These features can be divided into defining and characteristic features. Unfortunately, the theory does not include rules that stipulate which features are defining and which are characteristic, and there are considerable doubts about the existence of defining features (e.g., Mervis & Rosch, 1981). However, the basic idea is that defining features are those that are common to all of the instances of a category, whereas characteristic features are not. Those instances that are judged to be typical or representative of a category will possess more characteristic features than atypical instances. Thus, for example, a typical bird may have a specific size and degree of ferocity as two of its characteristic features (Rosch, 1974).

The feature model predicts that someone having to decide on the truth or falsity of a statement, such as, "A robin is a bird," will initially retrieve both characteristic and defining features of the two nouns, and then assess the overall degree of feature similarity. If the overall feature similarity is high, then the person produces a rapid "true" response, whereas he or she rapidly responds "false" if the overall similarity is low. If there is an intermediate degree of overall similarity, then a second comparison occurs on the basis of just the defining features of the category and the instance.

What predictions follow from these theoretical assumptions? For "true" sentences, the greater the degree of semantic relatedness, the faster the response should be, because highly related nouns will require only the first comparison process. The opposite should be the case for "false" sentences, with low degrees of semantic relatedness being necessary for a decision to be based on the first comparison process. Smith *et al.* (1974) confirmed these predictions, but it now appears that they confounded semantic relatedness with the familiarity of the stimulus words (McCloskey, 1980). Furthermore, we have already seen that high degrees of semantic relatedness do not always lead to slow responding with false sentences (e.g., Glass & Holyoak, 1975).

One of the most obvious inadequacies with the feature model is that it does not seem to take sufficient account of the order of the two nouns in the sentence to be evaluated. If all that happens is feature comparison, then the sentence "All birds are robins" is just as likely to be regarded as true as the sentence "All robins are birds"! The importance of noun order was also shown by Loftus (1973). She presented instances and asked subjects to list categories that the instances belonged to, and also presented categories and asked for a list of instances. This provided measures of instance-to-category production frequency and of category-to-instance production frequency, respectively. She then measured reaction times in a verification task in which either the instance preceded the category (e.g., "wren–bird") or the category preceded the instance (e.g., "bird–wren"). According to the feature model, verification time should have been unaffected by manipulation of noun order. In fact, Loftus discovered that instance-to-category production frequency determined reaction time when the instance preceded the category, whereas the category-to-instance production frequency determined response speed when the category preceded the instance. This pattern of results is predictable by a network model such as that of Collins and Loftus (1975), in which activation spreads outwards from the first node to be activated.

The feature theory of Smith *et al.* (1974) is remarkably restricted in terms of its potential applicability to situations other than the time taken to respond to various "An S is a P" sentences. The theory is of little or no relevance to the task of understanding and verifying simple sentences, such as, "The man has a car." The abstract relationship of possession expressed by the verb "has" cannot readily be expressed by simply combining sets of features.

General evaluation

Having discussed three of the main theories based on the speeded verification task, it is now time to turn to a more general evaluation of this approach to semantic memory. There is a basic methodological problem, in that it is not usually possible to manipulate the independent variable in a satisfactory fashion. Pairs of concepts that are high or low in semantic relatedness can be selected, but the approach is essentially correlational rather than experimental. Since semantic relatedness correlates with hierarchical distance, familiarity, frequency, category size, production frequency, and perhaps with other undiscovered variables, it is extremely difficult to be sure that an effect is due to semantic relatedness rather than to some other variable that has not been controlled.

It had been hoped initially that research on the speeded verification task would indicate whether network or feature models provided a more adequate account of the workings of semantic memory. Although network models such as those of Collins and Loftus (1975) and Glass and Holyoak (1975) have proved more adequate than the feature model of Smith et al. (1974), it is not at all clear that further research can resolve this issue. Hollan (1975) demonstrated the mathematical equivalence of network and feature models, and this has rather spoiled the fun of attempting to adjudicate between them.

Smith (1978) argued that the major issue was the relative importance of storage and computation in performance. Feature models tend to claim that much of our knowledge is computed from the relatively meagre information stored in semantic memory, whereas network models assume that most knowledge is pre-stored in memory. Of course, complex performance can involve either simple computational processes operating on detailed representations of knowledge, or complex computational processes operating on simple knowledge structures. However, the data obtained from the sentence-verification paradigm do not provide a definitive answer. This may well be another issue that can never be resolved, because apparently quite different representation-process models can be shown to be equivalent (Anderson, 1978).

It is becoming increasingly clear that the data obtained from sentence verification studies are insufficient to constrain theoretical alternatives. It also seems likely that this entire approach to semantic memory is misconceived. As Kintsch (1980) pointed out, some of the contemporary theoretical ideas about semantic memory closely resemble those of Aristotle. Aristotle claimed that each class or genus was sub-divided into two or more sub-classes or species; members of the class or genus are similar in some crucial way, but different in other ways. It may seem like a good idea for psychologists to align themselves with a genius like Aristotle, but it needs to be borne in mind that Aristotle was proposing a logical scheme rather than a psychological one. It is tempting to simplify matters by incorporating such a logical structure into psychological theories, but it is probably not fruitful.

Another potential hazard with the speeded verification task is the emphasis it places on the individual word as the unit of analysis. If, as seems likely, the meaning of a word is determined by contextual factors and by the higher-order units in which it is included, there is little merit in focusing on words in isolation. A step in the right direction was taken by Miller and Johnson-Laird (1976). They argued that words gain their meaning from semantic fields, which in turn are affected by task and contextual factors. As a consequence, the meaning of a word or concept is not absolute, but rather is relative to the context in which it is encountered. In other words, the meanings of words and concepts are fairly flexible and context-dependent, rather than comprising fixed sets of features or being represented by static locations in a semantic network as is assumed by most recent theories of semantic memory.

CATEGORISATION

The Nature of Categories

One of the most striking characteristics of Nature is its endless diversity. In order to reduce this diversity to manageable proportions, we engage in a considerable amount of categorisation. A category or concept is said to exist when two or more distinguishable events, objects, or organisms are treated in a very similar fashion. The categories that we form guide our subsequent thinking and behaviour, and so it is obviously of importance to understand both how we construct categories and the nature of the categories themselves.

A very influential view of the nature of concepts or categories was provided in a famous series of studies carried out by Bruner, Goodnow and Austin (1956). There was a stimulus array containing items varying along four dimensions (number of borders, number of objects inside the borders, shape of the objects, and colour of the objects). As a result of receiving feedback as to whether each of several stimulus items was an exemplar of the concept the experimenter had in mind, the subject attempted to decide what that concept was. It was usually a relatively simple conjunctive concept (e.g., two objects and one border).

Implicit in this approach to concept or category learning are several crucial assumptions about the nature of concepts or categories. In the first place, the combination of attributes that comprises a concept is entirely arbitrary (e.g., the concept is just as likely to include one border as two borders, or one object as two). Secondly, all stimuli which fit the definition of the concept (i.e., possess the relevant attributes in the right combination) are equivalently "good" members of the category or concept. Thirdly, the boundaries of the concept are well-defined; in other words, it is clear whether a particular stimulus belongs to the concept. Fourthly, a concept is composed of, and is decomposable into, its constituent elements (e.g., two objects, one border).

Are there any inadequacies in this conceptualisation of the nature of concepts or categories? According to Mervis and Rosch (1981), virtually everything is wrong with it, at least with repsect to natural categories. The quintessential differences between the artificial concepts studied in the laboratory and natural categories is that the former are neat, logical, and well-defined, whereas the latter are rather untidy, not organised along logical grounds, and fuzzy. Some of the characteristics of natural objects were discussed with reference to the concept of "games" in a quotation by Wittgenstein (1958), which no self-respecting book of cognitive psychology can afford to leave out:

> Consider for example the proceedings that we call "games." I mean board-games, card-games, ball-games, Olympic games, and so on. What is common to them all... if you look at them you will not see something that is common to *all*, but similarities, relationships, and a whole series of them at that.... Look for example at board-games, with their multifarious relationships. Now pass to card-games; here you will find many correspondences with the first group, but many common features drop out, and others appear. When we pass next to ball-games, much that is common is retained, but much is lost... Is there always winning and losing, or competition between players? Think of patience. In ball-games there is winning and losing; but when a child throws his ball at the wall and catches it again, this feature has disappeared [pp. 31–32].

According to Wittgenstein (1958), the similarities between the members of a category can be characterised as "family resemblances." In other words, two members of a category do not have to possess exactly the same features. Indeed, it might even happen that two members belonging to the same category did not have any features at all in common. How, then, do we decide whether or not a particular stimulus object belongs to a category? The decision seems to be based on the number of features possessed by that stimulus object that are also possessed by several category members. However, the imprecise way in which most categories are defined means that there will sometimes be disagreements about category membership. McCloskey and Glucksberg (1978) asked 30 people whether a "stroke" was a disease; 16 said it was, and 14 said it was not. Exactly the same result was obtained when the same people were asked whether a "pumpkin" was a fruit. More surprisingly, when they tested the same subjects a month later, 11 had changed their minds about "stroke" being a disease, and 8 had altered their opinion about "pumpkin" being a fruit.

Some of Wittgenstein's notions about category membership and family resemblances were confirmed by Rosch and Mervis (1975). They selected 20 instances from each of six categories (vehicles, weapons, clothing, vegetables, furniture, and fruit), and asked their subjects to list the attributes of each instance. In line with Wittgenstein's ideas, for none of the six categories was there more than a single attribute that was common to all of the 20 instances of that category.

Rosch and Mervis (1975) asked other subjects to rate the typicality of each instance as a member of the category. They discovered that the more typical members tended to be those that shared the most features or attributes with other members of the category (i.e., high within-category similarity). They also found that more typical items had fewer attributes in common with members of other categories than did atypical items (i.e., low between-category similarity). When artificial categories were used in order to dissociate the factors of within-category similarity or family resemblance and between-category similarity, it transpired that both contribute to typicality ratings (Rosch, Simpson & Miller, 1976).

Perhaps the most important implication of this work is the notion that some category members are "better" members of that category than are others (e.g., a robin is a better bird than a chicken is). The factors that are responsible for this state of affairs were considered further by Hampton (1979). He argued that many categories are polymorphous, in the sense that all instances of the category possess a sufficient number of relevant features, none of which needs to be common to all instances. Thus, some features that are important may be neither necessary (i.e., essential for category membership) nor sufficient (i.e., guaranteeing membership). Hampton asked people to list those characteristics that are usually important for deciding whether an object belongs to a particular category (e.g., "fruit"). Those properties mentioned most frequently were regarded as featural definitions for that category. Instances or examples were then rated for the degree to which they belonged to the category. Although very few of the features defining a category were common to all of the members of the category, the number of key category features that a word possessed predicted accurately its rated degree of membership in that category.

If we accept that most natural categories defy logical definition, and that the members of a category differ in terms of how typical or representative of the category they are, then it seems reasonable to assume that their boundaries will often be fuzzy rather than well defined. This was shown very clearly by Labov (1973). He investigated the degree to which people thought that each of a number of drawings represented a cup. As the shape of the object varied, so there were gradual (rather than precipitous) changes in how often the objects were called cups. There was, for example, a progressive reduction in the number of "cup" responses as the ratio of width to depth increased, but the absence of a point at which the object suddenly ceased to be a cup suggests that there are no precise boundaries for the concept of "cup."

Labov (1973) did not rest content with demonstrating the role played by perceptual features in determining "cupness." He pointed out that a cup also has functional attributes, i.e., characteristic functions or uses. The primary function of a cup is to contain liquids for drinking. This aspect of "cupness" was investigated by using drawings suggesting that the objects were filled with coffee, mashed potatoes, or flowers. This manipulation had little effect on the extent to which very typical cups were called cups, but greatly affected responding to the less typical cups. Somewhat cup-like looking objects were called a cup when filled with coffee, but not when filled with flowers. The key observation was that an object is regarded as a cup if it has either the appropriate perceptual attributes or the appropriate functional attributes, thus showing that there is no single attribute that is essential to make an object an acceptable member of a category.

Basic Level Categories

Why do we have the concepts or categories that we do? In general terms, the answer is that we construct those categories that are maximally useful for the purposes of perception, thought, and action. However, most of the objects in the external world can be categorised at each of several different hierarchical levels. Thus, for example, an easy chair is an easy chair, but it is also a chair and an article of furniture. There has been considerable interest recently in attempting to demonstrate that one of these hierarchical levels is more basic or fundamental than the others. A possible criterion for determining the basic level of categorisation is that it is the level at which there is maximal within-category similarity relative to between-category similarity.

A major study of basic level categories was carried out by Rosch, Mervis, Gray, Johnson and Boyes-Braem (1976). They asked people to list all of the attributes or features that applied to the items of each of three levels within a hierarchy (e.g., furniture, chair, easy chair). Very few attributes were listed for the superordinate categories such as "furniture," presumably because the categories were rather abstract. Many attributes were listed for the categories at the other two levels, but at the lowest level very similar attributes were listed for different categories (e.g., "easy chair," "living-room chair"). The implication is that the intermediate level categories such as "chair" are the basic level categories, since it is at this level that there is the best balance between informativeness and economy. Informativeness is lacking at the highest level of the hierarchy, and economy is missing at the lowest level.

Rosch et al. (1976) adduced other evidence that basic level categories have special properties not shared by categories at other levels. The basic level is the one at which adults spontaneously name objects, and it is also the one that is usually acquired first by young children. Furthermore, the basic level is the most general level at which people use similar motor movements for interacting with category members, at which category members have fairly similar overall shapes, and at which a mental image can reflect the whole category. Finally, objects tend to be recognised more quickly as members of basic level categories than as members of categories at higher or lower levels.

It is reasonably clear, then, that much of the most important knowledge that we possess about the world is in the form of basic level categories or concepts. This primacy of basic level categories may occur for at least two different reasons. Firstly, it may simply be due to linguistic factors, with basic level terms being more familiar words that happen to be learned earlier than category names at other levels. Secondly, it may reflect the operation of fundamental perceptual and cognitive processes. Only the latter explanation accords the basic level of categorisation major psychological significance.

This issue was investigated by Mervis and Crisafi (1982) using artificial categories whose hierarchical structure resembled that of natural categories. They obviated the problem of differential familiarity with terms at various levels within the hierarchy by never naming the stimuli. Some people were instructed to sort the stimuli in any way that made sense to them, and others were told that a particular stimulus had been given a name, and they should decide which other stimuli should also be given the same name. Nearly all of the responses on both tasks corresponded to the basic level categories, thus suggesting that the importance of the basic level of categorisation does not merely reflect linguistic factors.

Prototypes

How do people initially acquire categories or concepts? A popular view (e.g., Franks & Bransford, 1971; Mervis & Rosch, 1981; Posner & Keele, 1968) is that exposure to a range of stimulus objects belonging to a particular category leads a person to form a prototype that best represents the total set of stimulus objects. According to prototype theory, this prototype is then used to represent that category in our thinking. These notions can be clarified by considering a concrete example. Posner and Keele (1968) initially created four prototypes, each of which consisted of a pattern of random dots. Each prototype served as the basis for a category, with Posner and Keele generating further category members from each prototype by moving some of the dots randomly. Subjects were given the members of all four categories (but not the prototypes themselves), and had to learn to classify all of the members of any particular category in the same way.

According to prototype theory, the subjects should have formed representations of the four prototypes in memory, even though the prototypes themselves had never been presented. The reason is that each prototype constitutes the common thread running through the category instances. Posner and Keele (1968) examined what the subjects had learned by presenting them with additional dot patterns that had to be assigned to one of the four categories. There were two kinds of new patterns that the subjects had not seen before; additional patterns generated from the four prototypes, and the prototypes themselves. The prototypes were more frequently assigned to the correct category than were the new patterns generated from the prototypes, which is consistent with the notion that prototypes were stored in memory. However, the prototypes were not categorised as accurately as the old patterns which had been presented during learning. This suggests that information about specific instances is stored in addition to prototypical information.

Further support for prototype theory has been obtained from studies showing that categories are learned more rapidly and more accurately when people are initially exposed to only typical or representative members than when they are exposed to only atypical or non-representative instances (e.g., Mervis & Pani, 1980). This certainly makes sense intuitively. It is, for example, difficult to imagine that anyone would try to teach a young child the concept of "bird" by exposing him or her only to ostriches and penguins!

Although prototype theory undoubtedly contains a grain of truth, it seems inadequate in various ways. A prototype is like an ordinary member of a category in that it specifies values on all dimensions. Thus, a prototypical bird would include among its features a certain colour and food preferences. This contrasts with a schema, which includes many features but may omit some. The advantage of the schema over the prototype is that some dimensions of a concept are essentially irrelevant (e.g., colour to the concept of a chair). These irrelevant dimensions can be excluded from the schema but not from the prototype. In other words, some features are more important than others to the definition of a category, and schema theories take more account of this fact than do prototype theories.

Can prototypes be found for all concepts or categories? Nearly all of the evidence supporting prototype theory has been concerned with relatively concrete categories, and it is less clear that prototypes will be discovered for broader and more abstract categories. For example, the category of "games" seems to be so extensive that no single prototype could possibly be representative of the entire category. Some other abstract concepts were considered by Hampton (1981). He discovered that some abstract categories (e.g., "a work of art," "a science," "a crime") exhibited the same kind of structure as concrete categories, but others did not (e.g., "a rule," "a belief;" and "an instinct"). Why is it that some abstract concepts do not appear to have prototypes? Membership of abstract categories often seems to be almost endlessly flexible in a way that is not true of concrete categories. Thus, for example, it is not remotely possible to specify the complete set of possible rules or beliefs. This marked lack of constraint on the membership of many abstract categories may be partially responsible for their apparent absence of structure.

It is manifest that people do not always make use of prototypical information when making decisions about category membership. A whale resembles the fish prototype more closely than it does the mammal prototype, and yet most adults would classify a whale as a mammal. On the other hand, many children believe that a whale is a fish. We can understand what is happening here by distinguishing between popular and technical definitions (Glass, Holyoak & Santa, 1979). When people have learned the technical definition, this overrides considerations of the similarity between a whale and the fish and mammal prototypes. Most children have not learned the technical definition, and so respond in the way predicted by prototype theory.

Perhaps the most potentially damaging attack on prototype theory was mounted by Osherson and Smith (1981). They claimed that we should distinguish between the core of a concept and its identification procedure. A concept's core consists of those aspects dealing with its relation to other concepts and to thoughts; in contrast, the identification procedure merely specifies the information used when making rapid decisions about membership of the concept. They illustrated the distinction by examining the concept "woman." Whereas the core might include information about the presence of a reproductive system, the identification procedures might include information about hair length, voice pitch, and body shape. The basic contention of Osherson and Smith was that prototype theory provides insights into identification procedures, but tells us little about the core of a concept. In other words, prototype theory is concerned with the relatively superficial aspects of concepts, and largely ignores some of the essential core elements.

Concepts, Categories and Semantic Memory

It is generally assumed that concepts or categories play a major role in the organisation of semantic memory. It is customary to assume that the various attributes of a concept, and the pieces of information we possess about that concept, are stored close to each other rather than being distributed randomly throughout semantic memory. The theories of semantic memory discussed earlier in this chapter differed greatly from each other, but were united in their emphasis on the importance of word concepts to the structure of semantic memory.

If information in semantic memory is actually organised around concepts rather than, say, attributes of concepts, then certain predictions can be made. It might be expected that information could be accessed more effectively from concepts than from attributes. This prediction was investigated by Freedman and Loftus (1971). They gave their subjects tasks such as thinking of the name of a fruit starting with the letter "P" as rapidly as possible. The information was either presented in the order "fruit" followed by the letter "P" or in the order "P" followed by the word "fruit", and the time to respond was measured from the presentation of the second stimulus (i.e., "P" in the first instance and "fruit" in the second).

The key finding was that performance was faster when the category name preceded the attribute than it was when the order was reversed. The most natural interpretation of this finding is that people given "fruit" first could activate their knowledge of fruits while waiting for the subsequent letter, whereas the letter cue "P" on its own was of little use in the absence of the category name. Thus, our knowledge of fruits beginning with "P" is organised in terms of fruits rather than in terms of words starting with the letter "P."

In sum, it is likely that concepts and categories play an important role in the organisational structure of semantic memory. However, there are two inherent dangers in the theoretical preconceptions informing research in this area. Firstly, there is the danger of assuming that semantic memory consists of a static and inflexible structure. Such an assumption does a serious injustice to the flexibility of knowledge utilisation and its dependence on the immediate context. Secondly, while concepts and categories may well be psychologically real, it is likely that semantic memory also contains other, and larger, units of knowledge.

SCRIPTS, FRAMES AND SCHEMATA

Basic Notions

The focus so far has been on relatively limited units of knowledge, such as those relating to concepts or categories and their interrelationships. However, it is also worth considering the possibility that we possess rather larger, well-integrated chunks of knowledge. These larger chunks facilitate our understanding of complex communications, and they also allow us to behave appropriately in various situations, such as, a restaurant or a cocktail party. Theorists differ in the term they use to refer to such organised knowledge structures; Rumelhart and Ortony (1977) used the term "schema," but others have referred to "frames" (Minsky, 1975) or to "scripts" (Schank & Abelson, 1977). These various terms are by no means synonymous with each other, but their meanings do overlap to a substantial extent, and it is this overlap that is of central concern.

It is usually assumed that scripts, frames and schemata consist of organised structures of stereotypic knowledge. They exists as a result of extracting the common elements from a range of situations or events. Rumelhart (1980) provided the following definition of the "schema" construct:

> A schema, then is a data structure for representing the generic concepts stored in memory. There are schemata representing our knowledge about all concepts: those underlying objects, situations, events, sequences of events, actions and sequences of actions. A schema contains, as part of its specification, the network of interrelations that is believed to normally hold among the constituents of the concept in question. A schema theory embodies a *prototype* theory of meaning. That is, inasmuch as a schema underlying a concept stored in memory corresponds to the *meaning* of that concept, meanings are encoded in terms of the typical or normal situations or events that instantiate [provide concrete examples of] that concept [p. 34].

Some of these notions can be illustrated by considering the schema for the verb "buy." Obviously there are an almost endless number of situations that involve buying, but there are some common elements. For example, there is always a seller, a purchaser, a medium of exchange (e.g., money), some merchandise, and bargaining, in which the seller agrees to give the merchandise to the purchaser in exchange for a particular amount of money or whatever. The schema for "buy" consists primarily of these common elements, and does not specify the identity of the seller or the purchaser, or the nature of the merchandise.

One of the problems with the construct of a script or schema as discussed so far is its inflexibility. For example, it has been claimed by Schank and Abelson (1977) that most people possess a restaurant script containing information about the typical sequence of events involved in going to a restaurant to have a meal. However, the exact sequence of events that is anticipated varies somewhat as a function of the type of restaurant. We know that several events normally occurring in a restaurant are lacking in a self-service restaurant, and conversing with the wine waiter is more probable in a French restaurant than in a coffee shop. How can a script theory handle these variations? According to Schank and Abelson, there is a restaurant script, plus a number of "tracks" specifying optional additions or deletions to the script.

How are schemata or scripts acquired? According to Rumelhart (1980), there are three main ways in which learning can occur in a schema-based system: accretion, tuning and restructuring. Learning by accretion involves the memory traces of comprehension processes; these traces are usually partial copies of the instantiated schemata. Tuning refers to the elaboration and refinement of concepts through experience. Restructuring involves the creation of new schemata. This can happen in two rather different ways: a new schema can be created by copying an old one with a few modifications (patterned generation), or via the repetition of a spatio-temporal configuration of schemata (schema induction).

Especially important schemata relate to our knowledge about the spatial relations between objects and about their locations in the physical environment. Tolman coined the term "cognitive map" to refer to the structure in which such information is held, and there appear to be many kinds of cognitive map which enable us to plan car trips, walk to the local shops, and so on. Lynch (1960) looked at the cognitive maps of their own cities possessed by inhabitants of Los Angeles, Boston, and Jersey City. He asked them various questions, such as, what they would encounter in travelling between two different points in the city, and what came to their minds first when they thought about the city, and they also drew a sketch-map of the city. The cognitive maps of cities were found to include features, such as, landmarks (which have the value of being easily spotted from a distance); paths or travellable routes, such as, roads; nodes (i.e., important points at which several paths meet); districts (i.e., specific regions identifiable on cultural or geographical grounds); and edges, which are visibly defined boundaries of districts or other areas. Rivers and city walls are two examples of edges.

In what form is the information contained in cognitive maps stored? We definitely know that language is not necessarily involved, because chimpanzees readily acquire cognitive maps. If a chimpanzee is carried around an enclosure in the company of an experimenter who hides pieces of fruit in 18 different locations, it is subsequently able to uncover most of the fruit (Menzel, 1973). What is especially revealing, however, is that the chimpanzee does not simply follow the pathway used by the experimenter; rather, it demonstrates the acquisition of something akin to a cognitive map by moving efficiently from one piece of fruit to another in reasonable accordance with the least distance principle.

Many theorists have argued that cognitive maps are stored in the form of images, but the evidence is inconclusive. However, it is clear that cognitive maps are by no means a direct reflection of the visual environment. People living in Cambridge were asked to judge the angles at which pairs of roads within the City of Cambridge met. The average estimate in nearly every case was close to 90°, despite the fact that half of the pairs of roads actually met at an angle of less than 70° and the remaining pairs of roads met at angle in excess of 110° (Byrne, 1979). This is reminiscent of an earlier finding by Lynch (1960), who discovered that many of the residents of Boston apparently believed that Boston Common was a square with five right-angled corners! Byrne found in another study that walking distances between pairs of prominent locations in St. Andrews were more likely to be over-estimated if they included several bends or were within the town centre. Thus, our cognitive maps of towns may resemble the London tube map in being in the form of networks which preserve topological connectedness but not the precise distances between locations or the angles at which routes join.

Empirical Evidence

In order for theories based on scripts, schemata, or frames to be of real scientific value, it is essential for there to be adequate ways of measuring these constructs. They all involve stereotypic knowledge, and so it is to be expected that there should be some consensus of opinion among people as to the knowledge incorporated in a given schema, perhaps coupled with some individual differences in the script details. Relevant evidence was obtained by Bower, Black and Turner (1979). They asked 32 people to indicate what they viewed to be the 20 most important events in each of a number of given episodes. No event was listed as part of an episode by all of the subjects, but there still a considerable measure of inter-individual agreement. When describing the events involved in going to a restaurant, at least 73% of the subjects mentioned sitting down, looking at the menu, ordering, eating, paying the bill, and leaving the restaurant. In addition at least 48% of the subjects included in their descriptions entering the restaurant, giving the reservation name, ordering drinks, discussing the menu, talking, eating a salad or soup, ordering dessert, eating dessert, and leaving a tip. In other words, there are at least 15 events that form part of many people's knowledge of what is involved in having a meal at a restaurant.

It has been suggested that schemata, scripts and frames influence several psychological processes including perception, learning, and retrieval. So far as perception is concerned, it seems likely that frames serve the useful purpose of reducing processing demands. When viewing an everyday scene, such as, an office, kitchen, or living room, most people have clear expectations about the objects likely to be present. There is no need to spend very long looking at expected objects, and this frees our resources for processing the more novel and unexpected aspects of any given scene.

Some of these notions were tested by Friedman (1979). She presented her subjects with detailed line drawings of six different scenes (city, kitchen, living room, office, kindergarten and farm). Each picture contained mainly objects that you would expect to see in that particular setting, but a few unexpected objects were also included. Perception was influenced by the extent to which objects conformed to the appropriate frame, with the duration of the first look being almost twice as long for unexpected as for expected objects. The differences between expected and unexpected objects were even more marked on the subsequent recognition-memory test. The subjects rarely noticed missing, new, or partially changed expected objects, even when only those expected objects that had been looked at were considered. In contrast, deletions or replacements of unexpected objects were nearly always detected. As Friedman concluded, "The episodic information that will be remembered about an event is the difference between that event and its prototypical frame representation in memory [p. 343]."

Rather similar findings with schematic passages were reported by Graesser, Woll, Kowalski and Smith (1980). They discovered that there was better recognition-memory discrimination for atypical than for typical actions. Of most interest, there was no memory discrimination at all for very typical actions (e.g., "Jack paid the bill" and "Jack sat down at the table" in a story about eating out at a restaurant). This suggests that much of the information that is very typical or expected in the context of the current schema is incorporated in long-term memory even if it is unstated.

Smith and Graesser (1981) replicated these findings when they used a recognition test, but discovered that typical events were better recalled than atypical events at long retention intervals. It may well be that schemata play a much more important role in guiding the retrieval process in recall than in recognition. Obviously, schemata would facilitate retrieval of schema-relevant information only.

Rather stronger evidence that schemata can enhance the retrieval of information from long-term memory was obtained by Anderson and Pichert (1978). After their subjects had read a story from the perspective of either a burglar or of someone interested in buying a home, and then recalled it, they were asked to shift to the alternative perspective and recall the story again. On the second recall, subjects recalled more information that was important only to the second perspective or schema than they had done on the first recall. These results confirm the notion of schema-driven retrieval, and further support comes from the subjects' introspective reports. For example, Anderson and Pichert (1978) quoted the following example:

When he gave me the homebuyer perspective, I remembered the end of the story, you know, about the leak in the roof. The first time through I knew there was an ending, but I couldn't remember what it was. But it just popped into my mind when I thought about the story from the homebuyer perspective [p. 10].

We have already seen that schemata affect several processes. They help to determine what is perceived, they sometimes impair memory discrimination, and they can be used to guide the retrieval process. Another key role played by schemata is to facilitate the comprehension of complex passages and stimulus events. Bransford and Johnson (1972) presented their subjects with a prose passage that was deliberately written so that the referents of the terms used were quite obscure. Provision of an appropriate schema-evoking context, in the form of a title, increased comprehension of the passage considerably, and also enhanced subsequent recall (a detailed account of this experiment can be found in Chapter 5).

How useful are schemata in everyday life? The fact that schemata sometimes lead us to process schema-relevant information inadequately, and to show very poor retention of such information subsequently, suggests that schemata may be more of a hindrance than a help. In fact, such a conclusion would be wildly inaccurate. In the great majority of situations, schemata allow us to capitalise on the regularities of events and situations, and to make accurate inferences about the real world. If you like, schemata permit us to engage in corner-cutting that is usually time-saving. Thus, for example, if you are in a strange house and need to find what the Americans call the comfort station, you would use schema-based knowledge to eliminate the living room as a likely place to find it. Making use of such information is effective perhaps 99% of the time, but there are undoubtedly some houses in which the toilet is immediately adjacent to the living room.

While the theoretical constructs of scripts, frames, and schemata appear to have potential explanatory power, they are all rather amorphous notions. Furthermore, the theoretical models in which they have been incorporated are sadly lacking in testability. If some predicted effect of a schema on performance fails to occur, it is always possible to explain the data away by arguing that the subjects did not actually possess the relevant schema, or that an inappropriate schema was used. The notion of complex, integrated pieces of information is plausible, but much more needs to be done to spell out the details of the processes determining which schemata are activated and how schema information is used in the performance of cognitive activities.

12 Stress, Arousal and Cognition

We all know from personal experience that our ability to think and reason is markedly affected by our current motivational and emotional state. If we do not carry out some task satisfactorily, we sometimes attribute our inadequate performance to motivational factors (e.g., "I just wasn't interested in the task," "It was boring"), or to our emotional state (e.g., "I felt very tense and anxious," "I couldn't cope with it"). Of course, there are several other factors that play a part in determining whether or not our internal state is appropriate for performing complex tasks. For example, most people find that they are best equipped to tackle demanding activities either early in the day ("larks") or relatively late ("owls"). In addition, some people like peace and quiet when they are working or studying, whereas others prefer to work in conditions that are noisy and stimulating.

Most cognitive psychologists have studiously avoided considering any of the factors mentioned above, and have tended to focus almost exclusively on the performance of people who are both reasonably motivated and unaffected by strong emotion. Of course, when neither motivational nor emotional states are manipulated, precisely nothing can be discovered about the impact of these states on cognition. In recent years, however, there have been sporadic attempts to remedy this state of affairs (e.g., Broadbent, 1971; Eysenck, 1982a; Kahneman, 1973), and some of these endeavours are discussed later.

The stress, emotional, and motivational factors that have been investigated include intense noise, failure feedback, electric shock, time of day, incentives, and sleep deprivation; and the personality factors considered include anxiety and introversion–extraversion. The central issue is the extent to which the effects of this gallimaufry of external and internal factors are mediated by the same mechanisms and processes. One extreme position is to argue that these various factors are so diverse that each requires a separate theory. This approach may have some merits, but is obviously lacking in parsimony. At the other extreme, it has been argued (e.g., Broadbent, 1971) that there are important similarities between the effects of many of these factors, and he and others have suggested that this is because they affect a common arousal mechanism. Although it is, of course, tempting to account for the effects of several different stress-related variables in terms of a single, uni-dimensional arousal theory, considerable doubts have been expressed about its adequacy (e.g., Eysenck, 1982a).

Arousal theory represents virtually the only systematic attempt to integrate the various findings. It seems appropriate, therefore, to start with this theoretical approach. The merits and shortcomings of arousal theory and related conceptualisations are then discussed, followed by a detailed consideration of emotional and motivational factors.

AROUSAL THEORY

Basic Assumptions and Predictions

The concept of "arousal" is rather amorphous, but there is presumed to be a continuum of arousal ranging from deep sleep or coma at one extreme, to panic-stricken terror or great excitement at the other extreme. One important difference of opinion between theorists concerns the extent to which arousal is thought of in physiological terms. Perhaps the most common contemporary viewpoint was expressed by Broadbent (1971): "The physiological concept of arousal is certainly of interest and of ultimate relevance to the one we have found from behaviour, but at this stage the connection of any suggested physiological measure and the psychological state is too remote to make it practical to attach one concept directly to the other [p. 413]."

As Eysenck (1982a) pointed out, it is possible to distinguish between a "strong" and a "weak" version of arousal theory. According to the "strong" arousal theory, virtually all of the effects of the various arousers are mediated by a single arousal system. In contrast, the "weak" arousal theory assumes that there is only a partial overlap in the behavioural effects of different arousers. Each arouser has two kinds of effects on performance: (1) a general arousing effect; and (2) specific or idiosyncratic effects.

It is rather difficult to evaluate the "weak" version of arousal theory, because the additional idiosyncratic effects of any particular arouser can always be postulated in a *post hoc* manner to account for findings that would otherwise be embarrassing. The "strong" arousal theory is more testable, and can be evaluated in terms of a number of criteria. The first, and most obvious, criterion is that of behavioural equivalence, i.e., the requirement that different arousers should have comparable effects on performance.

The degree of support for this criterion depends in part on the level of performance which is investigated. For example, high arousal produced in various different ways improves long-term memory. While this supports arousal theory, detailed perusal of the data indicates that the effects of different arousers are by no means the same. Long-term retention is better when learning occurs in the afternoon than in the morning because high arousal leads to deeper or more semantic processing (Folkard, 1979); whereas intense white noise enhances long-term memory in spite of the fact that noise-produced arousal often *reduces* semantic processing (Hockey, 1979). In contrast, incentive improves long-term memory by increasing the elaboration of processing without affecting the depth of processing (Eysenck & Eysenck, 1980a, 1982). Anxiety reduces the elaboration of processing rather than the depth of processing (Eysenck, 1979a), and it typically *reduces* long-term memory.

Some of these differences among arousers may be due to the varying task demands in the various studies. However, the almost complete schism between the effects of different arousers at the general and specific performance levels is puzzling from the perspective of the "strong" arousal theory.

The second criterion with which it is possible to evaluate the "strong" arousal theory is that of interaction among arousers. If two arousers are applied together, and they both affect the same internal arousal mechanism in the same way, then their combined effects may well differ from those predicted by simply adding together their effects when applied singly. On the other hand, if two arousing agents actually affect different mechanisms, then they should exert independent effects on performance.

In order to predict the form of interaction between two arousers, it is necessary to make certain assumptions, of which the most common is that an intermediate level of arousal is optimal for performance. Various interactions involving two arousers—white noise, and incentive in the form of knowledge of results (K.R.)—and one de-arouser—sleep loss—are shown in Fig. 12.1. In all cases a continuous serial reaction task was used. As can be seen in panel (a), intense white noise impaired performance among subjects who had slept normally, perhaps because it created too high a level of arousal. On the other hand, noise enhanced performance for sleep-deprived subjects, who would otherwise have been under-aroused. The same general explanation fits the data in panel (b), an arousing stimulus (noise) reduced performance in aroused subjects (i.e., those receiving incentive in the form of knowledge of results), but had the opposite effect on those subjects deprived of feedback. Once again, in panel (c), arousal in the form of knowledge of results or incentive improved performance to a greater extent among under-aroused subjects who had suffered sleep loss. All in all, these three sets of data suggest that there is some important similarity between noise, incentive and sleep deprivation in terms of their effects on performance.

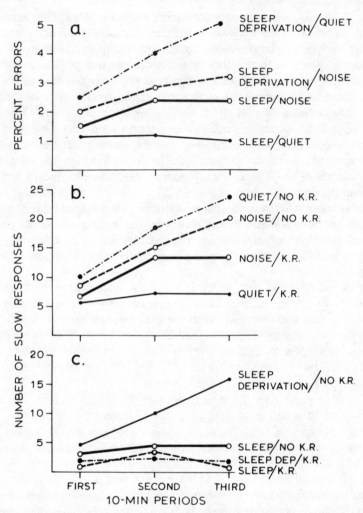

FIG. 12.1   Effects of arousal on the serial reaction task. Panel (a) sleep deprivation and white noise (Wilkinson, 1963); Panel (b) incentive (knowledge of results: K.R.) and white noise (Wilkinson, 1963); and Panel (c) Incentive (knowledge of results) and sleep deprivation (Wilkinson, 1961).

While these interactions are consistent with arousal theory, they provide less support for that theory than is generally thought to be the case. Depending on the precise assumptions made about the shape of the curve relating performance and arousal, and about the location of each condition on the arousal continuum, it is possible to "explain" virtually all possible forms of interaction between two arousers, and even to account for no interaction at all!

There is a third criterion which is relevant if arousal is thought of in physiological terms, namely, that the effects of different arousers on physiological response patterns should be comparable. A problem here is that different physiological measures of arousal (e.g., heart rate, skin conductance, and EEG) usually correlate only approximately, $+.2$ to $+.3$, with each other. Indeed, there are occasions when some measures indicate increased arousal at the same time as other measures reflect decreased arousal, a phenomenon which Lacey (1967) labelled "directional fractionation." For example, during the time interval between an alerting signal and the stimulus in reaction-time studies, some of the components of the EEG indicate high arousal, but concurrently there is a reduction in heart rate (i.e., cardiac deceleration).

There is a more detailed discussion of the experimental evidence relevant to these criteria later in this chapter. For the moment, it should be noted that there is rather limited support for all three criteria.

The Yerkes–Dodson Law

An extremely influential attempt to relate arousal and performance was put forward by Yerkes and Dodson (1908), and enshrined in the so-called Yerkes–Dodson Law. They made two crucial assumptions:

1. There is an inverted-U relationship between the level of tension, arousal, or motivation, and the level of performance, with optimal performance efficiency occurring at a moderate level of arousal.

2. The optimal level of motivation or arousal is inversely related to task difficulty.

In their 1908 study, Yerkes and Dodson used mice as subjects, arousal was created by electric shock, and task difficulty was determined by ease of discrimination along a brightness dimension. Their results were in line with the predictions of the Yerkes–Dodson Law, and so are the findings obtained by many other researchers who manipulated arousal and task difficulty in entirely different ways.

However, it is quite difficult to disprove the notion that there is an inverted-U relationship between arousal and performance. If three levels of arousal are compared, there are six possible orderings of these three levels with respect to performance. Of these six, only the two in which the middle level of arousal is associated with the worst level of performance are at variance with the Yerkes–Dodson Law. That means that two-thirds of such studies testing the Yerkes–Dodson Law would support it by chance alone!

This particular problem can be alleviated if four different levels of arousal are included in a study. There are 24 different possible orderings of four arousal conditions with respect to performance, and only one-third of them are consistent with the Yerkes–Dodson Law.

The evidence is rather stronger that the optimal level of arousal is inversely related to task difficulty (Eysenck, 1982a). However, it is not clear how the dimension of task difficulty can most appropriately be conceptualised. One suggestion (Kahneman, 1973) is that hard or difficult tasks make greater demands on attentional capacity or mental effort than do easy tasks. Alternatively, the most important aspect of task difficulty may be the extent to which the task requires concurrent processing.

The proper interpretation of the finding that the optimal level of arousal is inversely related to task difficulty is unclear. While the emphasis in the literature has been very much on the effects of arousal on task performance, the task itself is a source of arousal. Kahneman (1973) has discovered that arousal level as measured physiologically is higher when subjects are engaged in a difficult task than when they are performing a relatively simple task, presumably because the amount of mental effort demanded by a task is directly related to its complexity. In similar vein, it has been found that anxiety is much higher immediately after performing a difficult concept acquisition task than an easy one (Tennyson & Wooley, 1971). This may be due to the greater likelihood of experiencing failure when carrying out a difficult task.

Thus we cannot assume that the level of arousal remains equivalent across different task conditions, since task-induced arousal seems to increase in line with task difficulty. Eysenck (1982a) pointed out the implication of this state of affairs: "The simplest explanation of the interaction between arousal and task difficulty is to argue that the optimal level of arousal is actually *not* lower for difficult than for easy tasks: it merely appears so because the actual arousal level is underestimated [by researchers] for difficult tasks [p. 177]."

We have already seen that two of the theoretical constructs incorporated into the Yerkes–Dodson Law (i.e., arousal and task difficulty) were thought of in an over-simplified way by Yerkes and Dodson (1908). The same is true of the notion of "performance efficiency," which implies that the effects of arousal on performance can be readily assessed. In fact, arousal often increases the speed of performance but at the same time reduces accuracy. In such cases, it becomes meaningless to claim that arousal has either increased or decreased performance efficiency. The idea that arousal affects the overall efficiency with which a task is performed should be replaced by the notion that arousal increases the efficiency of some component processes involved in task performance and decreases the efficiency of other component processes.

A final inadequacy with the Yerkes–Dodson Law is that it is merely descriptive: All it does is to refer to certain predicted inter-relationships between arousal, task difficulty, and performance efficiency. The Law fails to explain *why* there is a curvilinear relationship between arousal and performance, and it is also uninformative with respect to the inverse relationship between the optimal level of arousal and task difficulty.

Easterbrook's Hypothesis

There have been various attempts to provide a theoretical underpinning for the Yerkes–Dodson Law, of which the most influential has probably been that of Easterbrook (1959). He claimed that states of arousal, high emotionality, and anxiety all affect the range of cue utilisation in the same way, defining the range of cue utilisation as, "the total number of environmental cues in any situation that an organism observes, maintains an orientation towards, responds to, or associates with a response [p. 183]." His key theoretical assumption was that there is a progressive reduction in the range of cues used as arousal increases, which "will reduce the proportion of irrelevant cues employed, and so improve performance. When all irrelevant cues have been excluded, however, ... further reduction in the number of cues employed can only affect relevant cues, and proficiency will fall [p. 193]."

Some of the implications of Easterbrook's hypothesis are shown in Fig. 12.2. The curvilinear relationship between arousal and performance is accounted for: performance is poor at low levels of arousal because many irrelevant cues are attended to, and it is poor at high levels of arousal because some of the task-relevant cues are ignored. The inverse relationship between the optimal level of arousal and task difficulty can also be explained provided that one makes the reasonable assumption that difficult tasks involve a greater number of relevant cues than do easy tasks. Task-relevant cues begin to be ignored at lower levels of arousal for difficult tasks than for easy tasks.

Easterbrook's hypothesis has been tested by using a paradigm in which a main or primary task and a secondary or incidental task are performed concurrently. The general expectation is that high arousal will have a relatively greater adverse effect on the subsidiary task than on the primary task, because the reduced range of cue utilisation excludes cues from the subsidiary task before those from the primary task. In other words, Easterbrook's hypothesis assumes that there is a reallocation of attention from less important to more important sources of information as arousal increases.

A slightly unfortunate feature of Easterbrook's hypothesis is that there are three different patterns of performance in dual task studies that are

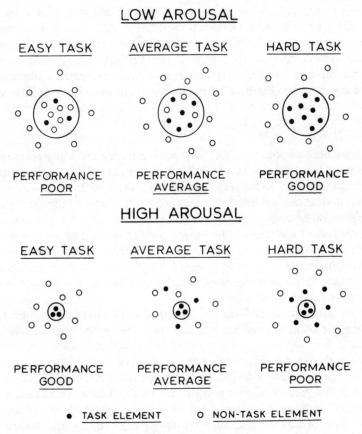

FIG. 12.2   Easterbrook's (1959) hypothesis applied to the interaction between arousal and task difficulty. The large circles represent the range of cue utilisation.

consistent with the notion that arousal increases attentional selectivity. Improved performance on the main task under high arousal combined with impaired performance on the subsidiary task; improved main-task performance coupled with no effect of arousal on the subsidiary task; and no effect of arousal on the main task in conjunction with reduced performance on the subsidiary task. *In toto* there are nine possible effects of high arousal on main task and subsidiary task performance, only three of which are manifestly incompatible with Easterbrook's hypothesis; in these three cases, arousal has either a less detrimental effect or a greater enhancing effect on the subsidiary task than on the main task.

Eysenck (1982a) has reviewed the literature on the effects of arousal on dual task performance. Of the studies in which arousal was induced by the threat of electric shock, six produced results clearly in line with Easterbrook's hypothesis and none of the studies was inconsistent with the hypothesis. There was exactly the same six/zero split in studies of anxiety, and the studies favourable and unfavourable to Easterbrook's hypothesis were eleven and one respectively in noise studies, and seven and two in incentive experiments. Across all these studies there were 30 cases in which the data clearly accorded with theoretical expectation, and only three in which the findings were at variance with the hypothesis.

There is obviously a grain of truth in the idea that high arousal leads to increased attentional selectivity. It is of particular interest and importance that this selectivity appears with such diverse arousers as electric shock and incentive. However, it is improbable that the only effect of arousal is to produce a narrowing of attention. Furthermore, Easterbrook (1959) regarded the narrowing of attention as a relatively automatic reaction to states of high arousal. It may well be preferable to regard attentional narrowing as an active coping response: When the total information-processing demands cannot be handled by the available processing capacity, aroused subjects may decide to restrict attention to a small number of information sources.

The most pronounced inadequacy of Easterbrook's hypothesis concerns the assumption that high arousal impairs task performance because it leads to intense concentration on some, rather than all, of the task elements. In fact, there is considerable evidence that high arousal in the form of anxiety has a very different effect, with anxious individuals finding it unusually difficult to concentrate on the task in hand. Anxious people report that they spend less of the available time than non-anxious people attending to the task (Deffenbacher, 1978), and they have also been found to look away from task stimuli more frequently (Nottelman & Hill, 1977).

One of the implications of the notion that high arousal increases concentration on task stimuli is that distractibility should be inversely related to the level of arousal. In fact, there are several studies in which the opposite findings were obtained. For example, Dornic and Fernaeus (1981) discovered in each of three experiments that neurotic introverts (i.e., subjects high in anxiety) were more adversely affected than stable extraverts (i.e., subjects low in anxiety) by distracting stimuli. In one of their experiments, each subject was given two three-digit numbers, and had to count backwards by threes alternately from each number. This task was either carried out in quiet conditions or with auditory distraction in the form of amusing anecdotes. Distraction increased the error rate for anxious subjects but actually decreased it for non-anxious subjects.

In sum, the notion that arousal increases attentional selectivity is an important one, and it clearly captures part of the effect of arousal on internal processes. However, Easterbrook's hypothesis really contains a number of explicit or implicit assumptions about the effects of arousal: (1) arousal reduces concurrent processing; (2) it increases attentional selectivity; and (3) it increases attentional control. The evidence in favour of each of these assumptions varies considerably, ranging from very strong in the case of the first assumption to rather weak for the third assumption.

Developments in Arousal Theory

It has been clear for a long time that the early versions of arousal theory were grossly over-simplified. This has led some theorists to consider each stressor or arouser separately, and to put forward relatively specific theories. An alternative is to replace the unitary concept of arousal with two or more rather more specific arousal-related concepts, an approach that has been adopted by several theorists (e.g., Broadbent, 1971; Eysenck, 1982a; Revelle & Humphreys, in press; Kahneman, 1973). This general approach receives some support from the physiological evidence, which was reviewed by Lacey (1967). He concluded that it was desirable to distinguish between behavioural, autonomic, and cortical arousal, the reason being that measures of each of these three kinds of arousal are often poorly related to each other.

Broadbent (1971) claimed that there are a number of grounds for abandoning the notion of a single arousal mechanism. He argued that one can assume that two stressors or arousers are affecting the same mechanism if the combined effects of the two stressors on performance greatly exceed additivity, i.e., if there is an interaction of the two stressors. The predicted interactions are often obtained, but there are sufficient exceptions to suggest the advisability of postulating more than one arousal mechanism (e.g., Wilkinson & Colquhoun, 1968).

Another complication for the arousal theory concerns some of the effects of noise (an arouser) and sleeplessness (a de-arouser). They resemble each other in that prolonged work is necessary before they affect performance, but dissimilar in that their effects are quite different when they do appear. Broadbent (1971) argued that these, and other, anomalous findings were potentially explicable if two interdependent arousal mechanisms were postulated: a Lower mechanism and an Upper mechanism. The Lower mechanism is primarily involved in the execution of well-established decision processes, and it is directly affected by sleeplessness, noise, amphetamine, and chlorpromazine. In contrast, the Upper mechanism monitors and alters the parameters of the Lower mechanism in an attempt to maintain the level of performance. Broadbent assumed that inefficiency in the Lower mechanism (i.e., sub-optimal or supra-optimal levels of arousal) does not impair performance provided that the Upper mechanism remains in an efficient state. Among the factors affecting the Upper mechanism rather than the Lower mechanism are introversion–extraversion, alcohol, time of day, and task duration. Although Broadbent did not do so, it makes sense to include incentive among the factors primarily affecting the Upper mechanism.

The quintessential difference between the early versions of arousal theory and the kind of theoretical position advanced by Broadbent (1971) and others can be expressed quite simply. The original theory assumed that behaviour was influenced *directly* by the prevailing level of arousal, whereas most contemporary theories are based on the assumption that the effects of arousal on behaviour are usually *indirect*. In particular, it is now assumed that the behavioural consequences of arousal on performance are affected systematically by cognitive processes. In other words, the early arousal theorists rather lost sight of the fact that people attempt to ameliorate the natural harmful effects of factors such as noise, caffeine, incentive, and sleep deprivation. It is not clear exactly how such control systems operate, but they are presumably influenced by feedback concerning the adequacy of the current level of performance. In sum, we are affected by our internal physiological states, but we are not as completely at their mercy as was implied by some of the original formulations of arousal theory.

The most striking support for Broadbent's kind of theory is the surprisingly modest effect on performance of manipulations which produce marked effects on arousal. The usual effects of intense noise on performance are considerably smaller than intuition would suggest, and it was thought until quite recently that the total loss of one or two nights' sleep had no effect on the performance of most tasks. This ability of the human processing system to cope with non-optimal levels of arousal, strongly suggests the existence of some compensatory system resembling Broadbent's Upper mechanism.

The same kind of explanation can be applied to the failure of sleep deprivation and noise to affect performance during the initial stages of the work period: At that time, the Upper mechanism is functioning efficiently, and thus reasonable levels of performance are maintained. The opposite effects of sleep deprivation and noise on performance start to appear after prolonged work because the increasing inefficiency of the Upper mechanism prevents appropriate compensatory activity from occurring.

Eysenck (1982a) argued for a similar distinction between two arousal systems. The first arousal system (similar to Broadbent's Lower mechanism) consists of a passive arousal state which is rather general and undifferentiated at the physiological level. The effects of activity on performance in this arousal system depend on the degree of appropriateness of the induced arousal state for the processing demands of the task. The second arousal system consists of an active and effortful reaction to the naturally occurring effects of arousal on performance. In general terms, the greater the extent of the adverse effects of the first arousal system on performance, the grosser will be the magnitude of compensatory activity in the second arousal system.

It is also possible that extra effort may be applied to a task simply because subjects who are, say, sleep-deprived or exposed to intense noise believe that their performance is certain to be impaired unless extra resources are allocated to the task. Such beliefs may be erroneous. Fisher (1984) found that subjects performing a reaction-time task in intense noise estimated their speed of responding as slower than subjects performing in quiet, despite the fact that reaction times were actually 300 milliseconds faster in noise. In other studies, subjects who performed a reaction-time task only in quiet conditions guessed that their subsequent performance on the task would be similar in quiet but slower in noisy conditions.

The proposed distinction between a passive arousal state and an active compensatory response can be clarified with reference to an important study by Wilkinson (1962) on sleep deprivation. The primary effect of sleep deprivation is to reduce the level of arousal in our first arousal system. However, Wilkinson found that those sleep-deprived subjects who performed best on a test of addition were the ones who had the greatest rise in the electromyogram (EMG) or muscle tension during the task. It is tempting to regard muscle tension as providing an approximate measure of compensatory effort or activity in the second arousal system. Wilkinson (1962) himself drew the following conclusions from his findings: "Sleep deprivation may cause inefficiency even in subjects who maintain performance if their raised EMG reflects greater effort or energy expenditure; this may be the cost of maintaining normal levels of arousal and performance in the face of the depressing influence of sleep deprivation per se [p. 570]."

It is probable that passively induced arousal and active compensatory processes both increase physiological arousal as that is conventionally assessed. However, the arousal state induced by white noise or caffeine is likely to be rather general, whereas the arousal state occurring as a by-product of active compensatory processing activities will typically be much more specific. Such specificity in the operation of the second arousal system is revealed by the ways in which patterns of physiological responding vary as a function of task requirements. Tasks involving active manipulation of information (e.g., reasoning, mental arithmetic) characteristically produce increased autonomic arousal on all of the major physiological measures; in contrast, tasks requiring attention to external sources of information produce directional fractionation in which most measures reflect greater autonomic arousal but heart rate decelerates.

It follows from Eysenck's (1982a) theoretical position that reasonably high levels of performance can be obtained in two rather different ways: Either by near-optimal arousal in the first arousal system and minimal involvement of the second arousal system; or by sub- or supra-optimal arousal together with considerable compensatory activity in the second arousal system. According to the theory, then, it is often misleading to conclude from a non-significant effect of some arousal manipulation on performance that the arouser has had no effect at all on internal processing: It is entirely possible that the more aroused subjects have achieved a comparable level of performance to less aroused subjects at greater cost to themselves in terms of involvement of the second arousal system. As a consequence, highly aroused subjects are less able to cope with any processing demands that are additional to those necessitated by the main task, such as performing a concurrent subsidiary task or rejecting extra-task distracting stimuli. We have seen already that there is overwhelming evidence that high arousal reduces the ability to perform a concurrent subsidiary task (Easterbrook, 1959), despite the fact that performance on the main task is rarely adversely affected by arousal. There is also some evidence (Dornic, 1977; Dornic & Fernaeus, 1981; Howarth, 1969; Morgenstern, Hodgson, & Law, 1974) that the ability to resist some kinds of distraction is reduced in states of high arousal.

One of the implications of this theoretical position is that there is an important conceptual distinction between processing efficiency and performance effectiveness. Effectiveness is a measure of the quality of performance, whereas efficiency refers to the relationship between the quality of performance and the effort invested in it. More specifically, the relationship between processing efficiency and performance effectiveness can be expressed in the following formula: processing efficiency = performance effectiveness/effort. Compensatory activity in the second arousal system tends to reduce the effects of arousal on performance effectiveness, and so arousal will often affect processing efficiency more than performance effectiveness, and measures of subsidiary task performance and resistance to distraction may reflect the effects of arousal on processing efficiency.

The 'Arousal Syndrome'

Most arousal theorists, whether they postulate one or two arousal systems, claim that different methods of producing arousal have broadly comparable effects on behaviour. How true is it that there is a characteristic arousal-induced pattern of performance? The answer to that question undoubtedly depends on the particular aspects of cognitive performance that are considered, but unfortunately little has as yet been achieved in the way of identifying the major dimensions of cognition. As a consequence, we will focus primarily on those aspects of performance that have received the most attention in the arousal literature.

Eysenck (1982a) has provided a detailed account of the effects of sleep deprivation, time of day, white noise, incentive, anxiety, and introversion–extraversion on performance, and so only a selective review of the evidence will be provided here. He argued that it is important to consider attention, because attentional mechanisms often mediate the effects of arousal on performance. One of the key attributes of attention is the extent to which attentional resources are allocated to one task or activity rather than to another, i.e., attentional selectivity. Easterbrook (1959) argued that high arousal in its various forms increases attentional selectivity, and the evidence broadly supports that position.

A related, but conceptually distinct, issue is that of attentional control, which can be assessed by measuring the extent to which irrelevant and distracting stimulation can be ignored. The data are somewhat inconsistent, and seem to vary somewhat from arouser to arouser. However, the usual finding is that high arousal leads to increased susceptibility to distraction, i.e., reduced attentional control.

There has been much theoretical controversy about the notion of a short-term store (see Chapter 4), but it is undeniable that the temporary "holding" of a limited amount of task-relevant information is essential in the performance of a very wide range of cognitive activities. It thus seems important to assess the effects of high arousal on the efficiency and/or capacity of this short-term storage system. The typical finding is that arousal impairs the functioning of this system, but there is at least one interesting exception: Incentive characteristically *increases* short-term storage capacity.

There has been some investigation of the effects of arousal on long-term memory as well as on short-term memory. The usual finding is that high arousal improves long-term memory (Eysenck, 1976), but there are some inconsistencies in the data. Anxiety usually worsens long-term memory, and, as we saw earlier in the chapter, the reasons why arousal improves long-term memory seem to vary from arouser to arouser.

One of the more robust phenomena in psychology is known as speed-accuracy trade-off. In essence, there is usually an inverse relationship between speed and accuracy, and on many tasks it is possible to produce predictable effects on both speed and accuracy by instructional manipulations. Does high arousal have any systematic effect on the relative emphasis accorded to speed and to accuracy? In general terms, the aroused state seems to be conducive to rapid and inaccurate responding, but this natural pattern can be altered and even reversed as a result of intervention by cognitive control systems.

The argument so far implies that there is a common behavioural pattern associated with high arousal. This pattern comprises increased attentional selectivity, reduced attentional control, greater performance speed, and increased proneness to errors. This pattern may underlie the inverse relationship between task difficulty and the optimal level of arousal, because easy tasks typically require rapid performance, make minimal demands on short-term storage, and are relatively impervious to distraction, whereas difficult tasks emphasise accuracy, impose substantial demands on short-term storage, and are easily disrupted by distracting stimuli.

It is tempting to assume that at least some of these effects of arousal on performance are interdependent. For example, reduced attentional control may be one reason for inaccurate performance, and reduced short-term storage capacity may facilitate rapid responding. The notion of inter-dependence is certainly intuitively appealing, but it is still unclear whether it is an appropriate conceptualisation.

The position outlined up to now is rather one-sided, and may even be regarded as a caricature of reality. It is true that different arousers tend to produce a certain degree of equivalence in a few aspects of cognitive performance, but a rather different conclusion is suggested when other behavioural measures are considered. For example, the effects of various arousers on retrieval from memory have been investigated. Introversion and anxiety generally reduce the efficiency of retrieval, incentive has no effect, and noise actually increases retrieval efficiency. It would thus be ludicrous to argue that there is any characteristic effect of arousal on retrieval.

Detailed examination of those aspects of performance generally affected in the same ways by different arousers also reveals some discrepancies. None of the arousers included in Table 12.1 (e.g. incentive, time of day) produces a behavioural pattern precisely in line with the allegedly characteristic arousal pattern, and there is no aspect of performance that is affected by all of the arousers in a uniform fashion. In other words, we are left in a rather frustrating situation: there is sufficient behavioural equivalence across

TABLE 12.1
Effects of High Arousal on Aspects of Performance*

Performance	Time of Day	White Noise	Incentive	Introversion	Anxiety	Sleep Deprivation
Attentional selectivity	?	+	+	+	+	+
Attentional control	?	?	−	−	−	?
Speed	+	+	+	−	0	+
Accuracy	−	−	−	+	−	0
Short-term storage	−	−	+	0	−	+
Long-term storage	+	+	0	+	−	+
Retrieval efficiency	+	+	0	−	−	?

*For time of day, later in the day is assumed to represent high arousal. The sleep-deprivation findings are reversed to facilitate comparisons.

+ = improved performance; − = impaired performance; 0 = no effect; and ? = effect unknown.

arousers to support an arousal-based theory, but the overlap is not great enough to justify any simple arousal theory.

In view of the usual assumption that there is a curvilinear relationship between arousal and performance (Yerkes & Dodson, 1908), it may seem strange that Table 12.1 refers to monotonic, or unidirectional effects of arousal on aspects of performance. If we assume that most tasks involve several component processes, each of which is monotonically related to arousal, then it is entirely possible for overall performance to be related to arousal in a curvilinear fashion.

The greatest weakness of most arousal theories is that they lead to an over-emphasis on the similarities between different arousers. Common sense indicates that all arousers have their own special characteristics. For example, intense noise is an auditory stimulus that may mask other auditory stimuli in addition to its role as an arouser, and most poeple would prefer to work under conditions of high incentive than to work exposed to ear-splitting noise or anxiety-inducing conditions, despite the fact that incentive, noise, and anxiety all increase the level of arousal. Progress may only be possible when we focus on the dissimilarities between arousers as well as the similarities. This can be done by considering different arousers separately in order to assess the behavioural pattern produced by each arouser, a task which is undertaken in the next section of the chapter. One motivational factor (i.e., incentive) and one major emotional factor (i.e., anxiety) are considered.

MOTIVATION AND EMOTION

Motivation and Incentive

Motivational states are affected by an amalgam of internal and external factors. For example, hunger is influenced by internal conditions related to the number of hours of food deprivation, but it is also affected by external stimuli that provide visual and olfactory information about food. The various internal and external influences often interact with each other in determining the intensity of hunger; pampered members of western society are less enthusiastic than starving peasants in Asia about a bowl of rice.

During the past 100 years or so there has been a shift in theoretical thinking away from an emphasis on internal determinants of motivation and towards an increasing recognition of the importance of external factors. The influence of Darwin led to an approach in which motivation was closely related to instinct, with the term "instinct" referring to a biologically determined internal source of energy. More recently, there has been increased theoretical and experimental interest in external factors relevant to motivation, such as, incentive and reinforcement.

Research into the effects of motivation on cognitive performance has typically manipulated motivation by varying the amount of incentive (usually money) offered for successful performance. The emphasis in such studies is very much on extrinsic motivation, in the sense that the incentives or rewards provide satisfaction that is independent of the activity itself, and they are controlled by someone other than the individual him- or herself. In contrast, intrinsic motivation is involved when the task activity itself provides the only apparent source of reward, possibly in the form of enhanced feelings of competence and self-determination (Deci, 1975).

The most natural assumption is that the effects of extrinsic and intrinsic motivation are additive and independent. However, this orthodoxy has been challenged by Deci (1975), who claimed that a frequent result of increasing extrinsic motivation is to *reduce* intrinsic motivation. One of the rewards associated with intrinsic motivation is the feeling that one's behaviour is self-determined; of course, extrinsic rewards or incentives make people feel that their behaviour is controlled by external forces, and this in turn reduces the feeling of self-determination. In other words, extrinsic rewards or incentives alter the perceived cause of the individual's behaviour, and it is this which undermines intrinsic motivation. This line of reasoning may explain the fact (if it is a fact!) that amateur sportsmen usually derive more pure enjoyment from sport than do professional sportsmen.

Support for the notion that extrinsic rewards can reduce intrinsic motivation was obtained in a classic study by Deci (1971). He found that people who had previously received payment for solving complex, block-arrangement problems were less inclined than those who had never been financially rewarded to spend their leisure time working on further problems. While this finding of extrinsic rewards reducing intrinsic motivation is reasonably robust (see Notz, 1975), there is some evidence (e.g., Calder & Staw, 1975) that extrinsic rewards actually *increase* intrinsic motivation when the task is boring or intrinsically uninteresting.

It is unfortunate that nearly all of our knowledge about the effects of motivation on cognition is based on extrinsic motivation. In view of the complex interactions between intrinsic and extrinsic motivation, it would obviously be desirable to consider both kinds of motivation together. Furthermore, there are signs that there may be crucial differences between extrinsic and intrinsic motivation. Intrinsic motivation is related to an individual's interests and aptitudes, and is thus presumably reasonably constant over time. In contrast, the effects of extrinsic rewards seem to be fairly transient. Shortly after extrinsic rewards cease to be available, there is often a reduction in response known as extinction.

It is well known that incentive or reinforcement often enhances performance, but there has been some disagreement as to whether or not this enhancement effect is always found. Skinner appears to believe that it is, defining a reward or reinforcer as a stimulus event that follows a response and thereby increases the strength or probability of occurrence of that response. A theoretical position that is almost exactly the opposite of that espoused by Skinner was put forward by Condry (1977):

> Compared to non-rewarded subjects, subjects offered a task-extrinsic incentive choose easier tasks, are less efficient in using the information available to solve novel problems, and tend to be answer oriented and more illogical in their problem-solving strategies. They seem to work harder and produce more activity, but the activity is of a lower quality, contains more errors, and is more stereotyped and less creative than the work of comparable non-rewarded subjects working on the same problems [pp. 471–472].

How can two such discrepant views be reconciled? The most obvious answer relates to the very different kinds of tasks considered by Skinner and by Condry. Skinner's preference has been to look at the effects of reinforcement on simple, repetitive tasks, such as lever pressing for food, in which little in the way of acquisition of new skills is required. In contrast, Condry has investigated the effects of incentive on more complex tasks such as problem solving and concept formation. As a first approximation, then, incentive or reward facilitates performance of simple, undemanding tasks, but worsens performance on complex cognitive tasks. This is, of course, consistent with the Yerkes–Dodson law (Yerkes & Dodson, 1908).

There are a few studies in which the effects of incentive on problem solving have been assessed. In one of the earliest, Glucksberg (1962) made use of a problem involving mounting a candle on a vertical screen. The solution to the problem necessitates using a small box as a platform for the candle. People experience difficulty with this problem because a box is normally regarded as a container and not a platform. This leads to what is known as functional fixedness, and this focusing on the irrelevant use of the box is greater when the box is presented full of drawing-pins than when it is empty. There was no effect of monetary incentive on solution speed when the easier version of the problem was used, but incentive increased the time taken to solve the more difficult version by an average of $3\frac{1}{2}$ minutes.

Perhaps incentive reduces the flexibility of thought, leading people to persist with previously established ways of thinking even when counterproductive. This conclusion is supported by the findings of McGraw and McCullers (1979). They used water-jar problems involving three jars. Liquid has to be poured from one jar to another in order to obtain a specified quantity in one of the jars. The initial nine problems all had the same three-jar solution, but the final problem had only a simple two-jar solution. Performance on this last problem reflects the ease or difficulty of breaking the mental set established by the previous problems. Solution speed on the first nine problems was unaffected by financial incentive, but subjects who were to receive an incentive took approximately 60% longer to solve the final problem than those subjects who did not. Once again, we have an example of incentive increasing the tendency to apply previously acquired skills inappropriately to a new situation.

We have so far considered tasks on which adverse effects of incentive have been demonstrated. Facilitatory effects are most pronounced on simple tasks where the emphasis is on speed of responding. Incentive typically produces increased response speed on reaction-time tasks (see Eysenck, 1982a, for details), and the same is true of performance speed on the five-choice serial reaction task. The apparatus for this task consists of five lights with a response key below each one. When a light comes on, it is switched off by pressing the corresponding key, and this in turn leads to another light at random becoming illuminated. While the effects of incentive on this task are predominantly positive, there is some evidence that the opposite happens with large incentives. When the subjects believed that their performance on the serial reaction task would play a part in determining whether or not they were accepted for a coveted apprenticeship, they produced fewer correct responses and twice as many errors (Willett, 1964).

It is important to note that incentive often increases speed at the cost of a reduction in accuracy, i.e., there is a speed-accuracy trade-off. Feldman (1964) found that high-incentive subjects (those seeking a desired apprenticeship) worked faster than low-incentive subjects (those previously accepted) on a digit-cancellation task, but they made considerably more errors. Bavelas and Lee (1978) observed the effects of incentive in the form of goal level (i.e., the number of objects they were asked to list), on the performance of an object-listing task (listing objects that are "hard, white, and edible"). The number of objects written down was positively related to incentive or goal level, but the quality of performance, in terms of the extent to which the objects matched up to the three criteria, was inversely related to goal level.

One of the most important effects of incentive on the processing system is that it increases attentional selectivity. There are several studies (discussed by Eysenck, 1982a) in which an intentional learning task took place at the same time as an incidental learning task. The most common finding is that incentive improves performance, or has no effect, on the intentional task, but that it worsens performance on the incidental task. Incentive acts as a kind of implicit instruction telling the subject to focus attention on stimuli associated with the incentive at the expense of other stimuli. This point of view was expressed succinctly by Simon (1967), who argued as follows: "We can use the term *motivation* . . . simply to designate that which controls attention at any given time [p. 34]."

This theoretical position can readily be applied to performance on a learning task in which there is a high monetary incentive for learning half of the items and a low incentive for learning the remaining items. Not surprisingly, the high-incentive items are better recalled than the low-incentive ones, presumably because more attention is paid to them. This account was fleshed out by Eysenck and Eysenck (1980b). They discovered that there was more extensive or elaborate processing of the high-incentive items, but there was no effect of incentive on the level or depth of processing (see Chapter 5). Eysenck and Eysenck (1982) subsequently found that the extra processing given to high-incentive stimuli was confined to those stimulus features that appeared to be relevant.

Working memory or some short-term memory system appears to play an important role in information processing, and it is of interest to investigate the ways in which it is affected by incentive. In a study by Eysenck and Gillan (1964), there was no effect at all of high incentive (a desired apprenticeship) on either forward or backward digit span. In an unpublished study, I found that word span was increased slightly, but significantly, by incentive. Eysenck and Eysenck made use of a letter-transformation task in which a specified number of letters must be added to each of between one and four letters (e.g., the answer to "SEG + 2" is "UGI"). The answer can be given only after all of the letters have been transformed, and so the demands on short-term storage increase systematically in line with the number of letters in the problem. Monetary incentive (£5 for being in the top 25% of the subjects) increased performance speed, especially on three- and four-letter problems; this suggests that incentive enhanced the efficiency of the short-term storage system.

In sum, incentive has various different effects on cognitive performance. It increases attentional selectivity, it increases performance speed, decreases accuracy of performance, produces some cognitive inflexibility, and in-creases short-term storage capacity. Some of these effects may be inter-dependent. Inaccurate performance may be attributable either to cognitive inflexibility or to high speed of performance, and cognitive inflexibility may result from increased attentional selectivity. The characteristic pattern of effects of incentive provides some basis for understanding the ways in which motivational factors interact with task demands: If this pattern is appropri-ate for any particular task, then performance on that task may be expected to improve with incentive, but incentive will impair performance if the pattern of effects is inappropriate.

An interesting attempt to make theoretical sense out of the various incentive effects was made by McGraw (1978). He claimed that two conditions needed to be satisfied in order for incentive to impair per-formance:

1. The task is of sufficient intrinsic interest that external incentives provide a redundant source of motivation.

2. The task is relatively open-ended, with the steps leading to task solution being non-obvious.

McGraw developed the second point by distinguishing between algorithmic and heuristic tasks; the path to solution is straightforward in algorithmic tasks, whereas the first requirement in heuristic tasks is to develop an appropriate algorithm.

According to this theoretical analysis, tasks can be allocated a position within the two-dimensional space formed by the attractive–aversive dimension and by the algorithmic-heuristic dimension. The emphasis in the literature has been very much on tasks that are aversive and algorithmic, and these are the kinds of tasks for which the beneficial effects of incentive are maximal. It is an interesting speculation that this bias in task selection is responsible for the widespread belief that incentive almost always enhances performance.

The importance of the algorithmic-heuristic distinction is exemplified by the work of Glucksberg (1962), who in a sense discovered that incentive only worsened performance when problem-solving tasks were presented in a heuristic form. Why should this be so? McGraw (1978) argued that the tendency for incentive to reduce incidental learning was responsible:

> Reward subjects might do less well on concept formation, problem solving, and those other tasks on which we have seen reward subjects to be inferior *precisely because* of their inferiority at incidental learning... The heuristic process needed for some intentional-task solutions can be said to feed on incidental thoughts and perceptions [p. 55].

McGraw's theory is consistent with much of the available evidence, but there are some exceptions. For example, incentive usually has no effect on intelligence-test performance, in spite of the fact that many of the items on such tests are both heuristic and interesting. If one compares those interesting, heuristic tasks that are adversely affected by incentive with those that are unaffected, the major difference seems to be the presence of accessible, but inappropriate, algorithms in the former tasks. This would explain why incentive only had a detrimental effect on that water-jar problem that was at variance with a previously established mental set, but had no effect on any of the other problems (McGraw & McCullers, 1979).

A further difficulty with McGraw's theoretical stance is that incentive sometimes harms performance on tasks that are neither intrinsically interesting nor heuristic. This is especially likely to happen when very strong incentives such as the possibility of a desired apprenticeship are provided. In view of the possibility that there is a curvilinear relationship between amount of incentive and level of performance on many tasks, it seems strange that McGraw did not include the amount of incentive as one of the determinants of the behavioural consequences of incentive manipulations.

We have implicitly assumed so far that there is a fairly direct relationship between the amount of incentive and the strength of motivation, but this assumption is not entirely accurate. One of the complicating factors is the subjective probability of performing the task sufficiently well to obtain the incentive; if there is a near-zero probability of success, then even very high incentive may be associated with a rather low level of motivation. If, for example, someone offered you £1,000,000 if you ran a marathon in under $2\frac{1}{2}$ hours, you would probably fail to respond to the challenge. It has been suggested (Revelle & Michaels, 1976) that tasks with subjective probabilities of success between .1 and .5 are highly motivating ("When the going gets tough, the tough get going"). If the probability of success falls below .1, then motivation may become extremely low ("There is no point in banging your head against a brick wall").

A theoretical position emphasising the cognitive and evaluative processes intervening between the offering of an incentive and the determination of the level of motivation was put forward by Locke (1968). The pivotal theoretical construct was the "goal," which Locke (1968) defined as, "what the individual is consciously trying to do (p. 159)." The goal that an individual has set himself or herself can be assessed, according to Locke, by direct questioning. The relevance of goal setting in predicting the behavioural consequences of incentive manipulations was spelled out by Locke, Bryan, and Kendall (1968): "Incentives such as money should affect action only if and to the extent that they affect the individual's goals and intentions (p. 104)."

How does goal setting relate to performance? Locke (1968) claimed with beguiling simplicity that there is a straightforward relationship between goal difficulty and performance: "the harder the goal the higher the level of performance (p. 162)." It is not entirely clear from Locke's theory exactly *why* goal setting should affect performance, but he implied that there is greater effort and utilisation of resources when difficult goals are set. He reviewed 12 relevant studies in which various different tasks (e.g., addition, toy construction, and reaction time) had been used, and assessed goal difficulty in terms of the percentage of the trials on which subjects attained their goal. Over the 12 studies, there was a rank-order correlation coefficient of +.78 between the level of performance and goal difficulty. In part, this high correlation reflects an inadequate assessment of performance. For example, an object-listing task was used in one of the studies, and the number of objects listed was directly related to goal level. However, since the quality of the responses usually varies inversely with goal level (Bavelas & Lee, 1978), such findings provide at best equivocal support for Locke's position.

The most glaring inadequacy in Locke's theory is the omission of any proper consideration of the ways in which motivational factors interact with task demands. In one programme of research (Eysenck, 1964), the effects of the incentive of a desired apprenticeship on the performance of several tasks were investigated. Performance on the Tsai-Partington Number Tracing Test and on serial reaction tasks was adversely affected by this incentive, whereas digit span and pursuit rotor learning were unaffected, and paired-associate learning and serial learning were improved. Such a complex pattern of findings cannot possibly be explained simply in terms of a direct effect of goal setting on performance.

Locke's claim that high goal setting is a necessary and sufficient condition for incentive-based improvements in performance is almost certainly erroneous. However, it is noticeable that the effects of incentive are minimal or non-existent when incentive fails to alter goal difficulty. Thus a necessary, but not sufficient, condition for incentive to enhance performance may be that it leads to the setting of harder goals.

There are some grounds for regarding incentive as an arouser that affects the same internal arousal mechanism as other manipulations such as sleeplessness and noise. According to Broadbent (1971), this arousal theory is supported by the fact that incentive has often been found to interact with these other factors. There are also some relevant physiological data. Wilkinson, El-Beheri and Gieseking (1972) discovered that incentive produced systematic changes in respiration rate, skin conductance level, and pulse rate, all of which were indicative of an elevated state of arousal. Fowles (1983) found that monetary incentive usually increased heart rate.

Are the behavioural effects of incentive comparable to those of other arousers? This is currently a matter of some controversy. Broadbent (1978) appeared to favour a positive answer to the question: "One of the interesting aspects of noise is the similarity of its effects to those of other conditions, such as financial incentives [p. 1060]." There are certain similarities, in that both noise and incentive characteristically produce enhanced attentional selectivity and rapid, inaccurate responding. However, there also appear to be some important differences. We have already seen that incentive tends, if anything, to increase the capacity and/or efficiency of the short-term storage system, but noise and other arousers usually reduce the capacity of short-term storage. The differences between noise and incentive are especially marked on the letter-transformation task described earlier. The beneficial effects of monetary incentive vary directly with the demands imposed on short-term storage capacity (Eysenck & Eysenck), whereas the effects of noise change from facilitatory (when storage demands are low) to detrimental (when such demands are high) (Hamilton, Hockey & Rejman, 1977).

The role played by individual differences in mediating the effects of incentive on performance has been relatively ignored. It has been argued

(Eysenck, 1967) that introverts are usually more aroused cortically than extraverts, and so the effects of an arouser, such, as incentive, should interact with introversion–extraversion. There is reasonable support for this prediction. In one study, Corcoran (1962) compared the effects of low and high motivation on introverts and extraverts performing a letter-cancellation task. There was a correlation of +.90 between introversion and performance speed under low motivation, but the correlation became negative under conditions of high motivation. Extraverts in the low motivation condition may have been sub-optimally aroused to a much greater extent than introverts, and thus they benefited more from incentive.

In sum, the ways in which incentive affects performance are determined by an amalgam of cognitive and physiological factors. Incentive only increases motivation provided that a cognitive appraisal indicates that there is a reasonable chance of performing well enough to attain the preferred incentive. Cognition is also involved in deciding how attentional and other resources should be allocated in response to the prevailing incentive conditions. The importance of physiological factors is suggested by the fact that the impact of incentive on performance is influenced considerably by the individual's current physiological state. In general terms, incentive is most likely to improve performance when the level of arousal is rather low (e.g., among the sleep-deprived), and least likely to do so when people are already highly aroused (e.g., exposed to intense noise).

Most theorists have assumed that the primary effect of incentive is on some internal motivational state, but this is clearly an over-simplification. If you were told that you would receive £100,000 if you performed your job unusually well tomorrow, you would undoubtedly be highly motivated. In addition, however, you might experience a considerable amount of anxiety at the thought of failing to obtain the financial incentive. It is possible that the characteristic pattern of incentive effects shown in Table 12.1 (p. 341) would come to resemble that of anxiety if large incentives were investigated.

Anxiety

The concept of "anxiety" is of central importance in a number of areas of psychology, most obviously in clinical and abnormal psychology, but also in personality research and work on emotion. Anxiety states are prevalent in western societies, and can be produced by an enormous range of environmental events ranging from snakes to failure feedback, and from an impending examination to flying in an aeroplane. Many definitions of the anxiety state have been proposed, of which the following one offered by Spielberger (1972) is typical: "Unpleasant, consciously-perceived feelings of tension and apprehension, with associated activation or arousal of the autonomic nervous system [p. 29]."

There are a number of theoretical distinctions that need to be made when discussing anxiety. The first is between trait anxiety and state anxiety (Spielberger, 1972). Trait anxiety is typically measured by means of a questionnaire, and it refers to an individual's semi-permanent susceptibility to anxiety. In contrast, state anxiety refers to the anxiety actually experienced by an individual in a particular situation. The level of state anxiety is interactively determined by an individual's proneness to anxiety (i.e., trait anxiety) and by the amount of stress in the situation. State anxiety is generally higher among individuals high in trait anxiety than among those low in trait anxiety, but the difference is much more pronounced in stressful environments, such as those involving threat to self-esteem (e.g., failure feedback). There is an interesting exception to this generalisation. The effects of stress in the form of physical danger (e.g., threat of electric shock) are comparable on individuals high and low in trait anxiety (Hodges, 1968). Thus trait anxiety reflects individual differences in reactions to ego threat rather than to physical danger.

A second important distinction is between worry and emotionality, which have been regarded as the two major components of anxiety. According to Liebert and Morris (1967), worry is "primarily *cognitive concern* about the consequences of failure [p. 975]," whereas emotionality relates to changes in physiological functioning. In view of this distinction, it is possible to move beyond the issue of the effects of anxiety on performance, and to investigate the role of its components. Adverse effects of anxiety seem to depend more on the worry component than on the emotionality component. For example, Spielberger, Gonzalez, Taylor, Algaze and Anton (1978) found with male students that worry correlated $-.47$ with grade point average (a measure of academic achievement), whereas the correlation of emotionality with grade point average was only $-.13$. The respective correlations for female students were $-.35$ and $.00$.

This study by Spielberger *et al.* illustrates a thorny problem. The negative relationship between worry and performance may reflect the adverse effect of worry on academic performance. On the other hand, it may be due to the influence of anticipated or actual poor performance on worry. The basic difficulty is that anxiety and performance exert bi-directional effects on each other: the level of anxiety undoubtedly affects performance, but the quality of performance in turn modifies the level of state anxiety.

A final theoretical distinction that has usually been ignored is between task-intrinsic and task-extrinsic anxiety. If the source of anxiety is intrinsic to the task, as is the case with failure feedback, then successful performance of the task should reduce anxiety. In such circumstances, anxiety can clearly be motivating. In contrast, if anxiety originates in events quite unrelated to the task itself, there is no reason why task motivation should increase. An example of task-extrinsic anxiety is a study in which a digit-span task was performed by subjects walking across a swaying rope bridge over a deep ravine (Capretta & Berkun, 1962). It seems unlikely that the anxiety induced by being in such a dangerous environment produced much motivation to repeat the digits back in the correct order.

One of the major issues concerns the degree of equivalence of different kinds of stress on anxiety and on performance. We have already seen that people high and low in trait anxiety are differentially responsive to ego threat but not to physical threat so far as state anxiety is concerned, and it is tempting to assume that there is a similar pattern with respect to behaviour. As expected, individuals of high trait anxiety are more detrimentally affected than those of low trait anxiety by failure experiences on a variety of learning tasks (Saltz, 1970), but the effects of electric shock on performance are more puzzling. Eysenck (1979a) uncovered a total of 14 relevant comparisons; in 13 cases, the learning performance of high-anxiety subjects was either less impaired or more facilitated by the threat of shock. In other words, there is a puzzling discrepancy between the state anxiety and performance data, in that threat of shock produces an equivalent increase in state anxiety for subjects high and low in trait anxiety, but has very different effects on their learning performance.

A promising starting point for understanding why the effects of ego threat and physical threat are so different is a study carried out by Morris and Liebert (1973). They considered the effects of failure and shock on the two main components of state anxiety, and found that failure increased worry but not emotionality, whereas threat of shock produced greater emotionality but did not affect worry significantly.

The effects of anxiety on performance are predominantly negative, but it would not be true to say that anxiety affects all tasks in the same way. Indeed, there are more than 20 studies in which anxiety has been found to interact with task difficulty, with anxiety usually having a more detrimental effect on difficult or complex tasks than on simple ones. The notion of "task difficulty" is rather amorphous, and so it obviously makes sense to attempt to identify the aspect or aspects of task complexity most affected by anxiety.

Spence and Spence (1966) argued that the critical factor in determining the effects of anxiety on learning was response competition rather than task difficulty *per se*. By response competition they meant the extent to which the correct response on a learning task must be discriminated from other competing responses. While there is some experimental support for the prediction that anxiety should only impair performance when there is response competition (see Eysenck, 1982a, for details), response competition was confounded with task difficulty in most of the studies. When these two factors are unconfounded, it turns out that the factor that interacts with anxiety is task difficulty rather than the degree of response competition (Saltz & Hoehn, 1957).

It is possible to look at the interaction between anxiety and task difficulty from a rather different perspective. People take longer to perform difficult tasks than easy ones and they also make more errors on complex tasks. It is likely, therefore, that difficult tasks provide more failure experiences and feelings of anxiety than do easy ones. It is certainly true that state anxiety tends to be higher both during and after the performance of difficult rather than of easy tasks (Tennyson & Wooley, 1971; Spielberger, O'Neil & Hansen, 1972). It may be that people high in trait anxiety learn poorly when they experience failure (e.g., on difficult tasks), but learn efficiently when they experience success (e.g., on easy tasks). Some support for the idea that the influence of anxiety on learning depends on the nature of the feedback received (i.e., success versus failure) rather than on task difficulty *per se* was obtained by Weiner and Schneider (1971).

Alternative approaches are possible. A major reason why some tasks are more difficult than others is that they make greater demands on some short-term storage system. For example, it is much harder to calculate the answer to $73 \times 16 = ?$ in your head than to work out $3 \times 6 = ?$ because of the additional storage demands imposed in the former case. This line of thinking leads to the hypothesis (Eysenck, 1982a) that anxiety reduces the efficiency of short-term storage, and this is responsible for the interaction between anxiety and task difficulty.

It has been known for some time that anxiety (at least of the state variety) has a disruptive influence on the transient holding of information. Eysenck (1979a) reviewed various digit-span studies, and reported that 11 out of 12 experiments in which there was a significant effect of state anxiety or situational stress obtained a detrimental effect of high anxiety. Eysenck (in preparation) made use of a series of tasks varying in the demands which they place on short-term storage of information. Between one and four letters had to be transformed by adding either two or four letters to each letter. One-letter problems (e.g., $F + 4 = ?$, for which the answer is "J") are very easy and require very little short-term storage, whereas four-letter problems (e.g., $FLUR + 4 = ?$; answer = JPYV) involve holding the accumulating answer as the later letters are transformed. The usual interaction between anxiety and task difficulty was obtained. Because the primary difference between easy and hard versions of the letter-transformation task is in the amount of short-term storage that is needed rather than in the nature of the requisite processing operations, it seems reasonable to argue that the adverse effect of anxiety on short-term storage efficiency is involved in producing the interaction between anxiety and task difficulty.

This conclusion is strengthened by a consideration of the effects of anxiety on the component processes involved in four-letter tasks. The processing of each letter requires the successive stages of accessing long-term memory to retrieve the alphabet, the actual transformation, and storage and rehearsal of the answer to date. Anxiety had its greatest negative effect towards the end of the problem, which is the time at which short-term storage demands are maximal. In addition, the adverse effects of anxiety were greatest during the stage of storage and rehearsal, which is the stage most intimately concerned with the transient storage of task-relevant information.

It seems fairly clear that anxiety reduces the efficiency of short-term storage, and it may be possible to extend this line of thinking to the somewhat broader working memory system proposed by Baddeley and Hitch (1974). Hitch and Baddeley (1976) obtained evidence that some verbal reasoning problems place greater demands on working memory than do others. A student of mine (Anna Eliatamby) used the same problems, and found that anxiety had a much greater detrimental effect on the more difficult problems, difficulty being assessed on the basis of the involvement of working memory.

In further unpublished research, Anna Eliatamby obtained more striking evidence that anxiety affects the functioning of the working memory system. An anagram task was performed either on its own, at the same time as an articulatory suppression task, or concurrently with the task of counting backwards by threes. Anxiety had a substantial effect on anagram-solution time only when the task of counting backwards was performed at the same time, with high-anxiety subjects taking an average of over 55 seconds to solve five-letter anagrams under these conditions against approximately 12 seconds for low-anxiety subjects. The task of counting backwards makes extensive use of the central executive component of working memory, and so the implication is that this component is adversely affected by anxiety.

A central issue concerns the effects of anxiety on attentional mechanisms. Easterbrook (1959) argued that anxiety produces increased attentional selectivity. It has been found, for example, that anxiety usually has no effect on intentional learning when subjects are given concurrent intentional and incidental learning tasks, but it does reduce the amount of incidental learning (see Eysenck, 1982a, for details). This suggests that there is a reallocation of processing resources favouring high-priority stimuli under high anxiety.

There has been less consensus about the ways in which anxiety affects attentional control. On the one hand, Easterbrook (1959) claimed that anxiety augments attention to task stimuli, and thus presumably increases the ability to resist distraction. On the other hand, Wachtel (1967) argued that anxiety leads to increased attentional lability, which implies that anxiety increases susceptibility to distraction (i.e., distractibility). The evidence is somewhat equivocal. When learning occurred in the presence of no cues, task-relevant cues, or task-irrelevant cues, the facilitatory effects of relevant cues on learning and the detrimental effects of irrelevant cues were reduced in high anxiety (Bruning, Capage, Kozul, Young & Young, 1968; Zaffy &

Bruning, 1966), suggesting that distractibility is inversely related to anxiety. In contrast, Pallak, Pittman, Heller and Munson (1975) found that anxious subjects performed the Stroop test better than non-anxious subjects when there was little distraction, but performed it worse under conditions of high distraction. Dornic and Fernaeus (1981) also found in each of three experiments that subjects high in anxiety were more susceptible to distraction. It is not clear why anxiety sometimes increases distractibility and sometimes decreases it, but it is probably true to say that those studies finding subjects with greater susceptibility to distraction under high anxiety have tended to use relatively complex tasks. It may be that anxious subjects maintain performance on complicated tasks at great "cost" to themselves, and this makes them more vulnerable to additional, distracting stimuli.

So far the focus has been on the ways in which anxiety influences susceptibility to distraction from external stimuli and events. It is also possible, of course, for people to be distracted from some current task by internal thoughts and ideas. It seems intuitively reasonable that anxiety greatly increases the tendency to be deflected from the task in hand by internal worries and preoccupations, and several theorists have emphasised this notion. Wine (1971) expressed this theoretical position in the following words: "The highly test-anxious person responds to evaluative testing conditions with ruminative, self-evaluative worry, and, thus, cannot direct adequate attention to task-relevant variables [p. 99]."

There has been a certain amount of interest in the effects of anxiety on memorial functioning, and some of the more recent research has made use of theoretical developments such as the levels-of-processing approach (Craik & Lockhart, 1972). It appeared at one time that anxiety reduced deep or semantic processing (Schwartz, 1975); if true, this would help to account for the fact that anxiety usually impairs long-term memory. However, a failure to replicate some of Schwartz's main findings was reported by Craig, Humphreys, Rocklin, and Revelle (1979), and further negative findings have been reported in several studies by Mueller (e.g., 1976). Mueller has usually found that anxiety reduces retention, but that it does so to the same extent for both semantic and shallow features or attributes.

If the adverse effects of anxiety on memory cannot be accounted for in terms of the depth of processing, then an alternative explanation must be sought. The notion that anxiety restricts processing activities suggests that fewer attributes or features are encoded under high anxiety. In contemporary terminology, it is hypothesised that anxiety reduces the elaboration or extensiveness of processing. This hypothesis is consistent with most of the available evidence, but has rarely been investigated directly. Eysenck and Eysenck tested retention of a list of words by means of recall cues that were either strongly or weakly related to particular list words as indicated by normative data. High anxiety had a negligible effect on recall with the strong cues, but substantially lowered recall with the weak cues. Because more elaborate or extensive processing is required for recall to weak cues, the implication is that anxiety reduced the elaboration of processing.

On the basis of the evidence discussed so far it is not difficult to explain why anxiety often disrupts performance. The reduction in short-term storage capacity as a function of high anxiety is one important reason, but increased attentional selectivity and reduced attentional control undoubtedly also play a part. Indeed, given these various effects of anxiety on the processing system, what is puzzling is the rather small effect of anxiety on performance which is usually found. Part of the solution may lie in a re-examination of the worry component of anxiety. It has frequently been assumed that the effects of worry on performance are invariably negative, because worry is a form of task-irrelevant processing. However, worry can also include constructive concern about performance inadequacies and the active search for more appropriate task strategies, in which case worry might actually enhance performance.

An alternative way of accounting for the surprisingly small influence of anxiety on most aspects of behaviour was proposed by Eysenck (1979a). He argued that anxiety may usually disrupt processing efficiency more than performance effectiveness (i.e., the quality of performance). The quality of performance is maintained under high anxiety despite reduced processing efficiency, because of the use of compensatory mechanisms. As Dornic (1980) concluded: "Individual differences in information-processing capacity may therefore remain hidden, taking the form of different 'subjective cost' for performance [p. 2]."

How can we show that processing efficiency has been impaired by anxiety? One way is to re-consider those dual-task studies in which main and subsidiary tasks were performed concurrently. Eysenck (1982a) reviewed the relevant studies, and discovered that anxiety had no effect on performance of the main task in 16 out of 20 experimental comparisons. This lack of effect of anxiety on performance effectiveness might lead one to conclude that anxiety had not affected the processing system. However, this conclusion is certainly erroneous. Among those 16 experimental studies in which anxiety had no effect on the main task, anxiety had a significantly detrimental effect on the subsidiary task in 11 cases, and no effect in the remaining 5 cases. This suggests that the non-significant effect on the main task masks some processing inefficiency that only becomes manifest when an additional task is included.

An alternative way of assessing processing efficiency is to relate the quality of performance to the amount of effort subjects feel they expended on the task. Anxiety had no effect on performance effectiveness on two tasks (counting backwards and visual search), but was associated with greater perceived effort (Dornic, 1980). Performance equivalence was achieved at greater "cost" by high-anxiety subjects, and, therefore, the implication is that they suffered from reduced processing efficiency.

In sum, anxiety typically increases attentional selectivity, reduces short-term storage capacity, reduces accuracy without increasing speed, impairs long-term memory, and often reduces attentional control. Some, or even all, of these anxiety-induced changes may occur because anxious individuals are dividing attention between task requirements and task-irrelevant cognitive activities such as worry and self-concern. Eysenck (1982a) argued that such task-irrelevant processing pre-empts some of the limited capacity of working memory, leaving reduced working memory capacity to process task-relevant information.

Perhaps the greatest inadequacy in previous formulations is the assumption that anxiety affects performance in a direct fashion. It is more likely that people attempt to compensate for any adverse effects of anxiety on performance, and the partial or total success of such attempts means that anxiety affects performance effectiveness less than processing efficiency.

Conclusions

The effects of motivation (in the form of incentive) and emotion (in the form of anxiety) on cognitive processes and performance have now been described. It is clear that these various effects cannot be encompassed by any single generalisation such as the Yerkes–Dodson Law or Easterbrook's hypothesis. Instead, what seems to happen is that these motivational and emotional factors have a number of discernible effects on the processing system, many of which are probably interdependent. As a result, we need to stop asking simple questions such as, "Does incentive improve performance?" or "Does anxiety impair performance?" We must recognise that incentive and anxiety both produce qualitative changes in the nature of information processing (cf. Eysenck & Folkard, 1980). It will usually be the case that some aspects of these qualitative changes will facilitate task performance, whereas other aspects will detract from task performance. Overall task performance represents the combined effects of all of these changes, and is not the most appropriate level of analysis.

Of course, our understanding of the detailed effects of incentive and anxiety on component processes remains incomplete. However, some progress has been made. We know that incentive typically increases speed, decreases accuracy, increases attentional selectivity, increases distractibility, increases short-term storage capacity, and has no effect on long-term memory or retrieval efficiency. The pattern of effects of anxiety on component processes is rather different; anxiety typically increases attentional selectivity, reduces accuracy, reduces short-term storage capacity, reduces long-term memory, and increases distractibility. It is quite likely that there are additional effects of incentive and of anxiety that have not as yet received systematic investigation, and the problem of attempting to make theoretical sense of these patterns of changes remains unsolved.

There is a growing awareness that the "natural" effects of motivational and emotional factors on performance are often obscured. If, for example, some motivational or emotional manipulation leads to an impairment of performance, then the subject may make use of various strategies and control processes to remedy matters. While we know relatively little about these compensatory systems, we can gain some insight into their effects by comparing performance effectiveness and processing efficiency. The use of compensatory control systems is at present most clearly revealed when a motivational or emotional factor has little or no effect on performance effectiveness but a marked adverse effect on processing efficiency. This pattern has been obtained a number of times in studies of anxiety.

In sum, we are beginning to understand some of the ways in which motivation and emotion shape cognitive processes. The effects are sometimes rather subtle, but they occur with sufficient consistency to indicate that cognitive psychology cannot be considered adequate if it continues to ignore the impact of motivation and emotion on cognition.

13

Cognitive Psychology: Present and Future

Contemporary research and theory in cognitive psychology have been discussed at some length in the previous chapters of this book. Notwithstanding the apparent vigour of cognitive psychology, there are many indications that all is not well, and that much so-called progress is illusory. However, I am less pessimistic than many other cognitive psychologists about the present state of affairs. It is certainly true that adequate theories of cognitive processes lie some way off in the future, but other kinds of progress are more evident. At the very least we know that certain theoretical approaches that seemed promising at one time are actually dead ends. Of course, eliminating erroneous approaches is not the same thing as discovering the correct approach, but the history of science reveals that it is usually an important step along the way.

In spite of some encouraging signs, I am not enough of a Pollyanna to believe that all is well with cognitive psychology. It is sometimes hard to escape the feeling that the vast amount of experimentation in the field of cognition has produced rather meagre dividends. What seem initially to be important empirical findings often turn out to be difficult to replicate or alternatively they become so hedged around with qualifications that their significance is dubious. Theoretical models proliferate at such a rate that it is rapidly becoming true that every self-respecting cognitive psychologist has his or her own theory, and the beleaguered researcher or student finds it almost impossible to compare theories because they are based on different sets of data, using separate constructs and terminology.

One of the main aims of this chapter is to provide an evaluation of contemporary cognitive psychology. Wherever deficiencies are discovered, constructive suggestions for remedying them are discussed. Finally, future lines of development in cognitive psychology are considered.

IS COGNITIVE PSYCHOLOGY IN TROUBLE?

General Criticisms

One of the earliest and best-known attacks on cognitive psychology was

359

delivered by Newell (1973). He argued that research tends to be phenomenon-driven, in the sense that the discovery of a new phenomenon (e.g., clustering in free recall; the visual icon; chunking in short-term memory) leads to a tremendous volume of research directed at exploring all of its ramifications. According to Newell, our investigation of a phenomenon often proceeds on the basis of binary oppositions. In other words, we attempt to play 20 questions with nature. Thus, for example, we ask of a phenomenon, "Does it depend on serial or parallel processing?," or "Does it depend on top-down or bottom-up processing?"

If we use the evidence of the past to extrapolate into the future, then we may discover another 60 or 70 phenomena and formulate a further seven or eight binary oppositions by the end of the century. Will this represent genuine progress? Newell (1973) argued that the answer is negative:

> As I examine the fate of our oppositions, looking at those already in existence as a guide to how they fare and shape the course of science, it seems to me that clarity is never achieved. Matters simply become muddier and muddier as we go down through time. Thus, far from providing the rungs of a ladder by which psychology gradually climbs to clarity, this form of conceptual structure leads rather to an ever increasing pile of issues, which we weary of or become diverted from, but never really settle [pp. 288–289].

Newell's major criticisms of the research strategies used by cognitive psychologists have been widely disseminated, and there has been much agreement with his contentions. However, it is not clear that he has diagnosed correctly the ills of contemporary psychology. As Cohen (1977) pertinently noted, the only way in which we can understand an interesting new phenomenon is by exploring it in detail and identifying the boundary conditions for its existence. Of course, such explorations often indicate the actual complexity of phenomena that initially appeared to be simple, but it would be misleading to characterise this as a shift from clarity to confusion.

What about the dangers of formulating hypotheses in terms of binary oppositions? Of course, such an approach can lead to an over-simplification of a complex reality. However, an examination of the evidence reveals that such hypotheses do not necessarily prevent more informed thinking. What typically happens in practice is that postulating binary oppositions is very helpful in getting the show on the road, but few cognitive psychologists are beguiled into remaining at that simplistic level of analysis for long. We saw an example of this in Chapter 6 in connection with retrieval from short-term memory on the Sternberg task. The early theories assumed that the retrieval process operated in either a parallel or serial fashion, whereas later theories often assumed a more complex, multi-stage retrieval process.

A further criticism of the state of cognitive psychology was put forward by Newell (1973), who argued that the usual procedure of averaging performance across subjects can be very misleading if subjects vary in the strategies they use to perform a given task. This is indisputable, but thankfully the problem can often be obviated. A detailed analysis of the pattern of performance of each individual subject will usually indicate fairly clearly whether or not qualitatively different processing strategies are being used. Sometimes this approach is very successful, as in the work of MacLeod, Hunt and Mathews (1978), which was discussed in Chapter 7. In their investigation of the sentence-picture verification task, they discovered that there were two quite different performance patterns among their subjects indicative of verbal and imaginal processing strategies. If such analyses at the level of the individual subject reveal the existence of a very large number of different task strategies, then the simplest solution is probably to look for another task that imposes greater constraints on processing strategies.

Allport (1975) endorsed most of the criticisms advanced by Newell (1973), and added some more of his own. In particular, he was concerned with the selective interpretation of results, in which researchers concentrate almost exclusively on those aspects of their own and other people's data which support their preferred interpretation, and ignore any conflicting evidence. It may well be true that experimental psychology would benefit from a greater degree of co-ordination of research endeavours, but it is not at all obvious how such cooperation could be achieved. The basic problem is that the future directions cognitive psychology should take are unclear, and there is no good reason for assuming that strong central control would solve the problem.

One of the most frequently mentioned criticisms of contemporary theorising is that it totally fails to match up to the complexity of human information processing. While there may be an element of truth in this criticism, it is also worth considering the opposite point of view, namely, that there are so many theoretical constructs available that any set of data can effortlessly be "explained" in a number of different ways. Consider this selection of terms taken from the memory literature by Eysenck (1977): "We have iconic, echoic, active, working, acoustic, articulatory, primary, secondary, episodic, semantic, short-term, intermediate-term, and long-term memories, and these memories contain tags, traces, images, attributes, markers, concepts, cognitive maps, natural-language mediators, kernel sentences, relational rules, nodes, associations, propositions, higher-order memory units, and features [p. 4]." With such a cornucopia to choose from, it would be a dull-witted researcher indeed who could find no way of accounting for his or her findings on any memory task!

There is a growing realisation among cognitive psychologists that any set of behavioural data can be accounted for by a number of different theories. For example, as we saw in Chapter 1 (pp. 3–5), the issue as to whether performance on a particular task reflects serial or parallel processing is in principle unresolvable, since any conceivable findings can be accounted for by both parallel and serial processing models. This suggests that there are important limitations on the potential precision of theorising in cognitive psychology.

If it is true that behavioural data are often unable to provide a basis for deciding between rival theoretical positions, what criteria can be used? Anderson (1976) has suggested three major requirements of a successful theory, over and above the obvious pre-condition that it provides accurate predictions of performance data: these are parsimony, effectiveness, and broad generality. The parsimony requirement is reasonable, since it is clearly more impressive to account for a set of experimental findings on the basis of, say, five theoretical assumptions rather than ten or fifteen. Effectiveness refers to the extent to which there are explicit procedures for deriving predictions from the theory. Generality is in some ways the most important requirement of all, because no theory tied closely to a single paradigm can possibly tell us much about everyday cognitive psychology.

Reductionism

Given that much of cognitive psychology is built on shifting sand, there is some appeal in the notion of attempting to explain psychological phenomena in physiological or biochemical terms. This approach is known as reductionism, and there has been much controversy about its merits. Those sceptical of the value of reductionism have claimed that all it achieves is a re-description of psychological phenomena in other terms, and that only relatively trivial aspects of behaviour are amenable to reductionist explanations.

One of the more outspoken critics of reductionism is Putnam (1973). His main argument was that reductionism is of little value to psychology because several factors other than basic biological and physiological processes need to be considered in order to understand human behaviour. For example, few psychologists would attempt to predict the results of a forthcoming election by examining in minute detail the brains of a random sample of the electorate! According to Putnam, "Psychology is as under-determined by biology as it is by elementary particle physics, and ... people's psychology is partly a reflection of deeply entrenched societal beliefs [p. 141]."

Surely Putnam is right to assume that many psychological phenomena cannot be adequately explained along purely reductionist lines? However, he over-stated his case, since reductionism is sometimes indispensable. Consider an analogy based on a motor car. Assume that the only information we have about the car comes from its external appearance and performance (as happens in psychology). Is the reductionist approach of peering under the bonnet at the internal workings of the car (as happens in physiology) of value in understanding the car's performance? If one wants to know whether or not the car will fit into a garage, then the answer is obviously negative. If we want to account for an apparent relationship between the amount of use of the car radio and lights and the difficulty of starting the car in the morning, then the answer is affirmative. Detailed examination of a reductionist kind will reveal that a common mechanism (i.e., the battery) is involved. It could be argued that physiology often operates at a more specific level, perhaps analogous to reading the maker's name on the battery, and thus provides us with relatively useless information. However, if we want to know why a particular car is more difficult to start than others, then this level of specificity may be required to answer the question. In other words, the relevance of the reductionist approach varies dramatically as a function of the questions we are asking, and neither a fervently pro- nor anti-reductionist position is tenable.

The most reasonable conclusion seems to be that there are considerable advantages to be gained from using as many different approaches as possible in psychological research. While every method is prone to error, it is unlikely that different methods will produce the same kinds of errors. Therefore, we can have real confidence when there is a convergence of findings from different approaches. For example, the distinction between verbal and imaginal processing has received support both from experimental research and from physiological data on hemispheric lateralisation of function. We may well agree with the conclusion of Cohen (1977): "Given the present fragmentary state of our knowledge, we should not neglect any source of evidence, nor put all our eggs into a single methodological basket [p. 229]."

Ecological Validity

As I am sure has become apparent from reading this book, much research in cognitive psychology seems rather artificial and removed from everyday events and concerns (i.e., it lacks ecological validity). A rapid inspection of the 59 experimental phenomena referred to by Newell (1973) confirms this, because only two of them have immediate relevance to everyday life; one relates to playing chess and the other to looking at the moon. The extent of this problem was spelled out by Claxton (1980), who observed that much of cognitive psychology does not:

> ... deal with whole people but with a very special and bizarre—almost Frankensteinian—preparation, which consists of a brain attached to two eyes, two ears, and two index fingers. This preparation is only to be found inside small, gloomy cubicles, outside which red lights burn to warn ordinary people away.... It does not feel hungry or tired or inquisitive; it does not think

extraneous thoughts or try to understand what is going on. It is, in short, a computer, made in the image of the larger electronic organism that sends it stimuli and records its responses [p. 13].

Claxton is obviously caricaturing contemporary cognitive psychology; nevertheless, many psychologists would be prepared to admit that there is at least a grain of truth in what he has to say. Most laboratory studies are also artificial in another important way: In everyday life, cognitive processes usually occur in the service of some higher purpose or goal, whereas they function as ends in themselves in the laboratory. Consider a standard laboratory task in which people decide on the answers to questions, such as, "Can canaries fly?" In the laboratory, such questions are answered readily, with no thought being given to any ulterior motives that the questionner might have. A rather different reaction would be forthcoming if the same question were asked in the context of a casual conversation. As Claxton (1980) pointed out, "If someone asks me 'Can canaries fly' in the pub I will suspect either that he is an idiot or that he is about to tell me a joke [p. 11]."

One of the aspects of the artificiality of much laboratory research that should be of great concern is what Reitman (1970) referred to as the decoupling problem. If a researcher wants to explore some facet of, say, human memory, then an attempt is usually made to decouple the memory system from other cognitive systems, and to minimise the impact of motivational and emotional factors on performance. Even if it is possible to study the memory system in isolation, it is manifestly obvious that the memory system usually operates in interaction with other functional systems; accordingly, the more successful we are in examining part of the cognitive system in isolation, the less our data are likely to tell us about cognition in everyday life. We saw in Chapter 12 that altering motivational and emotional factors may produce qualitative changes in internal cognitive processes. In consequence, ignoring motivational and emotional factors, as is usually done, cannot be recommended if we wish to extrapolate from the circumscribed motivational and emotional states studied in the laboratory to the very different states often found in everyday life.

Although many psychologists are aware that a sizeable proportion of laboratory research lacks ecological validity, they are quite rightly sceptical of a wholesale abandonment of experimental rigour and control in favour of a totally naturalistic approach. There are so many variables influencing behaviour in the real world, and it is so difficult to manipulate them systematically, that it becomes almost impossible to assess the relative importance of each variable in determining an individual's behaviour. It is no easy matter to obtain the required combination of experimental rigour and ecological validity, but some of the more successful endeavours in that direction have been discussed throughout this book.

The Way Ahead

The various criticisms that have been detailed in this chapter have made many cognitive psychologists reconsider the value of cognitive psychology. If there are significant deficiencies in cognitive psychology that cannot readily be rectified within the traditional approach, then the natural inclination is to look for alternative approaches that may turn out to be more productive. At the time of writing, three rather different approaches are all rapidly gaining adherents, and any of these may serve the purpose of allowing cognitive psychology to escape from at least some of its major limitations.

The three approaches are all discussed in detail in the following sections of the chapter. The first approach to be discussed is the neuropsychological one, which makes use of evidence concerning the patterns of cognitive impairment produced by different kinds of brain injury. The second approach takes the computer metaphor (i.e., the notion that human information processing resembles that of a computer), and develops and extends it in significant ways. This general approach is often referred to as "artificial intelligence," and the amalgamation of artificial intelligence, and cognitive psychology is increasingly termed "cognitive science." The third approach is the applied approach. Advocates of this approach take the problem of ecological validity very seriously indeed, and claim that cognitive psychology can make significant progress only when close attention is paid to cognitive performance in everyday situations.

Of course, the crucial question is, "Which of these approaches is the one likely to be of the greatest ultimate value?" The author does not pretend to know the answer to that. However, there is no sense in which the three approaches are mutually exclusive. As a result, the only sensible strategy seems to be to pursue all three approaches rigorously until their relative efficacy becomes apparent.

NEUROPSYCHOLOGY

There has been increased interest in recent years in the neuropsychological approach to cognitive psychology. In this approach, the effects of various kinds of brain injury on cognitive skills are examined in a systematic fashion. The hope is that neuropsychological findings will have relevance to psychological theories, lending additional support to some theoretical assumptions while tending to disprove others. Neuropsychological findings have been referred to from time to time in this book; for example, in connection with the distinction between short-term and long-term memory stores (Chapter

4), and also with respect to amnesia (Chapter 6). What is attempted here, is to address the more general issues concerning the value of the entire neuropsychological approach.

If we agree with the notion that most (or even all) psychological phenomena of a cognitive kind reflect the workings of specific brain mechanisms, then the neuropsychological approach seems entirely reasonable. However, the implicit assumption that there are two levels of representation (i.e., the psychological and the anatomical or physiological), with a direct one-to-one mapping between the two levels, may well turn out to be simplistic. Marshall (1982) argued that at least four levels of description may be required, and he cited approvingly Marr's discussion of the mathematical task of addition. At level four, there is the theory of computation, which represents the meaning and structure of addition in an abstract form. At level three, there is an algorithm or set of rules by means of which numbers may be added; unlike level four, the exact representation of the numbers (e.g., roman or arabic) is relevant. At level two, the algorithm is implemented in a specific calculating device, and, at level one, we have the neurophysiological elements of this device. Within such a multi-level conceptualisation, the relationship between brain mechanisms and psychological phenomena may be extremely varied and complex.

A crucial strategy in neuropsychology is that of double dissociation. The rationale is that if lesion *A* damages function 1 but not function 2, and lesion *B* damages function 2 but not function 1, then the brain area affected by lesion *A* plays a specific role in function 1, and the brain area affected by lesion *B* does the same for function 2. A concrete example of double dissociation concerns the work described in Chapter 4 (pp. 88–89), in which some patients were found to have impaired long-term memory but relatively intact short-term memeory, whereas others had intact long-term memory but impaired short-term memory. In spite of its popularity, there are significant problems with the double dissociation strategy. Since the two lesions at issue occur in different individuals, it is necessary to assume that different brains are organised in a similar fashion. A further difficulty is that the brain is extremely complex and its various parts function interdependently. In consequence, any lesion may produce a variety of direct and indirect effects. It is possible, for example, that lesions sometimes destroy fibres of passage between major centres rather than the centres themselves. Finally, the direct effects of a lesion on cognitive functioning may be masked as a result of special strategies that the patient has evolved in order to cope with his or her impairment.

The upshot of these various complexities is that the interpretation of neuropsychological evidence is by no means straightforward. Indeed, as Goldstein (1948) noted, we probably need to ask some more complex questions than used to be the case:

The question of the relationship between the symptom complex and a definitely localised lesion again becomes a problem, no longer, however, in the form: where is a definite function of symptom localised? but: *how does a definite lesion modify the function of the brain so that a definite symptom comes to the fore.*

We have focused so far on some of the interpretative difficulties with neuropsychological data. On the more positive side, neuropsychological evidence provides a distinctively different way of evaluating theories in cognitive psychology. Moreover, neuropsychological findings may suggest lacunae in such theories that otherwise might not have become apparent. Since the limitations of neuropsychological data are rather different from those of data collected from normal subjects, any convergence of findings from the two approaches must increase the probability that the data are valid. Matters are rather more problematic if the findings do not converge, because there are three possible explanations: The neuropsychological data are inadequate, or the data from normal subjects are inadequate, or both sets of data are inadequate.

Sometimes the neuropsychological approach provides us with unique insights into psychological phenomena. This may be the case with "deep" dyslexia, which is a condition invariably associated with extensive damage to the left hemisphere of the brain. The most important symptom of deep dyslexia is the existence of the semantic error, in which the patient is asked to read a printed word, and incorrectly says a word that is semantically related to it. According to Coltheart (1980), the presence of the semantic error virtually ensures that several other symptoms will also be present, including visual errors (e.g., saying "gallon" instead of "gallant" and derivational errors (e.g., saying "sick" instead of "sickness"). It has often been assumed that there are various "routes" from print to the internal lexicon, and it may be that deep dyslexics possess only the direct visual route to the lexicon. If so, the study of deep dyslexics may provide more direct information about the respective contributions of the visual access route and other, non-visual access routes than can be obtained in any other way.

Some interesting examples of neuropsychological findings that are relevant to cognitive theories have been obtained in connection with the effects of imagery on memory. It has often been assumed that there are functionally separate short-term and long-term stores, and the dichotomy is supported by a variety of neuropsychological evidence. Milner (1971) discussed the results of studies investigating spatial span (a non-verbal analogue of digit span) in which the subject has to attempt to tap a series of blocks in the same order as the experimenter has just done. There is usually no difference between normal subjects and those who have undergone a right temporal lobectomy on spatial span. However, rather different results were obtained with a version of the task involving non-verbal long-term memory. In this version, sequences of blocks just exceeding the spatial span are presented, and every third sequence is exactly the same. Recall of the repeated sequence increases progressively for normal subjects, due to the build-up of information in long-term memory. This enhancement effect for the repeated sequence was greatly reduced by right temporal lobectomy. Thus, the right temporal lobe appears to be implicated in non-verbal long-term memory, and other evidence suggests that the parietal lobes are involved in non-verbal short-term memory.

We argued in Chapter 5 that the psychological evidence largely fails to support Paivio's (1971) contention that concrete words are better remembered than abstract words because they are stored in verbal and imagery codes, whereas abstract words are stored only in verbal codes. For most people language functions are to be found primarily in the left cerebral hemisphere, whereas non-verbal functions occur mainly in the right hemisphere. The most natural expectation, therefore, is that damage to either hemisphere should produce an impairment on most verbal learning tasks involving concrete words or sentences. In fact, damage to the right hemisphere practically never disrupts verbal learning (see Richardson, 1980, for a review). While lesions of the right temporal lobe usually impair learning of pictorial material, they do not impair learning of concrete and abstract paired associates, nor do they reduce the usual superiority with concrete material. In sum, the neuropsychological evidence is entirely consistent with other evidence in indicating that Paivio's (1971) notions concerning qualitative differences in coding between concrete and abstract stimuli are erroneous.

A final way in which neuropsychological evidence can be of value to theories of cognition is via the discovery of important new phenomena. For example, the notion that people have conscious access to information which they have learned is implicit in the great majority of retention tests used in cognitive psychology (e.g., recall, recognition). While it has been known for some time that an individual's behaviour can show evidence of the effects of previous learning despite his or her lack of conscious awareness that learning has occurred, it is only recently that this phenomenon has been taken seriously. The turning point was the discovery that amnesics are often able to carry out a task reasonably well in spite of having no recollection of ever having done so before (e.g., Weiskrantz & Warrington, 1979). This phenomenon would seem to have important implications for theories of memory, especially since it has also been found with normal people who have weak memories (Meudell & Mayes, 1981).

In sum, the neuropsychological approach must at the very least be regarded as a useful adjunct to the traditional or cognitive approach. In fact, I think that a rather stronger endorsement of the neuropsychological approach is in order. The research discussed in this section provides illustrations of four kinds of contribution that neuropsychology can make to cognitive psychology:

1. It can permit us to study part of a complex system in relative isolation, as seems to be the case with deep dyslexia.
2. It can strengthen the evidential backing for theoretical formulations such as the dichotomy between short-term and long-term memory stores.
3. It can weaken the standing of theories in cognitive psychology by producing embarassing new findings; as happened with Paivio's (1971) dual-coding hypothesis.
4. It can lead to the discovery of theoretically significant phenomena, as in the case of successful learning in the absence of any conscious recollection of learning having occurred.

This diversity of benefits accruing from the neuropsychological approach in a relatively short period of time suggests strongly that it will have much to offer cognitive psychology in the future.

ARTIFICIAL INTELLIGENCE AND COMPUTATION

Cognitive psychologists have for many years made explicit or implicit use of the computer analogy in the construction of their theories. It is typical in computer systems to distinguish between an active processor and passive information storage, and the distinction is reflected in that between short-term and long-term storage. In similar fashion, most computers have a central processor of limited capacity, and this notion has been incorporated fairly directly into theories of attention. Recently, there have been attempts to extend and develop this computer analogy by writing programmes that enable computers to perform various tasks that apparently mirror the behaviour of people performing the same tasks. During the course of this book we have discussed a number of such computational theories, including Marr's theory of perception (Chapter 2), Kosslyn's imagery theory (Chapter 7), and Newell and Simon's General Problem Solver and Johnson-Laird's theory of mental models (Chapter 10).

There have been diverse reactions to the growth of artificial intelligence. Some have merely sneered at practitioners in this area, dismissing them as an "artificial intelligentsia" determined to avoid studying what is natural and human. Others have been markedly more enthusiastic, none more so than Allport (1980): "The advent of Artificial Intelligence is the single most important development in the history of psychology [p. 31]." The writer's own opinion of the potential value of artificial intelligence falls between these two extremes, perhaps closer to that of the enthusiasts than the critics.

What grounds do we have for supposing that people and computers function in broadly similar ways? Some plausible reasons were discussed by Simon (1980), who claimed that people and computers are both symbol systems that symbolise external and internal events, and then manipulate the resultant symbols. In addition, human information-processing and computer systems possess the property of being nearly decomposable, i.e., the rate of interaction between different components of the system is much smaller than the rate of intra-component interaction. As a result of these, and other, similarities, Simon (1980) was in no doubt about the resemblance between computer and human functioning:

> It might have been necessary a decade ago to argue for the commonality of the information processes that are employed by such disparate systems as computers and human nervous sytems. The evidence for that commonality is now overwhelming, and the remaining questions about the boundaries of cognitive science have more to do with information processing in genetic systems than with whether men and machines both think [p. 45].

In spite of the various similarities between human and computer functioning, it is important to note that there are also a number of major differences. Firstly, as Norman (1980) pointed out, human functioning can be regarded as dependent on an interplay of a cognitive system (which he calls the Pure Cognitive System) and a biological system (which he terms the Regulatory System). Much of the activity of the Pure Cognitive System is determined by the various needs of the Regulatory System, including the need for survival, for food and water, and for protection of oneself and one's family. Artificial intelligence, in common with most cognitive psychology, focuses on the Pure Cognitive System and virtually ignores the key role played by the Regulatory System. Secondly, and related to the first point, computers differ from people in that they do not possess any intrinsic purposes of their own. Thirdly, while it is indisputably the case that people have conscious awareness of many external and internal events, it seems improbable that computers are consciously aware of their own functioning.

It is a matter of continuing controversy whether these dissimilarities between people and computers are of sufficient magnitude to invalidate the computational approach. Of course, it is well known that all analogies break down at some point, and this does not prevent many analogies from proving extremely fruitful. However, the failures of the computer analogy described above seem potentially rather serious.

If we are prepared to assume that the computer analogy is a useful one, then the discovery (e.g., Newell & Simon, 1972) that computer programs can mimic the performance of people on several different tasks is an exciting one. However, there has been some disagreement about the status of such programs. Can they be regarded as psychological theories? Not really, because some of the ingredients of a complex computer program will simply reflect the constraints or idiosyncracies of a particular programming language, and will thus lack any true theoretical significance. Even if a program in artificial intelligence is not a theory *per se*, it can nevertheless possess a certain amount of theoretical relevance. The actual status of such programs was described in the following terms by Winograd (1977):

> If I have a complete blueprint for a complex mechanical device, it is not a "theory" of how that device works. But it would be foolish not to see a blueprint as a valuable part of an "explanation" of that device. Similarly, a program which completely duplicated the processes of human language use would still not be a theory. But any program which is built can be viewed as an hypothesised partial blueprint and can be a step towards understanding [p. 172].

In view of the status of computer programs, it can be difficult to know exactly what to do when a program produces an output that differs from human performance. The discrepancy may result from an inaccuracy in one or more of the central assumptions embodied in the program, in which case the problem is serious, or the discrepancy may be due to features of the computer having little or no theoretical importance for psychologists, in which case the problem is relatively trivial. The components of a computer program often interact with each other in complex ways, and so it is sometimes quite difficult to identify which particular assumption of the programmer is in error.

It is still early days to attempt an evaluation of the artificial intelligence approach. However, there are various indications that this approach can make a significant contribution to our understanding of cognition. A key characteristic of artificial intelligence is that the writing of a computer program requires explicit assumptions about all of the detailed processes involved in producing a particular kind of output. This precision is typically absent from traditional cognitive psychology, in which intractable problems have often been ignored. An extreme example of this is the multi-store model, in which there are three kinds of memory store (see Chapter 4). As information moves from one store to another it is transformed out of all recognition, and these mysterious transformations are mainly "explained" by inserting arrows pointing from one store to the next! Any systematic attempt to write computer programs based on the theoretical assumptions of multi-store theorists would rapidly have discovered these deficiencies.

A good example of how the computational approach can rectify such problems was discussed in Chapter 2. Marr initially found that previous assumptions about feature detectors in visual perception were inadequate by writing computer programs. Subsequently, he was able to use the computational approach to produce more complex programs that specified precisely how feature extraction might occur. In other words, artificial intelligence can be useful in two related ways: (1) by discovering the existence of previously unsuspected theoretical lacunae; and (2) by extending theoretical thinking to fill the gaps.

A further apparent advantage of the computational approach is that the emphasis is on the potential implications of various combinations of assumptions about processes and representations. This emphasis is obviously very theoretical, and sometimes leads workers in artificial intelligence to hold experimental data in rather low esteem. While such denigration of empirical research cannot be justified, there are significant advantages in a rather top-down approach as opposed to the bottom-up approach of much cognitive psychology. For example, artificial intelligence largely escapes the criticisms of cognitive psychology that it is phenomenon-driven (Newell, 1973) and obsessed by trivial experimental findings.

A final potential advantage of the artificial intelligence approach was emphasised by Allport (1979). He argued that the serial processing model favoured by many cognitive psychologists is unduly restrictive, and that artificial intelligence offers attractive alternative conceptualisations. Production systems are a case in point. A production system consists of a set of rules or productions and a data base. Each production consists of an action and of a condition for performing that action, and any complex system comprises a large number of such productions. In contrast, the data base corresponds to a working memory system (see Chapter 4), and the condition of each production is evaluated against the current contents of the data base. The details of different production systems vary, but a common principle is the combination of great parallelism via numerous independent productions and central integration represented by a data base that handles all integrative processes.

It is certainly true that production systems can be very powerful. A program known as DENDRAL (Nii & Feigenbaum, 1977) is written in the form of a production system, and is able to perform better than post-doctoral chemists in mass spectrometry. Modification of such systems is easily achieved, because all that is required is the substitution of a new production for an old one. The fact that the various productions are nearly independent means that changes in one production are unlikely to require compensating changes elsewhere in the system.

In sum, there are various reasons for arguing that artificial intelligence will ultimately make a significant contribution to cognitive psychology. Almost certainly it is unduly optimistic to claim (as proponents of artificial intelligence have done) that the relationship of artificial intelligence to traditional cognitive psychology is the same as that of astronomy to astrology. However, exciting developments may be on the way, especially if closer links can be forged between the theoretical tools of artificial intelligence and the rich experimental data provided by cognitive psychologists.

APPLIED COGNITIVE PSYCHOLOGY

Most of the research on cognitive psychology has been conducted under standard laboratory conditions, and the coverage in this book reflects that fact. However, as was stated earlier in this chapter, there are many psychologists who are critical of the laboratory-based approach on the grounds of its apparent artificiality and narrowness. Harré (1974) has gone further, describing the experimentalist as "tragically deceived," and arguing that, "experiments are largely worthless, except as descriptions of the odd way people carry on trying to make social sense out of the impoverished environments of laboratories [p. 146]."

Of course, there is another, more applied, tradition in cognitive psychology, many of the more interesting practical applications of which have been discussed in this book. There is no doubt that cognitive psychologists are increasingly concerned that their work should have relevance to cognition in everyday life. This work frequently takes the form of relatively naturalistic research carried out in "real-life" settings. Such an approach has a clear advantage over much laboratory experimentation in terms of realism, but often suffers from a lack of experimental rigour.

However, realism is by no means the only criterion that should be used when evaluating laboratory research. It should be obvious that laboratory-based research does not consist merely of more or less successful attempts to mimic aspects of everyday cognitive functioning. Amongst other uses of laboratory research, there is its use as a means of investigating theoretically interesting phenomena that for one reason or another could never be observed in every day life. This point was developed at some length by Henshel (1980), who gave as an example the well-known research into apes' ability to master sign language (see Chapter 8).

There are additional reasons why the artificiality of laboratory research is often advantageous. It may be possible to obtain support for a theoretical principle under the controlled conditions of the laboratory, but much more difficult (or even impossible) to do so under naturalistic conditions. While psychologists often regard this problem as unique to psychology, it is common to most scientific endeavours. For example, a physicist may have a profound understanding of the principles of heat and be able to demonstrate their validity in well-controlled conditions, and yet he or she may well be unable to apply those principles successfully to the task of predicting the temperature inside a particular room.

To some extent, the dichotomy between laboratory and "real-life" research is an artificial one. There are many cases in which research was carried out under standard laboratory conditions, but was nevertheless directly relevant to real-life concerns. One particularly good example of this is the work of Loftus and her colleagues on eyewitness testimony (see Chapter 5). She demonstrated in the laboratory that the recollections of eyewitnesses can be systematically distorted by leading questions asked after the event in question has been witnessed. Such research successfully straddles the divide between the laboratory and everyday life, since it is relevant to theories of memory representation, and to practical matters regarding police procedures.

The broad issue of whether our understanding of human cognition will benefit more from laboratory research or applied research seems to the author to be one that has no definite answer. The most fruitful strategy will probably involve both kinds of research being carried out concurrently, with the results of such research being compared and then (with luck) integrated. Laboratory research has in the past suffered in various ways from its failure to relate its findings adequately to everyday life:

1. What is studied may be of little relevance to ordinary human functioning. A clear case in point was the dominance of learning theory and its conditioning principles in the experimental psychology of the 1930s, 1940s, and 1950s. As Neisser (1978) pointed out, the notion that the learning abilities of the white rat can provide a satisfactory basis for understanding learning in general was weakened greatly by the ethologists. They studied animals in their natural habitats, and discovered that each and every species differs markedly in its range of learning abilities, and in those aspects of the environment to which it is especially sensitive.

2. Laboratory research has very often ignored important characteristics of the cognition of everyday life. For example, it is true of nearly all laboratory studies of memory that the experimenter provides explicit cues at the time of the retention test. In everyday life, by contrast, people often have to cue themselves to do something at a particular time (e.g., make a telephone call, take a pill). In other words, it is a matter of remembering *when* rather than *what*. Suggestive evidence that these kinds of memory may be quite different was obtained by Wilkins and Baddeley (1978). They discovered that those who did well on a free recall task were actually significantly worse than those who did poorly on the same recall task, at remembering to press a button at pre-specified times of day.

3. At least some laboratory findings may not extrapolate to "real-life" because of the artificiality of the laboratory situation. An interesting case in point is a recent study by Anderson and Brown (personal communication) on gambling. Nearly all laboratory studies of gambling have involved some

kind of artificial task, but Anderson and Brown attempted to make their "artificial casino" as realistic as possible by means of real chips, dim lights, a green table, soft music, a real casino shoe, and a real croupier. They compared the performance of experienced gamblers playing blackjack in this artificial casino and in a real casino. The increase in heart rate was more than three times as great in the real situation as in the artificial situation, and the betting strategies were quite different (e.g., bigger risks tended to be taken when behind in the artificial casino, but when ahead in the real casino). In other words, the comparison between gambling behaviour in the "real" world and in the laboratory sheds considerable doubt on the value of previous laboratory work.

There are other reasons why laboratory findings may not be readily replicated under more naturalistic conditions. Laboratory experimentation permits a degree of control over extraneous and confounding variables that is nearly always absent from the "real" world, and this difference in control means that only relatively large effects from the laboratory will be consistently obtainable in everyday life.

In sum, there is every likelihood that a cross-fertilisation between the laboratory and the more applied concerns of everyday life will prove of considerable ultimate value. Such a cross-fertilisation reduces the chances that cognitive psychologists will focus on trivial problems that have no potential social relevance, and it also provides the cognitive psychologist with additional data from naturalistic settings that can inform theoretical developments. What we are talking about is a wedding of insufficiencies: When the realistic but relatively contaminated data of everyday life are consistent with the somewhat artificial but pure data of the laboratory, then we may be reasonably confident that progress is being made.

CONCLUSIONS

It should have become apparent from reading this chapter that cognitive psychology is currently in a state of flux. There are significant differences between cognitive psychologists as to the most fruitful approach that should be taken when studying human cognition. Three approaches that may hold the key to the future have been discussed in this chapter: the neuropsychological, artificial intelligence, and applied approaches. The empirical evidence to date indicates that each approach has a positive contribution to make. Moreover, the advantages of each approach seem rather different, so that it makes sense to regard the approaches as complementary rather than directly competitive with each other. Obviously, the fact that various new avenues of potential expansion are being developed suggests that reports of the imminent demise of cognitive psychology are greatly exaggerated.

My own feeling about the future course of cognitive psychology is that there must be increased emphasis on the ways in which cognition, motivation, and emotion interact in human cognitive functioning. The research discussed in Chapter 12 (usually completely ignored in textbooks on cognitive psychology) indicates that cognitive functioning is altered in a number of systematic ways by the individual's motivational and emotional states, but work in this area is clearly in its infancy. Apart from the obvious relevance of such research to everyday cognition, it would be of great value to know and understand the optimal motivational and emotional conditions for different kinds of cognitive performance.

While the emphasis has been on the effects of motivation and emotion on cognitive functioning, we also need to consider the effects of cognitive processes on motivational and emotional states. Only when we have a theoretical understanding of the interplay of cognition, motivation, and emotion will a complete psychology of cognition, that will apply both inside and outside the laboratory, be a realistic possibility.

References

Allport, D. A. (1975) The state of cognitive psychology. *Quarterly Journal of Experimental Psychology, 27*, 141–152.

Allport, D. A. (1979) Conscious and unconscious cognition: A computational metaphor for the mechanism of attention and integration. In L.-G. Nilsson (Ed.), *Perspectives on Memory Research: Essays in Honor of Uppsala University's 500th Anniversary*. Hillsdale, N.J.: Lawrence Erlbaum Associates Inc.

Allport, D. A. (1980) Attention and performance. In G. Claxton (Ed.), *Cognitive Psychology: New Directions*. London: Routledge & Kegan Paul.

Allport, D. A., Antonis, B., & Reynolds, P. (1972) On the division of attention: A disproof of the single channel hypothesis. *Quarterly Journal of Experimental Psychology, 24*, 225–235.

Anderson, J. R. (1976) *Language, Memory, and Thought*. Hillsdale, N.J.: Lawrence Erlbaum Associates Inc.

Anderson, J. R. (1978) Arguments concerning representations for mental imagery. *Psychological Review, 85*, 249–277.

Anderson, J. R. (1980) *Cognitive Psychology and its Implications*. San Francisco: W. H. Freeman.

Anderson, J. R., & Bower, G. H. (1972) Recognition and retrieval processes in free recall. *Psychological Review, 79*, 97–123.

Anderson, J. R., & Bower, G. H. (1974) A propositional theory of recognition memory. *Memory & Cognitive, 2*, 406–412.

Anderson, J. R., & Reder, L. M. (1979) An elaborative processing explanation of depth of processing. In L. S. Cermak, & F. I. M. Craik (Eds.), *Levels of Processing in Human Memory*. Hillsdale, N.J.: Lawrence Erlbaum Associates Inc.

Anderson, R. C., & Pichert, J. W. (1978) Recall of previously unrecallable information following a shift in perspective. *Journal of Verbal Learning and Verbal Behavior, 17*, 1–12.

Anderson, R. C., & Watts, G. H. (1971) Response competition in the forgetting of paired-associates. *Journal of Verbal Learning and Verbal Behavior, 10*, 29–34.

Anzai, Y., & Simon, H. A. (1979) The theory of learning by doing. *Psychological Review, 86*, 124–140.

Arbib, M. A., Caplan, D., & Marshall, J. C. (1982) *Neural Models of Language Processes*. London: Academic Press.

Atkinson, R. C., & Juola, J. F. (1974) Search and decision processes in recognition memory. In D. H. Krantz, R. C. Atkinson, & P. Suppes (Eds.), *Contemporary Developments in Mathematical Psychology*. London: W. H. Freeman.

Atkinson, R. C., & Raugh, M. R. (1975) An application of the mnemonic keyword method to the acquisition of a Russian vocabulary. *Journal of Experimental Psychology: Human Learning and Memory, 104*, 126–133.

377

Atkinson, R. C., & Shiffrin, R. M. (1968) Human memory: A proposed system and its control processes. In K. W. Spence, & J. T. Spence (Eds.), *The Psychology of Learning and Motivation, Vol. 2.* London: Academic Press.

Atkinson, R. C., & Shiffrin, R. M. (1971) The control of short-term memory. *Scientific American, 225,* 82–90.

Attneave, F. (1954) Some informational aspects of visual perception. *Psychological Review, 61,* 183–193.

Averbach, E., & Coriell, E. (1961) Short-term memory in vision. *Bell System Technical Journal, 40,* 309–328.

Baddeley, A. D. (1976) *The Psychology of Memory.* New York: Basic Books.

Baddeley, A. D. (1979) Working memory and reading. In P. A. Kolers, M. E. Wrolstad, & H. Bouma (Eds.), *Processing of Visible Language.* New York: Plenum.

Baddeley, A. D. (1981) Reading and working memory. *Bulletin of the British Psychological Society, 35,* 414–417.

Baddeley, A. D. (1982) Domains of recollection. *Psychological Review, 89,* 708–729.

Baddeley, A. D., & Ecob, J. R. (1973) Reaction time and short-term memory: Implications of repetition effects for the high-speed exhaustive scan hypothesis. *Quarterly Journal of Experimental Psychology, 25,* 229–240.

Baddeley, A. D., Eldridge, M., & Lewis, V. J. (1981) The role of subvocalisation in reading. *Quarterly Journal of Experimental Psychology, 33A,* 439–454.

Baddeley, A. D., Grant, S., Wight, E., & Thomson, N. (1975) Imagery and visual working memory. In P. M. A. Rabbitt, & S. Dornic (Eds.), *Attention and Performance, Vol. V.* London: Academic Press.

Baddeley, A. D., & Hitch, G. (1974) Working memory. In G. H. Bower (Ed.), *The Psychology of Learning and Motivation, Vol. 8.* London: Academic Press.

Baddeley, A. D., & Lewis, V. J. (1981) Inner active processes in reading: The inner voice, the inner ear, and the inner eye. In A. M. Lesgold, & C. A. Perfetti (Eds.), *Interactive Processes in Reading.* Hillsdale, N.J.: Lawrence Erlbaum Associates Inc.

Baddeley, A. D., & Lieberman, K. (1980) Spatial working memory. In R. S. Nickerson (Ed.), *Attention and Performance, Vol. VIII.* Hillsdale, N.J.: Lawrence Erlbaum Associates Inc.

Baddeley, A. D., Thomson, N., & Buchanan, M. (1975) Word length and the structure of short-term memory. *Journal of Verbal Learning and Verbal Behavior, 14,* 575–589.

Baddeley, A. D., & Warrington, E. K. (1970) Amnesia and the distinction between long- and short-term memory. *Journal of Verbal Learning and Verbal Behavior, 9,* 176–189.

Bahrick, H. P. (1970) Two-phase model for prompted recall. *Psychological Review, 77,* 215–222.

Bahrick, H. P. (1979) Broader methods and narrower theories for memory research: Comments on the papers by Eysenck and Cermak. In L. S. Cermak, & F. I. M. Craik (Eds.), *Levels of Processing in Human Memory.* Hillsdale, N.J.: Lawrence Erlbaum Associates Inc.

Banks, W. P., & Atkinson, R. C. (1974) Accuracy and speed strategies in scanning active memory. *Memory & Cognition, 2,* 629–636.

Barclay, J. R., Bransford, J. D., Franks, J. J., McCarrell, N. S., & Nitsch, K. E. (1974) Comprehension and semantic flexibility. *Journal of Verbal Learning and Verbal Behavior, 13,* 471–481.

Barnes, J. M., & Underwood, B. J. (1959) "Fate" of first-list associations in transfer theory. *Journal of Experimental Psychology, 58,* 97–105.

Baron, J. (1973) Phonemic stage not necessary for reading. *Quarterly Journal of Experimental Psychology, 25,* 241–246.

Bartlett, F. C. (1932) *Remembering: A Study in Experimental and Social Psychology.* Cambridge: Cambridge University Press.

Bartley, S. H. (1969) *Principles of Perception.* London: Harper & Row.

Bavelas, J., & Lee, E. S. (1978) Effects of goal level on performance: A trade-off of quantity and quality. *Canadian Journal of Psychology, 32*, 219–240.

Beck, J. (1966) Perceptual grouping produced by changes in orientation and shape. *Science, 154*, 538–540.

Bellezza, F. S., Cheesman, F. L. & Reddy, B. G. (1977) Organisation and semantic elaboration in free recall. *Journal of Experimental Psychology: Human Learning and Memory, 3*, 539–550.

Berlyne, D. E. (1960) *Conflict, Arousal, and Curiosity.* London: McGraw-Hill.

Berzonsky, M. (1971) The role of familiarity in children's explanations of physical causality. *Child Development, 42*, 705–715.

Besner, D., & Davelaar, E. (1982) Basic processes in reading: Two phonological codes. *Canadian Journal of Psychology, 36*, 701–711.

Black, H. C. (1951) *Black's Law Dictionary.* St. Paul, Minn.: West Publishing.

Black, J. B. (1981) The effects of reading purpose on memory for text. In J. Long, & A. Baddeley (Eds.), *Attention and Performance, Vol. IX.* Hillsdale, N.J.: Lawrence Erlbaum Associates Inc.

Blake, M. (1973) Prediction of recognition when recall fails: Exploring the feeling-of-knowing phenomenon. *Journal of Verbal Learning and Verbal Behavior, 12*, 311–319.

Bolton, N. (1972) *The Psychology of Thinking.* London: Methuen.

Boomer, D. (1965) Hesitation and grammatical encoding. *Language and Speech, 8*, 145–158.

Borgida, E., & Nisbett, R. E. (1977) The differential impact of abstract vs. concrete information on decisions. *Journal of Applied Social Psychology, 7*, 258–271.

Bower, G. H. (1972) Mental imagery and associative learning. In L. Gregg (Ed.), *Cognition in Learning and Memory.* New York: Wiley.

Bower, G. H. (1973) How to... Uh... remember! *Psychology Today, 7*, 63–70.

Bower, G. H., Black, J. B., & Turner, T. J. (1979) Scripts in memory for text. *Cognitive Psychology, 11*, 177–220.

Bower, G. H., & Clark, M. C. (1969) Narrative stories as mediators for serial learning. *Psychonomic Science, 14*, 181–182.

Bower, G. H., Monteiro, K. P., & Gilligan, S. G. (1978) Emotional mood as a context for learning and recall. *Journal of Verbal Learning and Verbal Behavior, 17*, 573–585.

Bower, G. H., & Trabasso, T. (1963) Reversals prior to solution in concept identification. *Journal of Experimental Psychology, 66*, 409–418.

Bower, G. H., & Trabasso, T. (1964) Presolution reversal and dimensional shifts in concept identification. *Journal of Experimental Psychology, 67*, 398–399.

Bower, G. H., & Winzenz, D. (1969) Group structure, coding and memory for digit series. *Journal of Experimental Psychology Monograph, 80* (No. 2, Pt. 2), 1–17.

Bower, T. G. R. (1964) Discrimination of depth in premotor infants. *Psychonomic Science, 1*, 368.

Bower, T. G. R. (1965) Slant perception and shape constancy in infants. *Science, 151*, 832–834.

Bower, T. G. R. (1973) *Development in Infancy.* San Francisco: W. H. Freeman.

Bower, T. G. R., Broughton, J. M., & Moore, M. K. (1970) The coordination of visual and tactual input in infants. *Perception & Psychophysics, 8*, 51–53.

Bower, T. G. R., & Wishart, J. G. (1972) The effects of motor skill on object permanence. *Cognition, 1*, 165–172.

Bransford, J. D. (1979) *Human Cognition: Learning, Understanding and Remembering,* Belmont, Calif.: Wadsworth.

Bransford, J. D., Barclay, J. R., & Franks, J. J. (1972) Sentence memory: A constructive versus interpretive approach. *Cognitive Psychology, 3*, 193–209.

Bransford, J. D., Franks, J. J., Morris, C. D., & Stein, B. S. (1979) Some general comments on learning and memory research. In L. S. Cermak, & F. I. M. Craik (Eds.), *Levels of Processing in Human Memory*. Hillsdale, N.J.: Lawrence Erlbaum Associates Inc.

Bransford, J. D., & Johnson, M. K. (1972) Contextual prerequisites for understanding: Some investigations of comprehension and recall. *Journal of Verbal Learning and Verbal Behavior, 11*, 717–726.

Bransford, J. D., McCarrell, N. S., Franks, J. J., & Nitsch, K. E. (1977) Toward unexplaining memory. In R. Shaw, & J. D. Bransford (Eds.), *Perceiving, Acting, and Knowing*. Hillsdale, N.J.: Lawrence Erlbaum Associates Inc.

Brewer, W. F. (1974) The problem of meaning and the interrelations of the higher mental processes. In W. Weimer, & D. S. Palermo (Eds.), *Cognition and the Symbolic Processes*. Hillsdale, N.J.: Lawrence Erlbaum Associates Inc.

Broadbent, D. E. (1958) *Perception and Communication*. Oxford: Pergamon.

Broadbent, D. E. (1971) *Decision and Stress*. London: Academic Press.

Broadbent, D. E. (1978) The current state of noise research: Reply to Poulton. *Psychological Bulletin, 85*, 1052–1067.

Broadbent, D. E. (1982) Task combination and selective intake of information. *Acta Psychologica, 50*, 253–290.

Broadbent, D. E., & Broadbent, M. H. P. (1975) The recognition of words which cannot be recalled. In P. M. A. Rabbitt, & S. Dornic (Eds.), *Attention and Performance, Vol. V*. London: Academic Press.

Brown, R., Cazden, C. B., & Bellugi, U. (1969) The child's grammar from I to III. In J. P. Hill (Ed.), *Minnesota Symposium on Child Psychology, Vol. 2*. Minneapolis: University of Minnesota Press.

Brown, R., & McNeill, D. (1966) The 'tip of the tongue' phenomenon. *Journal of Verbal Learning and Verbal Behavior, 5*, 325–337.

Brown, R. W., & Lenneberg, E. H. (1954) A study in language and cognition. *Journal of Abnormal and Social Psychology, 49*, 454–462.

Bruce, D. J., Evans, C. R., Fenwick, P. B. C., & Spencer, V. (1970) Effect of presenting novel verbal material during slow-wave sleep. *Nature, 225* 873–874.

Bruner, J. S. (1957) On perceptual readiness. *Psychological Review, 64*, 123–152.

Bruner, J. S. (1974) From communication to language—A psychological perspective. *Cognition, 3*, 255–287.

Bruner, J. S. (1975) The ontogenesis of speech acts. *Journal of Child Language, 2*, 1–19.

Bruner, J. S., Goodnow, J. J., & Austin, G. A. (1956) *A Study of Thinking*. New York: Wiley.

Bruner, J. S., Olver, R. R., & Greenfield, P. M. (1966) *Studies in Cognitive Growth*. New York: Wiley.

Bruner, J. S., & Postman, L. (1949) On the perception of incongruity: A paradigm. *Journal of Personality, 18*, 206–223,

Bruning, J. L., Capage, J. E., Kozul, G. F., Young, P. F., & Young, W. E. (1968) Socially induced drive and range of cue utilisation. *Journal of Personality and Social Psychology, 9*, 242–244.

Bruno, K. J. (1980) Discrimination of assertions and implications: A training procedure for adults and adolescents. *Journal of Educational Psychology, 72*, 850–860.

Bryant, P. (1982) The role of conflict and of agreement between intellectual strategies in children's ideas about measurement. *British Journal of Psychology, 73*, 243–251.

Bryant, P. E., & Trabasso, T. (1971) Transitive inferences and memory in young children. *Nature, 232*, 456–458.

Burns, B., Shepp, B. E., McDonough, D., & Wiener-Ehrlich, W. (1978) The relation between stimulus analysability and perceived dimensional structure. In G. H. Bower (Ed.), *The Psychology of Learning and Motivation*, Vol. 12. London: Academic Press.

Butler, B. E. (1974) The limits of selective attention in tachistoscopic recognition. *Canadian Journal of Psychology, 28,* 199–213.

Butterworth, G. (1974) *The development of the object concept in human infants.* Unpublished Ph.D. thesis, University of Oxford.

Butterworth, G., & Jarrett, N. (1982) Piaget's stage 4 error: Background to the problem. *British Journal of Psychology, 73,* 175–185.

Butterworth, G. E., Jarrett, N., & Hicks, L. (1982) Spatiotemporal identity in infancy: Perceptual competence or conceptual deficit? *Developmental Psychology, 18,* 435–449.

Byrne, R. W. (1979) Memory for urban geography. *Quarterly Journal of Experimental Psychology, 31,* 147–154.

Calder, B. J., & Staw, B. M. (1975) Self-perception of intrinsic and extrinsic motivation. *Journal of Personality and Social Psychology, 31,* 599–605.

Caplan, D. (1972) Clause boundaries and recognition latencies for words in sentences. *Perception & Psychophysics, 12,* 73–76.

Capretta, P. J., & Berkun, M. (1962) Validity and reliability of certain measures of psychological stress. *Psychological Reports, 10,* 875–878.

Carpenter, P. A., & Eisenberg, P. (1978) Mental rotation and the frame of reference in blind and sighted individuals. *Perception & Psychophysics, 23,* 117–124.

Carpenter, P. A., & Just, M. A. (1975) Sentence comprehension: a psycholinguistic processing model of verification. *Psychological Review, 82,* 45–73.

Ceraso, J., & Provitera, A. (1971) Sources of error in syllogistic reasoning. *Cognitive Psychology, 2,* 400–410.

Cermak, L. S. (1979) Amnesic patients' level of processing. In L. S. Cermak and F. I. M. Craik (Eds.), *Levels of Processing in Human Memory.* Hillsdale, N.J.: Lawrence Erlbaum Associates Inc.

Cermak, L. S., & Moreines, J. (1976) Verbal retention deficits in aphasic and amnesic patients. *Brain and Language, 3,* 16–27.

Cermak, L. S., & Reale, L. (1978) Depth of processing and retention of words by alcoholic Korsakoff patients. *Journal of Experimental Psychology: Human Learning and Memory, 4,* 165–174.

Chapman, L. J., & Chapman, J. P. (1959) Atmosphere effect re-examined. *Journal of Experimental Psychology, 58,* 220–226.

Cherry, E. C. (1953) Some experiments on the recognition of speech with one and two ears. *Journal of the Acoustical Society of America, 25,* 975–979.

Chi, M. T. (1978) Knowledge, structure and memory development. In R. S. Siegler (Ed.), *Children's Thinking. What Develops?* Hillsdale, N.J.: Lawrence Erlbaum. Associates Inc.

Chomsky, N. (1957) *Syntactic Structures.* The Hague: Mouton.

Chomsky, N. (1959) Review of "Verbal Behaviour" by Skinner. *Language, 35,* 26–58.

Chomsky, N. (1965) *Aspects of the Theory of Syntax.* Cambridge, Mass.: MIT Press.

Chomsky, N. (1980) *Rules and Representations.* New York: Columbia University Press.

Clarapède, E. (1911) Récognition et moiité. *Archives de Psychologie, 11,* 75–90.

Clark, H. H. (1969) Linguistic processes in deductive reasoning. *Psychological Review, 76,* 387–404.

Clark, H. H., & Carlson, T. B. (1981) Context for comprehension. In J. Long, & A. Baddeley (Eds.), *Attention and Performance. Vol. IX.* Hillsdale, N.J.: Lawrence Erlbaum Associates Inc.

Clark, H. H., & Chase, W. G. (1972) On the process of comparing sentences against pictures. *Cognitive Psychology, 3,* 472–517.

Clark, H. H., & Clark, E. V. (1977) *Psychology and Language.* New York: Harcourt Brace.

Clark, H. H., & Haviland, S. E. (1977) Comprehension and the given-new contract. In R.O.

Freedle (Ed.), *Discourse Processes: Advances in Research and Theory, Vol. 1*. Norwood, N.J.: Ablex.

Clark, H. H., & Lucy, P. (1975) Understanding what is meant from what is said: A study in conversationally conveyed requests. *Journal of Verbal Learning and Verbal Behavior, 14,* 56–72.

Claxton, G. (1980) Cognitive psychology: A suitable case for what sort of treatment? In G. Claxton (Ed.), *Cognitive Psychology: New Directions*. London: Routledge & Kegan Paul.

Cohen, G. (1977) *The Psychology of Cognition*. London: Academic Press.

Collins, A. M., & Loftus, E. F. (1975) A spreading-activation theory of semantic processing. *Psychological Review, 82,* 407–428.

Collins, A. M., & Quillian, M. R. (1969) Retrieval time from semantic memory. *Journal of Verbal Learning and Verbal Behavior, 8,* 240–248.

Collins, A. M., & Quillian, M. R. (1970) Does category size affect categorisation time? *Journal of Verbal Learning and Verbal Behavior, 9,* 432–438.

Collins, A., & Gentner, D. (1980) A framework for a cognitive theory of writing. In L. W. Gregg, & E. R. Sternberg (Eds.), *Cognitive Processes in Writing*. Hillsdale, N.J.: Lawrence Erlbaum Associates Inc.

Coltheart, M. (1978) Lexical access in simple reading tasks. In G. Underwood (Ed.), *Strategies of Information Processing*. London: Academic Press.

Coltheart, M. (1980) The semantic error: Types and theories. In M. Coltheart, K. Patterson, & J. C. Marshall (Eds.), *Deep Dyslexia*. London: Routledge & Kegan Paul.

Coltheart, M. (1983) Ecological necessity of iconic memory. *The Behavioral and Brain Sciences, 6,* 17–18.

Coltheart, V. (1977) Recognition errors after incidental learning as a function of different levels of processing. *Journal of Experimental Psychology: Human Learning and Memory, 3,* 437–444.

Conrad, C. (1972) Cognitive economy in semantic memory. *Journal of Experimental Psychology, 92,* 149–154.

Conrad, R., & Hull, A. J. (1964) Information, acoustic confusion and memory span. *British Journal of Psychology, 55,* 429–432.

Cooper, W. E., & Ehrlich, S. F. (1981) Planning speech: Studies in choice reaction time. In J. Long, & A. Baddeley (Eds.), *Attention and Performance, Vol. IX*. Hillsdale, N.J.: Lawrence Erlbaum Associates Inc.

Cooper, L. A., & Shepard, R. N. (1973) Chronometric studies of the rotation of mental images. In W. G. Chase (Ed.), *Visual Information Processing*. London: Academic Press.

Corballis, M. C. (1975) Access to memory: An analysis of recognition time. In P. M. A. Rabbitt, & S. Dornic (Eds.), *Attention and Performance, Vol. V*. London: Academic Press.

Corcoran, D. W. J. (1962) Noise and loss of sleep. *Quarterly Journal of Experimental Psychology, 14,* 178–182.

Corkin, S. (1968) Acquisition of motor skill after bilateral medial temporal-lobe excision. *Neuropsychologia, 6,* 255–265.

Corrigan, R. (1978) Language development as related to stage 6 object permanence development. *Journal of Child Language, 5,* 173–189.

Condry, J. (1977) Enemies of exploration: Self-initiated versus other initiated learning. *Journal of Personality and Social Psychology, 35,* 459–477.

Corteen, R. S., & Dunn, D. (1974) Shock-associated words in a non-attended message: A test for momentary awareness. *Journal of Experimental Psychology, 102,* 1143–1144.

Craig, M. J., Humphreys, M. S., Rocklin, T., & Revelle, W. (1979) Impulsivity, neuroticism, and caffeine: Do they have additive effects on arousal? *Journal of Research in Personality, 13,* 404–419.

Craik, F. I. M. (1973) A "levels of analysis" view of memory. In P. Pliner, L. Krames, &

T. M. Alloway (Eds.), *Communication and Affect: Language and Thought*. London: Academic Press.

Craik, F. I. M., & Lockhart, R. S. (1972) Levels of processing: A framework for memory research. *Journal of Verbal Learning and Verbal Behavior, 11*, 671–684.

Craik, F. I. M., & Tulving, E. (1975) Depth of processing and the retention of words in episodic memory. *Journal of Experimental Psychology: General, 104*, 268–294.

Cromer, R. F. (1974) The development of language and cognition: The cognition hypothesis. In B. M. Foss (Ed.), *New Perspectives in Child Development*. Harmondsworth, England: Penguin.

Crowder, R. G. (1982) The demise of short-term memory. *Acta Psychologica, 50*, 291–323.

Cuvo, A. J. (1975) Developmental differences in rehearsal and free recall. *Journal of Experimental Child Psychology, 19*, 265–278.

Daneman, M., & Carpenter, P. A. (1980) Individual differences in working memory and reading. *Journal of Verbal Learning and Verbal Behavior, 19*, 450–466.

Darwin, C. J., Turvey, M. T., & Crowder, R. G. (1972) An auditory analogue of the Sperling partial report procedure: Evidence for brief auditory storage. *Cognitive Psychology, 3*, 255–267.

Day, R. H. (1980) Visual illusions. In M. A. Jeeves (Ed.), *Psychology Survey*, No. 3. London: Allen & Unwin.

Deci, E. L. (1971) Effects of externally mediated rewards on intrinsic motivation. *Journal of Personality and Social Psychology, 18*, 105–115.

Deci, E. L. (1975) *Intrinsic Motivation*. London: Plenum.

Deese, J. (1978) Thought into speech. *American Scientist, 66*, 314–321.

Deffenbacher, J. L. 1978) Worry, emotionality, and task-generated interference in test anxiety: An empirical test of attentional theory. *Journal of Educational Psychology, 70*, 248–254.

De Groot, A. D. (1966) Perception and memory versus thought: Some old ideas and recent findings. In B. Kleinmuntz (Ed.), *Problem Solving*. New York: Wiley.

Deutsch, J. A., & Deutsch, D. (1963) Attention: Some theoretical considerations. *Psychological Review, 70*, 80–90.

De Valois, R. L., & Jacobs, F. H. (1968) Primate colour vision. *Science, 162*, 533–540.

Dixon, N. F. (1981) *Preconscious Processing*. London: Wiley.

Doctor, E. A., & Coltheart, M. (1980) Children's use of phonological encoding when reading for meaning. *Memory & Cognition, 8*, 195–209.

Doise, W., & Mugny, G. (1979) Individual and collective conflicts of centrations in cognitive development. *European Journal of Social Psychology, 9*, 105–108.

Donaldson, M. (1978) *Children's Minds*. New York: Norton.

Donaldson, M. (1982) Conservation: What is the question? *British Journal of Psychology, 73*, 199–207.

Donders, F. C. (1968) Over de snelheid van psychische processen. *Onderzoekingen gedaan in het Psyiologish Laboratorium der Utrechtsche Hoogeschool: Tweede Reeks, II*, 92–120.

Dornic, S. (1977) Mental load, effort, and individual differences. *Reports of the Department of Psychology, University of Stockholm*, No. 509.

Dornic, S. (1980) Efficiency vs. effectiveness in mental work: The differential effect of stress. *Reports from the Department of Psychology, University of Stockholm*, No. 568.

Dornic, S., & Fernaeus, S.-E. (1981) Individual differences in high-load tasks: The effect of verbal distraction. *Reports from the Department of Psychology, University of Stockholm*, No. 569.

Doyle, A. C. (1974) *The Memoirs of Sherlock Holmes*. London: John Murray & Jonathan Cape.

Drachman, D. A., & Arbit, J. (1966) Memory and the hippocampal complex. *Archives of Neurology, 15*, 52–61.

Dresher, B. E., & Hornstein, N. (1977) Reply to Winograd. *Cognition, 5*, 379–392.

Duncan, J. (1979) Divided attention: The whole is more than the sum of its parts. *Journal of Experimental Psychology: Human Perception, 5*, 216–228.

Duncker, K. (1945) On problem solving. *Psychological Monographs, 58*, No. 5 (Whole No. 270), 1–113.

Easterbrook, J. A (1959) The effect of emotion on cue utilisation and the organisation of behaviour. *Psychological Review, 66*, 183–201.

Eich, J. E. (1980) The cue-dependent nature of state-dependent retrieval. *Memory & Cognition, 8*, 157–173.

Ellis, N. C., & Miles, T. R. (1978) Visual information processing in dyslexic children. In M. M. Gruneberg, P. E. Morris, & R. N. Sykes (Eds.), *Practical Aspects of Memory*. London: Academic Press.

Ellis, R., & Wells, G. (1980) Enabling factors in adult-child discourse. *First Language, 1*, 46–62.

Emler, N., & Valiant, G. L. (1982) Social interaction and cognitive conflict in the development of spatial co-ordination skills. *British Journal of Psychology, 73*, 295–303.

Erdelyi, M. H. (1974) A new look at the new look: Perceptual defence and vigilance. *Psychological Review, 81*, 1–24.

Ericsson, K. A., & Simon, H. A. (1980) Verbal reports as data. *Psychological Review, 87*, 215–251.

Ernst, G. W., & Newell, A. (1969) *GPS: A Case Study in Generality and Problem Solving*. London: Academic Press.

Ervin-Tripp, S. (1964) An analysis of the interaction of language, topic and listener. *American Anthropologist, 66*, 94–100.

Evans, J. St. B. T. (1972) Interpretation and "matching bias" in a reasoning task. *Quarterly Journal of Experimental Psychology, 24*, 193–199.

Evans, J. St. B. T. (1982) *The Psychology of Deductive Reasoning*. London: Routledge & Kegan Paul.

Evans, J. St. B. T., & Lynch, J. S. (1973) Matching bias in the selection task. *British Journal of Psychology, 64*, 391–397.

Evans, J. St. B. T., & Wason, P. C. (1976) Rationalisation in a reasoning task. *British Journal of Psychology, 63*, 205–212.

Eysenck, H. J. (1964) *Experiments in Motivation*. Oxford: Pergamon.

Eysenck, H. J. (1967) *The Biological Basis of Personality*. Springfield, Ill.: Thomas.

Eysenck, H. J., & Gillan, P. W. (1964) Immediate memory (digit span) as a function of drive. In H. J. Eysenck (Ed.), *Experiments in Motivation*. Oxford: Pergamon.

Eysenck, M. W. (1972) *Conditions Modifying Memory: The von Restorff and "Release" Effects*. Unpublished Ph.D. thesis, University of London.

Eysenck, M. W. (1976) Arousal, learning, and memory. *Psychological Bulletin, 83*, 389–404.

Eysenck, M. W. (1977) *Human Memory: Theory, Research and Individual Differences*. Oxford: Pergamon.

Eysenck, M. W. (1978) Verbal remembering. In B. M. Foss (Ed.). *Psychology Survey, No. 1*. London: Allen & Unwin.

Eysenck, M. W. (1979a) Anxiety, learning, and memory: A reconceptualisation. *Journal of Research in Personality, 13*, 363–385.

Eysenck, M. W. (1979b) Depth, elaboration, and distinctiveness. In L. S. Cermak, & F. I. M. Craik (Eds.), *Levels of Processing in Human Memory*. Hillsdale, N.J.: Lawrence Erlbaum Associates Inc.

Eysenck, M. W. (1979c) The feeling of knowing a word's meaning. *British Journal of Psychology, 70*, 243–251.

Eysenck, M. W. (1982a) *Attention and Arousal: Cognition and Performance*. Berlin: Springer.

Eysenck, M. W. (1982b) Incidental learning and orienting tasks. In C. R. Puff (Ed.), *Handbook of Research Methods in Human Memory and Cognition*. London: Academic Press.

Eysenck, M. W. (1983) Individual differences in human memory. In A. Mayes (Ed.), *Memory in Animals and Humans*. Wokingham, U.K.: Van Nostrand Reinhold.

Eysenck, M. W. (in preparation) *Ecphory and Encoding Specificity*.

Eysenck, M. W., & Eysenck, M. C. (1979) Processing depth, elaboration of encoding, memory stores, and expended processing capacity. *Journal of Experimental Psychology: Human Learning and Memory, 5*, 472–484.

Eysenck, M. W., & Eysenck, M. C. (1980a) Effects of monetary incentives on rehearsal and on cued recall. *Bulletin of the Psychonomic Society, 15*, 245–247.

Eysenck, M. W. & Eysenck, M. C. (1980b) Effects of processing depth, distinctiveness, and word frequency on retention. *British Journal of Psychology, 71*, 263–274.

Eysenck, M. W., & Eysenck, M. C. (1982) Effects of incentive on cued recall. *Quarterly Journal of Experimental Psychology, 34A*, 489–498.

Eysenck, M. W., & Folkard, S. (1980) Personality, time of day, and caffeine: Some theoretical and conceptual problems in Revelle *et al. Journal of Experimental Psychology: General, 109*, 32–41.

Fantz, R. L. (1961) The origin of form perception. *Scientific American, 204*, 66–72.

Fantz, R. L. (1966) Pattern discrimination and selective attention as determinants of perceptual development from birth. In A. H. Kidd, & J. F. Rivoire (Eds.), *Perceptual Development in Children*. New York: International Universities Press.

Feldman, M. P. (1964) Response reversal performance as a function of drive level. In H. J. Eysenck (Ed.), *Experiments in Motivation*. Oxford: Pergamon.

Finke, R. A. (1980) Levels of equivalence in imagery and perception. *Psychological Review, 87*, 113–132.

Finke, R. A., & Kosslyn, S. M. (1980) Mental imagery acuity in the peripheral visual field. *Journal of Experimental Psychology: Human Perception and Performance, 6*, 126–139.

Fischler, I., Rundus, D., & Atkinson, R. C. (1970) Effects of overt rehearsal procedures on free recall. *Psychonomic Science, 19*, 249–250.

Fisher, S. (1984) *Stress and the Perception of Control*. London: Lawrence Erlbaum Associates Ltd.

Flavell, J. H. (1963) *The Developmental Psychology of Jean Piaget*. London: Van Nostrand Reinhold.

Flavell, J. H. (1977) *Cognitive Development*. New York: Prentice-Hall.

Flavell, J. H., Beach, D. H., & Chinsky, J. M. (1966) Spontaneous verbal rehearsal in a memory task as a function of age. *Child Development, 37*, 283–299.

Flexser, A. J., & Tulving, E. (1978) Retrieval independence in recognition and recall. *Psychological Review, 85*, 153–171.

Folkard, S. (1979) Time of day and level of processing. *Memory & Cognition, 7*, 247–252.

Forster, K. (1979) Levels of processing and the structure of the language processor. In W. E. Cooper, & E. C. T. Walker (Eds.), *Sentence Processing: Psycholinguistic Studies Presented to Merrill Garrett*. Hillsdale, N.J.: Lawrence Erlbaum Associates Inc.

Fowles, D. C. (1983) Appetitive motivational influences on heart rate. *Personality and Individual differences, 4*, 393–401.

Franks, J. J., & Bransford, J. D. (1971) Abstraction of visual patterns. *Journal of Experimental Psychology, 90*, 65–74.

Freedman, J. L., & Loftus, E. F. (1971) Retrieval of words from long-term memory. *Journal of Verbal Learning and Verbal Behavior, 10*, 107–115.

Freud, S. (1943) *A General Introduction to Psychoanalysis*. New York: Garden City.

Friedman, A. (1979) Framing pictures: The role of knowledge in automatised encoding and memory for gist. *Journal of Experimental Psychology: General, 108*, 316–355.

Frisby, J. (1979) *Seeing: Illusion, Brain and Mind.* Oxford: Oxford University Press.

Furth, H. G. (1966) *Thinking Without Language.* New York: Free Press.

Galton, F. (1883) *Inquiries into Human Faculty and its Development.* London: Macmillan.

Garner, W. R. (1974) *The Processing of Information and Structure.* Potomac, Md: Lawrence Erlbaum Associates Inc.

Garrett, M. F. (1976) Syntactic processes in sentence production. In R. J. Wales, & E. Walker (Eds.), *New Approaches to Language Mechanisms.* Amsterdam: North Holland.

Gauld, A., & Stephenson, G. M. (1967) Some experiments relating to Bartlett's theory of remembering. *British Journal of Psychology, 58,* 39–50.

Ghiseli, B. (1952) *The Creative Process.* New York: Mentor.

Gibson, E. J. (1969) *Principles of Perceptual Learning and Development.* New York: Appleton-Century-Crofts.

Gibson, E. J., Shapiro, F., & Yonas, A. (1968) Confusion matrices of graphic patterns obtained with a latency measure. *The Analysis of Reading Skill: A Program of Basic and Applied Research.* Final report project No. 5–1213, Cornell University.

Gibson, E. J., & Walk, R. D. (1960) The visual cliff. *Scientific American, 202,* 64–71.

Gibson, J. J. (1950) *The Perception of the Visual World.* Boston: Houghton Mifflin.

Gibson, J. J. (1966) *The Senses Considered as Perceptual Systems.* Boston: Houghton Mifflin.

Gibson, J. J. (1972) A theory of direct visual perception. In J. R. Royce, & W. W. Rozeboom (Eds.), *The Psychology of Knowing.* London: Gordon & Breach.

Gibson, J. J. (1979) *The Ecological Approach to Visual Perception.* Boston: Houghton Mifflin.

Gick, M. L., & Holyoak, K. J. (1980) Analogical problem solving. *Cognitive Psychology, 12,* 306–355.

Glanzer, M., & Cunitz, A. R. (1966) Two storage mechanisms in free recall. *Journal of Verbal Learning and Verbal Behavior, 5,* 351–360.

Glass, A. L., & Holyoak, K. J. (1975) Alternative conceptions of semantic memory. *Cognition, 3,* 313–339.

Glass, A. L., Holyoak, K. J., & Santa, J. L. (1979) *Cognition,* London: Addison-Wesley.

Gleitman, L. R., & Wanner, E. (1982) Language acquisition: The state of the state of the art. In E. Wanner, & L.R. Gleitman (Eds.), *Language Acquisition: The State of the Art.* Cambridge: Cambridge University Press.

Glenberg, A., Smith, S. M., & Green, C. (1977) Type I rehearsal: Maintenance and more. *Journal of Verbal Learning and Verbal Behavior, 16,* 339–352.

Glucksberg, S. (1962) The influence of strength of drive on functional fixedness and perceptual recognition. *Journal of Experimental Psychology, 63,* 36–41.

Glucksberg, S., & Cohen, G. N. (1970) Memory for nonattended auditory material. *Cognitive Psychology, 1,* 149–156.

Godden, D. R., & Baddeley, A. D. (1975) Context-dependent memory in two natural environments: On land and under water. *British Journal of Psychology, 66,* 325–331.

Godden, D., & Baddeley, A. (1980) When does context influence recognition memory? *British Journal of Psychology, 71,* 99–104.

Goldstein, K. (1948) *Language and Language Disturbances.* New York: Grune and Stratton.

Gould, J. D. (1978) An experimental study of writing, dictating and speaking. In J. Requin (Ed.), *Attention and Performance, Vol. VII.* Hillsdale, N.J.: Lawrence Erlbaum Associates Inc.

Gould, J. D. (1979) Writing and speaking letters and messages. *IBM Research Report,* RC-7528.

Gould, J. D. (1980) Experiments on composing letters: some facts, some myths, and some observations. In L. W. Gregg, & E. R. Steinberg (Eds.), *Cognitive Processes in Writing.* Hillsdale, N.J.: Lawrence Erlbaum Associates Inc.

Graesser, A. C., Woll, S. B., Kowalski, D. J., & Smith, D. A. (1980) Memory for typical and atypical actions in scripted activities. *Journal of Experimental Psychology: Human Learning and Memory, 6,* 503–515.

Graf, R., & Torrey, J. W. (1966) Perception of phrase structure in written language. *American Psychological Association Convention Proceedings,* 83–88.

Gray, D. R., & Gummerman, K. (1975) The enigmatic eidetic image: A critical examination of methods, data, and theories. *Psychological Bulletin, 82,* 383–407.

Gray, J. A., & Wedderburn, A. A. (1960) Grouping strategies with simultaneous stimuli. *Quarterly Journal of Experimental Psychology, 12,* 180–184.

Greenberg, J. H. (1963) Some universals of grammar with particular reference to the order of meaningful elements. In J. H. Greenberg (Ed.), *Universals of Language.* Cambridge, Mass: MIT Press.

Greene, J. M. (1972) *Psycholinguistics: Chomsky and Psychology.* Harmondsworth, England: Penguin.

Greeno, J. G. (1974) Hobbits and Orcs: Acquisition of a sequential concept. *Cognitive Psychology, 6,* 270–292.

Gregg, V. (1976) Word frequency, recognition and recall. In J. Brown (Ed.), *Recall and Recognition.* New York: Wiley.

Gregory, R. L. (1970) *The Intelligent Eye.* New York: McGraw-Hill.

Gregory, R. L. (1972) Seeing as thinking. *Times Literary Supplement,* June 23.

Grice, H. P. (1967) Logic and conversation. In P. Cole and J. L. Morgan (Eds.), *Studies in Syntax, Vol. III.* New York: Seminar Press.

Griggs, R. A., & Cox J. R. (1982) The elusive thematic-materials effect in Wason's selection task. *British Journal of Psychology, 73,* 407–420.

Guilford, J. P. (1971) *The Nature of Human Intelligence.* London: McGraw-Hill.

Haber, R. N. (1983) The impending demise of the icon: A critique of the concept of iconic storage in visual information processing. *The Behavioural and Brain Sciences, 6,* 1–11.

Halff, H. M., Ortony, A., & Anderson, R. C. (1976) A context-sensitive representation of word meanings. *Memory & Cognition, 4,* 378–383.

Hamilton, E. (1961) *Plato: The Collected Dialogues.* New York: Bollingen Foundation.

Hamilton, P., Hockey, G. R. J., & Rejman, M. (1977) The place of the concept of activation in human information processing theory: An integrative approach. In S. Dornic (Ed.), *Attention and Performance, Vol. VI.* Hillsdale, NJ.: Lawrence Erlbaum Associates Inc.

Hampton, J. A. (1979) Polymorphous concepts in semantic memory. *Journal of Verbal Learning and Verbal Behavior, 18,* 441–461.

Hampton, J. A. (1981) An investigation of the nature of abstract concepts. *Memory & Cognition, 9,* 149–156.

Hardy, G. R., & Legge, D. (1968) Cross-modal induction of changes in sensory thresholds. *Quarterly Journal of Experimental Psychology, 20,* 20–29.

Hardyck, C. D., & Petrinovich, L. F. (1970) Subvocal speech and comprehension level as a function of the difficulty level of reading material. *Journal of Verbal Learning and Verbal Behavior, 9,* 647–652.

Harré, R. (1974) Some remarks on "rule" as a scientific concept. In T. Mischel (Ed.), *Understanding Other Persons.* Oxford: Blackwell.

Harris, M., Jones, D., & Grant, J. (In press) The non-verbal context of mothers' speech to infants. *First Language.*

Harris, P.L. (1982) Cognitive prerequisites to language? *British Journal of Psychology, 73,* 187–195.

Harris, R. J. (1977) Comprehension of pragmatic implications in advertising. *Journal of Applied Psychology, 62,* 603–608.

Harris, R. J. (1978) The effect of jury size and judge's instructions on memory for pragmatic implications from courtroom testimony. *Bulletin of the Psychonomic Society, 11*, 129–132.

Harris, R. J., Dubitsky, T. M., Perch, K. L., Ellerman, C. S., & Larson, M. W. (1980) Remembering implied advertising claims as facts: Extensions to the "real world". *Bulletin of the Psychonomic Society, 16*, 317–320.

Harris, R. J., & Monaco, G. E. (1978) Psychology of pragmatic implication: Information processing between the lines. *Journal of Experimental Psychology: General, 107*, 1–22.

Harris, R. J., Teske, R. R., & Ginns, M. J. (1975) Memory for pragmatic implications from courtroom testimony. *Bulletin of the Psychonomic Society, 6*, 494–496.

Hart, J. T. (1965) Memory and the feeling-of-knowing experience. *Journal of Educational Psychology, 56*, 208–216.

Haviland, S. E., & Clark, H. H. (1974) What's new? Acquiring new information as a process in comprehension. *Journal of Verbal Learning and Verbal Behavior, 13*, 512–521.

Hayes, J. R. (1973) On the function of visual imagery in elementary mathematics. In W. G. Chase (Ed.), *Visual Information Processing*. London: Academic Press.

Hayes, J. R., & Flower, L. S. (1980) Identifying the organisation of writing processes. In L. W. Gregg, & E. R. Steinberg (Eds.), *Cognitive Processes in Writing*. Hillsdale, N.J.: Lawrence Erlbaum Associates Inc.

Heider, E. R. (1972) Universals in colour naming and memory. *Journal of Experimental Psychology, 93*, 10–20.

Henle, M. (1962) On the relation between logic and thinking. *Psychological Review, 69*, 366–378.

Henshel, R. L. (1980) The purposes of laboratory experimentation and the virtues of deliberate artificiality. *Journal of Experimental Social Psychology, 16*, 466–478.

Hirst, W., Spelke, E. S., Reaves, C. C., Caharack, G., & Neisser, U. (1980) Dividing attention without alternation of automaticity. *Journal of Experimental Psychology: General, 109*, 98–117.

Hitch, G. J. (1978) The role of short-term working memory in mental arithmetic. *Cognitive Psychology, 10*, 302–323.

Hitch, G. J. (1980) Devloping the concept of working memory. In G. Claxton (Ed.), *Cognitive Psychology: New Directions*. London: Routledge & Kegan Paul.

Hitch, G. J., & Baddeley, A. D. (1976) Verbal reasoning and working memory. *Quarterly Journal of Experimental Psychology, 28*, 603–621.

Hochberg, J. (1978) Art and perception. In E. C. Carterette, & H. Friedman (Eds.), *Handbook of Perception*, Vol. 10. London: Academic Press.

Hockett, C. D. (1960) . The origin of speech. *Scientific American, 203*, 88–96.

Hockey, R. (1979) Stress and the cognitive components of skilled performance. In V. Hamilton, & D. M. Warburton (Eds.), *Human Stress and Cognition: An Information Processing Approach*. London: Wiley.

Hockey, G. R. J., Davies, S., & Gray, M. M. (1972) Forgetting as a function of sleep at different times of day. *Quarterly Journal of Experimental Psychology, 24*, 386–393.

Hockey, R., MacLean, A., & Hamilton, P. (1981) State changes and the temporal patterning of component resources. In J. Long, & A. Baddeley (Eds.), *Attention and Performance*, Vol. IX. Hillsdale, N.J.: Lawrence Erlbaum Associates Inc.

Hodges, W. F. (1968) Effects of ego threat and threat of pain on state anxiety. *Journal of Personality and Social Psychology, 8*, 364–372.

Holding, D. H. (1975) Sensory storage reconsidered. *Memory & Cognition, 3*, 31–41.

Hollan, J. D. (1975) Features and semantic memory: Set-theoretic or network model? *Psychological Review, 82*, 154–155.

Holmes, D. S. (1972) Repression of interference: A further investigation. *Journal of Personality and Social Psychology, 22*, 163–170.

Holmes, D. S. (1974) Investigations of repression: Differential recall of material experimentally or naturally associated with ego threat. *Psychological Bulletin, 81,* 632–653.

Hovland, C. I., & Weiss, W. (1953) Transmission of information concerning concepts through positive and negative instances. *Journal of Experimental Psychology, 45,* 178–182.

Howarth, E. (1969) Personality differences in serial learning under distraction. *Perceptual and Motor Skills, 28,* 379–382.

Howie, D. (1952) Perceptual defence. *Psychological Review, 59,* 308–315.

Hubel, D. H., & Wiesel, T. N. (1962) Receptive fields, binocular interaction and functional architecture in the cat's visual cortex. *Journal of Physiology, 160,* 106–154.

Huey, E. B. (1908) *The Psychology and Pedagogy of Reading.* New York: Macmillan.

Hughes, M. (1975) Egocentrism in pre-school children. Unpublished Ph.D. thesis, University of Edinburgh.

Hulme, C. (1981) *Reading Retardation and Multi-sensory Teaching.* London: Routledge & Kegan Paul.

Huppert, F. A., & Piercy, M. (1976) Recognition memory in amnesic patients: Effect of temporal context and familiarity of material. *Cortex, 4,* 3–20.

Huppert, F. A., & Piercy, M. (1978) The role of trace strength in recency and frequency judgments by amnesic and control subjects. *Quarterly Journal of Experimental Psychology, 30,* 347–354.

Huttenlocher, J. (1968) Constructing spatial images: A strategy in reasoning. *Psychological Review, 75,* 750–760.

Hyde, T. S., & Jenkins, J. J. (1973) Recall for words as a function of semantic, graphic, and syntactic orienting tasks. *Journal of Verbal Learning and Verbal Behavior, 12,* 471–480.

Inhelder, B., & Piaget, J. (1958) *The Growth of Logical Thinking from Childhood to Adolescence.* New York: Basic Books.

Jacoby, L. L., & Craik, F. I. M. (1979) Effects of elaboration of processing at encoding and retrieval: Trace distinctiveness and recovery of initial context. In L. S. Cermak, & F. I. M. Craik (Eds.), *Levels of Processing in Human Memory.* Hillsdale, N.J.: Lawrence Erlbaum, Associates Inc.

Jacoby, L. L., & Witherspoon, D. (1982) Remembering without awareness. *Canadian Journal of Psychology, 36,* 300–324.

James, W. (1890) *Principles of Psychology.* New York: Holt.

Janis, I. L., & Frick, F. (1943) The relationship between attitudes towards conclusions and errors in judging logical validity of syllogisms. *Journal of Experimental Psychology, 33,* 73–77.

Jenkins, J. G., & Dallenbach, K. M. (1924) Obliviscence during sleep and waking. *American Journal of Psychology, 35,* 605–612.

Jenkins, J. J. (1974) Remember that old theory of memory? Well, forget it! *American Psychologist, 29,* 785–795.

Johnson-Laird, P. N. (1977) Procedural semantics. *Cognition, 5,* 189–214.

Johnson-Laird, P. N. (1983a) *Mental Models.* Cambridge: Cambridge University Press.

Johnson-Laird, P. N. (1983b) Ninth Bartlett memorial lecture: Thinking as a skill. *Quarterly Journal of Experimental Psychology, 34A,* 1–29.

Johnson-Laird, P. N., Gibbs, G., & de Mowbray, J. (1978) Meaning, amount of processing, and memory for words. *Memory & Cognition, 6,* 372–375.

Johnson-Laird, P. N., & Steedman, M. (1978) The psychology of syllogisms. *Cognitive Psychology, 10,* 64–98.

Johnson-Laird, P. N., & Wason, P. C. (1970) A theoretical analysis of insight into a reasoning task. *Cognitive Psychology, 1,* 134–148.

Johnston, W. A., & Heinz, S. P. (1978) Flexibility and capacity demands of attention. *Journal of Experimental Psychology: General, 107,* 420–435.

Johnston, W. A., & Heinz, S. P. (1979) Depth of non-target processing in an attention task. *Journal of Experimental Psychology*, *5*, 168–175.

Johnston, W. A., & Wilson, J. (1980) Perceptual processing of non-targets in an attention task. *Memory & Cognition*, *8*, 372–377.

Jones, G. V. (1976) A fragmentation hypothesis of memory: Cued recall of pictures and of sequential position. *Journal of Experimental Psychology: General*, *105*, 277–293.

Jones, G. V. (1978) Recognition failure and dual mechanisms in recall. *Psychological Review*, *85*, 464–469.

Jones, G. V. (1979) Analysing memory by cueing: Intrinsic and extrinsic knowledge. In N. S. Sutherland (Ed.), *Tutorial Essays in Psychology: A Guide to Recent Advances*, Vol. 2. Hillsdale, N.J.: Lawrence Erlbaum Associates Inc.

Jones, G. V. (1982) Tests of the dual-mechanism theory of recall. *Acta Psychologica*, *50*, 61–72.

Jorm, A. F. (1981) Children with reading and spelling retardation: Functioning of whole-word and corresponding-rule mechanisms. *Journal of Child Psychology and Psychiatry*, *22*, 171–178.

Jorm, A. F. (1983) Specific reading retardation and working memory: A review. *British Journal of Psychology*, *74*, 311–342.

Kahneman, D. (1973) *Attention and Effort*. Englewood Cliffs: Prentice Hall.

Kahneman, D., & Henik, A. (1979) Perceptual organisation and attention. In M. Kubovy, & J. R. Pomerantz (Eds.), *Perceptual Organization*. Hillsdale, N.J.: Lawrence Erlbaum Associates Inc.

Kahneman, D., & Tversky, A. (1973) On the psychology of prediction. *Psychological Review*, *80*, 237–251.

Keeney, T. J., Cannizzo, S. R., & Flavell, J. H. (1967) Spontaneous and induced verbal rehearsal in a recall task. *Child Development*, *38* 953–966.

Kinchla, R. A., & Wolf, J. M. (1979) The order of visual processing: "Top-down," "bottom-up," or "middle-out." *Perception & Psychophysics*, *25*, 225–231.

Kintsch, W. (1968) Recognition and free recall of organised lists. *Journal of Experimental Psychology*, *78*, 481–487.

Kintsch, W. (1970) Models for free recall and recognition. In D. A. Norman (Ed.), *Models of Human Memory*. London: Academic Press.

Kintsch, W. (1980) Semantic memory: A tutorial. In R. S. Nickerson (Ed.), *Attention and Performance*, Vol. VIII. Hillsdale, N.J.: Lawrence Erlbaum Associates Inc.

Kintsch, W., & Keenan, J. (1973) Reading rate and retention as a function of the number of propositions in the base structure of sentences. *Cognitive Psychology*, *5*, 257–274.

Kleiman, G. M. (1975) Speech recording in reading. *Journal of Verbal Learning and Verbal Behavior*, *14*, 323–339.

Kobasigawa, A. (1974) Utilisation of retrieval cues by children in recall. *Child Development*, *45*, 127–134.

Kochevar, J. W., & Fox, P. W. (1980) Retrieval variables in the measurement of memory. *American Journal of Psychology*, *93*, 355–366.

Koffka, K. (1935) *Principles of Gestalt Psychology*. New York: Harcourt Brace.

Köhler, W. (1925) *The Mentality of Apes*. New York: Harcourt Brace, & World.

Kolers, P. A. (1972) *Aspects of Motion Perception*. New York: Pergamon.

Kolers, P. A., & Palef, S. R. (1976) Knowing not. *Memory & Cognition*, *4*, 553–558.

Kosslyn, S. M. (1980) *Image and Mind*. Cambridge, Mass.: Harvard University Press.

Kosslyn, S. M. (1981) The medium and the message in mental imagery: A theory. *Psychological Review*, *88*, 46–66.

Kosslyn, S. M., & Jolicoeur, P. (1980) A theory-based approach to the study of individual differences in mental imagery. In R. E. Snow, P.-A. Federico, & W. E. Montague (Eds.),

Aptitude, Learning, and Instruction: Cognitive Processes Analysis of Learning and Problem Solving, Vol. 2. Hillsdale, N.J.: Lawrence Erlbaum Associates.

Kosslyn, S. M., & Pomerantz, J. R. (1977) Imagery, propositions, and the form of internal representations. *Cognitive Psychology, 9,* 52–76.

LaBerge, D. (1981) Automatic information processing: A review. In J. Long & A. Baddeley (Eds.), *Attention and Performance, Vol. IX.* Hillsdale, N.J.: Lawrence Erlbaum Associates Inc.

Labov, W. (1973) The boundaries of words and their meanings. In C. J. Bailey, & R. Shuy (Eds.), *New Ways of Analysing Variation in English.* Washington: Georgetown University Press.

Lacey, J. I. (1967) Somatic response patterning and stress: Some revisions of activation theory. In M. H. Appley, & R. Trumbull (Eds.), *Psychological Stress.* New York: Appleton-Century-Crofts.

Leask, J., Haber, R. N., & Haber, R. B. (1969) Eidetic imagery in children: II. Longitudinal and experimental results. *Psychonomic Monograph Supplements,* 3 (3, Whole No. 35), 25–48.

Lenneberg, E. H., & Roberts, J. M. (1956) *The language of experience Memoir 13.* University of Indiana, Publications in Anthropology and Linguistics.

Lennie, P. (1980) Parallel visual pathways: A review. *Vision Research, 20,* 561–594.

Levine, M. (1966) Hypothesis behaviour by humans during discriminating learning. *Journal of Experimental Psychology, 71,* 331–338.

Levine, M. (1971) Hypothesis theory and non-learning despite ideal S–R-reinforcement contingencies. *Psychological Review, 78,* 130–140.

Levine, M. W., & Schefner, J. M. (1981) *Fundamentals of Sensation and Perception.* London: Addison-Wesley.

Levy, B. A. (1971) Role of articulation in auditory and visual short-term memory. *Journal of Verbal Learning and Verbal Behavior, 10,* 123–132.

Levy, B. A. (1978) Speech processing during reading. In A. M. Lesgold, J. W. Pellegrino, S. D. Fokkema, & R. Glaser (Eds.), *Cognitive Psychology and Instruction.* New York: Plenum.

Levy, B. A. (1981) Interactive processing during reading. In A. M. Lesgold, & C. A. Perfetti (Eds.), *Interactive Processes in Reading.* Hillsdale, N.J.: Lawrence Erlbaum Associates Inc.

Liben, L. (1975) Long-term memory for pictures related to seriation, horizontality, and verticality concepts. *Developmental Psychology, 11,* 795–806.

Liberman, I. Y., & Mann, V. A. (1981) *Should Reading Instruction and Remediation Vary with the Sex of the Child?* New Haven, Conn.: Haskins Laboratories Report on Speech Research SR-65.

Libet, B. (1973) Electrical stimulation of cortex in humans and conscious sensory aspects. In A. Iggo (Ed.), *Handbook of Sensory Physiology,* Vol. 2. New York: Springer.

Lichtenstein, S., & Fischhoff, B. (1977) Do those who know more also know more about how much they know? *Organizational Behavior and Human Performance, 20,* 159–183.

Liebert, R. M., & Morris, L. W. (1967) Cognitive and emotional components of test anxiety: A distinction and some initial data. *Psychological Reports, 20,* 975–978.

Light, P., Buckingham, N., & Robbins, A. H. (1979) The conservation task as an interactional setting. *British Journal of Educational Psychology, 49,* 304–310.

Locke, E. A. (1968) Toward a theory of task motivation and incentives. *Organizational Behavior and Human Performance, 3,* 157–189.

Locke, E. A., Bryan, J. F., & Kendall, L. M. (1968) Goals and intentions as mediators of the effects of monetary incentives on behaviour. *Journal of Applied Psychology, 52,* 104–121.

Lodico, M. G., Ghatala, E. S., Levin, J. R., Pressley, M., & Bell, J. A. (1983) The effects of strategy-monitoring training on children's selection of effective memory strategies. *Journal of Experimental Child Psychology, 35,* 263–277.

Loftus, E. F. (1973) Category dominance, instance dominance, and categorisation time. *Journal of Experimental Psychology, 97,* 70–74.

Loftus, E. F. (1975) Leading questions and the eyewitness report. *Cognitive Psychology, 7,* 560–572.

Loftus, E. F., Altman, D., & Geballe, R. (1975) Effects of questioning upon a witness's later recollections. *Journal of Police Science and Administration, 3,* 162–165.

Loftus, E. F. & Loftus, G. R. (1980) On the permanence of stored information in the human brain. *American Psychologist, 35,* 409–420.

Loftus, E. F., Miller, D. G., & Burns, H. J. (1978) Semantic integration of verbal information into a visual memory. *Journal of Experimental Psychology: Human Learning and Memory, 4,* 19–31.

Loftus, E. F., & Palmer, J. C. (1974) Reconstruction of automobile destruction: An example of the interaction between language and memory. *Journal of Verbal Learning and Verbal Behavior, 13,* 585–589.

Loftus, E. F., & Suppes, P. (1972) Structural variables that determine the speed of retrieving words from long-term memory. *Journal of Verbal Learning and Verbal Behavior, 11,* 770–777.

Loftus, E. F., & Zanni, G. (1975) Eyewitness testimony: The influence of the wording of a question. *Bulletin of the Psychonomic Society, 5,* 86–88.

Logan, G. D. (1979) On the use of a concurrent memory load to measure attention and automaticity. *Journal of Experimental Psychology: Human Perception, 5,* 189–207, 1–95.

Luchins, A. S. (1942) Mechanisation in problem-solving behaviour. *Psychological Monographs, 54,* No. 6 (Whole No. 248).

Luria, A. R. (1968) *The Mind of a Mnemonist.* New York: Basic Books.

Lynch, K. (1960) *The Image of the City.* Cambridge, Mass.: MIT Press.

MacKay, D. G. (1973) Aspects of the theory of comprehension, memory and attention. *Quarterly Journal of Experimental Psychology, 25,* 22–40.

Maclay, H., & Osgood, C. E. (1959) Hesitation phenomena in spontaneous English speech. *Word, 15,* 19–44.

MacLeod, C. M., Hunt, E. B., & Mathews, N. N. (1978) Individual differences in the verification of sentence-picture relationships. *Journal of Verbal Learning and Verbal Behavior, 17,* 493–507.

Madison, P. (1956) Freud's repression concept: A survey and attempted clarification. *International Journal of Psychoanalysis, 37,* 75–81.

Mahl, G. F., Rothenberg, A., Delgado, J. M. R., & Hamlin, H. (1964) Psychological responses in the human to intracerebral electrical stimulation. *Psychosomatic Medicine, 26,* 337–368.

Maier, N. R. F. (1931) Reasoning in humans: The solution of a problem and its appearance in consciousness. *Journal of Comparative and Physiological Psychology, 11,* 181–194.

Mandler, G. (1967) Organisation and memory. In K. W. Spence, & J. T. Spence (Eds.), *The Psychology of Learning and Motivation: Advances in Research and Theory, Vol. 1.* London: Academic Press.

Mandler, G. (1972) Organisation and recognition. In E. Tulving, & W. Donaldson (Eds.), *Organisation of Memory.* London: Academic Press.

Mandler, G. (1980) Recognising: The judgment of previous occurrence. *Psychological Review, 87,* 252–271.

Mandler, G., & Boeck, W. (1974) Retrieval processes in recognition. *Memory & Cognition, 2,* 613–615.

Mandler, G., Pearlstone, A., & Koopmans, H. S. (1969) Effects of organisation and semantic similarity on recall and recognition. *Journal of Verbal Learning and Verbal Behavior, 8,* 410–423.

Marr, D. (1976) Early processing of visual information. *Proceedings of the Royal Society of London, Series B, B275,* 483–524.

Marr, D. (1982) *Vision: A Computational Investigation into the Human Representation and Processing of Visuals Information.* San Francisco: W. H. Freeman.

Marshall, J. C. (1982) Models of the mind in health and diseases. In A. W. Ellis (Ed.), *Normality and Pathology in Cognitive Functions.* London: Academic Press.

Marslen-Wilson, W., & Tyler, L. K. (1980) The temporal structure of spoken language understanding. *Cognition, 8,* 1–71.

Martin, M. (1978) Memory span as a measure of individual differences in memory capacity. *Memory & Cognition, 6,* 194–198.

Martin, M. (1980) Attention to words in different modalities: Four-channel presentation with physical and semantic selection. *Acta Psychologica, 44,* 99–115.

Mathews, N. N., Hunt, E. B., & MacLeod, C. M. (1980) Strategy choice and strategic thinking in sentence-picture verification. *Journal of Verbal Learning and Verbal Behavior, 19,* 531–548.

McCloskey, M. (1980) The stimulus familiarity problem in semantic memory research. *Journal of Verbal Learning and Verbal Behavior, 19,* 485–502.

McCloskey, M. E., & Glucksberg, S. (1978) Natural categories: Well defined or fuzzy sets? *Memory & Cognition, 6,* 462–472.

McCloskey, M., & Watkins, M. J. (1978) The seeing-more-than-is-there phenomenon: Implications for the locus of iconic storage. *Journal of Experimental Psychology: Human Perception and Performance, 4,* 553–564.

McConkie, G. W. (1979) On the role and control of eye movements in reading. In P. A. Kolers, M. E. Wrolstad, & H. Bouma (Eds.), *Processing Visible Language,* Vol. 1. New York: Plenum.

McGarrigle, J., & Donaldson, M. (1974) Conservation accidents. *Cognition, 3,* 341–350.

McGeoch, J. A. (1932) Forgetting and the law of disuse. *Psychological Review, 39,* 352–370.

McGraw, K. O. (1978) The detrimental effects of reward on performance: A literature review and a prediction model. In M. R. Lepper, & D. Greene (Eds.), *The Hidden Costs of Reward: New Perspectives on the Psychology of Human Motivation.* Hillsdale, N.J.: Lawrence Erlbaum Associates Inc.

McGraw, K. O., & McCullers, J. C. (1979) Evidence of a detrimental effect of extrinsic incentives on breaking a mental set. *Journal of Experimental Social Psychology, 15,* 285–294.

McKoon, G., & Ratcliff, R. (1981) The comprehension processes and memory structures involved in instrumental inference. *Journal of Verbal Learning and Verbal Behavior, 20,* 671–682.

McLaughlin, B. (1978) *Second Language Acquisition in Childhood.* Hillsdale, N.J.: Lawrence Erlbaum Associates Inc.

McLeod, P. (1977) A dual task response modality effect: Support for multiprocessor models of attention. *Quarterly Journal of Experimental Psychology, 29,* 651–667.

McNemar, Q. (1964) Lost: Our intelligence? Why? *American Psychologist, 19,* 871–882.

Melton, A. W., & Irwin, J. M. (1940) The influence of degree of interpolated learning on retroactive inhibition and the overt transfer of specific responses. *American Journal of Psychology* **53,** 173–203.

Menzel, E. W. (1973) Chimpanzee spatial memory organisation. *Science, 182,* 943–945.

Mervis, C. B., & Crisafi, M. A. (1982) Order of acquisition of subordinate-, basic-, and superordinate-level categories. *Child Development, 53,* 258–266.

Mervis, C. B., & Pani, J. R. (1980) Acquisition of basic object categories. *Cognitive Psychology, 12,* 496–522.

Mervis, C. B., & Rosch, E. (1981) Categorisation of natural objects. *Annual Review of Psychology, 32,* 89–115.

Meudell, P., & Mayes, A. (1981) The Clarapède phenomenon: A further example in amnesics, a demonstration of a similar effect in normal people with attenuated memory, and a reinterpretation. *Current Psychological Research*, *1*, 75–88.

Meudell, P., & Mayes, A. (1982) Normal and abnormal forgetting: Some comments on the human amnesic syndrome. In A. Ellis (Ed.), *Normality and Pathology in Cognitive Function*. London: Academic Press.

Miller, G. A., & Johnson-Laird, P. N. (1976) *Language and Perception*. Cambridge, Mass.: Harvard University Press.

Miller, G. A., & McNeill, D. (1969) Psycholinguistics. In G. Lindzey, & E. Aronson (Eds.), *The Handbook of Social Psychology*, *Vol. III*. Reading, Mass.: Addison-Wesley.

Miller, G. A., & Nicely, P. (1955) An analysis of perceptual confusions among some English consonants. *Journal of the Acoustic Society of America*, *27*, 338–352.

Milner, B. (1971) Inter-hemispheric differences in the localisation of psychological processes in man. *British Medical Bulletin*, *27*, 272–277.

Minsky, M. (1975) A framework for representing knowledge. In P. H. Winston (Ed.), *The Psychology of Computer Vision*. New York: McGraw-Hill.

Monaco, G. E. (1976) *Construction as a Storage Phenomenon*. Unpublished M.A. thesis, Kansas State University.

Moray, N. (1959) Attention in dichotic listening: Affective cues and the influence of instructions. *Quarterly Journal of Experimental Psychology*, *11*, 56–60.

Moray, N. (1969) *Attention: Selective Processes in Vision and Hearing*. London: Hutchinson.

Morgenstern, F. S., Hodgson, R. J., & Law, L. (1974) Work efficiency and personality: A comparison of introverted and extraverted subjects exposed to conditions of distraction and distortion of stimulus in a learning task. *Ergonomics*, *17*, 211–220.

Morris, C. D., Bransford, J. D., & Franks, J. J. (1977) Levels of processing versus transfer appropriate processing. *Journal of Verbal Learning and Verbal Behavior*, *16*, 519–533.

Morris, P. E. (1979) Strategies for learning and recall. In M. M. Gruneberg, & P. E. Morris (Eds.), *Applied Problems in Memory*. London: Academic Press.

Morris, P. E., Gruneberg, M. M., Sykes, R. N., & Merrick, A. (1981) Football knowledge and the acquisition of new results. *British Journal of Psychology*, *72*, 479–483.

Morris, P. E., Jones, S., & Hampson, P. (1978) An imagery mnemonic for the learning of people's names. *British Journal of Psychology*, *69*, 335–336.

Morris, P. E., & Reid, R. L. (1970) The repeated use of mnemonic imagery. *Psychonomic Science*, *20*, 337–338.

Morris, P. E., & Stevens, R. (1974) Linking images and free recall. *Journal of Verbal Learning and Verbal Behavior*, *13*, 310–315.

Morris, L. W., & Liebert, R. M. (1973) Effects of negative feedback, threat of shock, and level of trait anxiety on the arousal of two components of anxiety. *Journal of Counseling Psychology*, *20*, 321–326.

Morton, J. (1979) Facilitation in word recognition: Experiments causing change in the logogen model. In P. A. Kolers, M. E. Wrolstad, & H. Bourma (Eds.), *Processing of Visible Language*, Vol. 1. New York: Plenum.

Moscovitch, M., & Craik, F. I. M. (1976) Depth of processing, retrieval cues, and uniqueness of encoding as factors in recall. *Journal of Verbal Learning and Verbal Behavior*, *15*, 447–458.

Mueller, J. H. (1976) Anxiety and cue utilisation in human learning and memory. In M. Zuckerman, & C. D. Spielberger (Eds.), *Emotions and Anxiety: New Concepts, Methods and Applications*. Hillsdale, N.J.: Lawrence Erlbaum Associates Inc.

Murray, D. J. (1968) Articulation and acoustic confusability in short-term memory. *Journal of Experimental Psychology*, *78*, 679–684.

Navon, D., (1977) Forest before trees: The precedence of global features in visual perception. *Cognitive Psychology*, *9*, 353–383.

Navon, D., & Gopher, D. (1979) On the economy of the human processing system. *Psychological Review, 86*, 214–225.

Neely, J. H. (1977) Semantic priming and retrieval from lexical memory: Roles of inhibitionless spreading activation and limited-capacity attention. *Journal of Experimental Psychology: General, 106*, 226–254.

Neill, W. T. (1979) Switching attention within and between categories: Evidence for intra-category inhibition. *Memory & Cognition, 7*, 283–290.

Neisser, U. (1963) The multiplicity of thought. *British Journal of Psychology, 54*, 1–14.

Neisser, U. (1967) *Cognitive Psychology.* New York: Appleton-Century-Crofts.

Neisser, U. (1972) Changing conceptions of imagery. In P. W. Sheehan (Ed.), *The Function and Nature of Imagery.* London: Academic Press.

Neisser, U. (1976) *Cognition and Reality.* San Francisco: W. H. Freeman.

Neisser, U. (1978) Memory: What are the important questions? In M. M. Gruneberg, P. E. Morris, & R. N. Sykes (Eds.), *Practical Aspects of Memory.* London: Academic Press.

Nelson, T. O. (1977) Repetition and depth of processing. *Journal of Verbal Learning and Verbal Behavior, 16*, 151–171.

Nelson, T. O. (1978) Detecting small amounts of information in memory: Savings for non-recognised items. *Journal of Experimental Psychology: Human Learning and Memory, 4*, 453–468.

Nelson, T. O., Metzler, J., & Reed, D. A. (1974) Role of details in the long-term recognition of pictures and verbal descriptions. *Journal of Experimental Psychology, 102*, 184–186.

Nelson, T. O., & Vining, S. K. (1978) Effect of semantic versus structural processing on long-term retention. *Journal of Experimental Psychology: Human Learning and Memory, 4*, 198–209.

Newell, A. (1973) You can't play 20 questions with nature and win. In W. G. Chase (Ed.), *Visual Information Processing.* New York: Academic Press.

Newell, A. (1980) Reasoning, problem solving, and decision processes: The problem space as a fundamental category. In R. Nickerson (Ed.), *Attention and Performance, Vol. VIII.* Hillsdale, N.J.: Lawrence Erlbaum Associates Inc.

Newell, A., & Simon, H. A. (1972) *Human Problem Solving.* Englewood Cliffs, N.J.: Prentice-Hall.

Nii, H. P., & Feigenbaum, E. A. (1977) *Rule-based Understanding of Signals.* Stanford, Calif.: Stanford University (Tech. Rep. HPP-77-7).

Nisbett, R., & Ross, L. (1980) *Human Inference: Strategies and Shortcomings of Social Judgment.* Englewood Cliffs, N.J.: Prentice-Hall.

Nisbett, R. E., & Wilson, T. D. (1977) Telling more than we can know: Verbal reports on mental processes. *Psychological Review, 84*, 231–259.

Nitsch, K. E. (1977) *Structuring Decontextualised Forms of Knowledge.* Unpublished Ph.D. thesis, Vanderbilt University, Nashville, Tennessee.

Norman, D. A. (1969) Memory while shadowing. *Quarterly Journal of Experimental Psychology, 21*, 85–93.

Norman, D. A. (1980) Twelve issues for cognitive science. *Cognitive Science, 4*, 1–32.

Norman, D. A., & Bobrow, D. G. (1975) On data-limited and resource-limited processes. *Cognitive Psychology, 7*, 44–64.

Nottelman, E. D., & Hill, K. T. (1977) Test anxiety and off-task behaviour in evaluative situations. *Child Development, 48*, 225–231.

Notz, W. W. (1975) Work motivation and the negative effects of extrinsic rewards: A review with implications for theory and practice. *American Psychologist, 30*, 884–891.

Olson, D. R. (1970) Language and thought: Aspects of a cognitive theory of semantics. *Psychological Review, 77*, 257–273.

HCP–N*

Osherson, D. N., & Smith, E. E. (1981) On the adequacy of prototype theory as a theory of concepts. *Cognition, 9,* 35–58.

Pachella, R. G. (1974) The interpretation of reaction time in information processing research. In B. Kantowitz (Ed.), *Human Information Processing: Tutorials in Performance and Cognition.* Hillsdale, N.J.: Lawrence Erlbaum, Associates Inc.

Paivio, A. (1971) *Imagery and Verbal Processes.* New York: Holt, Rinehart, & Winston.

Paivio, A. (1979) Psychological processes in the comprehension of metaphor. In A. Ortony (Ed.), *Metaphor and Thought.* Cambridge: Cambridge University Press.

Paivio, A., & Begg, I. (1981) *Psychology of Language.* Englewood Cliffs, N.J.: Prentice-Hall.

Paivio, A., & Csapo, K. (1969) Concrete-image and verbal memory codes. *Journal of Experimental Psychology, 80,* 279–285.

Paivio, A., & Csapo, K. (1973) Picture superiority in free recall: Imagery or dual coding? *Cognitive Psychology, 5,* 176–206.

Paivio, A., Yuille, J. C., & Madigan, S. A. (1968) Concreteness, imagery, and meaningfulness values for 925 nouns. *Journal of Experimental Psychology Monograph Supplement, 76* (1, Pt. 2), 1–25.

Pallak, M. S., Pittman, T. S., Heller, J. F., & Munson, P. (1975) The effect of arousal on Stroop colour-word task performance. *Bulletin of the Psychonomic Society, 6,* 248–250.

Palmer, S. E. (1977) Hierarchical structure in perceptual representation. *Cognitive Psychology, 9,* 441–474.

Paris, S. G., & Lindauer, B. K. (1976) The role of inference in children's comprehension and memory for sentences. *Cognitive Psychology, 8,* 217–227.

Parkin, A. J. (1979) Specifying levels of processing. *Quarterly Journal of Experimental Psychology, 31,* 175–195.

Patterson, K. E. (1971) *Retrieval Limitations in Categorised Free Recall.* Unpublished Ph.D. thesis, University of California, San Diego.

Penfield, W. (1969) Consciousness, memory, and man's conditioned reflexes. In K. Pribram (Ed.), *On the Biology of Learning.* New York: Harcourt, Brace, & World.

Perfetti, C. A., & Lesgold, A. M. (1977) Discourse comprehension and sources of individual differences. In M. A. Just, & P. A. Carpenter (Eds.), *Cognitive Processes in Comprehension.* New York: Wiley.

Phillips, W. A., & Christie, D. F. M. (1977) Interference with visualisation. *Quarterly Journal of Experimental Psychology, 29,* 637–650.

Piaget, J. (1967) *The Child's Conception of the World.* Totowa, N.J.: Littlefield, Adams.

Piaget, J. (1970) Piaget's theory. In J. Mussen (Ed.), *Carmichael's Manual of Child Psychology, Vol. 1.* New York: Basic Books.

Piaget, J., & Inhelder, B. (1973) *Memory and Intelligence.* New York: Basic Books.

Poltrock, S. E., Lansman, M., & Hunt, E. (1982) Automatic and controlled attention processes in auditory target detection. *Journal of Experimental Psychology: Human Perception and Performance, 8* 37–45.

Popper, K. (1959) *The Logic of Scientific Discovery.* London: Hutchinson.

Posner, M. I. (1978) *Chronometric Explorations of Mind.* Hillsdale, N.J.: Lawrence Erlbaum Associates Inc.

Posner, M. I., & Keele, S. W. (1968) On the genesis of abstract ideas. *Journal of Experimental Psychology, 77,* 353–363.

Posner, M. I., & Snyder, C. R. R. (1975) Attention and cognitive control. In R. L. Solso (Ed.), *Information Processing and Cognition: The Loyola Symposium.* Hillsdale, N.J.: Lawrence Erlbaum Associates Inc.

Postman, L. (1976) Interference theory revisited. In J. Brown (Ed.), *Recall and Recognition.* New York: Wiley.

Postman, L., & Keppel, G. (1977) Conditions of cumulative proactive inhibition. *Journal of Experimental Psychology, 106,* 376–403.

Postman, L., & Stark, K. (1969) Role of response availability in transfer and interference. *Journal of Experimental Psychology, 79,* 168–177.

Postman, L., Thompkins, B. A., & Gray, W. D. (1978) The interpretation of encoding effects in retention. *Journal of Verbal Learning and Verbal Behavior, 17,* 681–705.

Premack, D. (1976) Language and intelligence in ape and man. *American Scientist, 64,* 674–683.

Putnam, B. (1979) Hypnosis and distortions in eyewitness memory. *International Journal of Clinical and Experimental Hypnosis, 27,* 437–448.

Putnam, H. (1973) Reductionism and the nature of psychology. *Cognition, 2,* 131–146.

Pylyshyn, Z. W. (1973) What the mind's eye tells the mind's brain: A critique of mental imagery. *Psychological Bulletin, 80,* 1–24.

Pylyshyn, Z. W. (1979) Imagery theory: Not mysterious—just wrong. *Behavioral and Brain Sciences, 2,* 561–563.

Rabbitt, P. M. A. (1964) Ignoring irrelevant information. *British Journal of Psychology, 55,* 403–414.

Rabbitt, P. M. A. (1967) Ignoring irrelevant information. *American Journal of Psychology, 80,* 1–13.

Rabinowitz, J. C., Mandler, G., & Barsalou, L. W. (1979) Generation-recognition as an auxiliary retrieval strategy. *Journal of Verbal Learning and Verbal Behavior, 18,* 57–72.

Rabinowitz, J. C., Mandler, G., & Patterson, K. E. (1977) Determinants of recognition and recall: Accessibility and generation. *Journal of Experimental Psychology: General, 106,* 302–329.

Ratcliff, R., & McKoon, G. (1981) Does activation really spread? *Psychological Review, 88,* 454–462.

Rayner, K., Carlson, M., & Frazier, L. (1983) The interaction of syntax and semantics during sentence processing: Eye movements in the analysis of semantically biased sentences. *Journal of Verbal Learning and Verbal Behavior, 22,* 358–374.

Reason, J. T. (1979) Actions not as planned. In G. Underwood, & R. Stevens (Eds.), *Aspects of Consciousness.* London: Academic Press.

Reitman, J. S. (1974) Without surreptitious rehearsal, information in short-term memory decays. *Journal of Verbal Learning and Verbal Behavior, 13,* 365–377.

Reitman, W. (1970) What does it take to remember? In D. A. Norman (Ed.), *Models of Human Memory.* London: Academic Press.

Revelle, W., & Humphreys, M. S. (In press) *Personality, Motivation, and Performance: A Theory of Individual Differences.*

Revelle, W., & Michaels, E. J. (1976) The theory of achievement motivation revisited: The implications of intertial tendencies. *Psychological Review, 83,* 394–404.

Richardson, J. T. E. (1980) *Mental Imagery and Human Memory.* London: Macmillan.

Richardson, J. T. E., & Baddeley, A. D. (1975) The effect of articulatory suppression in free recall. *Journal of Verbal Learning and Verbal Behavior, 14,* 623–629.

Rips, L. J., & Marcus, S. L. (1977) Suppositions and the analysis of conditional sentences. In M. A. Just, & P. A. Carpenter (Eds.), *Cognitive Processes in Comprehension.* New York: Wiley.

Rips, L. J., Shoben, E. J., & Smith, E. E. (1973) Semantic distance and the verification of semantic relations. *Journal of Verbal Learning and Verbal Behavior, 12,* 1–20.

Roediger, H. L. (1980) Memory metaphors in cognitive psychology. *Memory & Cognition, 8,* 231–246.

Rollman, G. B., & Nachmias, J. (1972) Simultaneous detection and recognition of chromatic flashes. *Perception & Psychophysics, 12,* 308–314.

Rosch, E. (1973) Natural categories. *Cognitive Psychology, 4*, 328–350.

Rosch, E. (1974) Universals and cultural specifics in human categorisation. In R. Breslin, W. Loner, & S. Bochner (Eds.), *Cross-Cultural Perspectives*. London: Sage.

Rosch, E., & Mervis, C. B. (1975) Family resemblances: Studies in the internal structure of categories. *Cognitive Psychology, 7*, 573–605.

Rosch, E., Mervis, C. B., Gray, W. D., Johnson, D. M., & Boyes-Braem, P. (1976) Basic objects in natural categories. *Cognitive Psychology, 8*, 382–439.

Rosch, E., Simpson, C., & Miller, R. S. (1976) Structural bases of typicality effects. *Journal of Experimental Psychology: Human Perception and Performance, 2*, 491–502.

Ross, J., & Lawrence, K. A. (1968) Some observations on memory artifice. *Psychonomic Science, 13*, 107–108.

Rubenstein, H., Lewis, S. S., & Rubenstein, M. A. (1971) Evidence for phonemic recording in visual word recognition. *Journal of Verbal Learning and Verbal Behavior, 10*, 645–657.

Rubin, E. (1921) *Visuell Wahrgenommene Figuren*. Copenhagen: Glydendalske.

Rugel, R. P. (1974) WISC sub-test scores of disabled readers: A review with respect to Bannatyne's recategorisation. *Journal of Learning Disabilities, 7*, 48–55.

Rumelhart, D. E. (1980) Schemata: The building blocks of cognition. In R. Spiro, B. Bruce, & W. Brewer (Eds.), *Theoretical Issues in Reading Comprehension*. Hillsdale, N.J.: Lawrence Erlbaum Associates Inc.

Rumelhart, D. E., & Ortony, A. (1977) The representation of knowledge in memory. In R. C. Anderson, R. J. Spiro, and W. E. Montague (Eds.) *Schooling and the Acquisition of Knowledge*. Hillsdale, N.J.: Lawrence Erlbaum Associates Inc.

Rundus, D. (1977) Maintenance rehearsal and single-level processing. *Journal of Verbal Learning and Verbal Behavior, 16*, 665–681.

Rundus, D. & Atkinson, R. C. (1970) Rehearsal processes in free recall, a procedure for direct observation. *Journal of Verbal Learning and Verbal Behavior, 9*, 99–105.

Sakitt, B. (1976) Iconic memory. *Psychological Review, 83*, 257–276.

Salapatek, P. (1975) Pattern perception in early infancy. In L. B. Cohen and P. Salapatek (Eds.), *Infant Perception: From Sensation to Cognition. Vol. 1: Basic Visual Processes*. London: Academic Press.

Saltz, E. (1970) Manifest anxiety: Have we misread the data? *Psychological Review, 77*, 568–573.

Saltz, E., & Hoehn, A. J. (1957) A test of the Taylor-Spence theory of anxiety. *Journal of Abnormal and Social Psychology, 54*, 114–117.

Salzberg, P. M. (1976) On the generality of encoding specificity. *Journal of Experimental Psychology: Human Learning and Memory, 2*, 586–596.

Schaffer, H. R. (1977) *Mothering*. London: Open Books.

Schank, R. C. (1976) The role of memory in natural language processing. In C. N. Cofer (Ed.), *The Structure of Human Memory*. San Francisco: W. H. Freeman.

Schank, R. C., & Abelson, R. P. (1977) *Scripts, Plans, Goals and Understanding*. Hillsdale, N.J.: Lawrence Erlbaum Associates Inc.

Schneider, W., & Fisk, A. D. (1982) Concurrent automatic and controlled visual search: Can processing occur without resource cost? *Journal of Experimental Psychology: Learning, Memory, and Cognition, 8*, 261–278.

Schneider, W., & Shiffrin, R. M. (1977) Controlled and automatic human information processing: I. Detection, search and attention. *Psychological Review, 84*, 1–66.

Schwartz, R. M., & Humphreys, M. S. (1974) Recognition and recall as a function of instructional manipulations of organisation. *Journal of Experimental Psychology, 102*, 517–519.

Schwartz, S. (1975) Individual differences in cognition: Some relationships between personality and memory. *Journal of Research in Personality, 9*, 217–225.

Segal, S. J., & Fusella, V. (1970) Influence of imaged pictures and sounds on detection of visual and auditory signals. *Journal of Experimental Psychology*, *83*, 458–464.

Seidenberg, M. S., & Petitto, L. A. (1979) Signing behaviour in apes: A critical review. *Cognition*, 7, 177–215.

Shaffer, L. H. (1975) Multiple attention in continuous verbal tasks. In P. M. A. Rabbit, & S. Dornic (Eds.), *Attention and Performance, Vol. V*. London: Academic Press.

Shallice, T., & Butterworth, B. B. (1977) Short-term memory impairment and spontaneous speech. *Neuropsychologia*, *13*, 729–736.

Shallice, T., & Warrington, E. K. (1970) Independent functioning of the verbal memory stores: A neuropsychological study. *Quarterly Journal of Experimental Psychology*, *22*, 261–273.

Shankweiler, D., Liberman, I. Y., Mark, L. S., Fowler, C. A., & Fischer, F. W. (1979) The speech code and learning to read. *Journal of Experimental Psychology: Human Learning and Memory*, *5*, 531–545.

Shatz, M. (1982) On mechanisms of language acquisition: Can features of the communicative environment account for development? In E. Wanner, & L. R. Gleitman (Eds.), *Language Acquisition: The State of the Art*. Cambridge: Cambridge University Press.

Shepard, R. N. (1978) The mental image. *American Psychologist*, *33*, 125–137.

Shepp, B. E., Burns, B., & McDonough, D. (1980) The relation of stimulus structure to perceptual and cognitive development: Further tests of a separability hypothesis. In F. Wilkering, J. Becker, & T. Trabasso (Eds.), *The Integration of Information by Children*. Hillsdale, N.J.: Lawrence Erlbaum Associates Inc.

Shiffrin, R. M. (1976) Capacity limitations information processing, attention, and memory. In W. K. Estes (Ed.), *Handbook of Learning and Cognitive Processes*, Vol. 4. Hillsdale, N.J.: Lawrence Erlbaum Associates Inc.

Shiffrin, R. M., & Schneider, W. (1977) Controlled and automatic human information processing: II. Perceptual learning, automatic attending, and a general theory. *Psychological Review*, *84*, 127–190.

Silveira, J. (1971) *Incubation: The Effect of Interruption Timing and Length on Problem Solution and Quality of Problem Processing*. Unpublished Ph.D. thesis, University of Oregon.

Simon, C. W., & Emmons, W. H. (1956) Responses to material presented during various stages of sleep. *Journal of Experimental Psychology*, *51*, 89–97.

Simon, D. P., & Simon, H. A. (1978) Individual differences in solving physics problems. In R. Seigler (Ed.), *Children's Thinking: What Develops?* Hillsdale, N.J.: Lawrence Erlbaum Associates Inc.

Simon, H. A. (1967) Motivational and emotional controls of cognition. *Psychological Review*, *74*, 29–39.

Simon, H. A. (1974) How big is a chunk? *Science*, *183*, 482–488.

Simon, H. A. (1980) Cognitive science: The newest science of the artificial. *Cognitive Science*, *4*, 33–46.

Simon, H. A., & Reed, S. K. (1976) Modelling strategy shifts in a problem-solving task. *Cognitive Psychology*, *8*, 86–97.

Sinclair-de-Zwart, H. (1969) Developmental psycholinguistics. In D. Elkind, & J. Flavell (Eds.), *Studies in Cognitive Development*. Oxford: Oxford University Press.

Skinner, B. F. (1957) *Verbal Behavior*. New York: Appleton-Century-Crofts.

Slobin, D. I. (1982) Universal and particular in the acquisition of language. In E. Wanner, & L. R. Gleitman (Eds.), *Language Acquisition: The State of the Art*. Cambridge: Cambridge University Press.

Smith, D. A., & Graesser, A. C. (1981) Memory for actions in scripted activities as a function of typicality, retention interval, and retrieval task. *Memory & Cognition*, *9*, 550–559.

Smith, E. E. (1978) Theories of semantic memory. In W. K. Estes (Ed.), *Handbook of Learning and Cognitive Processes*, *Vol. 6*. Hillsdale, N.J.: Lawrence Erlbaum Associates Inc.

Smith, E. E., Shoben, E. J., & Rips, L. J. (1974) Structure and process in semantic memory: A featural model for semantic decisions. *Psychological Review, 81*, 214–241.

Smith, S. M. (1979) Remembering in and out of context. *Journal of Experimental Psychology: Human Learning and Memory, 5*, 460–471.

Smith, S. M., Brown, H. O., Toman, J. E. P., & Goodman, L. S. (1947) Lack of cerebral effects of D-tubocurarine. *Anaesthesiology, 8*, 1–14.

Snow, C. E. (1977) Mothers' speech research: From input to interaction. In C. E. Snow, & C. A. Ferguson (Eds.), *Talking to Children: Language Input and Acquisition.* Cambridge: Cambridge University Press.

Solso, R. L. (1974) Theories of retrieval. In R. L. Solso (Ed.), *Theories in Cognitive Psychology.* Potomac, Md.: Lawrence Erlbaum Associates Inc.

Spearman, C. E. (1927) *The Abilities of Man: Their Nature and Measurement.* London: Macmillan.

Spelke, E. S., Hirst, W. C., & Neisser, U. (1976) Skills of divided attention. *Cognition, 4*, 215–230.

Spence, J. T., & Spence, K. W. (1966) The motivational components of manifest anxiety: Drive and drive stimuli. In C. D. Spielberger (Ed.), *Anxiety and Behaviour.* London: Academic Press.

Sperling, G. (1960) The information available in brief visual presentations. *Psychological Monographs, 74* (Whole No. 498), 1–29.

Spielberger, C. D. (1972) Anxiety as an emotional state. In C. D. Spielberger (Ed.), *Anxiety: Current Trends in Theory and Research, Vol. 1.* London: Academic Press.

Spielberger, C. D., Gonzalez, H. P., Taylor, C. J., Algaze, B., & Anton, W. D. (1978) Examination stress and test anxiety. In C. D. Spielberger, & I. G. Sarason (Eds.), *Stress and Anxiety, Vol. 5.* Hillsdale, N.J.: Lawrence Erlbaum Associates Inc.

Spielberger, C. D., O'Neill, H. F., & Hansen, D. N. (1972) Anxiety, drive theory, and computer-assisted learning. In B. A. Maher (Ed.), *Progress in Experimental Personality Research, Vol. 6.* London: Academic Press.

Spoehr, K. T., & Lehmkuhle, S. W. (1982) *Visual Information Processing.* San Francisco: W. H. Freeman.

Spring, C., & Capps, C. (1974) Encoding speed, rehearsal and probed recall or dyslexic boys. *Journal of Educational Psychology, 66*, 780–786.

Stacey, B., & Pike, R. (1970) Apparent size, apparent depth and the Müller–Lyer illusion. *Perception & Psychophysics, 7*, 125–128.

Standing, L., Conezio, J., & Haber, R. N. (1970) Perception and memory for pictures: Single-trial learning of 2500 visual stimuli. *Psychonomic Science, 19*, 73–74.

Steedman, M. J., & Johnson-Laird, P. N. (1977) A programmatic theory of linguistic performance. In P. Smith, & R. Campbell (Eds.), *Proceedings of the Stirling Conference on Psycholinguistics.* London: Plenum.

Stein, B. S., Morris, C. D., & Bransford, J. D. (1978) Constraints on effective elaboration. *Journal of Verbal Learning and Verbal Behavior, 17*, 707–714.

Stern, L. D. (1981) A review of theories of human amnesia. *Memory & Cognition, 9*, 247–262.

Sternberg, R. J. (1977) *Intelligence, Information Processing, and Analogical Reasoning.* Hillsdale, N.J.: Lawrence Erlbaum Associates Inc.

Sternberg, R. J. (1980) Representation and process in linear syllogistic reasoning. *Journal of Experimental Psychology, 109*, 119–159.

Sternberg, R. J., & Bower, G. H. (1974) Transfer in part-whole and whole-part free recall: A comparative evaluation of theories. *Journal of Verbal Learning and Verbal Behavior, 13*, 1–26.

Sternberg, R. J., & Weil, E. M. (1980) An aptitude X strategy interaction in linear syllogistic reasoning. *Journal of Educational Psychology, 72*, 226–239.

Sternberg, S. (1969) The discovery of processing stages: Extensions of Donders' method. *Acta Psychologica, 30,* 276–315.

Sternberg, S. (1975) Memory scanning: New findings and current controversies. *Quarterly Journal of Experimental Psychology, 27,* 1–32.

Storms, M. D., & Nisbett, R. E. (1970) Insomnia and the attribution process. *Journal of Personality and Social Psychology, 2,* 319–328.

Stromeyer, C. F., & Psotka, J. (1970) The detailed texture of eidetic images. *Nature, 225,* 346–349.

Sullivan, L. (1976) Selective attention and secondary message analysis: A reconsideration of Broadbent's filter model of selective attention. *Quarterly Journal of Experimental Psychology, 28,* 167–178.

Tenebaum, J. M., Witkin, A. P., & Wandell, B. A. (1983) Review of 'Vision: A computational investigation into the human representation and processing of visual information' by D. Marr. *Contemporary Psychology, 28,* 583–584.

Tennyson, R. D., & Wooley, F. R. (1971) Interaction of anxiety with performance on two levels of task difficulty. *Journal of Educational Psychology, 62,* 463–467.

Terrace, H. S. (1979) *Nim.* New York: Alfred Knopf.

Terrace, H. S., Petitto, L. A., Sanders, D. J. & Bever, T. G. (1979) On the grammatical capacities of apes. In K. Nelson (Ed.), *Children's Language, Vol. 2.* New York: Gardner Press.

Thomson, D. M., & Tulving, E. (1970) Associative encoding and retrieval: Weak and strong cues. *Journal of Experimental Psychology, 86,* 255–262.

Thorndike, E. L. (1898) Animal intelligence: An experimental study of the associative processes in animals. *The Psychological Review Monograph Supplements, 2,* No. 4 (Whole No. 8).

Thorndike, E. L. (1924) Mental discipline in high school studies. *Journal of Educational Psychology, 15,* 1–22.

Thorndyke, P. W. (1976) The role of inferences in discourse comprehension. *Journal of Verbal Learning and Verbal Behavior, 15,* 437–446.

Torgesen, J. K. & Houck, D. J. (1980) Processing deficiencies of learning—disabled children who perform poorly on the digit span test. *Journal of Educational Psychology, 72,* 141–160.

Treisman, A. M. (1964) Verbal cues, language, and meaning in selective attention. *American Journal of Psychology, 77,* 206–219.

Treisman, A. M. (1977) Focused attention in the perception and retrieval of multidimensional stimuli. *Perception & Psychophysics, 22,* 1–11.

Treisman, A. M., & Davies, A. (1973) Divided attention to ear and eye. In S. Kornblum (Ed.), *Attention and Performance, Vol. IV.* London: Academic Press.

Treisman, A. M., & Geffen, G. (1967) Selective attention: Perception or response? *Quarterly Journal of Experimental Psychology, 19,* 1–18.

Treisman, A. M., & Gelade, G. (1980) A feature-integration theory of attention. *Cognitive Psychology, 12,* 97–136.

Treisman, A. M., & Riley, J. G. A. (1969) Is selective attention selective perception or selective response: A further test. *Journal of Experimental Psychology, 79,* 27–34.

Tronick, E., & Clanton, C. (1971) Infant looking patterns. *Vision Research, 11,* 1479–1486.

Tulving, E. (1972) Episodic and semantic memory. In E. Tulving and W. Donaldson (Eds.), *Organisation of Memory.* London: Academic Press.

Tulving, E. (1974) Cue-dependent forgetting. *American Scientist, 62,* 74–82.

Tulving, E. (1979) Relation between encoding specificity and levels of processing. In L. S. Cermak, & F. I. M. Craik (Eds.), *Levels of Processing in Human Memory.* Hillsdale, N.J.: Lawrence Erlbaum Associates Inc.

Tulving, E. (1982) Synergistic ecphory in recall and recognition. *Canadian Journal of Psychology*, *36*, 130–147.

Tulving, E. (1983) *Elements of Episodic Memory*. Oxford: Oxford University Press.

Tulving, E., & Psotka, J. (1971) Retroactive inhibition in free recall: Inaccessibility of information available in the memory store. *Journal of Experimental Psychology*, *87*, 1–8.

Tulving, E., & Thomson, D. M. (1971) Retrieval processes in recognition memory: Effects of associative context. *Journal of Experimental Psychology*, *87*, 116–124.

Tulving, E., & Thomson, D. M. (1973) Encoding specificity and retrieval processes in episodic memory. *Psychological Review*. *80*, 353–373.

Tulving, E., Mandler, G., & Baumal, R. (1964) Interaction of two sources of information in tachistoscopic word recognition. *Canadian Journal of Psychology*, *18*, 62–71.

Tuma, D. T., & Reif, F. (1980) *Problem Solving and Education: Issues in Teaching and Research*. Hillsdale, N.J.: Lawrence Erlbaum Associates Inc.

Tversky, A., & Kahneman, D. (1973) Availability: A heuristic for judging frequency and probability. *Cognitive Psychology*, *5*, 207–232.

Tversky, A., & Kahneman, D. (1974) judgement under uncertainty: Heuristics and biases. *Science*, *185*, 1124–1131.

Tversky, A., & Kahneman, D. (1978) Causal schemata in judgments under uncertainty. In M. Fishbein (Ed.), *Progress in Social Psychology*. Hillsdale, N.J.: Lawrence Erlbaum Associates Inc.

Tversky, B. (1969) Pictorial and verbal encoding in a short-term memory task. *Perception & Psychophysics*, *6*, 225–233.

Underwood, B. J. (1957) Interference and forgetting *Psychological Review*, *64*, 49–60.

Underwood, B. J., Broder, P. K., & Zimmerman, J. (1973) Retention of verbal discrimination lists as a function of number of prior lists, word frequency, and type of list. *Journal of Experimental Psychology*, *100*, 101–105.

Underwood, B. J., & Ekstrand, B. R. (1967) Word frequency and accumulative proactive inhibition. *Journal of Experimental Psychology*, *74*, 193–198.

Underwood, G. (1974) Moray vs. the rest: The effects of extended shadowing practice. *Quarterly Journal of Experimental Psychology*, *26*, 368–372.

Underwood G. (1977) Contextual facilitation from attended and unattended messages. *Journal of Verbal Learning and Verbal Behavior*, *16*, 99–106.

Vellutino, F. R., Steger, J. A., Harding, C. J., & Phillips, F. (1975) Verbal vs. non-verbal paired-associates learning in poor and normal readers. *Neuropsychologia*, *13*, 75–82.

Von Restorff, H. (1933) Über die Wirkung von Bereichsbildungen im Spurenfeld. In W. Köhler and H. von Restorff, *Analyse von Vorgängen in Spurenfeld, I. Psychologische Forschung*, *18*, 299–342.

Von Wright, J. M., Anderson, K., & Stenman, U. (1975) Generalisation of conditioned GSRs in dichotic listening. In P. M. A. Rabbitt, & S. Dornic (Eds.), *Attention and Performance*, *Vol. V*. London: Academic Press.

Wachtel, P. L. (1967) Conceptions of broad and narrow attention. *Psychological Bulletin*, *68*, 417–429.

Walker, P. (1975) The subliminal perception of movement and the "suppression" in binocular rivalry. *British Journal of Psychology*, *66*, 347–356.

Wallas, G. (1926) *The Art of Thought*. London: Jonathan Cape.

Warr, P. B. (1964) The relative importance of proactive interference and degree of learning in retention of paired associate items. *British Journal of Psychology*, *55*, 19–30.

Warren, R. M., & Warren, R. P. (1970) Auditory illusions and confusions. *Scientific American*, *223*, 30–36.

Warrington, E. K., & Weiskrantz, L. (1974) The effect of prior learning on subsequent retention in amnesic patients. *Neuropsychologia*, *12*, 419–428.

Wason, P. C. (1960) On the failure to eliminate hypotheses in a conceptual task. *Quarterly Journal of Experimental Psychology*, *12*, 129–140.

Wason, P. C. (1966) Reasoning. In B. Foss (Ed.), *New Horizons in Psychology*. London: Penguin.

Wason, P. C. (1968) Reasoning about a rule. *Quarterly Journal of Experimental Psychology*, *20*, 273–281.

Wason, P. C., & Shapiro, D. (1971) Natural and contrived experience in a reasoning problem. *Quarterly Journal of Experimental Psychology*, *23*, 63–71.

Watkins, M. J. (1973) When is recall spectacularly higher than recognition? *Journal of Experimental Psychology*, *102*, 161–163.

Watkins, M. J., & Todres, A. K. (1978) On the relation between recall and recognition. *Journal of Verbal Learning and Verbal Behavior*, *17*, 621–633.

Waugh, N. C., & Norman, D. (1965) Primary memory. *Psychological Review*, *72*, 89–104.

Weiner, B., & Schneider, K. (1971) Drive versus cognitive theory: A reply to Boor and Harmon. *Journal of Personality and Social Psychology*, *18*, 258–262.

Weisberg, R. W., & Alba, J. W. (1981) An examination of the alleged role of "fixation" in the solution of several "insight" problems. *Journal of Experimental Psychology: General*, *110*, 169–192.

Weiskrantz, L., & Warrington, E. K. (1970) A study of forgetting in amnesic patients. *Neuropsychologia*, *8*, 281–288.

Weiskrantz, L., & Warrington, E. K. (1979) Conditioning in amnesic patients. *Neuropsychologia*, *17*, 187–194.

Weisstein, N., & Harris, C. S. (1974) Visual detection of line segments: An object-superiority effect. *Science*, *186*, 752–755.

Weist, R. M. (1972) The role of rehearsal: Recopy or reconstruct. *Journal of Verbal Learning and Verbal Behavior*, *11*, 440–450.

Welch, J. (1898) On the measurement of mental activity through muscular activity and the determination of a constant attention. *American Journal of Psychology*, *1*, 288–306.

Wellman, H. M., Ritter, K., & Flavell, J. H. (1975) Deliberate memory behaviour in the delayed reactions of very young children. *Developmental Psychology*, *11*, 780–787.

Wertheimer, M. (1958) *Productive Thinking*. 2nd ed., New York: Harper & Row.

Wertheimer, M. (1962) Psychomotor co-ordination of auditory-visual space at birth. *Science*, *134*, 1692.

Wheldall, K., & Poborca, B. (1980) Conservation without conversation: An alternative, non-verbal paradigm for assessing conservation of liquid quantity. *British Journal of Psychology*, *71*, 117–134.

Whorf, B. L. (1956) *Language, Thought, and Reality*. Cambridge, Mass.: MIT Press.

Wilkins, A. J., & Baddeley, A. D. (1978) Remembering to recall in everyday life: An approach to absent mindedness. In M. M. Gruneberg, P. E. Morris, & R. N. Sykes (eds.), *Practical Aspects of Memory*. London: Academic Press.

Wilkinson, R. T. (1961) Interaction of lack of sleep with knowledge of results, repeated testing and individual differences. *Journal of Experimental Psychology*, *62*, 263–271.

Wilkinson, R. T. (1962) Muscle tension during mental work under sleep deprivation. *Journal of Experimental Psychology*, *64*, 565–571.

Wilkinson, R. T. (1963) Interaction of noise with knowledge of results and sleep deprivation. *Journal of Experimental Psychology*, *66*, 332–337.

Wilkinson, R. T., & Colquhoun, W. P. (1968) Interaction of alcohol with incentive and with sleep deprivation. *Journal of Experimental Psychology*, *76*, 623–629.

Wilkinson, R. T., El-Beheri, S., & Gieseking, C. C. (1972) Performance and arousal as a function of incentive, information load, and task novelty. *Psychophysiology*, *9*, 589–599.

Willett, R. A. (1964) Experimentally induced drive and performance on a five-choice serial reaction task. In H. J. Eysenck (ed.), *Experiments in Motivation*. Oxford: Pergamon.

Wine, J. (1971) Test anxiety and direction of attention. *Psychological Bulletin, 76*, 92–104.

Winnick, W. A., & Daniel, S. A. (1970) Two kinds of response priming in tachistoscopic recognition. *Journal of Experimental Psychology, 84*, 74–81.

Winocur, G., & Weiskrantz, L. (1976) An investigation of paired-associate learning in amnesic patients. *Neuropsychologia, 14*, 97–110.

Winograd, T. (1977) On some contested suppositions of generative linguistics about the scientific study of language. *Cognition, 5*, 151–179.

Wiseman, S., & Neisser, U. (1974) Perceptual organisation as a determinant of visual recognition memory. *American Journal of Psychology, 87*, 675–681.

Wiseman, S., & Tulving, E. (1976) Encoding specificity: Relation between recall superiority and recognition failure. *Journal of Experimental Psychology: Human Learning and Memory, 2*, 349–361.

Wittgenstein, L. (1958) *Philosophical Investigations*. New York: Macmillan.

Woodworth, R. S., & Sells, S. B. (1935) An atmosphere effect in syllogistic reasoning. *Journal of Experimental Psychology, 18*, 451–460.

Yates, F. A. (1966) *The Art of Memory*. London: Routledge & Kegan Paul.

Yerkes, R. M., & Dodson, J. D. (1908) The relation of strength of stimulus to rapidity of habit formation. *Journal of Comparative and Neurological Psychology, 18*, 459–482.

Zaffy, D. J., & Bruning, J. L. (1966) Drive and the range of cue utilisation. *Journal of Experimental Psychology, 71*, 382–384.

Subject Index

Author Index